John Burroughs
and the Place of Nature

John Burroughs
and the Place of Nature

JAMES PERRIN WARREN

The University of Georgia Press   *Athens & London*

© 2006 by The University of Georgia Press
Athens, Georgia 30602
All rights reserved
Designed by Kathi Dailey Morgan
Set in Electra by BookComp, Inc.
Printed and bound by Maple-Vail
The paper in this book meets the guidelines for
permanence and durability of the Committee on
Production Guidelines for Book Longevity of the
Council on Library Resources.

Printed in the United States of America
10 09 08 07 06 C 5 4 3 2 1

Library of Congress Cataloging-in-Publication Data
Warren, James Perrin
John Burroughs and the place of nature
/ James Perrin Warren.
p. cm.
Includes bibliographical references (p.) and index.
ISBN-13: 978-0-8203-2788-4 (hardcover : alk. paper)
ISBN-10: 0-8203-2788-3 (hardcover : alk. paper)
1. Burroughs, John, 1837–1921—Criticism and
interpretation. 2. Muir, John, 1838–1914—
Criticism and interpretation. 3. Roosevelt, Theodore,
1858–1919—Knowledge—Natural history.
4. Burroughs, John, 1837–1921—Influence.
5. Nature in literature. 6. American prose literature—
19th century—History and criticism. 7. Natural history
literature—United States—History. 8. Natural history—
United States—History. I. Title.
PS1227 .W37 2006
814'.4—dc22   2005021230

British Library Cataloging-in-Publication Data available

Photograph of John Burroughs reading letters at Roxbury,
Catskills by Clifton Johnson reproduced by permission of
the Jones Library, Inc., Amherst, MA.

For Sylvia and Eline

CONTENTS

List of Illustrations / *ix*

Acknowledgments / *xi*

Introduction. The Power of Place / *1*

One. Great Neighbors: Emerson, Thoreau, and the Writer's Place / *14*

Two. Whitman Land: John Burroughs's Pastoral Criticism / *42*

Three. Pastoral Illustration: Burroughs, Muir, and the

  Century Magazine / *73*

Four. Landscapes Beginning to Be Born: Alaska and the

  Pictorial Imagination / *113*

Five. The "Best of Places": Roosevelt as Literary Naturalist / *150*

Six. The Divine Abyss: Burroughs and Muir in the New Century / *194*

Conclusion. The Place of Elegy / *227*

Notes / *235*

Bibliography / *251*

Index / *259*

ILLUSTRATIONS

1. Map of the Merced Range near Yosemite / 77

2. Glacier of Mount Ritter / 77

3. Bergschrund of Black Mountain Glacier / 79

4. The Sierra from Mount Diablo / 80

5. Gathering Butter / 83

6. A Wind Storm in the California Forests / 86

7. A Bee-Ranch in Lower California / 91

8. Wild Bee Garden / 92

9. Flight of the Birds / 96

10. John Muir / 106

11. John Burroughs (photograph) / 108

12. John Burroughs (drawing) / 110

13. Landscapes Beginning to Be Born / 131

14. Lynn Canal Glacier, First Draft / 133

15. Lynn Canal Glacier, Second Draft / 133

16. Lynn Canal Glacier, Final Draft / 134

17. East Side, St. Matthew Island / 135

18. Muir Glacier / 141

19. Before the Great Berg Fell / 141

20. "The Two Jonnies [*sic*]" / 148

21. Roosevelt as Wilderness Hunter / 162

22. Close Quarters with Old Ephraim / 163

23. Bear at Elk Carcass / 165

24. Sunset on Plateau / 167

25. A Night in the Open / 167

26. An Episode in the Opening Up of a Cattle Country / 171

27. Bronco Busters Saddling / 171

28. "Hands Up!" — The Capture of Finnigan / 174

ACKNOWLEDGMENTS

IN WRITING *John Burroughs and the Place of Nature*, I have experienced as much community as solitude. Even when I was sitting at my study desk in Still House Hollow, delving into ideas and finding words to put on paper, I was never really alone. Scholarship is always collaborative, and that remains a humbling and valuable lesson.

Colleagues in the Association for the Study of Literature and Environment (ASLE) have nurtured and supported me in more ways than I can name or they can know. I name many now, but there are scores of others I do not name to whom I owe the debt of community. Foremost, Michael Branch, Michael Cohen, and John Tallmadge encouraged and supported this project from the very beginning. From Missoula to the White Mountains, other ASLE friends participated in conferences and symposia, sharing in work devoted to nineteenth-century American culture and nature: Matt Bolinder, Larry Buell, Pavel Cenkl, Laird Christensen, Terry Gifford, Ellen Goldey, Annie Ingram, Rochelle Johnson, Lauren LaFauci, John Lane, Corey Lewis, Eric Lupfer, Ian Marshall, T. Scott McMillin, Stephen Mercier, Ash Nichols, Dan Payne, Dan Philippon, Eve Quesnel, Randall Roorda, Kent Ryden, Lee Schweninger, Bill Stowe, Charlotte Walker, Jeff Walker, Alan Weltzien, and Maria Windell. Ed Renehan, Charlotte Walker, and an anonymous referee commented extensively and helpfully on the manuscript. An earlier version of chapter 2 appeared in *ISLE*, and I benefited greatly from the editorial suggestions of my anonymous referees and editors at that journal. Christa Frangiamore, environmental acquisitions editor at the University of Georgia Press, has been all that one could wish for as an editor and friend. The rest of the editorial staff at the University of Georgia Press have treated me so well that I will undoubtedly be bothering them again. Molly Thompson was an expert copy editor and indexer.

In a work so devoted to archival research on the idea of place, I count some of my deepest debts to places of learning, especially libraries and librarians. My research at the Berg Collection of the New York Public Library was facilitated by Isaac Gewirtz, Curator; Stephen Crook, Librarian; Diana Burnham, Librarian; and Philip Milito, Technical Assistant. The staff in the Manuscripts and Archives Division of the NYPL were equally helpful in meeting my photocopying requests. Barnard College provided needed housing for a middle-aged professor. Dean Rogers, Special Collections Librarian at Vassar College Library, was unfailingly generous in guiding me through the Burroughs Papers and helping me arrange my stays in Poughkeepsie. Wallace Dailey, Curator of the Theodore Roosevelt Collection at Harvard University, became my personal librarian for intensely productive work in the Houghton Library. The librarians of the Houghton are rightly legendary in their efficiency and good will. I also wish to acknowledge the permission of the Trustees of Harvard University for use of manuscript materials from the Roosevelt Collection and the Houghton Mifflin Archives. During a monthlong fellowship at the Huntington Library, I learned much about the many beauties, both natural and cultural, in that amazing place. The institution was generous and accommodating without fail. Librarians Romaine Ahlstrom and Dan Lewis extended expertise as well as friendship, enabling me to add several species to my life-list of birds. Though I was never able to work in the Holt-Atherton Collection of the University of the Pacific or in the Harriman Expedition Collection of the University of Washington, both libraries were efficient and professional in filling my requests for reproductions of images. The argument is clearer, and the book itself more appealing, for their work. Closer to home, the librarians at Alderman Library and the Albert and Shirley Small Special Collections Library of the University of Virginia were always hospitable to a small-town visitor from over the mountain. I gratefully acknowledge the permission of the University of Virginia to reproduce materials from the Clifton Waller Barrett Library of American Literature. Finally, my home librarians and technology specialists at Washington and Lee University have helped me in more ways than I can specify. Carole Bailey, John Blackburn, Flash Floyd,

Lisa McCown, Yolanda Merrill, Vaughan Stanley, Elizabeth Teaff, Laura Turner, and April Washburn deserve special praise.

My colleagues and friends at Washington and Lee University deserve special thanks. The Hewlett-Mellon and Class of '62 Award allowed me to devote a full year to research and writing. John M. Glenn Summer Research Grants have been a steady source of funding and recognition. The Glenn Grant Publication Fund defrayed the cost of some illustrations. The S. Blount Mason, Jr., Endowed Professorship has given me a research fund for the purchase of scholarly books. My excellent colleagues in the English Department have encouraged the new direction in my scholarship, and I continue to learn from the many young faculty who surround me. My students maintain a lively curiosity in American environmental writing, and I have been blessed to teach many brilliant undergraduates during the research phase of the project. Lauren LaFauci holds a special place in that regard, since she is carrying on the work in Michigan and Mainz and has gone from being my student to being my colleague and friend.

Ed Folsom, my fellow-Whitmaniac and editor of WWQR, gave me his usual unflagging support as I cast about for sabbatical fellowships. Dick and Cindy Brodhead, despite misrecognizing my respectability, have always seen me and my work for what they are. Steve and Sandy Cushman are likewise irreplaceable causes for thanksgiving.

After the travel to important places and people, I always return to my family. During the sabbatical year especially, I was grateful for my parents, my brothers, and all of that growing extended family. The generations teach us deep, intertwined lessons about nature and culture. Deepest of all, without doubt, are the lessons I learn from my daughters, Sylvia and Eline. The dedication expresses my abiding love for them.

The Power of Place

An American Literary Naturalist

For the fifty years from 1870 through 1920, John Burroughs was the most famous and widely published nature writer in America. Today, less than a century after his death, he is largely unread, even by teachers of environmental writing. He shares his fate, of course, with scores of writers whose style and vision find little sympathy among modern readers. But Burroughs may not deserve that fate. He gave voice to the art of simple living and to the beauty and power of nature found near at hand. In both respects, his work may speak to modern readers who seek an inclusive, diverse sense of nature, a nature that finds a place in close proximity to culture and exercises a healthy influence upon it.

Death came to John Burroughs on a railroad train somewhere in Ohio. For the sake of his health, he had wintered in southern California in 1920 and again in 1921, but toward the end of February 1921 he was hospitalized there for four weeks. After midnight on March 29, aboard an eastbound train, the dying Burroughs awoke and asked his friend Dr. Clara Barrus, "How far are we from home?" He died twelve hours before the train arrived at his Hudson Valley home in West Park, New York. The circumstances of his death point toward the deep elegiac strain in Burroughs's writing and to his profound sense of displacement in the modern world.

Born on a Catskill dairy farm on April 3, 1837, Burroughs led the existence of a farm boy until he left home to become a rural schoolteacher in the spring of 1854. For the rest of his days, he blended the life of a farmer with the life of a literary writer, though he always insisted that his work was humble in its aims: "I always read the best books of English literature eagerly, but I could never acquire any of the marks or accomplishments of a scholar. . . . I got much out of books, but not what the schools and colleges give. I lack the pride of scholarly accomplishments. My farmer ancestry rules me in this respect. . . . Perhaps I should say that it is the technical part of literature and science that I fail in. My natural-history knowledge is more like that of the hunter and trapper than like that of the real scientist. I know our birds well, but not as the professional ornithologist knows them. I know them through my heart more than through my head" (*Life and Letters* 1:16).

Burroughs's nearly thirty books present the modern reader with an intriguing mixture of direct, concrete experiences of nature; bluff, unsentimental evaluations of literature; and abstract meditations on time, the cosmos, and religion. At their best, his nature essays convey through the imagery and tone of unadorned discovery the experiential quality of walking in the woods. He was most famous for his descriptions of birds, but in his essay "The Invitation" he notes that "ornithology cannot be satisfactorily learned from the books. The satisfaction is in learning it from nature. One must have an original experience with the birds. The books are only the guide, the invitation" (*Writings* 1:221). His own books effectively deliver his original experiences with the birds, inviting a host of readers to walk in the woods and learn the birds by heart.

In addition to his role as the most famous and prolific American nature writer of his day, Burroughs exercised an important role as a literary critic. In numerous essays on Emerson, Thoreau, Whitman, and other nineteenth-century writers, he advanced the principle of nature as the standard for judging literature, and this marks him as an early writer of ecocriticism. His fourth book, *Birds and Poets* (1877), combines nature essays and literary criticism so that the two types of writing reflect upon each other, and the conjunction often creates moments of profound insight into the relationship between nature and culture. In the complex mosaic called "Touches of Nature," for instance, Burroughs notes, "It is well to let down our metropolitan pride a little. Man thinks himself at the top, and that the immense display and prodigality of Nature are for him. But they are no more for him than they are for the birds and beasts, and he is no more at the top than they are" (*Writings* 3:53–54). The tone of humility is commanding, for

Burroughs undercuts the anthropocentric hierarchy of the culture-nature relationship.

Burroughs's lifelong ruminations on nature and culture led him to write many essays in which he grappled with the competing claims of science, religion, philosophy, and literature. His goal was often reconciliation, and at their best the later essays achieve a rhetorical balance. In *The Light of Day* (1900), for example, he presents scientific theories of knowledge along with the necessary roles of religious sentiment and aesthetic sensibility, and many times he faces what he calls the "cosmic chill" of the indifferent universe, insisting that "we must face it, and still find life sweet under its influence" (*Writings* 11:133). In *Time and Change* (1912), Burroughs develops a geological perspective for the vastness of the physical universe, and by seeing "through the geologist's eyes" he conceives of a scientific imagination "working in new fields and under new conditions, and achieving triumphs that mark a new epoch in the history of the race. Nature, which once terrified man and made a coward of him, now inspires him and fills him with love and enthusiasm" (*Writings* 16:88). In his own lengthy career, Burroughs was himself an exemplary figure of the imagination that combines science, natural history, philosophy, and literature.

Place in Ecocriticism

As a proponent of interdisciplinary studies for opening "new fields . . . under new conditions," Burroughs has much to offer current students of ecocriticism, nature writing, and environmental studies. For example, in his book *Practical Ecocriticism*, Glen Love argues precisely for viewing the emerging field of ecocriticism within the context of "new fields . . . under new conditions." One of the new conditions we face now, a century after Burroughs was a celebrity author, is the rise of ecological consciousness throughout our culture. Love calls for a "nature-conscious, nature validating literature and criticism" to correct the insular theories of postmodernism and social constructionism. Such an ecocriticism would recognize the need for humanism to "embrace" the nonhuman, for the humanities to embrace the sciences, and for our complex technological culture to embrace nature in all its complexity.[1]

Even in these first arguments concerning the new field of ecocriticism we can see productive and problematic metaphors. The act of embracing is figurative in several ways, since the agents engaged in the embrace are metaphorical rather than physical. Indeed, some canny readers would immediately protest that the metaphors suggest that the objects of the embracing—the nonhuman, the sciences, and nature—are rendered less powerful and less significant by the implied assignment of agency. The metaphors imply a hierarchy of power and domination. Moreover, the series of metaphors raises a further problem by including the sciences in the trio of the embraced. Who would argue that the sciences are less powerful than the humanities? Are the sciences somehow more "natural" or more closely allied to the "nonhuman" than the humanities? Aren't the sciences just like the humanities in being constructions of human culture? These questions are not frivolous but necessary.

An even more productive metaphor occurs in the phrase "new fields." There is no hierarchy of power and agency in the phrase, but it employs a spatial or geographical figure for human knowledge. In Burroughs's case, we can be confident that the word "fields" implies an agricultural sense as well; for him, knowledge is a form of cultivation. Forecasting the work of Wendell Berry, the single word figures human culture as dependent on the basic agricultural relationship of human beings to the earth. Burroughs's metaphor thus subverts, at least partly, the implied hierarchy of culture and nature. It raises questions about the relationship between nature and culture, especially when that relationship is mediated by language.

One of the most persistent metaphors we encounter in investigating the relationship between culture and nature is that of *place*, a privileged metaphor in ecocriticism. The English word has a fascinating etymology and usage history, revealing a complex play of literal and figural meanings. Its fundamental, literal meaning is "an open space in a city; a square, a market-place," and in that sense it renders the Latin original *platea*. It also signifies material space, both general and specific, and in most of these senses it suggests a dwelling place for human beings. *Place* can signify position in some scale, order, or series—as in arithmetical progressions or athletic competitions—or a position with reference to its occupation or occupant, such as the proper place for definitions. Moreover, it functions in a host of phrases and combinations to create specific meanings for other substantives—for instance, in the "place of nature." These meanings overlap, resulting in such a network of usages and meanings that the editors of the *Oxford English Dictionary* comment that the senses of "place" are "very numerous and difficult to arrange."

Ecocritics approach what Aristotle called "the power of place" (*Physics* 208b) in a variety of ways, both practical and theoretical, and an unscientific survey of recent works on my study bookshelves suggests that place retains all of its potency in contemporary ecocriticism. Much of my thinking about Burroughs, Muir, and Roosevelt began with Lawrence Buell's chapter on place in *The Environmental Imagination* (1995). Buell develops his reading of place throughout *Writing for an Endangered World* (2001), most thoroughly in the chapter called "The Place of Place" (55–83). Noting the highly flexible, elusive, and dynamic characteristics of the concept, Buell maps five dimensions of "place-connectedness" or sense of place. First, the sense of place can be figured as concentric zones of affiliation, decreasing in intimacy as one fans out from a central point (64–65). Second, the experience of place involves both the near and the far, so that a "scattergram or archipelago of locales" more accurately represents the sense of place (65–66). Third, places are shaped by forces from inside and outside, so that they are unstable processes that occur over time, both on a communal level and on an individual level (67–69). Fourth, the sense of place is a composite of all the places that have been significant over time to a person or a people (69–71). Fifth, the sense of place includes fictive or virtual places as well as real places, so that unseen actual places and imagined utopian places exercise a powerful influence (71–74). The five dimensions chart the ways in which individuals and communities form a sense of *belonging* to a place.

Interdisciplinary approaches to literature and environment repeatedly focus on the power of place. Kent Ryden explores the interdisciplinary sense of place in relation to New England in two important books, *Mapping the Invisible Landscape* (1993) and *Landscape with Figures* (2001). A recent

anthology, *The Greening of Literary Scholarship* (2002), includes essays by
James Tarter, Andrea Blair, Eleanor Hersey, and Rick Van Noy that explore
representations of place in literary works involving environmental justice,
ecofeminism, and literary theory. Place-based interdisciplinary scholarship
abounds in the pages of *ISLE* (*Interdisciplinary Studies in Literature and
Environment*), as we see clearly in the anthology *The ISLE Reader: Ecocriticism, 1993–2003*. On the border between criticism and creative nonfiction,
Ian Marshall charts new directions for narrative scholarship in *Story Line*
(1998) and *Peak Experiences* (2003). In the fourth chapter of *Practical
Ecocriticism* (2003), "Place, Style, and Human Nature in Willa Cather's
The Professor's House," Love uses the concept to show how to approach
literature from a biocultural perspective.[2]

A sharper eye would find other place-based titles on my bookshelves.
In particular, the writings of Gary Snyder, Wendell Berry, Barry Lopez,
and Rick Bass have been important to my thinking about place over the
past decade. More recently, works by Linda Hogan and Simon Ortiz have
helped me develop the sense of place as a mysterious, immanent power. In
the remote past of my undergraduate and graduate days, William Faulkner,
Flannery O'Connor, and Walker Percy loomed large, as did the myriad
imagined and real landscapes of the Deep South. Perhaps the most important part of those days, however, I spent translating Snyder's *Turtle Island*
(1974) with a French friend in the provincial city of Angers. There a displaced native southerner experienced a sense of place by struggling to
squeeze a California poet's American idioms into French! I name these
names because the personal dimension of place fits complexly into a larger
cultural dimension, and in this case my own intellectual and emotional
attachments illustrate the large-scale significance of place-based literature
in the field we now call ecocriticism.

The power of place comes to ecocriticism from many directions. The
philosophy of place, for example, has become important in the past few
decades. In *The Fate of Place*, Edward S. Casey aims "to thrust the very idea
of place, so deeply dormant in modern Western thinking, once more into
the daylight of philosophical discourse" by tracing theories of place from
Plato and Aristotle to the present.[3] In an earlier volume, *Getting Back into*

Place, Casey examines the relationship between nature and culture from a phenomenological perspective that owes a signal debt to Heidegger. In the section "Wild Places," Casey considers the conjoining of culture and nature, finding much more than a combination, compromise, or synthesis:

> Something is gained, something *emerges* from the conjunction itself that is not present when the factors are held apart. Let us call the process of this emergence "thickening." By this I mean the dense coalescence of cultural practices and natural givens. . . .
>
> Thickening occurs when each party to the interaction gains in concert with the other. Wendell Berry cites the instance of small-scale farming. He observes that a plowed field on the edge of wilderness attracts animals, e.g., the red-tailed hawk, which would not otherwise be drawn out of its wild habitat. Meanwhile, the cultivation of this same field, if carefully accomplished, falls in with and enhances natural cycles. The field's marginal position augments the interaction of the agriculturalist with the wild life beyond, furnishing a common arena for both.[4]

Casey's phenomenological concept of "thickening" suggests that culture and nature exert their powers reciprocally. The etymologies of words signify fundamentally that "the cultural leads us inexorably back to the natural," but in turn "to pursue nature into its own lair—its wild places—is still to adhere to culture. Even stationed squarely in the midst of the wilds of nature, *we cannot get away from, or around, the cultural*" (230).

Phenomenology has especially influenced the power of place in the discipline of geography. The most important figure in contemporary geography is Yi-Fu Tuan, whose work over the last thirty years has led to the development of humanistic geography as a field.[5] Two of Tuan's books are of particular interest to ecocritics: *Topophilia* (1974) and *Space and Place* (1977). In both, Tuan focuses on the role played by sense perception and experience in forging human beings' affective ties to the physical environment. Like more traditional geographical work, his arguments often present diagrams and spatial interpretations of landscape in cities and suburbs, but he moves beyond disciplinary boundaries to explore a wide variety of topics, including sexuality, religion, and wilderness. Although his work is theoretically astute, Tuan's arguments for the aesthetic and ethical values of individual agency mark him as an opponent of poststructuralist theory. In all of his writing he practices a style of disarming generosity.[6]

Robert David Sack delineates a theoretical framework for humanistic geography in *Homo Geographicus* (1997), dedicated to Tuan, "the Consummate Geographer." Like Tuan, Sack resists the divisions and skepticisms of postmodernism, insisting on the connections between place and self. Indeed, at one point Sack asserts that "the entire book is a geographic view of the self" (127). Sack relates self to place through a set of homologies. Place is structured by nature, social relations, and meaning, a relational model that Sack represents by three overlapping circles. Likewise, the self is a composite of nature, social relations, and meaning, and Sack argues from the homology that place acts as "an agent in the formation of the self" (132). As Buell's five dimensions suggest, moreover, the self can influence place, so that the two form a reciprocal web of connections through time.[7]

Sack investigates the relationship between nature and culture in the chapter "Structure and Dynamics of Place and Space." He posits a geographical continuum as a way of understanding the relationship, with primary or pure nature at one end and "least" nature—culture—at the other. Nature is comprised of "elements and forces that would exist and operate without us" (79), though any knowledge inserts the mind and its symbolic systems into nature. The power of place "transforms nature into 'second' nature, and subjects it to the structure and dynamics of place" (80). This means, according to Sack's relational model, that place "interweaves nature with social relations and meaning":

> When people say that nature is socially constructed, that it is being transformed, that it is in danger and must be saved, they are referring to this "second" nature that comes about because of place. We do not, of course, affect in the least the laws of gravity, or electromagnetism, or the other planets, stars, and galaxies in the solar system. Nor will we extinguish genes and evolution. Rather it is nature that is part of the environment we control—our place, home, or world—that is the object of concern, and this nature, as part of place, is already entwined with culture. (81)

According to Sack's reciprocal model, then, even the most remote natural area of the world is touched by culture, even if the influence is mainly the cultural act of designating and regulating the area as wilderness in order to minimize or disguise the dependence of nature upon culture. But the reverse is also true: not even the least natural place of culture—say, the city—is completely devoid of nature, and even the attenuation of nature bespeaks its power to disturb or inconvenience human inhabitants.

Two brief stories about walking may illustrate the explanatory appeal of Sack's model. On a bright morning in July 1997, I rode a rented mountain bike north of Missoula, Montana, in order to explore the Rattlesnake Wilderness National Recreation Area. I left the green campus of the University of Montana, rode northeast through the city of Missoula, and then quickly entered a rural environment of farms, barns, and stables. Soon I was biking through the southwest tip of the Lolo National Forest. The few hikers I met along the way repeatedly warned me that there had been a cougar sighting earlier that morning. I continued north, along Rattlesnake Creek, and then climbed up through a spectacular meadow in Sawmill Gulch, full of flowers and butterflies. Bearing northeast, I started climbing, and within a half hour I found myself alone in the woods, surrounded by big conifers draped in horsehair lichen. The trail climbed steadily, and at last I was reduced to walking the path with my bike beside me. Beargrass and paintbrush were blooming on the open slopes. Finally, I locked the bike to a sapling and continued climbing by foot. At about six thousand feet, I came to the boundary marker of the wilderness area. A mountain bike was locked to the signpost, and as I continued my hike up to a saddle between Stuart Peak and an unnamed mountain, I followed the tracks of a solitary hiker—probably, I figured, the person who had dutifully left the bike at the boundary, since the sign said bikes were not allowed in the wilderness area. My bike was at least a thousand feet below the wilderness boundary, so I was in no danger of breaking the law. I scrambled up the rocky slope of Stuart Peak and looked down on Twin Lakes far below. I was at eight thousand feet, and I felt drained and slightly lonely, maybe depressed by the elevation change and the treeline landscape. I could look out across a wide valley at mountains into the Flathead Indian Reservation. After a snack and a rest, I made my way down to the bike and retraced my route to Missoula. Back on the university campus before sundown, I was struck by how far away I had seemed and how nearby I had actually been.

In the summer of 2003, a former student of mine named Michael was told to leave his workplace in Times Square on Manhattan Island at two in the afternoon. The electrical grid of the entire New York area was out of power, and the office buildings were already becoming stuffy and uncomfortable. After some fruitless waiting at bus stops, Michael decided to walk to his apartment in Brooklyn, though he had no real idea how many miles away it was. In the late afternoon, he walked north to the edge of Central Park, turned right, and crossed the East River on the Queensboro Bridge. After a couple more hours, he arrived at a friend's apartment in Queens, but then he discovered that he couldn't reach his friend because the telephones and doorbells were not working. Tired, he stared up at the sixth floor of the apartment building, but telepathy did not work, either. As the sun set, he began walking south toward Brooklyn. Along the way, he realized he would have to cross some "bad" neighborhoods in the dark, so he decided to recross the river and seek out another friend on the Lower East Side of Manhattan. He thought he might find her in her neighborhood pub. He veered southwest and walked across the Williamsburg Bridge to Manhattan. By this time, after nine o'clock, darkness had fallen. Mike found hordes of people in the streets along Houston and Second Avenue, drinking and smoking like there was no tomorrow. Emotions and voices struck every chord he could imagine. When he neared his friend's apartment, he realized she was on vacation at the beach. So he crossed the river for a third time, circling back along Roosevelt Drive and the East River Park to the Williamsburg Bridge. This time the river was simply black, like the rest of the city. The utter blackness was strangely disorienting, too, and Mike stumbled over himself and others several times. Finally, after midnight, he hailed a cab, gladly paying more than twenty dollars for a brief ride to his apartment door. His odyssey had lasted nearly twelve hours.

Sack's unifying framework, along with its dynamic loops and circuits, is far too complex to apply to these anecdotes, but the two stories of walking illustrate the interweaving of nature and culture. In both cases, the walker traverses a complex, layered landscape. The loss of power in New York City leads to both a new sense of place and a new sense of the power nature exerts simply by being part of place. The inhabitants of that most urban of cities may wish to limit the power of nature in their place, but such desires are at best temporarily fulfilled. Nature's power is evident in the overheated buildings, the setting of the sun, and the darkness that follows. In the Rattlesnake Wilderness, on the other hand, culture repeatedly designates boundaries, functions, and ways of occupying the landscape. The power of culture is clear even at eight thousand feet, and ultimately the wilderness is not so far away from the university campus. Thus the Rattlesnake Wilderness is a form of "second" nature, but then this means that even New York City is a kind of "second" culture.[8]

Burroughs and the Place of Nature

In a trenchant essay on the present state of ecocriticism, Michael P. Cohen concludes that "books are tools for seeing the world" and asks, "Which tools help perception?"[9] Cohen raises several questions concerning the tools and methods of ecocritics, but this last is the most telling. Which tools help perception? That is a question John Burroughs himself might ask.

John Burroughs and the Place of Nature is meant to help perception in several ways. By mapping American nature writing from 1865 to 1920, I argue that John Burroughs, John Muir, and Theodore Roosevelt form the core of major American nature writing from the end of the Civil War to the end of World War I. The word "major" may seem exaggerated, for these three writers do not appear in standard college anthologies of American literature. Most contemporary college students have heard of Muir and Roosevelt, but few have read more than a passage or two by Muir, and Roosevelt's nature writing is largely unfamiliar. Burroughs's essays are so rarely read and taught as to be virtually unknown to the academic audience in the twenty-first century. But such blindness should not determine the description of the world. In their own day, all three of these writers were celebrities within the dominant literary institutions of American culture.

Second, I have tried to "make a book," as Huck Finn says, as an experimental tool in ecocriticism. Although the interdisciplinary study of place has fascinated me over the last seven years, I have not attempted to apply any particular model to the three writers or to the place of nature they create in American culture. True, I have tried to practice a healthy self-awareness in my own critical choices, but I have also found that my best writing came in moments of textual topophilia. Like all readers, I am drawn to particular places in books, and I have sought a balance between self-awareness and self-trust in making my analyses. My readings seek to explore the complex relationship between nature and culture, and in doing so they map the place of nature in late-nineteenth-century and early-twentieth-century America.

Third, I have tried to make a tool for understanding literary affiliation. If John Burroughs is an unjustly neglected writer, he is perhaps most important for the company he keeps. His rich understanding of Emerson, Thoreau, and Whitman constitutes an early form of ecocriticism, for he constantly invokes the power of place in reading these three major literary antecedents and in presenting them to his own generation of readers. Burroughs's relationship with Muir, moreover, is equally significant and complex. The two writers define the place of nature in markedly different ways, but they also share a number of characteristics in their representations of nature and its relationship to the industrial, capitalistic America of the late nineteenth century and early twentieth century. Finally, Burroughs's friendship with Roosevelt gives him the role of literary mentor for the younger generation of nature writers. In effect, then, I argue for a core literary tradition of nature writing in postbellum American literature.

Fourth, the project has constantly called for interdisciplinary understanding. While I cannot claim to relate Burroughs's work to the science of ecology in the manner of Glen Love, I do attempt to interpret verbal and visual representations of nature in cultural context. Cultural history is therefore at least as relevant as literary criticism to my understanding of Burroughs, Muir, and Roosevelt. That becomes most evident in chapter 3, in which the cultural power of magazine illustrations forms the focus of interpretation. At the same time, however, I do not argue that nature is a cultural construction or that culture is a refuge from nature. I view nature and culture as intertwined, creating a complex array of meanings through a complex array of places both natural and cultural. *Place* is always a crossroads of dynamic forces and processes, demanding interdisciplinary ways of understanding natural history, literature, art history, and cultural history. This is not the only map for the place of nature, but it charts a territory for future explorations.

Finally, I have shaped this tool by studying the manuscripts, sketches, journals, letters, magazine articles, and books of Burroughs, Muir, and Roosevelt. That is, I have used many other tools to shape this one. Those tools, in turn, were shaped by other tools—the works of Emerson, Thoreau, and Whitman most important among them. Doubtless one could argue that those tools lead back to other, previous tools—back, for instance, to Aristotle and the power of place. But in my case they always lead back to John Burroughs and his abiding sense of place.

Like Lawrence Buell's map of place, Burroughs's sense of place reveals several dimensions. First and foremost, it emerges from the way in which Burroughs occupies and inhabits his literal, physical place in the Hudson River Valley and the Catskill Mountains of New York state. It also appears in the changing ways in which Burroughs uses language to describe and represent place; it shows how he makes a place for the local, common, and familiar aspects of nature in his writing; it gives him a way to read literature ecocritically; and it makes a cultural place for the version of nature he perceives and represents in his essays. Finally, it provides the means for mapping a place for Burroughs, Muir, and Roosevelt in our new century of ecocriticism.

Whether or not these dimensions of Burroughs's place are permanent is another question. But if we are to see our way clear to an answer, we will surely need all of these tools and more.

1 *Great Neighbors*

Emerson, Thoreau, and the Writer's Place

The Moving-Picture Brain

Nearing the end of his long life and lengthy career, John Burroughs made plans for publishing three volumes of essays over a three-year period, in return for which the publisher Houghton Mifflin guaranteed him an annuity of two thousand dollars. Burroughs regarded the amount as insufficient. On October 12, 1918, he wrote to the editor Ferris Greenslet that he would need double the sum; a year later, he lowered his request to twenty-five hundred dollars. Greenslet resisted, pointing out in a letter of November 26, 1919, that the sales of all of Burroughs's books in 1918 had dipped below five hundred dollars. By the end of 1919, Burroughs was ready to accept the two thousand dollars and promised Greenslet "a book of about 40.000 words, or half the size of one of my other volumes. Emerson & his Journals, & Thoreau, a Critical Study, would be the contents. Perhaps we can find a good title later." On January 5, 1920, Burroughs sent his editor the manuscript of the proposed volume on Emerson and Thoreau, and ten days later he wrote again, expressing his confidence that he would be able to bring out the three volumes within the three years of the annuity. But his health had already begun to fail, and the octogenarian's plans never materialized. Despite two winters spent recuperating in southern California, within fifteen months he was dead.[1]

The material from the final years appears in the two posthumous volumes of Burroughs's *Writings*, edited by Dr. Clara Barrus under the titles *Under the Maples* and *The Last Harvest*.[2] Most of these brief essays are not of great importance, but the three essays on Emerson and Thoreau in *The Last Harvest* form the core of a forty-thousand-word book that Burroughs never finished. "Emerson and His Journals," "Flies in Amber," and "Another Word on Thoreau" are significant critical essays in their own right, and they indicate the abiding importance of Emerson and Thoreau for Burroughs as a literary naturalist and ecocritic. The three essays show how Burroughs tends to see Emerson and Thoreau together, interpreting the two predecessors in terms of one another. The project also suggests that at the end of his life Burroughs was attempting to interpret the work of Emerson and Thoreau for a new generation. His fundamental angle of interpretation features ideas of place, particularly the place of nature in American culture.

Burroughs may already have suspected that the interpretive attempt would fail, not for lack of health and time, but because the new generation was no longer interested in nature writers like him. In his journal for November 9, 1916, for instance, he noted that his audience was slipping away from him:

> The magazine writer has a new problem: how to address himself to the moving-picture brain—the brain that does not want to read or think, but only to use its eager shallow eyes, eyes that prefer the shadow and ghosts of things to the things themselves, that rather see the ghosts of people flitting around on the stage, than to see real flesh and blood. How an audible dialogue would tire them! It might compel them to use their minds a little—horrible thought!
>
> For my own part, I am sure I cannot interest this moving-picture brain, and do not want to. It is the shallowest brain that has yet appeared in the world. What is to be the upshot of this craze over this mere wash of reality which the "movies" (horrible word!) offer our young people?[3]

As amusing as the private diatribe against silent "movies" may be, it expresses a real sense of the writer's cultural displacement, and it clearly indicates the widening gulf between Burroughs and the modern world. Ironically, the moving-picture brain has not dissolved into shallow shadows; instead, Burroughs has nearly disappeared from the literary landscape of American literature. And whatever else one thinks of the radical shift in sensibility—not all moviegoers need think of themselves as possessing "the shallowest brain that has yet appeared in the world"—it suggests that

Burroughs seeks to retrieve a literary audience by educating readers about a common ancestry and refreshing their memory of the American literary map.

The first paragraphs of "Flies in Amber" clearly support the suggestion. Burroughs notes that "younger writers" now "speak slightingly and flippantly of Emerson, referring to him as outworn, and as the apostle of the obvious" (*Writings* 23:86), but he attributes their view to "our hurrying, materialistic age" and echoes his journal when he imagines Emerson attempting to deliver a winter lyceum lecture in the modern West: "What chance would he stand, even in university towns, as against the 'movies' (a word so ugly I hesitate to write it) in the next street?" (87). In both essays Burroughs defends Emerson by admitting the difficulties of Emerson's writing—the lack of logic and organization, for instance—while pointing out that the difficulties do not undermine his real influence, which rests on "spiritual power and insight." For Burroughs, the minor defects are "like flies in amber" (90). Still, the majority of "Flies in Amber" is taken up with Emerson's flaws, and Burroughs especially takes him to task for misinterpreting nature, drawing far-fetched, incongruous, and false analogies, and exaggerating. As he closes the essay, Burroughs himself laments the rhetorical stance he has taken: "I cherish and revere the name of Emerson so profoundly, and owe him such a debt, that it seems, after all, a pity to point out the flaws in his precious amber" (102). Such a pity, in fact, that Burroughs added a final paragraph to the essay, according to a note by Clara Barrus the last words he ever wrote. Here Burroughs exhorts his readers to value the past, and his words could just as easily apply to himself:

> Let us keep alive the Emersonian memories: that such a man has lived and wrought among us. Let us teach our children his brave and heroic words, and plant our lives upon as secure an ethical foundation as he did. Let us make pilgrimages to Concord, and stand with uncovered heads beneath the pine tree where his ashes rest. He left us an estate in the fair land of the Ideal. He bequeathed us treasures that thieves cannot break through and steal, nor time corrupt, nor rust nor moth destroy. (102)

The imagery of place is concrete, evoking Sleepy Hollow Cemetery in Concord, Massachusetts, as well as the "ethical foundation" and "fair land of the Ideal" that the graveyard scene signifies. In imagining the grave, Burroughs is a bit sly at the last, altering the biblical verse: "Lay up for yourselves treasures in heaven, where neither moth nor rust doth corrupt, and where thieves do not break through nor steal" (Matthew 6:20). Inserting "nor time corrupt" he brings the treasures back to earth. Here, in a place marked by time, we remember the past and bequeath its treasures to the future. The dying writer bequeaths his readers the task of remembering the past, both in the remote shape of Emerson and in the nearer form of Burroughs himself.

When we consider the "brave and heroic words" of Emerson, the irony of Burroughs's final words deepens. As Burroughs keenly points out in "Emerson and His Journals," Emerson "knew that the past and the present, the near and the far, were made of one stuff. . . . His doctrine of self-reliance, which he preached in season and out of season, was based upon the conviction that Nature and the soul do not become old and outworn, that the great characters and great thoughts of the past were the achievements of men who trusted themselves before custom or law. The sun shines to-day; the constellations hang there in the heavens the same as of old. God is as near us as ever He was—why should we take our revelations at second hand?" (31–32). The word "outworn" echoes the charge that the new generation of writers lays at Emerson's feet, but in this passage there is no aging or wearing-out of nature and the soul. Both are, like God, "as near us as ever." Burroughs interprets Emerson's poetry in similar terms, praising it for "the extent to which it takes hold of the concrete, the real, the familiar" and yet maintains an "elusive, mystical suggestiveness. . . . Its cheerful and sunny light of the common day enhances instead of obscures the light that falls from the highest heaven of the spirit" (10). As in the evocation of the Concord graveyard, the imagery of place creates a union of real and ideal realms. Emerson's poetry becomes the figurative place that merges the light of common day and the light of highest heaven.

Despite the visionary, unifying light of Emerson's writing, Burroughs is equally drawn to the writer's dark sense of limitation and division. For example, he raises the specter of Emerson's "uncertainty and blind groping for adequate expression" concerning God, asking pointedly, "How can we put the All, the Eternal, in words?" And he uses the same imagery to draw a striking analogy: "As the sunlight puts out our lamp or candle, so our mental lights grow pale in the presence of the Infinite Light" (49). Burroughs responds to this dilemma by focusing on the concrete, real, and familiar rather than the abstract ideal. Thus he notes, "I am not looking for ethical or poetic values. I am looking for natural truths. I am less interested in the sermons in stones than I am in the life under the stones" (54). The allusion to Duke Senior's famous speech in Shakespeare's *As You Like It* appropriately suggests the writer's familiarity with pastoral literature, but it also asserts Burroughs's self-reliant choice to focus upon natural history rather than ethics or aesthetics. Burroughs thus answers Emerson's limitations with limitations of his own.

Indeed, limitation becomes his avowed technique, since in adopting it he proves himself Emerson's true disciple. In section 14 of "Emerson and His Journals," Burroughs quotes a February 1859 entry in Emerson's journal in which Emerson asks why, after thirty years of writing and speaking "what were once called novelties," he now has not one disciple. Emerson's answer recurs to the centrality of self-reliance, since his lectures and essays "did not go from any wish in me to bring men to me, but to themselves. I delight in driving them from me."[4] Burroughs then notes that "it is never easy to stray far from the master in high moral, aesthetic, and literary matters." Instead, the disciple can merely "break over his limitations and 'brave the landscape's look' with our own eyes" (73). By recognizing Emerson's limitations, Burroughs enhances his own self-reliant critical stance. In addition, he presents a model of reading and writing for the new generation he addresses. If we see Emerson as outworn or obvious, the limitation may lie at least partly with our own "mental lights." On the other hand, we must not be blind to Emerson's limitations, or they will become ours. At the deepest level, Burroughs understands that limitation and power are made of one stuff, like past and present, near and far. For the critic and nature writer alike, the landscape calls for new eyes. That is the sense of the allusion to

Emerson's poem "Waldeinsamkeit," though Burroughs slightly misquotes the poem:

> See thou bring not to field or stone
> The fancies found in books;
> Leave author's eyes, and fetch your own,
> To brave the landscape's looks. (41–44)

Braving Thoreau's Landscape

Burroughs faces a different critical problem in the eleven-part essay "Another Word on Thoreau." From the outset he notes that Thoreau's "fame is more alive than ever" and that "after Emerson, the name of no New England man of letters keeps greener and fresher than that of Thoreau" (103). Rather than recall a neglected master's place for the new generation, Burroughs places Thoreau next to Emerson and measures the two against one another. Already in "Emerson and His Journals," Burroughs remarks that Thoreau is "characteristically Emersonian" (20) and that "he was undoubtedly deeply and permanently influenced by Emerson both in his mental habits and in his manner of life" (21). Yet he also asserts that Thoreau is "original and unadulterated," that his "literary style is in many respects better than that of Emerson," and that *Walden* "will last as long as anything Emerson has written, if not longer. It is the fruit of a sweeter solitude and detachment from the world than Emerson ever knew, a private view of nature, and has a fireside and campside quality that essays fashioned for the lecture platform do not have. Emerson's pages are more like mosaics, richly inlaid with gems of thought and poetry and philosophy, while Thoreau's are more like a closely woven, many-colored textile" (21). The analogies suggest no inherent value judgment but an appreciation of two different kinds of beauty.

In evaluating Thoreau's detachment from the world, Burroughs answers a common charge, first leveled by James Russell Lowell in 1864, that "Thoreau's experiment . . . actually presupposed all that complicated civilization which it theoretically abjured" (107). Rather than rejecting all civilization, however, Thoreau makes "no claims to living independently of the rest of mankind. His only aim in his Walden experiment was to reduce life to its lowest terms, to drive it into a corner, as he said, and question and cross-question it, and see, if he could, what it really meant. And he probably came as near cornering it there in his hut on Walden Pond as any man ever did anywhere" (108). Burroughs employs Emersonian rhetoric in answering Lowell. He locates the experiment, not by analyzing the abstract and general relationship of culture versus nature, but by placing it within the hut on Walden Pond and driving Thoreau's principles into the corner, where he can question and cross-question them. By using the concept of place, Burroughs in effect joins Thoreau and Emerson in answering Lowell's famous criticism.[5]

Burroughs employs the concept of place to evaluate both Emerson and Thoreau. It is clear that Burroughs holds Thoreau in high regard, for in *Walden* he "gave us our first and probably only nature classic" (108). He calls the book "a wonderful and delightful piece of brag, but it is much more than that. It is literature; it is a Gospel of the Wild" (110). In the third section of the essay, he turns to Thoreau's essay "Walking" as a practical example of the gospel, contrasting both Emerson and Thoreau to Wordsworth:

> Wordsworth gathered his finest poetic harvest from common nature and common humanity about him—the wayside birds and flowers and waterfalls, and the wayside people. Though he called himself a worshiper of Nature, it was Nature in her half-human moods that he adored—Nature that knows no extremes, and that has long been under the influence of man—a soft, humid, fertile, docile Nature, that suggests a domesticity as old and as permanent as that of cattle and sheep. His poetry reflects these features, reflects the high moral and historic significance of the European landscape, while the poetry of Emerson, and of Thoreau, is born of the wildness and elusiveness of our more capricious and unkempt Nature. (131)

Differences in landscape drive the contrast between Wordsworth and the two American writers, giving rise to markedly different styles and tones. Wordsworth's pastoral poetry evokes a domesticated, humanized nature, a landscape of "second" nature that places "common nature" and "common humanity" together. Emerson and Thoreau, on the other hand, inhabit and reflect the wildness of American nature, and their writing is marked by its elusive, capricious, unkempt style. Burroughs's position as judicious critic allows him to place the English poet in the pastoral tradition while he defines America as a new, wild, and inherently more poetic landscape. Although it is tempting to place Burroughs in that same American landscape, the passage does not actually produce such a map. For many readers, moreover, Burroughs's nature writings have more in common with Wordsworth's pastoral poetry than with the "wildness and elusiveness" of Emerson and Thoreau.

Burroughs develops a critical distance from Thoreau as the essay progresses. As in the two essays on Emerson, he employs a strategy of limited praise. He disputes Thoreau's reputation as a naturalist, defining him as "not a born naturalist, but a born supernaturalist" because he was "too intent upon the bird behind the bird to take careful note of the bird itself" (134). He reveals several "little slips" in the published works and the journals, but he also praises "the rich harvest of natural-history notes with which his work abounds" (137). Thoreau's rhetorical excesses call for harsher criticism, and Burroughs takes him to task for his false analogies, exaggerations, moralizing interpretations, and paradoxes. Tellingly, he quotes Emerson's criticism of Thoreau: "'The trick of his rhetoric is soon learned; it consists in substituting for the obvious word and thought, its diametrical antagonist'" (141). This sentence directly echoes a lengthier set of criticisms that Burroughs quotes in "Emerson and His Journals," focusing especially on "the old fault of unlimited contradiction" and giving several examples of Thoreau's antagonistic rhetoric (22). In addition, Burroughs quotes the disparaging passage from Emerson's journal in which he notes, "I am very familiar with all his thoughts,—they are my own quite originally drest" (22). In the eighth section of "Another Word on Thoreau," Burroughs quotes more of Emerson's criticisms in order to portray Thoreau's crusty fractiousness (156–58).

As he moves toward the conclusion of the essay, Burroughs focuses on the "radical idealism" that underlies Thoreau's contradictions and inconsistencies (166), but that does not prevent him from seeing Thoreau as "often simply grotesque" (169). He ends "Another Word on Thoreau" in much the same vein as "Flies in Amber," but in this case he is not apologetic about his critical views, since he believes that Thoreau's merits and flaws are equally appreciated. In the final sentence, however, he once again implies that Emerson deserves better: "[Thoreau] drew a gospel out of the wild; he brought messages from the wood gods to men; he made a lonely pond in Massachusetts a fountain of the purest and most elevating thoughts, and, with his great neighbor Emerson, added new luster to a town over which the muse of our colonial history had long loved to dwell" (171). Along with the filiopietism about Walden, Concord, and our colonial history, Burroughs accurately summarizes Thoreau's literary contributions by considering Thoreau in terms of wildness and the place of nature in human thought. The idea of place figures prominently in all three essays of the Emerson-Thoreau book, and in the final sentence Burroughs creates a literary geography, including the wild, the wood gods, the lonely pond in Massachusetts, and the town of Concord. On the map that Burroughs draws, Emerson is Thoreau's "great neighbor," and clearly Emerson occupies the central, empowering position. The final sentence recalls the last paragraph of "Flies in Amber" because in both essays Burroughs in effect makes a literary pilgrimage to Concord, bequeathing readers the mythic landscape of nineteenth-century transcendentalism and encouraging them to treasure it.

Emerson's Place

Burroughs's intense, sixty-year relation to Emerson is no secret, but it is well worth recalling and reinterpreting. Burroughs first read Emerson in the summer of 1856, when he was a nineteen-year-old farm boy struggling to educate himself between stints as a country schoolteacher. He tells the story in the 1889 essay "An Egotistical Chapter": "I carried to my room one volume of his, but I could do nothing with it. What, indeed, could a Johnsonian youth make of Emerson? A year or so later I again opened one of his books in a Chicago bookstore, and was so taken with the first taste of it that I then and there purchased the three volumes,—the 'Essays' and the

'Miscellanies'" (*Writings* 8:267). In a February 1901 interview, Burroughs embellished the account: "For a long time afterward I lived, moved, and had my being in those books. I was like Jonah in the whale's belly—completely swallowed by them. They were almost my whole intellectual diet for two or three years. I kept my Emerson close at hand and read him everywhere. I would go up under the trees of the sap-bush there at home and read and be moved to tears by the extreme beauty and eloquence of his words. For years all that I wrote was Emersonian. It was as if I was dipped in Emerson."[6] In a notebook entry from April 1858, Burroughs lists Emerson as a topic for an essay, and an 1859 notebook in the Berg Collection, titled "A Note Book: containing a few smooth pebbles and pearly shells which the waves of thought leave, from time to time, upon my shores," contains over 150 pages of trial essays, written in broadly Emersonian style. A third notebook, also from 1859, contains yet other Emersonian trials.[7] By 1860 Emerson had become "the master-enchanter" of the young Burroughs, who imitated Emerson's thought and style so well that when he submitted the essay "Expression" to James Russell Lowell at the *Atlantic*, Lowell thought the essay had been plagiarized and even asked Emerson if it was his (*Writings* 8:267).

"Expression" was published in the November 1860 issue of the *Atlantic*, Burroughs's first major publication and the first of scores of *Atlantic* articles he would pen over the next sixty years.[8] Even though Burroughs claims that the essay "had not much merit" (267), it in fact shows how thoroughly he absorbed Emersonian transcendentalism in the 1850s, for the essay is a remarkable performance by a talented literary chameleon. In the second paragraph, for instance, the writer could easily be mistaken for Emerson, and we can surely appreciate Lowell's doubts:

> Nature exists to the mind not as an absolute realization, but as a condition, as something constantly becoming. It is neither entirely this nor that. It is suggestive and prospective; a body in motion, and not an object at rest. It draws the soul out and excites thought, because it is embosomed in a heaven of possibilities, and interests without satisfying. The landscape has a pleasure to us, because in the mind it is canopied by the ideal, as it is here canopied by the sky. (572)

Not only does Burroughs provide a succinct summary of Emersonian ideas of nature, but he also expresses the ideas in Emerson's characteristic style, employing analogy and antithesis most prominently. The symbolic character of nature underlies the paragraph, as it underlies Emerson's 1836 *Nature*, and that insight calls for a figurative, doubling style. Hence Burroughs notes that "we cannot know one thing alone; two ideas enter into every distinct act of the understanding" (573). Because of this inherent duality, no thought is whole when it is given expression: "We cannot speak entire and unmixed truth, because utterance separates a part from the whole, and consequently in a measure distorts and exaggerates and does injustice to other truths. The moment we speak, we are one-sided and liable to be assailed by the reverse side of the fact" (573). Already in "Expression," Burroughs is formulating the dominant ideas he delineates in "Emerson and His Journals" and "Flies in Amber," especially the duality of power and limitation.

The other implied duality is that of nature and soul, the fundamental duality in Emerson's essays. Burroughs understands the duality well in 1860, remarking that a well-expressed idea is, like nature itself, "suggestive and prospective" and that "analogy is the highest form of expression, the poetry of speech" (574). In focusing on language, Burroughs summarizes the ideas and echoes the phrasing of the "Language" chapter in *Nature* and the 1844 essay "The Poet." Poetry, for Emerson and Burroughs, is the "perpetual marrying of thought with things," and it depends upon poets who "grow earnest and impassioned, and speak from their inmost heart" (575).

Manuscript evidence shows that the young Burroughs was perpetually attempting to marry thoughts with things through his writing. In his copy of Emerson's *Essays: First Series*, for instance, he marked a passage from "The Over-Soul," underlining a particularly important phrase: "But the soul that ascends to worship the great God is plain and true; has no rose-color, no fine friends, no chivalry, no adventures; does not want admiration; dwells in the hour that now is in the earnest *experience of the common day,*—by reason of the present moment and the mere trifle having become porous to thought, and bibulous of the sea of light." On the back flyleaf of his copy of *Essays: Second Series*, he wrote this note, dated March 19, 1864: "I find that my familiarity with common objects—with cows, horses, woods, rivers, mountains &c helps me to judge and estimate men, books, art. I see the commonest experiences such as that of the farmer, teamster, drover, tanner, mechanic, mason, sailor, soldier &c would be useful to one in any sphere, in aesthetics, morals, art &c."[9] The cataloguing style of the note suggests that by 1864 Burroughs was already under the strong influence of Walt Whitman. The duality of objects and subjects organizes the passage, but there are two other dualisms at work: the languages of experience and art, and the languages of Emerson and Whitman.

As Burroughs closes his first significant Emersonian essay, he draws a specific, individual conclusion concerning the relationship between the languages of experience and art:

> The language of life, and of men who speak to be understood, should be used more in our books. A great principle anchored to a common word or a familiar illustration never looses its hold upon the mind; it is like seeing the laws of Astronomy in the swing of a pendulum, or in the motion of the boy's ball,—or the law of the tides and the seasons appearing in the beating of the pulse, or in inspiring and expiring the breath. The near and the remote are head and tail of the same law, and good writing unites them, giving wholeness and continuity. The language of the actual and the practical applied to the ideal brings it at once within everybody's reach, tames it, and familiarizes it to the mind. (577)

At first this passage seems to echo Emerson's *Nature*, especially the concluding chapter, "Prospects." The key relationship is between near and remote, the real and the ideal, and that remains the key relationship in Burroughs's old-age meditations on the master-enchanter. But the young Burroughs is not merely echoing the master.

As Emerson ends *Nature*, he calls for the restoration of the world to its "original and eternal beauty" through the redemption of the soul. In his famous formulation, "the ruin or the blank, that we see when we look at nature, is in our own eye. The axis of vision is not coincident with the axis of things, and so they appear not transparent but opake [*sic*]. The reason why the world lacks unity, and lies broken and in heaps, is, because man is disunited with himself. He cannot be a naturalist, until he satisfies all the demands of the spirit."[10] If the naturalist manages to combine detachment and affection, learning and prayer, he will find that the world abounds with objects of knowledge:

> The invariable mark of wisdom is to see the miraculous in the common. What is a day? What is a year? What is summer? What is woman? What is a child? What is sleep? To our blindness, these things seem unaffecting. We make fables to hide the baldness of the fact and conform it, as we say, to the higher law of the mind. But when the fact is seen under the light of an idea, the gaudy fable fades and shrivels. We behold the real higher law. To the wise, therefore, a fact is true poetry, and the most beautiful of fables. These wonders are brought to our own door. (*Nature* 44)

For Emerson, the most seemingly common fact embodies the ideal, or "real higher law," and for that reason nature does not exist in some world apart from human beings or separated from the human spirit. It *is* that world itself, if only we can open our eyes to see the miraculous ideal within the common, ordinary, and near-at-hand reality.

Burroughs understands this fundamental Emersonian insight, but "Expression" concludes with a very different emphasis. Rather than seeking the restoration of the world and the redemption of the soul, the young Burroughs attempts to bring the ideal "within everybody's reach." This taming and familiarizing of the ideal in effect reverses the direction of Emerson's argument in *Nature*, even though Burroughs echoes Emerson's concern with the near and the remote, the actual and the ideal. For Emerson, the ideal is ever-present and ready to be seen, if we could open the eye of Reason from within. For Burroughs, language itself remains the less-than-transparent mediator between the near and the remote: "Though the genealogy of our ideas be traceable to Jove and Olympus, they must marry their human sisters, the facts of common life and experience, before they can be productive of anything positive and valuable" (577).

For the young writer starting out, this simultaneous reversal and preservation of the relationship between near and far is both empowering and necessary. The influence of Emerson is by no means simple, nor is it simply benign. In "An Egotistical Chapter," Burroughs notes his complicated sense of the influence immediately after he considers "Expression" as having "not much merit," and he responds by recalling how he escaped the master's power:

> It was mainly to break the spell of Emerson's influence and to get upon
> ground of my own that I took to writing upon outdoor themes. I wrote half
> a dozen or more sketches upon all sorts of open-air subjects, which were
> published in the New York "Leader." The woods, the soil, the waters, helped
> to draw out the pungent Emersonian flavor and restore me to my proper
> atmosphere. But to this day I am aware that a suggestion of Emerson's manner
> often crops out in my writings. His mind was the firmer, harder substance, and
> was bound to leave its mark upon my own. But, in any case, my debt to him is
> great. He helped me to better literary expression, he quickened my perception
> of the beautiful, he stimulated and fertilized my religious nature. (8:268)

In this passage, place exercises a counterinfluence on the young writer, drawing out "the pungent Emersonian flavor" of his style. Landscape imagery appears in the description of Emerson's manner as an outcropping in his own writings, and Emerson's mind is geological in character, underlying Burroughs's work like an ancient substrate of rock. Even the term "fertilized" smacks of the soil. The imagery suggests that Burroughs understands his career most fundamentally in terms of place, but he also sees Emerson's active influence underlying and supporting his literary landscape.

The outdoor sketches appeared under the title "From the Back Country," and they elicited the admiring response of Myron Benton, a young poet-farmer who is best known for having received Thoreau's final letter. Like Thoreau, Burroughs was gratified by Benton's letters. On August 27, 1862, he replied to Benton, evoking the same sense of literary consumption as the phrase "pungent Emersonian flavor." He says that he wrote the sketches "for a change of mental diet" and because his "style needed limbering up a little, needed more play and movement. . . . Writing about common and familiar objects, I find, is a good exercise." The imagery of change and freedom is physical, and Burroughs joins it to the "good exercise" of writing about common and familiar objects. Later in the letter, he locates himself physically: "Fifty miles from the railroad, twelve miles from the stage-coach, and two miles from the Post Office—is not that Back Country? This is my native place." Again Burroughs links the physical to the literary, since for the young writer the Back Country is the "native place" he has discovered as a subject. Finally, Burroughs connects the new friendship to his literary models: "I see your name in the Leader quite often. Your papers and essays are good. I should like to talk with you about Emerson and Thoreau, but could not do it on this sheet." The correspondence with Benton opens a series of important possibilities for Burroughs. He discovers an appreciative reader with whom he can exchange ideas; he engages his skills as a critical reader of Benton, of himself, and of their common mentors; he defines himself and his literary place in physical terms, since he shares with Benton the vocabulary of the Back Country.[11]

The measure of Emerson's influence is less in the power of his ideas and literary style than in the sheer staying power of the influence itself. Like a good Emersonian, Burroughs resists the master-enchanter, but he also appreciates the enchantment. It is not quite as simple as Emerson himself says in the journal entry of 1859, when he claims that he delights in driving men from him. Rather, Burroughs reads both Emerson and Thoreau in order to define his own place as a writer of nature essays and literary criticism. Burroughs extends the complicated calculus of this relationship beyond the writers, too. In confronting the influence of Emerson and Thoreau, he defines a place that embraces both the nature essay and place-based literary criticism. If Emerson drives Burroughs toward the outdoor themes and the literary Back Country, he also drives him toward reading culture in terms of nature.

Burroughs's response to Emerson leads in the direction of "Emerson and His Journals" and "Flies in Amber," but equally interesting are the three essays Burroughs wrote about Emerson in the earlier phases of his career. The first, titled simply "Emerson," appears in *Birds and Poets* (1877); the second, "Arnold's View of Emerson and Carlyle," appears in *Indoor Studies* (1889); the third, "Another Word on Emerson," appears in *Literary Values* (1902). In addition, Burroughs discusses Emerson repeatedly in other essays, such as "A Sunday in Cheyne Row" in *Fresh Fields* (1884),

"A Spray of Pine" in *Signs and Seasons* (1886), and "Style and the Man" and "Recent Phases of Criticism" in *Literary Values*. Burroughs's view of Emerson does not change dramatically over the sixty years of his career, but it grows and deepens considerably.

Birds and Poets is a remarkable mixture of nature writing and ecocriticism. In the title essay, originally published as "The Birds of the Poets" in *Scribner's Monthly* (September 1873), Burroughs claims that "the poets are the best natural historians, only you must know how to read them. They translate the facts largely and freely" (*Writings* 3:13–14). Factual accuracy becomes a standard for judging the English and American poets, but Burroughs also uses a more figurative understanding. In discussing Emerson, for instance, he notes that his "best natural history poem is the 'Humble-Bee,'" but that "his later poem, 'The Titmouse,' has many of the same qualities, and cannot fail to be acceptable to both poet and naturalist" (39). Then Burroughs discusses the chickadee as "a truly Emersonian bird," a paragraph that depends both on the ornithological kinship between titmouse and chickadee (both of the family Paridae) and on the reader's acceptance of the chickadee as "a New England bird, clad in black and ashen gray" (40). This blend of science and metaphor leads to a paragraph on Emerson as "a northern hyperborean genius,—a winter bird with a clear, saucy, cheery call, and not a passionate summer songster. His lines have little melody to the ear, but they have the vigor and distinctness of all pure and compact things. They are like the needles of the pine—'the snow loving pine'—more than the emotional foliage of the deciduous trees, and the titmouse becomes them well" (40). In three sentences, Burroughs effectively creates a winter New England landscape as Emerson's characteristic poetic style. Emerson's poetry thus inhabits the place as surely as the pines, chickadees, and titmice.

The characterization of Emerson in "Birds and Poets" depends fundamentally on Burroughs's sense of Emerson as a poet of place. That place is New England, of course, but it is also a crossroads of science and poetry, criticism and natural history. In the essay "Emerson," Burroughs fully develops the literal and literary geography fully. He begins by considering what "the race has so far lost and gained, in being transplanted from

Europe to the New England soil and climate," and he finds that "Emerson is undoubtedly a master on the New England scale,—*such* a master as the land and race are capable of producing" (179). Burroughs considers Emerson "an essence, a condensation" (180), and he calls him "the master Yankee, the centennial flower of that thrifty and peculiar stock" (182–83). Instead of emphasizing Emerson's transcendentalism, Burroughs focuses on the hard-edged practicality and penetrating style of the late Emerson. For these reasons, Burroughs describes Emerson as "a man who occupies every inch of his rightful territory; he is there in proper person to the farthest bound" (186). In Burroughs's reading, that territory is defined by the lyceum circuit of New England and its demand "for ceaseless intellectual friction and chafing" (188), and the forum prompts Emerson's characteristic style of electric, startling surprise:

> Emerson's peculiar quality is very subtle, but very sharp and firm and unmis-
> takable. It is not analogous to the commoner, slower-going elements, as heat,
> air, fire, water, but is nearer akin to that elusive but potent something we call
> electricity. It is abrupt, freaky, unexpected, and always communicates a little
> wholesome shock. It darts this way and that, and connects the far and the near
> in every line. (187)

Burroughs's search for an elemental analogy leads him to the freaky electricity of Emerson's darting style, and it forecasts the unmistakable connection of far and near that he develops most fully in "Emerson and His Journals." In both movements, Burroughs shows that he grounds his criticism of Emerson in a concrete sense of place and in a concept of nature as a primal, electric force.

Emerson's place, in Burroughs's formulation, encompasses both nature and culture. Thus he calls Emerson "the fruit of extreme culture" (190), a figure that metaphorically joins the two. But because Emerson is a condensation or essence, Burroughs faults him for being "balked by the cloud of materials" and for writing "a bloodless kind of poetry" (192–93). Emerson's vision, though penetrating, is limited; he is "one of those men whom the gods drive with blinders on, so that they see fiercely in only a few directions" (195). As in "Expression," Burroughs calls for "good red blood and plenty of it" (196). Thus he finds that Emerson is too fixed in place, incapable of movement and change:

> Emerson's limitation or fixity is seen also in the fact that he has taken no new step in his own direction, if indeed another step could be taken in that direction and not step off. He is a prisoner on his peak. He cannot get away from the old themes. His later essays are upon essentially the same subjects as his first. He began by writing on nature, greatness, manners, art, poetry, and he is still writing on them. He is a husbandman who practices no rotation of crops, but submits to the exhaustive process of taking about the same things from his soil year after year. (197)

The critical metaphor suggests that Emerson has exhausted his imaginative landscape by harvesting too exclusively the great themes of his early essays. Emerson's strategy reveals a certain lack of sympathy for others, and Burroughs notes that this lack is apparent in Emerson's performance at the lecture stand, where "he might be of wood, so far as he is responsive to the moods and feelings of his auditors" (200). Burroughs figures Emerson as emotionally imprisoned, even if the prison is the transcendental peak he alone has climbed.

Despite the limitations, Burroughs concludes the essay by noting Emerson's power, for the "prisoner on his peak" occupies a higher altitude than most writers and readers: "His thought is far above the great sea level of humanity, where stand most of the world's masters. He is like one of those marvelously clear mountain lakes whose water-line runs above all the salt seas of the globe" (201). Burroughs reads literature as a landscape of masters, assigning Emerson a topographical place on the map he draws. Burroughs's sense of place shows him how Emerson acts upon his readers like a "living force" (202). With more confidence than he would find in the last two essays on Emerson, Burroughs therefore predicts that "his work has the seal of immortality upon it" and that it will continue to appeal to youth and to genius (205).

In addition to the central role in "An Egotistical Chapter," Emerson plays a major part in two other essays in *Indoor Studies*: "Science and the Poets" and "Arnold's View of Emerson and Carlyle." The first essay describes Emerson's interest in science in succinct and telling detail, discussing both prose and poetry and finding that his writings "seem curiously to imply science, as if he had all these bold deductions and discoveries under his feet, and was determined to match them in the ideal" (83). The essay effectively adds the scientific element to the blending of discursive modes in Emerson's work. In the account of Matthew Arnold's lectures on Emerson and Carlyle, delivered in 1883 and 1884, Burroughs makes a critical rejoinder to the English critic, but the essay is more important for the general ground it takes than for any particular defense it makes of Emerson or Carlyle. Burroughs views Arnold as representing classical formalism, and by such standards he is ready to admit that both Emerson and Carlyle are barbarians. But Burroughs defends them on their own terms, for they represent a "new turn-up in literature,—men whose highest distinction is the depth and fervor of their moral conviction, whose greatness of character is on a par with their greatness of intellect" (151). While this response certainly echoes the "language of life" passage in "Expression," the defense of Emerson and Carlyle does not employ the place-based arguments that mark Burroughs's first and last essays on the master. In replying to Arnold, Burroughs focuses on character and therefore does not evoke his sense of place as a combination of culture and nature.

In "Another Word on Emerson," published in 1902, Burroughs recurs to the prisoner on his peak, describing Emerson's "remoteness from the common thoughts, aims, attractions, of everyday humanity" (*Writings* 12:212). The remoteness can be praiseworthy, as when Burroughs calls him "the most astral genius in English or any other literature," but it can also be a limitation or defect, preventing Emerson from sympathizing with human life (213). Despite the limitations, however, Burroughs defines Emerson's leading trait as "eminently American; I mean his hospitality toward the new" (214). This looks forward to the idea in "Emerson and His Journals," in which Burroughs praises Emerson for seeing that "the past and the present, the near and the far, [are] made of one stuff" (*Writings* 23:31). But in "Another Word on Emerson," Burroughs finds that Emerson's "hospitality toward the new" causes his thinking and writing to become fragmentary and random, though occasionally brilliant and bold. He characteristically ends by affirming Emerson's ability to marry the ideal and the real: "He is abstract in his aim, and concrete in his methods. He fixes his eye on the star, but would make it draw his wagon" (216). The essay is itself a fragment, more remarkable for its bold willingness to criticize Emerson than for its brilliant insight or figuration. Burroughs opens the door to a place-based criticism, one that would view Emerson as "eminently American" by seeing him in the context of the relationship between nature and culture. But he does not seize the opportunity he gives himself until he returns for final words on Emerson in *The Last Harvest*.

The Thoreau Charge

If Emerson provides Burroughs with opportunities for critical discovery and literary development, Thoreau acts more like a goad or prod. In the three published essays on Thoreau, Burroughs is restrained and judicious, but in journals, letters, and interviews, he often breaks out in impatience with what he calls "the Thoreau charge." In February 1878, for instance, he wrote this telling note to himself in his journal:

> I take it as a great compliment when my friends, those who have known me longest and best, say of my writings, "They sound just like you; I see you in every page," as a doctor who knew me when a boy, and who knew my people, has just written me. This removes much of the Thoreau charge; if it is my flavor, it is not his. I really see very little of Thoreau in myself. There is a whiff of him, now and then, in a few of my pieces, as in "Exhilarations of the Road." I know his quality is very penetrating and contagious; reading him is like eating onions—one must look out or the flavor will reach his own page. But my current is as strong in my own channel as Thoreau's in his. Thoreau preaches and teaches always. I never preach or teach. I simply see and describe. I must have a pure result. I paint the bird for its own sake, and for the pleasure it affords me, and am annoyed at any lesson or moral twist. Even the scholar in me (a very poor one he is!) must not show his head when

I am writing on natural themes. I would remind of books no more than the things themselves do. [12]

Burroughs speaks here as an ambitious forty-year-old writer of nature essays and literary criticism. The "Thoreau charge" had been repeated from the beginning of his career as a nature writer, and he clearly chafed at it. Indeed, the journal entry may have been in response to Henry James's review in the January 27, 1876, issue of the *Nation*, in which James called Burroughs "a sort of reduced but also more humorous, more available, and more sociable Thoreau." [13] The volume under review, *Winter Sunshine*, includes the "Exhilarations of the Road" essay, in which Burroughs himself detects a "whiff" of Thoreau, and the eight essays in the book are arranged seasonally, beginning in winter and running around the year to October. Thus it is tempting to find whiffs of "Walking" and *Walden* in *Winter Sunshine*, and we know from "Another Word on Thoreau" how much Burroughs admired those two works. Just as the young Burroughs steeped himself in Emerson and then sought to purge himself of "the pungent Emersonian flavor," so in the journal entry he finds Thoreau's flavor altogether too strong.

Burroughs repeats the humorous image of onions in the essay "Before Genius," from *Birds and Poets*, but in doing so he takes away the stinging aftertaste of the journal passage:

With two or three exceptions, there is little as yet in American literature that shows much advance beyond the merely conventional and scholastic,—little, I mean, in which one gets a whiff of the strong, unbreathed air of mountain or prairie, or a taste of rude, new power that is like the tonic of the sea. Thoreau occupies a niche by himself. Thoreau was not a great personality, yet his writings have a strong characteristic flavor. He is anti-scorbutic, like leeks and onions. He has reference, also, to the highest truths. (3:163)

Here the "whiff" is not unpleasant, being the "unbreathed" air of a vast landscape. Even though Thoreau's onion flavor returns, it is medicinal, "anti-scorbutic," and in that way is analogous to the "tonic of the sea." The images of place and taste combine the far and near, just as Burroughs reads Thoreau as combining the ideal and the real—highest truths and onions.

For over a decade after the publication of *Birds and Poets*, Burroughs had very little to say about Thoreau, but Concord functioned as a special place for him during the period. In June 1883, he made a literary pilgrimage to Concord in the company of Richard Watson Gilder, editor of *Century Illustrated Monthly Magazine* and one of Burroughs's best friends. The two men traveled to Boston, walking by Longfellow's home and Lowell's grounds, and then took a train to Concord, where they met Dr. Edward Waldo Emerson, the youngest child and eventual biographer of Emerson and editor of his father's works.[14] On June 28, according to Burroughs's journal, the two friends made their way to Walden Pond:

> Gilder & I walk to Walden Pond; much talk & loitering by the way. Walden a clear bright pond, not very wild. Look in vain for the site of Thoreau's hut. Two boys in a boat row up & ask us the question we have on our tongues to ask them. Day hot, we sit in the woods & try to talk about immortality; don't get very near together; on such a theme, like ships at sea, we soon part company, words have no meaning when we leave this solid ground of earth. The language is for this life—not the next. . . . I saw nothing in Concord that recalled Thoreau, except that his ripe culture & tone might well date from such a place. On the whole Concord is the most pleasing country village I ever saw. Nothing like it in England, where only the poor live in villages. It impressed me much. Its amplitude, its mellowness, its home-like air, its great trees, its broad avenues, its good homes, &c. Emerson & Hawthorne are its best expression in literature. It seems fit that they should come from this place.[15]

Burroughs creates a vivid sense of place, both in the descriptive narrative and in his reflections on the place itself. He first of all tempers the idea of Walden Pond as potentially remote or wild, finding it "not very wild" at all. Nor is Walden a place for abstract, transcendental talk. Gilder and Burroughs attempt a kind of Hawthorne-Melville dialogue on immortality, but Burroughs ultimately has little use for language of this kind, and his reflections echo the theory of common, concrete language that he develops in "Expression" and in his essays on Emerson. Remarkably, in a description of Walden and Concord, Burroughs claims to find "nothing . . . that recalled Thoreau." It is as if he were erasing Thoreau from the landscape, and by the time he finishes his laudatory description of the village, Emerson and Hawthorne occupy the place like an exclusive neighborhood. The rhetoric of the journal entry thus enacts a subtle and aggressive displacement of Thoreau.

Subtle aggression marks Burroughs's discussion of Thoreau in "An Egotistical Chapter." Immediately after explaining how he read Emerson and then began writing on outdoor themes in the New York *Leader*, Burroughs notes that "about this period I fell in with Thoreau's 'Walden,' but I am not conscious of any great debt to Thoreau: I had begun to write upon outdoor themes before his books fell into my hands, but he undoubtedly helped confirm me in my own direction. He was the intellectual child of Emerson, but added a certain crispness and pungency, as of wild roots and herbs, to the urbane philosophy of his great neighbor" (8:268–69). The phrase "great neighbor" looks forward to the last sentence of "Another Word on Thoreau," and the image of pungency looks back to the journal entry of 1876 and its "whiff" of onions. In combination, the two elements crystallize Burroughs's abiding sense of Thoreau's influence, an influence he "falls" in with rather than seeks out. If Thoreau is the intellectual child of Emerson, Burroughs is Thoreau's competitive younger brother.

This sense of influential rivalry makes "Henry D. Thoreau" the most interesting essay of *Indoor Studies* (1889), especially because it is the lead article in the book. Burroughs begins the essay in the same vein as "Another Word on Thoreau," noting the posthumous fame and the eleven-volume Riverside edition of Thoreau's works (*Writings* 8:4–6).[16] Echoing the language of "Before Genius" and "An Egotistical Chapter," Burroughs notes that Thoreau "fills his own niche well" (6) but was "a little too near his friend and master, Emerson, and brought too directly under his influence. If he had lived farther from him, he would have felt his attraction less. But he was just as positive a fact as Emerson. The contour of his moral nature was just as firm and resisting. He was no more a soft-shelled egg, to be dented by every straw in the nest, than was his distinguished neighbor" (7). The relationship between Emerson and Thoreau clearly becomes a means by which Burroughs can negotiate his relationship to both. Moreover, the concrete language of place measures the strength of the relationships, for literary influence is a function of physical and moral "nearness" to a great or distinguished "neighbor."

In many respects, Burroughs treats Thoreau as a lesser Emerson, in that way echoing Henry James's view of Burroughs. But he also focuses sharply on the particular aspects of Thoreau's work that mark him as a unique writer, the most important of which is the theme of wildness:

> Thoreau was, probably, the wildest civilized man this country has produced, adding to the shyness of the hermit and woodsman the wildness of the poet, and to the wildness of the poet the greater ferity and elusiveness of the mystic. An extreme product of civilization and of modern culture, he was yet as untouched by the worldly and commercial spirit of his age and country as any red man that ever haunted the shores of his native stream. He put the whole of nature between himself and his fellows. A man of the strongest local attachments,—not the least nomadic, seldom wandering beyond his native township,—yet his spirit was as restless and as impatient of restraint as any nomad or Tartar that ever lived. He cultivated an extreme wildness, not only in his pursuits and tastes, but in his hopes and imaginings. He says to his friend, "Hold fast your most indefinite waking dream." Emerson says his life was an attempt to pluck the Swiss edelweiss from the all but inaccessible cliffs. The higher and the wilder, the more the fascination for him. Indeed, the loon, the moose, the beaver, were but faint types and symbols of the wildness he coveted and would have reappear in his life and books; not the cosmical, the universal,—he was not great enough for that,—but simply the wild as distinguished from the domestic and the familiar, the remote and the surprising as contrasted with the hackneyed and the commonplace, arrow-heads as distinguished from whetstones or jackknives. (14–15)

In this remarkable passage, Burroughs's analysis of Thoreau creates a meeting-place for opposites, though he does not indulge in the extreme paradoxes that mark Thoreau's own language. The character of wildness dominates the paragraph, but so does the idea of place. For Thoreau— especially the Thoreau of "Walking"—the wild *is* place, *is* nature, and his extremity is an attempt to distance himself from culture. Thus Burroughs can remark, with some humor, that Thoreau "cultivated an extreme wildness." In that extremity, Thoreau goes beyond Emerson's sense of place, even though he remains invested in the local. Unlike Emerson's, Thoreau's sense of place does not include "the cosmical, the universal," but it is also too remote from our familiar world. It occupies a remote, exotic past, signified by the arrowheads Thoreau collected. According to Burroughs, then, Thoreau's wildness is more an artifact than a useful tool.

When Burroughs considers Thoreau's style, he finds that "his literary art, like that of Emerson, is in the unexpected turn of his sentences" (29). But rather than finding wisdom in common things, as Emerson does, Thoreau "must make the commonest facts and occurrences wear a strange and unfamiliar look." According to Burroughs, Walden Pond provides the best example of that tendency, and Thoreau makes the "whole world interested in his private experiment . . . by the strange and, on the whole, beaming face he put[s] upon it." The result, however, is that "we are not buoyed up by great power, we do not swim lightly as in deep water, but we are amused and stimulated, and now and then positively electrified" (30). Despite the praise, Burroughs clearly undercuts any claims for Thoreau's greatness. He characterizes the tone of *Walden* as "clear, saucy, cheery, triumphant," noting Thoreau's own comparison of himself to Chanticleer and claiming that the book "is a challenge and a triumph, and has a morning freshness and *élan*" (33). By simultaneously limiting and praising Thoreau's achievement, Burroughs effectively domesticates his wild rival. He reads his great neighbor carefully but not generously.

In reading Thoreau's journal, Burroughs considers him more talented in supernatural history than in natural history. This must have been a surprising claim even in 1889. To support it, Burroughs quotes a passage from the journal: "Man cannot afford to be a naturalist, to look at Nature directly, but only with the side of his eye. He must look through and beyond her." He then suggests that Thoreau misses "seeing much there was in her; the jealous goddess had her revenge," and he offers a disingenuous disclaimer: "I do not make this remark as a criticism, but to account for his failure to make any new or valuable contribution to natural history" (37–38). Burroughs sees Thoreau as an "industrious and persistent" natural historian, but not as a gifted one, and he finds no "felicitous and happy seeing," no "inspiration of the eye," in the journals (39).[17]

By limiting Thoreau's powers of observation, Burroughs transforms him into a persistently bad naturalist. But he does not doubt Thoreau's sincere attempts to know the place around him. "From his journal," he writes, "it would appear that Thoreau kept nature about Concord under a sort of police surveillance the year round" (43). All of Thoreau's efforts, however, are fruitless, for nature is always a step ahead of his knowledge: "Thus he went through the season, Nature's reporter, taking down the words as they fell from her lips, and distressed if a sentence was missed" (45). Thoreau emerges, then, as a distressed and displaced person, a writer who, despite his best efforts, knows little of his place. Burroughs seals the effect by quoting the famous passage about the azad from the "Economy" chapter of *Walden*. He notes that there is no source for the passage in the Gulistan, implying that the passage is invented and therefore especially significant. In effect, Thoreau is the azad, like a cypress tree that bears no fruit. The azad is independent, but the cost of freedom is to have "nothing to give away" (47). For Thoreau, the parable relates directly to the encumbrances of nineteenth-century American capitalism; for Burroughs, it relates directly to the poverty of place in Thoreau.

Burroughs does not always represent Thoreau as impoverished and displaced. In "Thoreau's Wildness," published in *Literary Values* (1902), Burroughs calls him "the wildest man New England has turned out since the red aborigines vacated her territory" and claims that "his whole life was a search for the wild, not only in nature but in literature, in life, in morals" (*Writings* 12:217). In Burroughs's definition, wildness is more than a state of nature, more than an absence of culture or civilization. It includes, for instance, the indigenous cultures of America, and Burroughs eventually concludes that Thoreau's literary art is itself arrow-like, letting fly "with a kind of quick inspiration; and though his arrows sometimes go wide, yet it is always a pleasure to watch their aerial course" (220). Thoreau becomes an "Emersonian or transcendental red man," in Burroughs's formulation, not a naturalist. In this brief essay, however, Burroughs does not take Thoreau to task for his errors or exaggerations. Instead, he portrays the writer as a seeker after truth:

> He went to Nature as to an oracle; and though he sometimes, indeed very often, questioned her as a naturalist and a poet, yet there was always another question in his mind. He ransacked the country about Concord in all seasons and weathers, and at all times of the day and night he delved into the ground, he probed the swamps, he searched the waters, he dug into woodchuck holes, into muskrats' dens, into the retreats of the mice and squirrels; he saw every bird, heard every sound, found every wildflower, and brought home many a fresh bit of natural history; but he was always searching for something he did not find. This search of his for the transcendental, the unfindable, the wild that will not be caught, he has set forth in a beautiful parable in "Walden:" —
>
> > "I long ago lost a hound, a bay horse, and a turtledove, and am still on their trail. Many are the travelers I have spoken concerning them, describing their tracks, and what calls they answered to. I have met one or two who had heard the hound, and the tramp of the horse, and even seen the dove disappear behind a cloud; and they seemed as anxious to recover them as if they had lost them themselves." (222–23)

Nature is an oracular place, but it does not always give a clear message to the seeker. Beyond his roles as naturalist and poet, Thoreau pursues the ineffable, the sense of the wild that Burroughs develops most tellingly. Of course such a hunt must fail, since the ineffable is by definition "the wild that will not be caught." But in "Thoreau's Wildness" the failure does not lead to a sense of Thoreau's limitations. Instead, Burroughs celebrates Thoreau's close contact with the local, concrete place. Thoreau is in every way an active and successful seeker after knowledge. But there is always more to seek, and other places to search. Thus the essay concludes with the very parable of the pursuit itself, the search for the unfindable. Some travelers recognize and recall a sign of what Thoreau seeks. One of them, finally, is John Burroughs. Rather than undercut Thoreau's accomplishments by detailing his failed pursuit of knowledge, Burroughs eagerly celebrates the wildness that leads Thoreau to pursue the unfindable in "the country about

Concord in all seasons and weathers." Burroughs is at his most generous in "Thoreau's Wildness," and as a result he writes his best essay on his elder rival. He draws very near to Thoreau, so near that the two seem to occupy nearly the same place of nature. In such nearness, Burroughs most resembles both his great neighbors, Emerson and Thoreau.

2 *Whitman Land*
John Burroughs's Pastoral Criticism

Ecocentric Aesthetics

As important as Emerson and Thoreau were to John Burroughs as a literary naturalist and critic, Walt Whitman exercised the longest-lasting and most profound influence on his career as a writer. The two first met in Washington, D.C., in 1863, and they were close friends to the very end of Whitman's life, when he spoke to Burroughs from his deathbed. In his journal of December 1891, Burroughs recorded that he stepped out of Whitman's bedroom, "for fear of fatiguing him. He says, 'It is all right, John,' evidently referring to his approaching end." Though Whitman lived another three months, Burroughs never saw him again. At the graveside in Harleigh Cemetery in Camden, New Jersey, on March 30, 1892, Burroughs was an honorary pallbearer but was too overcome by grief to deliver a eulogy.[1]

Just as the publication of "Expression" in the pages of the *Atlantic* suggests the powerful effect of Emerson on the outsetting writer, Burroughs's first four books reveal Whitman's influence as fundamental. The poet edited Burroughs's first book, *Notes on Walt Whitman, as Poet and Person*, published in the spring of 1867. He helped Burroughs with his first book of nature essays, especially in selecting the title *Wake-Robin* (1871), which became the best known of Burroughs's nearly thirty books. Whitman's direct influence came most tellingly in the drafting and naming of Burroughs's fourth book, *Birds and Poets* (1877). On January 7, 1877, Burroughs wrote to the editors of Houghton Mifflin Company, proposing "a new vol. for next spring or summer to be called 'Nature and Genius.'" But just over three weeks later, on January 29, he sent the publishers part of the manuscript and said it was to be titled *"Birds and Poets,* instead of Nature & Genius as I first thought."* The intervening event was a letter from Whitman on January 24, 1877:

> I think **Birds and Poets** not only much the best name for the book, but a first-rate good name, appropriate, original & fresh, without being at all affected or strained. The piece you put 4th should be *first*—should lead the book giving it its title, & having the name of the piece changed to "Birds and Poets"—which I think would be an improvement. The whole collection would be sufficiently homogeneous, (and it were a fault to be too much so)—you just want *a hint* for the name of a book—Only it must be in the spirit of the book—& not too much so either. *"Nature & Genius"* is *too Emersony altogether.*[2]

Within a matter of a few days, then, Burroughs took Whitman's "too Emersony altogether" comment to heart, making precisely the changes in title and arrangement of contents the poet recommended. The phrase itself suggests that Whitman was aware of Burroughs's "Emersony" tendencies and therefore spoke emphatically against using the abstract, transcendental title.

Even though Whitman exercises the most profound influence on Burroughs of all his literary mentors, Burroughs is no mere disciple of the poet. Rather, he accepts Whitman's editorial advice without feeling threatened or manipulated, partly because of his sincere and absolute admiration for Whitman, but also because he is writing in genres that are outside Whitman's direct expertise. Nature essays and literary criticism were never Whitman's strongest genres, even in the Timber Creek essays that open *Specimen Days & Collect* (1884) or in the literary essays that close it. For his part, Burroughs never ventures into the kind of imitative writing that marks "Expression." He studiously avoids producing any versions of Whitman's revolutionary verse, and he definitely does not imitate the orotund, heavily qualified style of Whitman's post–Civil War prose. Whitman empowers Burroughs as a young writer, and his influence is as practical and concrete as it is profound.

As an old man, Burroughs readily admitted that "substantial portions of *Notes on Walt Whitman, as Poet and Person,* were read and revised by

Whitman himself. The poet reviewed sections as they were completed, discussed drafts with Burroughs, and even wrote a section entitled 'Standard of the Natural Universal.'"[3] The thirteen pages of "Standard of the Natural Universal" contain Whitman's most important statement on the role of nature in his work, and they suggest how Burroughs understands Whitman in the 1860s and 1870s. The argument of the chapter, moreover, indicates how the work of the literary naturalist and the ecocritic merge in Burroughs's writing, beginning with its first, largely rhetorical, question: "What is the reason that the inexorable and perhaps deciding standard by which poems, and other productions of art, must be tried, after the application of all minor tests, is the standard of absolute Nature?" (*Notes* 37). In developing the standard of "absolute Nature," Whitman argues that the human spirit and spirit of nature are convertible:

> I assert that every true work of art has arisen, primarily, out of its maker, apart from his talent of manipulation, being filled fuller than other men with this passionate affiliation and identity with Nature. Then I go a step further, and, without being an artist myself, I feel that every good artist of any age would join me in subordinating the most vaunted beauties of the best artificial productions, to the daily and hourly beauty of the shows and objects of outward Nature. I mean inclusively, the objects of Nature in their human relations. (*Notes* 38)

Whitman boldly asserts the primacy of the object-world as a standard for judging artworks, but in the last sentence he subtly places the environment in relation to humanity. The key to the relationship is "passionate affiliation and identity," so that the artist expresses a sense of spiritual kinship with the "shows and objects of outward Nature."

Whitman develops the nature-culture relationship as "intimate and precious," according the "objects of Nature" a primary power "which nothing at second hand can supply." The spiritual power of the object-world is figured as the *only* source of healthy spirituality and aesthetic balance: "Their spirit affords to man's spirit, I sometimes think, its only inlet to clear views of the highest Philosophy and Religion. Only in their spirit can he himself have health, sweetness, and proportion; and only in their spirit can he give any essentially sound judgment of a poem, no matter what the subject of it may be" (38). Whitman follows this statement by lamenting the utter lack of the natural spirit in the poetry and criticism of the age. The rhetoric of the American jeremiad dominates "Standard of the Natural Universal," but it also functions to answer the call and fill the lack it defines. So Whitman himself contradicts the claim that the spirit of nature is "entirely lacking," since "the whole stress of Walt Whitman is the supply of what is wanted in this direction" (39).

Whitman attempts to supply the spirit of nature in one long sentence, a verbal analogy to the cosmos:

> The image Walt Whitman seems generally to have in his mind is that of the Earth, "round, rolling, compact," and he aims to produce effects analagous [*sic*] to those produced by it; to address the mind as the landscape or the mountains, or ideas of space or time, address it; not to excite admiration by fine and minute effects, but to feed the mind by exhibitions of power; to make demands upon it, like those made by Nature; to give it the grasp and wholesomeness which come from contact with realities; to vitalize it by bringing to bear upon it material forms, and the width of the globe, as the atmosphere bears upon the blood through the lungs; working always by indirections, and depending on a corresponsive working of the mind that reads or hears, with the mind that produces, as the female with the male; careless of mere art, yet loyally achieving the effects of highest art; not unmindful of details, yet subordinating everything to the total effect. (40–41)

Like the 1855 Preface to *Leaves of Grass*, this sentence is as much a practical demonstration as a theoretical proposition. Syntactic parallelism, analogy, and antithesis, together with Whitman's dynamic vocabulary, create the characteristic effects of a "round, rolling, compact" style. In the background, too, one senses the "corresponsive working of the mind that reads or hears," for in this sentence Whitman lists the aspects of his work that would correspond most nearly to the demands Burroughs makes upon it. The gendered relationship of reader and writer ("as the female with the male") corresponds, moreover, to the relationship between poet and nature: in the previous section, Whitman had described the receptive poet as "him that is pregnable" (38). Thus Whitman demonstrates a certain gender bias in his figurations, but he also practices a fluid convertibility of gender identity.

The sense of "corresponsiveness" between writer and reader suggests that Whitman's jeremiad also laments the lack of literary criticism based on the spirit of nature and that, rather than Whitman filling that lack, Burroughs himself could become "the supply of what is wanted in this direction." Nor is Burroughs lacking in the text of *Notes*, despite Whitman's large and vital presence. For example, Burroughs describes himself in the opening chapter of *Notes* as a farm boy, cataloguing the "homely facts of the barn, and of cattle and horses; the sugar-making in the maple woods in early spring; the work of the corn-field, hay-field, potato-field; the delicious fall months, with their pigeon and squirrel shootings; threshing of buckwheat, gathering of apples, and burning of fallows; in short, everything that smacked of, and led to, the open air and its exhilarations" (9). Although the catalogue is suspiciously Whitmanesque, it is not nearly so round and rolling as the sentence from "Standard of the Natural Universal." Indeed, the fact that Burroughs and Whitman are practically indistinguishable is precisely the point. Both the critic and the poet imbibe the spirit of nature, and for that reason their spirits correspond to one another. As Burroughs details the effects of farm labor and life upon him, he sounds like the principal figure in "There Was a Child Went Forth": "I belonged, as I may say, to them; and my substance and taste, as they grew, assimilated them as truly as my body did its food. I loved a few books much; but I loved Nature, in all those material examples and subtle expressions, with a love passing all the books of the world. Appropriately enough, I at this time, 1861, first made the acquaintance of LEAVES OF GRASS, in the woods" (9–10). The autobiographical account traces a sequence of preparatory growth and experience leading to the discovery of Whitman's poetry, which appears as the appropriate stage in Burroughs's growth as a lover of nature. The book is figured as a person, and that figure accords with Burroughs's characteristic assessment of Whitman's poetry as presenting a powerful personality and voice. Thus boundaries dissolve—between art and nature, artist and critic, Whitman and Burroughs.

A clear example of how Whitman and Burroughs mingle perspectives can be seen in the discussion of Wordsworth, who had been Burroughs's favorite poet before 1861. The penultimate section of "Standard of the Natural Universal," for instance, registers Burroughs's turn from Wordsworth to Whitman, but it does so in Whitman's terms:

> Wordsworth was truly a devout and loving observer of Nature, and perhaps has indicated more surely than any other poet the healthful moral influence of the milder aspects of rural scenery. But to have spoken in the full spirit of the least fact which he describes would have rent him to atoms. To have accepted Nature in her entirety, as the absolutely good and the absolutely beautiful, would have been to him tantamount to moral and intellectual destruction. He is simply a rural and metaphysical poet whose subjects are drawn mostly from Nature, instead of from society, or the domain of romance; and he tells in so many words what he sees and feels in the presence of natural objects. He has definite aim, like a preacher or moralist as he was, and his effects are nearer akin to those of pretty vases and parlor ornaments than to trees or hills.
>
> In Nature everything is held in solution; there are no discriminations, or failures, or ends; there is no poetry or philosophy—but there is that which is better, and which feeds the soul, diffusing itself through the mind in calm and equable showers. To give the analogy of this in the least degree was not the success of Wordsworth. Neither has it been the success of any of the so-called poets of Nature since his time. Admirable as many of these poets are in some respects, they are but visiting-card callers upon Nature, going to her for tropes and figures only. In the products of the lesser fry of them I recognize merely a small toying with Nature—a kind of sentimental flirtation with birds and butterflies. (*Notes* 47)

The strategy in both paragraphs is to reduce the subject to its smallest dimension, to belittle the subject in the guise of judicious praise or clear-eyed appraisal. Wordsworth emerges as delicate, sincere, and severely limited, with little real kinship to "trees or hills." The followers of Wordsworth are even more limited and ineffectual, for the figuration infantilizes and feminizes them. The passage discriminates between small fry (Wordsworth) and "lesser fry" (his derivative disciples), and there is little doubt as to who is the ultimate big fish. Finally, the entire passage looks forward in both theme and style to Burroughs's discussion of Wordsworth's pastoral poetry in "Another Word on Thoreau." There he opposes the poetry of Emerson and Thoreau, "born of the wildness and elusiveness of our more capricious and unkempt Nature," to Wordsworth's more domesticated poetic landscape (*Writings* 23:131). And as we have seen, Burroughs applies this rhetoric of domestication to Thoreau in the lead essay of *Indoor Studies* (1889). In 1867, however, the rhetoric is reserved for English poets and their disciples.

Burroughs makes his presence felt more strongly in the chapter on "Beauty," immediately following the "Standard of the Natural Universal." The topic itself is one Burroughs had been writing about since the 1850s, and the aesthetic principles he outlines in the chapter remain central to his thinking for the rest of his career. Three fundamental principles stem as much from Burroughs's ideas of nature as they do from Whitman's: beauty is not the goal of nature, but it follows as the result of nature's powerful processes; beauty in art should likewise follow as a result of the creator's powerful imaginative processes; aesthetic appreciation of nature or art requires participation, not a distanced spectatorship (*Notes* 50–51).

The corollary to these three principles could come from Whitman, Burroughs, Emerson, or Thoreau: "The commonest and the nearest are at last the most acceptable" (52). But Burroughs develops the idea in his own terms:

> It must be ever present to the true artist in his attempt to report Nature, that every object as it stands in the sequence of cause and effect has a history which involves its surroundings, and that the depth of the interest which it awakens in us is in proportion as its integrity in this respect is preserved. In Nature we are prepared for any opulence of color, or vegetation, or freak of form, or display of any kind, by the preponderance of the common, ever-present features of the earth. I never knew how beautiful a red-bird was till I saw one darting through the recesses of a shaggy old hemlock wood. In like manner the bird of the naturalist can never interest us like the thrush the farm boy heard singing in the cedars at twilight as he drove the cows to pasture,

or like the swallow that flew gleefully in the air above him as he picked the stones from the early May meadow. (52–53)

The entire passage echoes Emerson's poem of environmental aesthetics, "Each and All," which emphasizes the interdependence of all beautiful particulars within the perfect whole. Equally important, however, is Burroughs's sense of place. The first sentence focuses on the complex embedding of every object in nature, arguing that the interest awakened in the observer by the object depends on the integrity of the relationship between the object and its surroundings. Burroughs makes a vital claim for American criticism in one of the earliest statements of an ecocritical position regarding the aesthetics of literature and landscape. It is certainly a clear statement of an ecocentric view. The surroundings form the ground of "common, ever-present features" that make the particular object beautiful. Thus, says Burroughs, the beauty of the "red-bird" depends upon the moment he perceives it darting through the hemlocks, and the thrush and swallow are beautiful when the farm boy hears or sees them while he works. The idea could come from Emerson, but the examples are most closely associated with Burroughs, his childhood on a Catskill dairy farm, and his work as a literary naturalist. If there are also echoes of Whitman and Thoreau in the passage, they are tertiary. Whitman celebrates the "commonest, cheapest, nearest, easiest" in section 14 of "Song of Myself," but he is most concerned with how they become the "Me."[4] And while Thoreau may appreciate the common, ever-present features of the landscape, in Burroughs's view he tends to defamiliarize those features, making them uncommon and rare.

Burroughs applies the principles of ecocentric aesthetics to Whitman most fully, seeing Whitman's poetry as exemplifying the principles he elaborates in the chapter. Current poetry, he asserts, "is an attempt to give us beauty without the lion" (53), but Whitman's poems "seem dressed for work, with hands and arms bare. At first sight they appear as careless of mere beauty, or mere art, as do the leaves of the forest about numbers, or the snow-flakes as to where they shall fall; yet his poems do more to the mind, for this very reason, than the most ostentatiously elaborated works.

They indicate fresh and near at hand the exhaustless sources of beauty and art" (55). The analogies suggest that *Leaves of Grass* operates in the same way nature operates, unconsciously powerful and always "near at hand."

While it may be impossible to ascribe sole authorship to Burroughs, a remarkable fact is the reappearance of the "Beauty" chapter of *Notes* in his fourth book, *Birds and Poets*, the volume Whitman fretted over as "too Emersony," both in the original title and in the contents themselves.[5] The eighth essay in *Birds and Poets* is titled "Before Beauty," pairing it with the seventh essay, "Before Genius." But though "Before Genius" was published in the April 1868 issue of the *Galaxy*, there is no record of the essay "Before Beauty" being published in a magazine prior to the book publication in 1877. Parts of "Before Beauty" do appear in the essay "What Makes the Poet?" published in the *Galaxy* in July 1876. The second section of "Before Beauty," for example, repeats paragraphs and shorter passages from the 1876 *Galaxy* essay.[6]

The most interesting parallels occur in the first section of "Before Beauty," where Burroughs repeats whole sections of the "Beauty" chapter from *Notes*. Most tellingly, the three principles of ecocentric aesthetics reappear in exactly the same form as in the 1867 text (*Writings* 3:168–70). Burroughs does not repeat the corollary statement concerning "the commonest and the nearest," nor does he employ the three birds from the paragraph on perceiving objects in relation to their surroundings. But he repeats verbatim the key assertions concerning the object, its surroundings, and the "common, ever-present features of the earth" (3:171). Moreover, he closes the first section of "Before Beauty" with several paragraphs taken from the "Beauty" chapter, although he omits all direct references to Whitman and *Leaves of Grass*. Thus he revises the specific defense of Whitman's aesthetics in *Notes* to make a general statement concerning the aesthetics of "translating nature into another language" (3:173). Indeed, Whitman had made exactly that recommendation in the April 1, 1875, letter to Burroughs: "My name might be brought in, in one or two places, as foil or suggestive comparison—but *my name only*, without any praises or comments" (*Correspondence* 2:327). The image of the "foil" reappears in several places in "Before Beauty," most saliently in two sentences that

Burroughs inserts in place of his redbird, thrush, and swallow: "The foil is always at hand. In like manner in the master poems we are never surfeited with mere beauty" (171). Because of the context of the April 1, 1875, letter, focusing on the "too Emersony" tone of Burroughs's literary criticism, it is clear that Whitman is the open-air foil to Emerson's claustrophobic culture. In "Before Beauty," however, the foil is the power of common, "always at hand" features of the earth, which are antecedent to beauty and the necessary ground for its appearance. In effect, Burroughs uses Emerson and Whitman as master foils, always at hand, to create his own ecocentric aesthetics.

The same strategy and similar effects appear in "Before Genius." The essay promotes "simple manhood" (3:158) as the source of literary and artistic genius, and it does so in terms that accord well with the ecocentric aesthetics of "Before Beauty":

> Literature dies with the decay of the *un*-literary element. It is not in the spirit
> of something far away in the clouds or under the moon, something ethereal,
> visionary, and anti-mundane, that Angelo, Dante, and Shakespeare work, but
> in the spirit of common Nature and of the homeliest facts; through these, and
> not away from them, the path of the creator lies. (3:158)

Once again Burroughs omits all direct mention of Whitman as the theorist of democracy and *Leaves of Grass* as the first original American poem. In the *Galaxy* article, these references were especially germane, since Whitman had published the essay "Democracy" in the December 1867 issue of the magazine and would follow Burroughs with the essay "Personalism" in the May 1868 issue. In several passages, the *Galaxy* version of "Before Genius" does sound much like Whitman. Two paragraphs lamenting the "absence of anything like strong and matured personalities in the mass of American productions" and "the sleepless anxiety which possesses most writers to make a sensation" could come directly from Whitman's jeremiads on American democratic culture. For that very reason, it is all the more telling that Burroughs deletes the two paragraphs in the *Birds and Poets* version of the essay, since by doing so he establishes fundamental principles of criticism rather than specific problems in postbellum American literature.[7]

The final chapter in *Birds and Poets,* "The Flight of the Eagle" is one of Burroughs's most important essays on Whitman. It follows the essay "Emerson," which develops a powerful sense of literary geography, grounding Emerson in the place of nature. Not surprisingly, then, in "The Flight of the Eagle" Burroughs develops Whitman as the foil to Emerson, "the fruit of extreme culture" (190). Burroughs's strategy of limitation and domestication drives the contrast. For instance, in the most developed discussion of Emerson in the "Eagle" essay, Burroughs praises him for the "first-class service" he has delivered in the moral sphere of literature. But after him, he argues, "the need is all the more pressing for a broad, powerful, opulent, human personality to absorb these ideals, and to make something more of them than fine sayings. With Emerson alone we are rich in sunlight, but poor in rain and dew, — poor, too, in soil, and in the moist, gestating earth principle. Emerson's tendency is not to broaden and enrich, but to concentrate and refine" (227). The analogies create images of Emerson as a natural element and as a landscape. But while the element of sunshine is praiseworthy, the landscape of Emerson's work is sunbaked and infertile. Characteristically, Burroughs employs the pastoral imagery of agricultural production to portray the strengths and weaknesses of Whitman's predecessor.

The rhetoric of sources, both natural and literary, runs consistently through "The Flight of the Eagle," as it does in "Before Genius" and "Before Beauty." Just as Burroughs argues that manhood is the source of genius, and power is the source of beauty, so he focuses on the qualities of Whitman's personality that give rise to the poetry. The effect is remarkably intimate, though Burroughs presents himself as a kind of poetic naturalist: "I have studied him as I have studied the birds, and have found that the nearer I got to him the more I saw" (210). For Burroughs as a student of nature, Whitman presents "volcanic emotional fires" and "the largest emotional element that has appeared anywhere" (211). But as he attempts to account for Whitman's power, Burroughs recurs to the "Standard of the Natural Universal" and its abstractions:

> The influence of books and works of art upon an author may be seen in all
> respectable writers. If knowledge alone made literature, or culture genius,

there would be no dearth of these things among the moderns. But I feel bound to say that there is something higher and deeper than the influence or perusal of any or all books, or all other productions of genius,—a quality of information which the masters can never impart, and which all the libraries do not hold. This is the absorption by an author, previous to becoming so, of the spirit of nature, through the visible objects of the universe, and his affiliation with them subjectively and objectively. Not more surely is the blood quickened and purified by contact with the unbreathed air than is the spirit of man vitalized and made strong by intercourse with the real things of the earth. The calm, all-permitting, wordless spirit of nature,—yet so eloquent to him who hath ears to hear! The sunrise, the heaving sea, the woods and mountains, the storm and the whistling winds, the gentle summer day, the winter sights and sounds, the night and the high dome of stars,—to have really perused these, especially from childhood onward, till what there is in them, so impossible to define, finds its full mate and echo in the mind,—this only is the lore which breathes the breath of life into all the rest. Without it, literary productions may have the superb beauty of statues, but with it only can they have the beauty of life. (215–16)

As in "Before Genius" and "Before Beauty," Burroughs makes a genetic argument concerning the sources of poetry. In this paragraph, as in most of Burroughs's literary criticism, the ultimate source is the "spirit of nature," which manifests itself "through the visible objects of the universe." The author must absorb that spirit before he or she can become an author, and a means of this absorption seems to be the "affiliation with [the objects] subjectively and objectively." The word "affiliation" directly echoes Whitman's phrase, "this passionate affiliation and identity with Nature," used in "Standard of the Natural Universal" (*Notes* 38). For Whitman, the spirit of nature is the cosmic force that drives the universe and "feeds the mind by exhibitions of power" (*Notes* 40). Burroughs does not elaborate on the term, nor does he clarify what he means by it. Instead, he simply lists several "real things of the earth" and concludes that "what there is in them" is "impossible to define." The catalogue is general, evoking large-scale elements of nature rather than a specific place or power, and Burroughs does not cite examples from Whitman's poems, even though "There Was a Child Went Forth" or "Out of the Cradle Endlessly Rocking" would certainly illustrate his points.

Although the ideas surely recall Whitman's hand in "Standard of the Natural Universal," Burroughs expresses his own creed as a literary naturalist and ecocritic. The subject is Whitman's poetry, but the passage does not limit itself to that. Rather, Burroughs employs the language of spiritual origins in order to explore the source of literary power. The language is in part biblical, echoing the gospels of Matthew, Mark, and Luke with the oft-repeated command, "He that hath ears to hear, let him hear," and pointing toward the mixed genesis of humankind: "And the Lord God formed man of the dust of the ground, and breathed into his nostrils the breath of life; and man became a living soul" (Gen. 2:7). Burroughs's language is also formal in its performative rhetoric: "I feel bound to say that there is something higher and deeper." Ultimately, these rhetorical elements cohere around the central "spirit of nature," which is the calm, all-permitting, wordless origin of true literature. Only by finding that source can the "beauty of life" find its genesis.

To complement the "spirit of nature" genetic argument, Burroughs denies prevailing critical opinions that Whitman's poems are formless and prosaic. In the second section of the essay, for instance, he argues that the critics who seek a "fair verbal structure, a symmetrical piece of mechanism, whose last stone is implied and necessitated in the first," will necessarily be disappointed in Whitman's poems (233). But, he argues, that is not the only sense of form or design possible:

> There is a want of form in the unfinished statue, because it is struggling into form; it is nothing without form; but there is no want of form in the elemental laws and effusions, — in fire, or water, or rain, or dew, or the smell of the shore or the plunging waves. And may there not be the analogue of this in literature, — a potent, quickening, exhilarating quality in words, apart from and without any consideration of constructive form? Under the influence of the expansive, creative force that plays upon me from these pages, like sunlight or gravitation, the question of form never comes up, because I do

not for one moment escape the eye, the source from which the power and
action emanate. (234)

Burroughs first focuses upon nature and its elemental laws, listing common
elements to evoke active, dynamic forms. The analogue in literature is
verbal power or creative force, and in encountering such qualities the reader
is in effect brought into the poet's presence, "the eye, the source from which
the power and action emanate." The analogy suggests that the poet is a
godlike power, a human embodiment of the "spirit of nature."

Burroughs turns the theories of organic analogy and dynamic form to
account in several innovative ways. Because he focuses on the personal,
physical presence of the poet himself, he argues that Whitman's poems
are most important for teaching "the great lesson of nature . . . that a sane
sensuality must be preserved at all hazards." Whitman shows that "there
is still sap and fecundity, and depth of virgin soil in the race, sufficient to
produce a man of the largest mould and the most audacious and uncon-
querable egotism" (228). For Burroughs, the genetic account becomes a
way of understanding human sexuality and its role in art, and the agricultural analogy makes literary production both sexual and natural. When he
considers Whitman's catalogue style, he argues that the objects listed "serve
as masses of shade or neutral color in pictures, or in nature, or in character,"
and that the poet "will not put in the dainty and pretty things merely,—he
will put in the coarse and common things also, and he swells the list till even
his robust muse begins to look uneasy" (237). The general theory clearly
gives him a way of understanding a particular formal feature of Whitman's
work. In addition, Burroughs associates the "common things" with what
he calls, in the first section of the essay, "the commonness of humanity"
(220). That is, he suggests that Whitman's poems are "consistent with, and
the outcome of, that something which secures to the race ascendancy,
empire, and perpetuity" (241). By making Whitman's poetry part of an
evolutionary process, Burroughs justifies the democratic and progressivist
rhetoric of *Leaves of Grass*. The theme of evolution allows Burroughs to
claim that Whitman's poetry is the most scientifically accurate and therefore the most modern in the world, and he praises Whitman for developing

an evolutionary theory before Darwin and Spencer (249–50). The realistic requirements of Burroughs's theory lead him to conclude the essay by balancing Whitman's idealism and realism: "It is because Whitman's ideal is clothed with rank materiality, as the soul is clothed with the carnal body, that his poems beget such warmth and desire in the mind, and are the reservoirs of so much power. . . . Indeed, the spirituality of Walt Whitman is the chief fact after all, and dominates every page he has written" (262).

Poetry as Place

Burroughs's most developed critical view of Whitman's achievement appears in *Whitman: A Study*, published in 1896. In that book, Burroughs produces a spatialized figure of Whitman's work, reading Whitman's poetry as a place. The strategy merges literature and the environment, the human and nonhuman, in the twin acts of reading and writing. In the very first section of the "Preliminary" chapter, for example, Burroughs stages his summation of thirty years spent in mapping the landscape of Whitman's imagination:

> The writing of this preliminary chapter, and the final survey and revision
> of my Whitman essay, I am making at a rustic house I have built at a wild
> place a mile or more from my home upon the river. I call this place Whitman
> Land, because in many ways it is typical of my poet,—an amphitheatre of
> precipitous rock, slightly veiled with a delicate growth of verdure, enclosing a
> few acres of prairie-like land, once the site of an ancient lake, now a garden of
> unknown depth and fertility. Elemental ruggedness, savageness, and grandeur,
> combined with wonderful tenderness, modernness, and geniality. There rise
> the gray scarred cliffs, crowned here and there with a dead hemlock or pine,
> where, morning after morning, I have seen the bald-eagle perch, and here
> at their feet this level area of tender humus, with three perennial springs of
> delicious cold water flowing in its margin; a huge granite bowl filled with the
> elements and potencies of life. The scene has a strange fascination for me, and
> holds me here day after day. From the highest point of rocks I can overlook a
> long stretch of the river and of the farming country beyond; I can hear owls

hoot, hawks scream, and roosters crow. Birds of the garden and orchard meet birds of the forest upon the shaggy cedar posts that uphold my porch. At dusk the call of the whippoorwill mingles with the chorus of the pickerel frogs, and in the morning I hear through the robins' cheerful burst the sombre plaint of the mourning-dove. When I tire of my manuscript, I walk in the woods, or climb the rocks, or help the men clear up the ground, piling and burning the stumps and rubbish. This scene and situation, so primitive and secluded, yet so touched with and adapted to civilization, responding to the moods of both sides of the life and imagination of a modern man, seems, I repeat, typical in many ways of my poet, and is a veritable Whitman land. Whitman does not to me suggest the wild and unkempt as he seems to do to many; he suggests the cosmic and the elemental, and this is one of the dominant thoughts that run through my dissertation. Scenes of power and savagery in nature were more welcome to him, probably more stimulating to him, than the scenes of the pretty and placid, and he cherished the hope that he had put into his "Leaves" some of the tonic and fortifying quality of Nature in her more grand and primitive aspects. (*Writings* 10:1–2)

The opening paragraph strategically crosses boundaries in order to enlarge the dimensions of the subject. The first sentence frames the paragraph as a combination of writing and reading, and the "final survey" of the critical landscape crosses into a survey of the actual landscape surrounding Burroughs's retreat, Slabsides. As Burroughs surveys the "wild place" he names "Whitman Land," he describes it in terms that negotiate between the human and nonhuman: "amphitheatre," "veiled," and "garden" merge with the descriptive terms for the landscape. The effect is to make the place less wild but more complex, for it combines "elemental ruggedness, savageness, and grandeur" with "wonderful tenderness, modernness, and geniality." As the paragraph proceeds, Burroughs refers to "Whitman Land" three times as a "scene," evoking an aesthetic and dramatic sense of place. It is a scene of "strange fascination" to the writer, a scene that combines the "primitive and secluded" with "civilization," and yet a scene that is finally characterized more by "power and savagery in nature" than by the "pretty and placid." The boundless landscape provides for and includes the bounded landscape. Thus Whitman Land becomes a meeting ground for opposites. When Burroughs notes that "birds of the garden and orchard meet birds of the forest upon the shaggy cedar posts that uphold my porch," the birds meet in a landscape of wildness and cultivation, a place in which cedars "uphold" the writer's retreat.

If the pastoralism of Burroughs's Whitman Land seems facile, it may be because I have failed to describe an important aspect of the figural place— the element of elegy. When Whitman died in March 1892, Burroughs responded at first by being dumbstruck with grief, but then he produced a flood of writing on the poet; over the four years from 1892 to the 1896 publication of *Whitman: A Study*, Burroughs published eighteen major essays on the poet in addition to the book.[8] This was also during a period in which Burroughs produced comparatively few nature essays. In 1894, he published *Riverby*, but it was "the first volume of his nature essays to be published in seven years and a book that included no piece of writing less than three years old."[9] In short, Burroughs wrote *Whitman: A Study* as a "final survey" of Whitman Land, and he did so from an elegiac perspective that combines his roles as an ecocritic and literary naturalist.

The initial paragraph does not strictly follow the conventions of pastoral elegy. We could find those conventions more clearly at work in Whitman's "When Lilacs Last in the Door-yard Bloom'd," a work that Burroughs certainly influenced, especially in the poet's use of the hermit thrush's song.[10] But Burroughs does suggest that a shadow of loss looms over Whitman Land. So, for example, he points like a guide to particular aspects of the landscape "typical of my poet": "There rise the gray scarred cliffs, crowned here and there with a dead hemlock or pine, where, morning after morning, I have seen the bald-eagle perch." The eagle image rewrites Whitman's "The Dalliance of the Eagles," which Whitman had based on written and spoken descriptions by Burroughs.[11] Whereas Whitman focuses on the "rushing amorous contact" between two eagles "high in space together" (3), Burroughs figures the lone eagle perched high above scarred cliffs in a dead hemlock or pine, converting *eros* into *thanatos*. The image of the eagle also recalls the 1877 "The Flight of the Eagle," especially in Burroughs's evocation of Whitman at the beginning and end of the essay:

His wings do not glitter in their movement from rich and vari-colored plumage, nor are his notes those of the accustomed song-birds; but his flight is the flight of the eagle. (*Writings* 3:186)

He who wanders through the solitudes of far-off Uist or lonely Donegal may often behold the Golden Eagle sick to death, worn with age or famine, or with both, passing with weary waft of wing from promontory to promontory, from peak to peak, pursued by a crowd of rooks and crows, which fall back screaming whenever the noble bird turns his indignant head, and which follow frantically once more, hooting behind him, whenever he wends again upon his way. (*Writings* 3:232)[12]

The "strange fascination" the scene has for Burroughs would seem to be that of grief. Thus the meeting ground becomes the elegiac landscape Burroughs traverses from grief to consolation, for it includes "the robins' cheerful burst" as well as "the sombre plaint of the mourning-dove." The paragraph closes with an expression of hope, projected into the memory of a still-living Whitman: "Scenes of power and savagery in nature were more welcome to him, probably more stimulating to him, than the scenes of the pretty and placid, and he cherished the hope that he had put into his 'Leaves' some of the tonic and fortifying quality of Nature in her more grand and primitive aspects." Burroughs figuratively resuscitates Whitman, imbuing the poet and his book with the "tonic and fortifying quality of Nature." Three doublets insist on the large and vibrant reality of Whitman's poetry and the spirit of nature it represents: "power and savagery," "tonic and fortifying," "grand and primitive." They contrast sharply with the pejorative doublet, "pretty and placid," which we can now associate with Wordsworthian nature. The doublets also move from "nature" to the personified "Nature," as if they have gained a grand and primitive title. Finally, Burroughs's figural strategies create an oscillating tension and a tone of urgency.

The passage I have been explicating at such length is interesting in its own right, and it also suggests an interesting complication of American pastoralism. Burroughs creates a scene of refuge and retreat, but it is not exactly what Lawrence Buell calls "a form of willed amnesia" (*Environmental*

Imagination 49). Burroughs himself rejects such a retreat in the distinction he draws between Wordsworth and Whitman: "There was no privacy in Whitman; he never sat me down in a corner with a cozy, comfortable shut-in feeling, but he set me upon a hill or started me upon an endless journey. Wordsworth had been my poet of nature, of the sequestered and idyllic; but I saw that here was a poet of a larger, more fundamental nature, indeed of the Cosmos itself. Not a poet of dells and fells, but of the earth and the orbs" (10:6). Buell's argument on pastoral ideology is that no example is pure, that every example of American pastoral is subject to crosscurrents of "the centripetal pull of consensualism" and "the centrifugal impulse . . . for pastoral to form itself in opposition to social institutions of whatever sort" (50). Burroughs may wish to forget the political and social complexities of late-nineteenth-century America, but he does not practice a form of willed amnesia in regard to Whitman. Instead, the ecocriticism of *Whitman: A Study* is a form of willed imagination and memory.

The objects of Burroughs's imagination and memory come together in the image of Whitman Land, which figuratively stands for *Leaves of Grass*, for Whitman's place in American literature and culture, for Burroughs's place as disciple and critic of Whitman, and for his fundamental principle of criticism. In the chapter called "His Relation to Art and Literature," for instance, Burroughs merges these four identities in one singular passage on beauty:

> Is there not in field, wood, or shore something more precious and tonic
> than any special beauties we may chance to find there, — flowers, perfumes,
> sunsets, — something that we cannot do without, though we can do without
> these? Is it health, life, power, or what is it?
>   Whatever it is, it is something analogous to this that we get in Whitman.
> There is little in his "Leaves" that one would care to quote for its mere beauty,
> though this element is there also. One may pluck a flower here and there
> in his rugged landscape, as in any other; but the flowers are always by the
> way, and never the main matter. We should not miss them if they were
> not there. What delights and invigorates us is in the air, and in the look of
> things. The flowers are like our wild blossoms growing under great trees or

amid rocks, never the camellia or tuberose of the garden or hot-house, — something rude and bracing is always present, always a breath of the untamed and aboriginal. (133)

Burroughs describes the "rugged landscape" of Whitman's poetry in terms that do not exclude particular beauties but put them in a secondary position. The primary elements of the landscape are "health, life, power," or some invigorating presence, "rude and bracing." The word "tonic" recalls the "tonic and fortifying quality of Nature" from the initial paragraph of the book. Burroughs emphasizes the "untamed and aboriginal" aspects of the landscape in the present passage, and those aspects accord with the figure of Whitman Land with which he began the study. In both passages, we can see that Burroughs's tendency as a critic is to apply what he calls "open-air standards" to Whitman and, in doing so, to emulate the boundless effects he experiences in Whitman's poetry.

The purpose behind Burroughs's figural strategies is, on one level, rather straightforward. Repeatedly in his critical accounts of Whitman, Burroughs employs the figures of boundless, elemental nature in order to make a place for Whitman in the map of American culture. So, for instance, he asserts that "his book is not a temple: it is a wood, a field, a highway; vista, vista, everywhere" (120). But in such statements — and there are dozens like it — Burroughs also suggests that the conventional standards of literary value in late-nineteenth-century America are restrictive, limited, and even trivial: "We make a mistake," he says, "when we demand of Whitman what the other poets give us, — studies, embroidery, delicate tracings, pleasing artistic effects, rounded and finished specimens. We shall understand him better if we inquire what his own standards are, what kind of a poet he would be. He tells us over and over again that he would emulate the great forces and processes of Nature. He seeks for hints in the sea, the mountain, in the orbs themselves. In the wild splendor and savageness of a Colorado canyon he sees a spirit kindred to his own" (156).

In the chapter on "His Relation to Culture," Burroughs goes so far as to use Whitman as a means of redefining the fundamental relationship between nature and culture:

We constantly mistake culture for mere refinement, which it is not: it is a liberating process; it is a clearing away of obstructions, and the giving to inherent virtues a chance to express themselves. It makes savage nature friendly and considerate. The aim of culture is not to get rid of nature, but to utilize nature. The great poet is always a "friendly and flowing savage," the master and never the slave of the complex elements of our artificial lives.

Though our progress and civilization are a triumph over nature, yet in an important sense we never get away from nature or improve upon her. Her standards are still our standards, her sweetness and excellence are still our aim. Her health, her fertility, her wholeness, her freshness, her innocence, her evolution, we would fain copy or reproduce. We would, if we could, keep the pungency and aroma of her wild fruit in our cultivated specimens, the virtue and hardiness of the savage in our fine gentlemen, the joy and spontaneity of her bird-songs in our poetry, the grace and beauty of her forms in our sculpture and carvings. (10:210–11)

Burroughs's pastoralism may be nostalgic and regressive in some of its modes and perspectives, but it effectively represents the claims of the environment in reading and evaluating literature. Nor is it merely a limited form of realism, an irritable searching after fact. Instead, the figural strategies of *Whitman: A Study* suggest that pastoralism is itself a means of arguing that "her standards are still our standards, her sweetness and excellence are still our aim." Though Burroughs's optimism is conditional, his pastoral criticism reminds us that we still live in Whitman Land, and that our maps are both old and new.

Rambles in the Place of Nature

John Burroughs is a compelling literary critic, fashioning an early version of ecocriticism, and he is most compelling because he writes as both an ecocritic and a nature writer. Burroughs's literary criticism owes much to Emerson, Thoreau, and Whitman, but it owes just as much to his work as a literary naturalist. Likewise, his nature writing owes a signal debt to the three writers he admires most, but it owes its deepest debt to his own work as an ecocritic. These relationships are complex, intense, and fruitful. As a result, the essays of *Wake-Robin, Winter Sunshine,* and *Birds and Poets* create a groundbreaking literary geography. Lawrence Buell is only the latest reader to see Burroughs as a minor figure of genteel pastoralism, a writer who promotes a retreat to nature as a form of "willed amnesia" concerning humanity's social demands. But while there is certainly an element of truth to that representation of his work, in his best essays he attempts to counter the prevailing literary and cultural values of nineteenth-century America.

The essays of *Wake-Robin* develop the theme of knowledge from a place-based perspective, locating the literary naturalist on the border between nature and art. It is a border Burroughs crosses repeatedly. In the introduction to the 1895 "Riverside Edition" of the book, Burroughs specifically addresses the situation he faces as a nature writer:

> Do such books as mine give a wrong impression of Nature, and lead readers to expect more from a walk or a camp in the woods than they usually get? I have a few times had occasion to think so. I am not always aware myself how much pleasure I have had in a walk till I try to share it with my reader. The heat of composition brings out the color and the flavor. We must not forget the illusions of all art. If my reader thinks he does not get from Nature what I get from her, let me remind him that he can hardly know what he has got till he defines it to himself as I do, and throws about it the witchery of words. Literature does not grow wild in the woods. Every artist does something more than copy Nature; more comes out in his account than goes into the original experience. (*Writings* 1:xiv–xv)

Burroughs clearly understands that writing itself has the power to create knowledge, rather than simply report it. Even though he always insists on factual accuracy in his criticisms of literary naturalists and poets, he admits that there is a "witchery of words" and that no essay or poem simply copies the experience of nature. Language heightens the senses, "bring[ing] out the color and the flavor." It also creates the powerful illusion of the heightened experience itself. If literature does not grow wild in the woods, it creates the illusion that experience and knowledge do.

The mixture of realism and witchery works well in much of *Wake-Robin*, especially in the essay "In the Hemlocks," first published in the June 1866 issue of the *Atlantic Monthly*. Burroughs describes the intense difficulty of identifying warblers in an old hemlock wood, though he counts over forty species in one summer day's walk through the forest (42). One of the ways of surmounting the difficulty is to "watch and watch till my head grows dizzy and my neck is in danger of permanent displacement" (49), but when patience fails, the naturalist uses his gun, for "no sure and rapid progress can be made in the study without taking life, without procuring specimens" (49–50). The offhand authority may repel modern readers, but the gun does allow Burroughs to describe a Blackburnian warbler and what he calls a "blue yellow-back." The detail with which he describes the latter warbler allows the modern reader to identify it as a northern parula, with its "slight bronze-colored triangular spot between the shoulders" and the "throat yellow, becoming a dark bronze on the breast" (1:50–51). Burroughs's descriptive technique makes the naming of the bird seem to emerge from the details, but it also leads to the writer's reflections:

> He is remarkably delicate and beautiful,—the handsomest as he is the smallest of the warblers known to me. It is never without surprise that I find amid these rugged, savage aspects of nature creatures so fairy and delicate. But such is the law. Go to the sea or climb the mountain, and with the ruggedest and the savagest you will find likewise the fairest and the most delicate. The greatness and the minuteness of nature pass all understanding. (1:51)

The meeting of "greatness and minuteness" is similar to the description of Whitman Land that opens *Whitman: A Study*, and it resembles the sense of the near and far that Burroughs develops in his treatment of Emerson and Thoreau. Here the two qualities are joined in the landscape itself, but it would be foolhardy to assume that this is actually the "law" of the landscape. Rather, it is the law of Burroughs's perceptive style, which continually balances opposing elements and levels of scale. The law even seems to arise from God, since the greatness and minuteness "pass all understanding." That phrase echoes Philippians 4:7: "And the peace of God, which passes all understanding, will keep your hearts and your minds in Christ Jesus." The biblical echo is ambiguous—just as the last words Burroughs ever wrote, closing the "Flies in Amber" essay on Emerson, bring the "treasures in heaven" ambiguously back to earth. In both passages, Burroughs suggests that nature is an adequate substitute for God.

The spiritual quality of nature is one of the most fundamental principles that Burroughs takes from Emerson, Thoreau, and Whitman. As in the description of the northern parula, it is often difficult to discern which influence is working its witchery most tellingly. In the case of Whitman, the "corresponsiveness" of the two writers creates the complicated possibility of mutual influence. A suggestive example of the situation occurs immediately following the description of the northern parula. Burroughs notes a bird song that he calls "the finest sound in nature—the song of the hermit thrush," and then describes it as "rising pure and serene, as if a spirit from some remote height were slowly chanting a divine accompaniment. This song appeals to the sentiment of the beautiful in me, and suggests a serene religious beatitude as no other sound in nature does" (51). The hermit thrush embodies, in its beautiful song, the spirit of nature, and Burroughs embodies the poetic spirit that affiliates itself with the spirit of nature. Thus the bird song enacts the dynamic spiritual relationship that Whitman delineates in "Standard of the Natural Universal" and that Burroughs applies to Whitman in "The Flight of the Eagle."[13] In the next two pages of the essay, Burroughs describes the hermit thrush in great detail, employing religious language to balance the writer's heightened response to the song and his evocation of the song itself (51–53).

The hermit thrush returns twice more in the essay. In the first instance, it functions to punctuate the descriptions of other birds: "I lie on my back with eyes half closed, and analyze the chorus of warblers, thrushes, finches, and flycatchers; while, soaring above all, a little withdrawn and alone rises the divine contralto of the hermit" (60). The effect of the sentence is to mark both the special beauty of the hermit thrush and the naturalist's ability to perceive that beauty within the context of the surrounding chorus. The second instance closes the essay with the image of nightfall:

> Mounting toward the upland again, I pause reverently as the hush and still-
> ness of twilight come upon the woods. It is the sweetest, ripest hour of the day.
> And as the hermit's evening hymn goes up from the deep solitude below me, I
> experience that serene exaltation of sentiment of which music, literature, and
> religion are but the faint types and symbols. (75)

Artfully effecting closure, the passage evokes the spirit of nature and its
echo in the writer's experience. The passage exemplifies the kind of witchery that Burroughs describes in the Riverside introduction of 1895, and it
subtly suggests the combined, choral influence of Emerson, Thoreau, and
Whitman. Burroughs's successful gesture depends on his apparent scorn
for the "faint types and symbols" of culture. By pointing toward the wordless
source of exaltation, he paradoxically vivifies his own types and symbols.

The tension between culture and nature reappears in other essays in
Wake-Robin. In two narrative essays, "The Adirondacks" and "Birch Browsings," Burroughs recounts two separate camping excursions in the Adirondacks and the Catskills. Both essays echo Thoreau's excursions in *The
Maine Woods,* a book Burroughs praised more consistently than *Walden.*
In the first, Burroughs tells of a hunting and fishing trip in the summer of
1863, when he was "in the first flush of [his] ornithological studies" (77).
The essay develops the theme of experiential knowledge, and Burroughs
subtly celebrates his prowess with rod and gun. More subtle is the way in
which he notes "a new song that I was puzzled in tracing to the author,"
at last discovering that it is the white-throated sparrow (78). The prose
recreates the experience of being puzzled, then noting characteristics of
habitat and habits, and finally divulging the name of the bird. He does not
detail the use of gun, field-glass, or field guide in arriving at the identity
of the bird; rather, the name emerges "at last." The description of the
mountain lake also plays upon the sense of discovery: the narrator finds the
"wild, desolate lake" a mysterious place, "as if some secret of Nature might
here be revealed," since water is "the place for wonders and miracles to
happen" (82–83). The lake becomes an emblem of both art and wildness,
making "the wild more wild, while it enhances culture and art" (83).

Wildness characterizes the Catskills of "Birch Browsings," but it does not enhance the narrator's aesthetic excursion. Instead, the experience teaches him a lesson in humility: "I was taught how poor an Indian I should make, and what a ridiculous figure a party of men may cut in the woods when the way is uncertain and the mountains high" (176). Most of the essay is taken up with the flustered mechanics of getting lost in the woods. In this story, the gun serves to signal the intrepid, pathfinding narrator's companions, but his efforts are fruitless. Though Burroughs notes wryly that the firing "must have aroused many long-dormant echoes from a Rip Van Winkle sleep," there is no magical or religious tone in the story (189). The point of the essay is the difficulty in knowing a place and, more important, in knowing one's own place.

In the ramble essay "Spring at the Capital," Burroughs evokes the city of Washington, D.C., as a meeting ground of the wild and the civilized: "One need but pass the boundary of Washington city to be fairly in the country, and ten minutes' walk in the country brings one to real primitive woods. The town has not yet overflowed its limits like the great Northern commercial capitals, and Nature, wild and unkempt, comes up to its very threshold, and even in many places crosses it" (141–42). The phrase "wild and unkempt" recalls Burroughs's description of the poetry of Emerson and Thoreau, "born of the wildness and elusiveness of our more capricious and unkempt Nature," in "Another Word on Thoreau" (*Writings* 23:131). Nature appears more powerful than the city, since it is able to cross the city's threshold, while the city remains within its limits. As a result, the place of nature is fluid and dynamic.

For most of the essay, Burroughs describes the woods along Rock Creek, making the descriptions seem to be part of one intensely experiential walk. But the essay actually compiles many walks, many experiences of birding along the creek and in the city. Along with this illusion of heightened experience, the essay often seems to move chronologically, from early spring to early summer, but Burroughs artfully mixes temporal, spatial, and thematic structures. In common with other essays in the volume, Burroughs develops the descriptions of birds, but he also describes wildflowers and their habitats. In developing these mixed modes, he recurs to the mixture of nature and culture in one place. So, for instance, he notes that "the national capital is situated in such a vast spread of wild, wooded, or semi-cultivated country, and is in itself so open and spacious, with its parks and large government reservations, that an unusual number of birds find their way into it in the course of the season" (154). Rock Creek itself becomes emblematic of the close relationship between the wild and the cultivated:

> Rock Creek has an abundance of all the elements that make up not only pleasing but wild and rugged scenery. There is, perhaps, not another city in the Union that has on its very threshold so much natural beauty and grandeur, such as men seek for in remote forests and mountains. A few touches of art would convert this whole region, extending from Georgetown to what is known as Crystal Springs, not more than two miles from the present State Department, into a park unequaled by anything in the world. There are passages between these two points as wild and savage, and apparently as remote from civilization, as anything one meets with in the mountain sources of the Hudson or the Delaware. (158)

For Burroughs, the wild is not confined to some remote world beyond the limits of civilization. It is available within the limits of the District, a ramble away from the State Department. If he heightens the possibilities for Rock Creek, that is less important than the sense of possibility itself. Nature does not reside completely outside human ken; instead, the place of nature lies at the threshold of our perception and knowledge. Nature is as close as it is remote.

The place of nature and the figure of the rambler occupy Burroughs's attention in the most important essays of *Winter Sunshine* (1875). "The Exhilarations of the Road," published in the June 1873 issue of the *Galaxy*, owes a signal debt to Thoreau's "Walking," but Whitman's "Song of the Open Road" and "Standard of the Natural Universal" are just as important to the ramble. Burroughs develops his aesthetic principles in a whimsical, accessible language, humorously naming his followers "the Order of Walkers" and deliberately parodying *Walden*—"I am going to brag as lustily as I can on behalf of the pedestrian" (27–28). The essay insists on cheerfulness because that is the tonic effect of walking. Unlike Thoreau in "Walking," however, Burroughs does not freight his essay with symbolic import concerning western discovery and wildness of spirit. Rather, he notes that the tonic of walking comes from its pedestrian qualities: "A man must invest himself near at hand and in common things, and be content with a steady and moderate return, if he would know the blessedness of a cheerful heart and the sweetness of a walk over the round earth" (30).

For Burroughs, the "corresponsive" affiliation between the human spirit and the spirit of nature depends on the walker's ability to see wonders in the commonplace. Nor can the walker remain aloof and apart from nature:

> The vital, universal currents play through him. He knows the ground is alive; he feels the pulses of the wind, and reads the mute language of things. His sympathies are all aroused; his senses are continually reporting messages to his mind. Wind, frost, rain, heat, cold, are something to him. He is not merely a spectator of the panorama of nature, but a participator in it. He experiences the country he passes through, —tastes it, feels it, absorbs it; the traveler in his fine carriage sees it merely. (37)

In this passage, the walker is synonymous with Whitman's poet of nature, participating in the landscape rather than merely seeing or describing it. In addition, Burroughs echoes the famous "transparent eyeball" passage from Emerson's *Nature*: "I become a transparent eye-ball. I am nothing. I see all. The currents of the Universal Being circulate through me; I am part or particle of God" (*Nature, Addresses, and Lectures* 10). Burroughs is characteristically playful in the allusion to Emerson, since the walker is more than a spectator or Emersonian eyeball, and the "vital, universal currents" are not as divine as the Emersonian currents of "Universal Being." Burroughs brings Emerson back to earth.

Burroughs's pedestrian is not merely pedestrian, though it is concretely and physically earthbound. As he says, the walker "does not need a large territory," for the possibilities for interpretation lie everywhere: "When you get into a railway car you want a continent, the man in his carriage requires a township; but a walker like Thoreau finds as much and more along the shores of Walden Pond. The former, as it were, has merely time to glance at the headings of the chapters, while the latter need not miss a line, and Thoreau reads between the lines" (37). Walking, like careful reading, offers a heightened experience of the landscape. Moreover, it actively creates a heightened landscape, investing it with significant emotions and memories: "The roads and paths you have walked along in summer and winter weather, the fields and hills which you have looked upon in lightness and gladness of heart, where fresh thoughts have come into your mind, or some noble prospect has opened before you, and especially the quiet ways where you have walked in sweet converse with your friend, pausing under the trees, drinking at the spring,—henceforth they are not the same; a new charm is added; those thoughts spring there perennial, your friend walks there forever" (44). Through the witchery of commonplace words, Burroughs transforms a landscape into the place of nature.

Repeatedly in the four parts of "An October Abroad," Burroughs uses modes of locomotion and perception to reflect on place and his sense of place as the meeting ground of nature and culture.[14] The landscape is Wordsworthian, and Burroughs emphasizes the human, domesticated, benignly settled qualities of England as a garden. The descriptions move fluidly between country and city. In addition, his meditations develop both the sense of an American in England and the knowledge of the American's own country. That leads to cultural criticisms of the United States and its landscapes, marked by "poverty and nakedness" of ornamentation and the domestic arts, and Burroughs accepts the idea that American landscape and American art are alike in that respect (242–45). But the reflections and criticisms do not lead to a jeremiad like Whitman's *Democratic Vistas* or Thoreau's "Economy" chapter in *Walden*, nor do they become an occasion, such as Henry James's *Hawthorne* (1884), for attacking the thin soil of American culture. In the late 1870s, Burroughs seems completely at home in American culture, sure of his place in the literary scene, and certain of his ability to convey the sense of place to his readers. Such certainties may account for James's belittling of Burroughs and *Winter Sunshine*, the "Thoreau charge" that Burroughs was "a sort of reduced but also more humorous, more available, and more sociable Thoreau." But that is to miss the enlargement of place in *Winter Sunshine*, a failing that reduces James more than it does Burroughs.

Perhaps Burroughs had James in mind in "Touches of Nature," one of the most interesting nature essays in *Birds and Poets*, for he meditates there on the "metropolitan pride" of human beings regarding the "immense display and prodigality of Nature" as for us (*Writings* 3:53). The essay is a seventeen-section mosaic, combining natural history, literary criticism, concrete observation, and theoretical meditation. Burroughs creates a kind of mental ramble, moving flexibly from one topic to another and joining ideas in surprising ways. In section 7, for instance, he begins with "a feeling in heroic poetry, or in a burst of eloquence," which he then finds in a long night train hauled by two engines. The description recalls Thoreau's "Sounds" chapter from *Walden* and Whitman's "To a Locomotive," and it insists on finding wild nobility in the mass of motion (63–64). That hymn to industrial power leads to section 8, in which the mowing machines are "in tune with the voices of Nature at this season" (65–66). The mosaic method is Emersonian, and it is often surprisingly electric and original.

The next essay in the collection, "A Bird Medley," plays with the musical image by creating a loose gathering of bird songs. Both "Touches of Nature" and "A Bird Medley" ramble, in subject and in style, just as they *are* rambles and evoke the physical act of rambling over a landscape. At the same time, however, they maintain a strong sense of place. Describing the "calling and chirping" snow bunting, for example, the whitest of eastern songbirds, Burroughs notes that "in its plumage it reflects the winter landscape,—an expanse of white surmounted or streaked with gray and brown; a field of snow with a line of woods or a tinge of stubble. It fits into the scene, and does not appear to lead a beggarly and disconsolate life, like most of our winter residents" (97). The implied analogy of bird and winter landscape resides within the explicit assertion of how the plumage "reflects" the landscape. Thus the bird becomes as large as a field of snow, or the field of snow becomes as surprising as the flight and song of the snow bunting. In such imaginative sentences, Burroughs uses the witchery of words to create new ways of seeing—ways of seeing nature, its place, and our place within it. His prose reflects the combined influence of Emerson, Thoreau, and Whitman, but it expands beyond those figures to make a place for the writer as a literary naturalist and ecocritic, creating a reflectively complex and dynamic place of nature.

3 Pastoral Illustration

Burroughs, Muir, and the *Century Magazine*

Codes of Illustration

John Burroughs never spared his friends. Writing on February 1, 1891, to Richard Watson Gilder, editor of the *Century Illustrated Monthly Magazine*, Burroughs criticized the magazine, especially the latest issue, which featured illustrations of poor white southerners, for printing "ugly pictures of ugly objects." The right purpose of an illustration, said Burroughs, is to suggest "something pleasing," for "why should the eye be greeted with something ugly in an illustrated magazine, any more than the nose should be greeted by a bad odor in a house, or the ear by a discordant sound? These Georgia crackers are hideous. Think what their effect might be upon a sensitive, imaginative pregnant woman who might be fascinated by their very ugliness! If I were a woman I think they would make me miscarry." Burroughs lambasted illustrator E. W. Kemble as "the worst realist who has yet turned up" and asked his friend Gilder rhetorically, "When one sees a defect in a great public institution like the Century, why should he not point it out?"[1] The diatribe is unintentionally humorous in its hyperbole. The only "hideous" aspect of Clare de Graffenreid's article is the writing, which portrays the Georgia "cracker" as an illiterate and shiftless cog in the industrial machine. The men come in for special condemnation, since they exhibit remarkable skill in avoiding all manner of work, whereas the women and children perform the majority of household duties and factory labor. Kemble's illustrations are realistic, and they consist mainly of portraits, of "heads" and "types," not grotesque distortions or exaggerations. The details of illustrations such as "Cooking in the Yard," "Around the Grocery," "In the Mill," and "A Race Problem" are spare and

73

characteristic. So, for example, the grandmotherly figure who stirs a pot over an open fire in the first-named illustration is smoking a hand-rolled cigarette, and the dominance of tobacco among the subjects is a major point in de Graffenried's article. Only in the last-named engraving does the illustrator imply a criticism, since the poor whites' "race problem" is the whiskey jug. To a modern reader, the article and illustrations seem well intentioned and condescending, but they are hardly the stuff to make an imaginative, fascinated young woman miscarry.

The letter to Gilder reveals Burroughs's sense of propriety, his hyperbolic imagination, and his acute image of the typical reader as a sensitive, imaginative woman. In all of these aspects, he is characteristic of American literary culture at the end of the nineteenth century. From 1881 to 1910, the *Century* was indeed a "great public institution." The leading illustrated monthly magazine in America, the *Century* exerted a powerful influence on the formation of American culture during the period. As an insider and frequent contributor to the magazine, Burroughs participated actively in the cultural formation. Along with John Muir, who would become his friend and associate during the last two decades of the nineteenth century, Burroughs established the place of nature in mainstream American periodicals. In addition, both Muir and Burroughs made a place for the nature essay, developing the genre within the pages of the illustrated monthly magazine.

A set of remarkable convergences in the cultural history of postbellum America is especially pertinent to the rise of the nature essay as a genre in American periodicals. In the 1870s, *Scribner's Monthly*, edited by Josiah Gilbert Holland, became a culturally influential illustrated magazine, appealing to the burgeoning urban, middle-class readership that was also attracted to *Harper's New Monthly Magazine*.[2] A commonplace of American cultural history accords elite status to the *Atlantic Monthly*, which never succumbed to the temptation to use illustrations for its articles and reviews; the older *Harper's Monthly*, on the other hand, was expressly begun to attract readers for its book publications and aimed at "the great mass of the American people."[3] The growth of periodical literature in the second half of the nineteenth century suggests that there were in fact many kinds of readers for an amazing variety of newspapers, weeklies, monthlies, and quarterlies. Moreover, specialized journals grew at least as rapidly as general literary magazines. The first convergence, then, is that just as John Muir and John Burroughs were becoming writers in the late 1860s and early 1870s, new magazines were springing up, eager to print and illustrate their articles.

This phenomenon is clear in the early work Muir published in the *Overland Monthly*. Founded in 1868 and modeled on the *Atlantic Monthly*, the San Francisco magazine published seventeen articles by Muir between 1872 and 1875.[4] By the time Muir reached the pages of the magazine, its celebrity editor, Bret Harte, had published his famous stories "The Luck of Roaring Camp" and "The Outcasts of Poker Flat," demanded a substantial raise for his efforts, and then left the West behind. The *Overland Monthly* published California's first wave of professional writers, including Ina Coolbrith, Clarence King, Joaquin Miller, and Charles Warren Stoddard, and it counted Mark Twain among its first contributors. By using the magazine as a springboard for his literary career back east, Harte was simply following a pattern that Twain and William Dean Howells had used. In a certain sense the same can be said of Muir himself.

Muir's first article in the *Overland Monthly*, "Yosemite Valley in Flood," appeared in April 1872, and the last, "Flood-Storm in the Sierra," in June 1875. Between the two floods, Muir established himself as the most knowledgeable writer on the Yosemite and the Sierra Nevada. Some of the essays are experiential, poetic, and descriptive, while the seven essays of "Studies in the Sierra," published between May 1874 and January 1875, are technical articles on the glacial origins of the Sierra mountain landforms. Like the *Atlantic*, the *Overland Monthly* tended to eschew illustrations (it began printing them regularly in the late 1880s), but the "Studies in the Sierra" articles include a large number of diagrams and drawings by Muir himself, showing the direction and force of glaciers flowing over the land. Muir's illustrations are clearly more technical than aesthetic, but they do suggest Muir's talents as a draftsman. In the third article, "Ancient Glaciers and Their Pathways," his sketch of the channel of the South Lyell Glacier is as pictorial as it is scientific.[5] In general, however, Muir's early drawings for the *Overland Monthly* serve the purpose of explanation, not representation.

Muir's first publication in an eastern monthly magazine shows how illustration can be used for dramatic representational effects. The November 1875 issue of *Harper's New Monthly Magazine* carried Muir's "Living Glaciers of California" as the lead article, featuring seven wood engravings as illustrations. A short, enthusiastic version of "Living Glaciers of California" was published in the December 1872 issue of the *Overland Monthly*, and the *Harper's* article repeats the basic story of Muir's October 1871 discovery of an active glacier in the Sierra Nevada.[6] The later article is less personal and more scientific in tone than the early sketch, which dramatizes the discovery rather humorously: "Dirt-stained lines curved across the snow-bank from side to side, and when I observed that these curved lines coincided with the curved moraine, and that the stones and dirt were most abundant near the bottom of the bank, I shouted, '*A living glacier!*'" (*Overland Monthly* 9:547). By 1875, Muir had made a long, arduous, and painstaking study of the Sierra that resulted in the seven "Studies in the Sierra" articles. The *Harper's Monthly* essay summarizes and elaborates Muir's observations and theory of glaciation. But the most visible difference between the two essays is the effect of wood engravings.

Only one illustration in the *Harper's Monthly* article has any relation to Muir's earlier publications in the *Overland Monthly*. The diagram of the Mount Ritter glaciers (772) is clearly indebted to the kind of schematic diagrams that fill the "Studies in the Sierra" articles. An illustration in "Mountain-Building" (see figure 1) gives an aerial view along the spine of the Merced spur of mountains, with arrows indicating the backward erosion of the cirques, which Muir calls "glacial wombs" (Gifford 475). This two-dimensional schematic drawing becomes, in the hands of the *Harper's Monthly* engravers, a three-dimensional rendering of Mount Ritter and the Minarets, again in an aerial view but with the palpable texture of cirques and ridges (see figure 2).

The other six engravings in the *Harper's* article render particular landscapes in the high Sierra, and they employ details from Muir's descriptions for both illustrative and aesthetic effects. The second engraving, "The

Figure 1. Map of the Merced Range near Yosemite, *Studies in the Sierra* VII: "Mountain Building" (*Overland Monthly* 14 [January 1875]: 69).

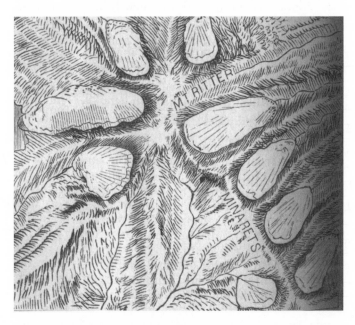

Figure 2. Glacier of Mount Ritter, from "Living Glaciers of California" (*Harper's New Monthly Magazine* 51 [November 1875]: 772).

Bergschrund of Black Mountain Glacier," appears before Muir actually describes the bergschrund in his essay, but it starkly contrasts the deep, wide crevasse and clustered icicles to the dark figure of a tiny mountaineer in the foreground (see figure 3). The sublime effect of the pictorial technique recalls such Romantic artists as Caspar David Friedrich or, closer to Muir's own time, Thomas Moran and Albert Bierstadt.

The other engravings develop a similar sublime effect. In "Mount Shasta Glacier," for instance, a group of six tiny human figures occupy the center foreground, while behind them yawn a series of lateral crevasses. The very first illustration, "The Sierra from Mount Diablo," does not follow Muir's description, which takes a perspective from the summit of Mount Diablo across the San Joaquin Valley. Instead, it leads the viewer from a darkened position in the lower foreground, nearly in the waters of the San Joaquin River, up the whitened surface of a vast, unnamed glacier that would seem to be the northeast glacier of the Mount Ritter system (see figure 4). Two other engravings evoke specific aspects of Ritter's glaciers—the descent of the north Ritter glacier into a glacial lake and the ice tongue of the northeast glacier protruding from beneath the snow below the summit. In these engravings, the perspective moves from a low foreground to the heights of the receding background, taking the reader-viewer's eye from the flat page toward an invisible sublime. It is as if we were at eye level with the glacial lake, looking up at the ice pouring into the surface, or as if we were standing below the ice tongue and crevasses of the northeast glacier, staring up at the summit of Mount Ritter.

The *Harper's Monthly* engravings suggest a code for viewing Muir's Sierra Nevada. Humanity is dwarfed by the vast ice fields and deep crevasses. Human beings gaze up into a hazy boundary between mountain and ice and sky, or else they huddle at the edge of a frozen abyss. The human figures are mere smudges of ink on the page, hardly larger than a capital letter, while the Sierra Nevada is, as Muir calls it, "one grand wrinkled sheet of glacial records. For the scriptures of the ancient glaciers cover every rock, mountain, and valley of the range, and are in many places so well preserved, and are written in so plain a hand, they have long been recognized even by those who were not seeking for them" (569). Nature

Figure 3. Bergschrund of Black Mountain Glacier
(*Harper's New Monthly Magazine* 51:771).

Figure 4. The Sierra from Mount Diablo
(*Harper's New Monthly Magazine* 51:769).

is represented as forbidding, foreign, and distant, even if it is at the same time beautifully terrifying.

From Muir's journal sketches to the rudimentary, schematic diagrams of the "Studies in the Sierra" articles, and thence to the culturally coded engravings of *Harper's Monthly*—the illustration functions differently along this path. In the journal, the sketch is a visual mnemonic device and an immediate record of experience. In the "Studies in the Sierra" articles, the diagrams are geometrical and scientific, functioning as algorithmic guides to the reader. So Muir asserts, in "Mountain-Building," "Thus [in figure 1], let A B represent a section of a portion of the summit of a mountain chain, and C D E F G H, etc., the wombs of glaciers dead or active, then the residual masses 1 2 3 will be the so-called mountains" (Gifford 473). Illustrated monthlies like *Harper's Monthly* subordinate the explanatory function to emotional and interpretive effects. From a record of immediate experience, then, the visual image is transformed into a powerful cultural code. In this particular instance, the transformation creates a peculiar distancing between the reader-viewer and the place depicted. Muir emphasizes the distancing effect in the last line of "Living Glaciers of California": "In the Swiss Alps carriage roads approach within a few hundred yards of some of the low-descending glaciers, while the comparative remoteness and inaccessibility of the Sierra glaciers may be inferred from the fact that, during the prosecution of my own explorations in five summers, I never met a single human being, not even an Indian or a hunter" (776). The text and illustrations combine to enforce a strong sense of nature as a remote and inaccessible wilderness.

Pastoral Convergences

The second convergence of the nature essay and illustrated magazines relates to the founding of *Scribner's Monthly* in 1870 and the development of periodical illustrations from 1870 to 1910. With Josiah Gilbert Holland as editor, Alexander Drake as art director, and Theodore Low DeVinne as printer, *Scribner's Monthly* quickly became a major competitor with *Harper's Monthly*. By 1881, when *Scribner's Monthly* was sold and

renamed the *Century Illustrated Monthly Magazine*, it already wielded
immense cultural power. Robert Scholnick attributes "the most important
improvements in the art and technology of reproducing images in periodicals" (46) to the first decade of *Scribner's Monthly*, but the *Century* not
only maintained but also developed the illustrations of the 1870s.[7] The
illustrations of the *Century* became known as the New School of American
wood engraving, which featured the technique called photoxylography, or
photographing illustrations directly on the engraving block. The magazine
continued to be a source of both tradition and innovation until the rise of
half-tone plates effectively ended the golden age of wood engraving. Until
Richard Watson Gilder's death in 1909, however, the *Century* attracted the
finest new American artists and engravers.[8]

In several important ways, the rise of the nature essay and the rise of
magazine illustration intersect, giving a new line of direction to American
periodicals. Muir and Burroughs in effect meet in the pages of *Scribner's
Monthly* and the *Century*. By virtue of this convergence, these two dis-
similar writers develop remarkable similarities, and just as they are reaching their first maturity, magazine illustrations reach a new technical and
aesthetic level. The pages of these two magazines, more than any other,
become the vivid figurative place of nature for Muir, Burroughs, and their
readers.

An early example of these convergences appears in the November 1878
Scribner's Monthly. The issue features consecutive articles by Burroughs
and Muir: "Picturesque Aspects of Farm Life in New York" (17:41–54) and
"A Wind Storm in the Forests of the Yuba" (17:55–63). Burroughs's essay is
lavishly illustrated with eleven "process" reproductions of drawings by Mary
Hallock Foote.[9] The first page of the article features a nearly page-length
engraving titled "Gathering Butter," in which a young farmwife bends over
a butter churn in a cellar, subtly lit by a screened window and a latticed
window. The stucco walls are richly textured and cracked, and the drawing
is framed in a polygon, as if the reader were viewing the subject through an
archway. The tone of the drawing, especially the woman's face and body,
is peacefully monastic (see figure 5). Other drawings contribute to the
atmosphere of rural health. Labor is rendered as a form of near repose in

Figure 5. Gathering Butter, from "Picturesque Aspects of Farm Life in New York"
(*Scribner's Monthly* 17 [November 1878]: 41).

"Strawberry Pickers," "The Hay-Wagon after the Harvest," "Driving Sheep to be Washed," and "Twilight in the Fields." Several illustrations feature no human figures at all but instead create an atmosphere of bucolic solitude: "Milking-Time," for instance, features two cows in a barnyard, framed by a barn; "Old barn with cattle sheds" suggests a charcoal sketch, especially since the caption is given in handwritten script. The engravings create a pastoral, nostalgic perspective.[10]

Burroughs emphasizes the same perspective in his prose, but he clearly opens the way to a more nuanced reading of the nature essay and its place. First, he repeats the adjective "picturesque" so often that the editors of *Scribner's Monthly* do not repeat the word in the running titles. As Burroughs puts it in the essay, reprinted in *Signs and Seasons* (1886), "Indeed, the picturesque in human affairs and occupations is always born of love and humility, as it is in art or literature; and it quickly takes to itself wings and flies away at the advent of pride, or any selfish or unworthy motive" (*Writings* 7:239). Burroughs expressly mingles the aesthetic and moral in his theory of the picturesque. The term also refers constantly and accurately to the "pictures" in the magazine article. As in Burroughs's letter to Gilder about the "hideous," miscarriage-inducing illustrations of E. W. Kemble, the magazine illustration he appreciates most must be picturesque rather than harshly realistic. Foote's renderings of farm life in New York State are detailed and honest, but they are also highly selective, grouping human beings, farm animals, and buildings in stable compositions that are both humble and loving.

The picturesque creates several ironies in conjunction with sentimental nostalgia and honest detail. The pastoral artworks depend on their effect of offhandedness, as if they were pages in an artist's sketchbook, but they are produced by the innovative technologies of photoxylography, the New School process that the contemporary critic W. J. Linton disparages as "mechanical." In addition, Burroughs notes that the picturesque, both in actual farm life and in represented farm scenes, has declined over the past fifty to one hundred years. According to Burroughs, this is "owing partly to the advent of machinery, which enables the farmer to do so much of his work by proxy, and hence removes him farther from the soil, and partly to the growing distaste for the occupation among our people" (239). But as Raymond Williams argues, the picturesque and pastoral both depend on the aesthetic distance from the actual soil and toil of farming. The picturesque may be declining in the real farming communities of New York, but it thrives in the pages of *Scribner's Monthly*. Only by removing the place from contact with the urban, industrial world of New York City can Burroughs point to the tonic of farm life. So he concludes the article by noting that "we long for the more elegant pursuits, or the ways and fashions of the town," but the farmer alone "has a home," and "nothing will take the various social distempers which the city and artificial life breed out of a man like farming, like direct and loving contact with the soil. It draws out the poison. It humbles him, teaches him patience and reverence, and restores the proper tone to his system" (260–61). This clarion call for a return to simple rural life depends most fundamentally on the distance between the reader's "artificial life" and the ideal of a natural antidote. Burroughs is by no means naïve or disingenuous. Rather, the pastoral imagination depends on fundamental gaps between real and ideal, life and literature.

Burroughs's innocent perspective is thorough and substantial, for it springs from his dual occupations as a fruit farmer and writer. The two vocations depend on one another, and they also depend on the tension between Burroughs's farm at Riverby, a train ride up the Hudson River Valley from New York City, and the largest metropolis in the country. The gaps and contradictions are paradoxical, and they are also productive. Burroughs maintains a distance from the city, but he also maintains a distance from farm life, especially in its industrial form. The tensions allow Burroughs to write and publish in the most prestigious literary journals of the day, while he remains remote enough from the city to create a "more simple and imaginative" place (256).

Similar tensions between proximity and remoteness, the near and far, dominate John Muir's article, "A Wind Storm in the Forests of the Yuba." Although the essay runs only five pages in the original magazine version and features only one illustration (see figure 6), it creates some of the same effects as Burroughs's pastoral study of the picturesque. First, the illustration, from Muir's own sketch, reproduces the sketchbook quality

Figure 6. A Wind Storm in the California Forests (After a Sketch by the Author), from "A Wind Storm in the Forests of the Yuba" (*Scribner's Monthly* 17 [November 1878]: 56).

of Mary Hallock Foote's picturesque drawings. The illustration creates an effect of immediacy and accuracy, but the reality it portrays is far from the peace and calm of farm life. Instead, the unpopulated landscape is full of powerful motion. Despite the invisibility of wind, the engraving delivers a clear visual sense of the storm. The wind appears to be rushing from left to right, across the frame of the illustration, and it is so forceful that large conifers are bending in one direction, as if an invisible hand were brushing across them. The white lines of the individual tree trunks, together with the traces of white space across the foreground, create an ominous, otherworldly effect, since there is no source of light anywhere in the scene. The darkness of forest, rocks, and distant mountains dominates the tone of the drawing to such an extent that it resembles a photographic negative. Although the landscape does not resemble the vast and terrifying ice fields of the "Studies in the Sierra" series in the *Overland Monthly*, it does evoke sublime, elemental power. As in the earlier series, too, the illustration gestures toward the wilderness as an inhuman, alien place.

The illustration functions quite differently from those of "Picturesque Aspects of Farm Life" or the "Studies in the Sierra" series, however, when we look at it in relation to the text of Muir's article. In those earlier examples, the writing and engraving are in close accord with one another. Here, on the contrary, the sublime effect of the illustration runs directly counter to Muir's tone. From the opening sentence, Muir insists on the beneficial beauty of the winds: "The mountain winds, like the dew and rain, sunshine and snow, are measured and bestowed with love on the forests to develop their strength and beauty."[11] The passive voice does not disguise Muir's sense of divine guidance and loving design. He notes the sublime power of the wind, but only in a comparative sense: "The waving of a forest of the giant Sequoias is indescribably impressive and sublime, but the pines seem to me the best interpreters of winds. They are mighty waving goldenrods, ever in tune, singing and writing wind-music all their long century lives" (*Mountains* 174). The anthropomorphism and scale of the passage bring the otherworldly pine forest of the illustration into close, familiar relationship with the reader. In that way, Muir's style counters the tone of the engraving.

The "Wind Storm" essay features Muir's wild ride in the windy top of a young Douglas fir tree, over a hundred feet high. From beginning to end, the description emphasizes the trees "rocking and swirling in wild ecstasy" (176), the racing light and shadows, the surprising color in the "wild sea of pines," and the sounds that "corresponded gloriously with this wild exuberance of light and motion." But the wildness is not remote from human emotions: "We hear much nowadays concerning the universal struggle for existence, but no struggle in the common meaning of the word was manifest here; no recognition of danger by any tree; no deprecation; but rather an invincible gladness as remote from exultation as from fear" (177). Muir undercuts the sublime and terrifying aspects of the storm, just as he subverts the intrepid quality of his own climb and ride. He pointedly refuses to admit any harsh evolutionary mechanism to the description, and in parallel fashion he refuses to recognize any emotion but gladness. After ruminating on the "one grand anthem" of mountain streams, Muir concludes that the "storm-streams of air in the mountain woods" are even more sublime and substantial, and that leads to this famous insight:

> We all travel the milky way together, trees and men; but it never occurred to me until this storm-day, while swinging in the wind, that trees are travelers, in the ordinary sense. They make many journeys, not extensive ones, it is true; but our own little journeys, away and back again, are only little more than tree-wavings—many of them not so much. (179)

The essay effectively brings humanity and nature together, and the strategy is more substantial than mere anthropomorphism. The key to the insight is Muir's shifting sense of scale, from the familiarity of waving goldenrods to the unifying motion of the Milky Way. The scale is not only vast, sublime, or elemental; rather, Muir also finds humility and generosity of spirit in recognizing the "littleness" of all travels and travelers.

Taken together, Burroughs's and Muir's two *Scribner's Monthly* essays form a matched pair. They create two different places of nature, on different scales, but ultimately nature is both picturesque and sublime, both near and far, and these different figurative places can appear quite literally on the opposite sides of the same sheet of paper. Both essays depend on the remoteness, in time or space, of the natural place described, but both bring that remote place into near relation with the reader. Both writers create a peculiar tension between nature and culture, and both give subtle new definitions to the place of nature within culture. Physically removed from the urban world of the illustrated magazine, both Burroughs and Muir insist on a necessary intimacy between culture and nature.

Muir and Burroughs thus emerge as much more complicated than the terms "wilderness" and "pastoral" suggest—or, at the very least, more than our common understanding of the terms suggests. One way of appreciating the complication is to look at Muir's first publications in the new *Century* magazine, which both continued and improved upon the work of *Scribner's Monthly*. In the June and July 1882 issues of the *Century*, Muir published the two-part essay "The Bee Pastures of California," which would later become, with minor revisions, the final chapter of *The Mountains of California*.[12] The essay marks the climax of Muir's first phase as a writer, since after this publication he goes into an eight-year silence, broken by the important essays commissioned by Robert Underwood Johnson in 1889–90: "The Treasures of the Yosemite" and "Features of the Proposed Yosemite National Park," which appeared in the August and September 1890 issues of the *Century*.[13]

In the two-part "Bee Pastures of California" essay, Muir strikes some of his characteristic themes, especially for modern readers who know such later works as *My First Summer in the Sierra*, published in 1911 but derived from the 1869 journal. At the beginning of the essay, for instance, he contrasts the former wild "glorious pastures" to the present "sad havoc" created by "plows and sheep" (*Mountains* 234). The contrast makes all cultivation seem tragic, all wilderness glorious. But the essay is not schematic. Muir focuses on the former glory of California as "one sweet bee-garden," "one smooth, continuous bed of honey-bloom" that stretches over four hundred miles, and "one sheet of plant gold, hazy and vanishing in the distance, distinct as a new map along the foot-hills" (234–35). The images of unity recall the figure of the Milky Way in "A Wind Storm in the Forests of the Yuba," and they implicitly contrast the present fragmented landscape to an idealized, unified past. Muir's mapping of California recalls Burroughs's nostalgic mapping of New York, for in both the contrast between past and present creates an intertwined sense of place and displacement.

Second, the map includes much more than the wilderness regions of the Sierra Nevada. In both parts of the essay, Muir explores the entire state—Coast Range, Sierra foothills, Central Valley, Sierra forests (even up the slopes of Mount Shasta), then Southern California, including the San Gabriel Valley, San Gabriel Mountains, Los Angeles and San Diego counties, and the desert east of the Sierra. The illustrations feature views of Southern California "bee-ranches" rather than the wilds of Shasta, and Muir finds more wilderness in the southern mountains than in the northern: "The Santa Lucia, San Rafael, San Gabriel, San Jacinto, and San Bernardino ranges are almost untouched as yet save by the wild bees"

(258). Ultimately, Muir concludes that the "bee-ranches" of the south are much advanced over those of the north, and both areas must contest the destruction of the "bee-gardens" by fire and axe and "sheep evil" (264). In effect, the essay holds out beekeeping as an alternative form of agriculture, one that harms the landscape far less than logging and grazing.

Third, the illustrations by Roger Riordan and Harry Fenn are exquisitely produced and printed engravings (see figures 7 and 8). They routinely combine one close-up image of a flowering plant or "honey-bloom" and at least one landscape scene. Most feature people engaged in the work of beekeeping, but like the illustrations of Burroughs's "Picturesque Aspects of Farm Life" the labor is downplayed in favor of pastoral scenes and noble prospects. The scale is human, even when the figures cannot be discerned in great detail. The art of engraving, clearly at its height in these works, accords nature an honored place within the established print culture of New York City. Muir's "Bee Pastures of California" essays create a figurative place between the real world and the printed page, between wilderness and pastoral, nature and culture, far and near. The perspective is simultaneously panoramic and microscopic. As a result, the essays create a paradoxical place of intimate remoteness, in which Muir guides readers into new territory and makes them familiar with it.

Giving Nature a Place

The paradoxical sense of place created in the illustrated essays of the 1870s and early 1880s suggests artful insights into the relationship of nature and culture, but it should not blind us to the fundamental power of culture in giving nature a place. One reason that Muir and Burroughs appear together in the pages of *Scribner's Monthly*, the *Century*, and the *Atlantic Monthly* is that they fulfill particular cultural roles as writers. These three magazines, along with a handful of others such as *Lippincott's*, *Harper's*, *North American Review*, the *Critic*, the *Nation*, and the *Galaxy*, exercised so much cultural authority that Nancy Glazener has recently named them "The *Atlantic* Group" and has detailed their institutional status and power in the literary marketplace from 1850 to 1910.[14] Glazener fastens the magazines

Figure 7. A Bee-Ranch in Lower California, from "The Bee-Pastures of California"
(*Century* 24 [June 1882]: 225).

Figure 8. Wild Bee Garden, from "The Bee-Pastures of California"
(*Century* 24 [June 1882]: 229).

to the formation of a bourgeois readership and a genteel, refined taste, and in this context Burroughs's hyperbolic outcry to Gilder in February 1891 is an excellent example of the writer as wounded reader—and, in Louis Althusser's terms, as interpellated subject.[15] Indeed, the three editors of *Scribner's Monthly* and the *Century* during the period—Josiah Gilbert Holland, Richard Watson Gilder, and Robert Underwood Johnson—functioned as moral and aesthetic guardians of their readers, schooling them to read and judge the art and literature of their magazines.[16]

The notion of cultural schooling has become familiar to students of American literature since the publication of Richard Brodhead's *School of Hawthorne*, and Glazener follows Brodhead in attributing the greatest cultural power to the fiction of high realism that dominated the periodical literature of the period.[17] The magazines depended heavily on short stories and serial novels to form their readership, but the *Century* increased its circulation most dramatically when it devoted significant numbers of pages to the illustrated historical "Civil War Series" from 1884 to 1887. In addition, the series of engravings by Timothy Cole of the Old Masters of Europe and drawings by Joseph Pennell of European monuments contributed significantly to the cultural authority and material success of the magazine.[18]

The essays of Burroughs and Muir cross generic boundaries in remarkably flexible ways. Indeed, that flexibility is the special strength of the nature essay as it is formed in the late nineteenth century. So, for instance, Muir's essays combine travel narrative, scientific observation, and poetic description, and they can present landscapes that are both wild and cultivated. Burroughs ranges yet more widely. Although he is celebrated for his ornithological rambles, an essay like "Picturesque Aspects of Farm Life in New York" is difficult to categorize. For over fifty years Burroughs filled the pages of the *Atlantic Monthly*, *Scribner's Monthly*, and the *Century* with dozens of essays on travel, literary criticism, poetry, philosophy of science, and theology. Fiction is perhaps the only form he never touched.

Unlike Muir, Burroughs maintained a steady record of publication in the pages of the *Century* during the 1880s and 1890s. In addition, he published several articles in *Appleton's Journal* until it stopped publication in

1876, and he contributed often to the *North American Review*, the *Atlantic Monthly*, the *Critic*, *Poet-Lore*, and the *Conservator* during the last three decades of the century. Only in the pages of *Scribner's Monthly* and the *Century*, however, did he present the combined power of artistic illustration and a genial style. In the March 1883 *Century*, for example, the essay "Signs and Seasons" admonishes the "student and lover of nature" to "stay at home and see the procession pass." Thus the "change of the seasons is like the passage of strange and new countries; the zones of the earth, with all their beauties and marvels, pass one's door, and linger long in the passing."[19] The passing of seasons becomes a kind of perpetual fascination for the observer, one that Burroughs gives a personal aspect in the first paragraph of the essay:

> One spring morning five swans flew above my barn in single file, going northward,—an express train bound for Labrador. It was a more exhilarating sight than if I had seen them in their native haunts. They made a breeze in my mind, like a noble passage in a poem. How gently their great wings flapped; how easy to fly when spring gives the impulse! On another occasion I saw a line of fowls, probably swans, going northward, at such a height that they appeared like a faint, waving black line against the sky. They must have been at an altitude of two or three miles. I was looking intently at the clouds to see which way they moved, when the birds came into my field of vision. I should never have seen them had they not crossed the precise spot upon which my eye was fixed. As it was near sundown, they were probably launched for an all-night pull. They were going with great speed, and as they swayed a little this way and that, they suggested a slender, all but invisible, aerial serpent cleaving the ether. What a highway was pointed out up there!—an easy grade from the Gulf to Hudson's Bay. (*Writings* 7:4–5)

For a reader familiar with Burroughs's first three books, this passage will seem characteristic in several ways. He transforms the observation of the five swans into an exhilarating experience, a sight more amazing than if he had seen them in their native habitat. He transfers the birds' motion into a figurative, mental breeze. He compares them to "a noble passage in a poem," making the experience into an aesthetic form. He uses the first sighting to shape his second observation—of the "line of fowls, probably swans." The second experience becomes more and more elaborate as an experiment in keeping a "sharp lookout" and seeing with all of one's self. Finally, the passage not only reports the two experiences but, more important, teaches a reader how to see, how to approach a place in order to find the extraordinary within the common.

Burroughs's description focuses especially on the fineness of perception necessary for having the second experience, just as his style emphasizes the nearly invisible "faint, waving black line against the sky." The style suggests the kind of pictorial imagination that dominates the pages of the *Century*, so it is no surprise to find on the following page a full-page engraving by Elbridge Kingsley, "Flight of the Birds" (figure 9). The engraving masterfully evokes the liminal. From a darkened foreground, dominated by the beautifully open conical crown of a red spruce, the eye travels to the reflected sunset in the waters of the Hudson River in the middle distance. The crown of the spruce and the light of the sky, rendered as gray and white space, draw the eye farther up the page, where the reader can barely discern the "all but invisible, aerial serpent cleaving the ether." Together, the illustration and text educate the reader in ways of seeing.

Burroughs's essay develops the mysteries of that educational project. Part of the mystery lies in observation, which demands patience and care; another lies in interpretation, which demands at least as much patience and care. But nature remains mysterious and elusive for all that: "All we know about the private and essential natural history of the bees, the birds, the fishes, the animals, the plants, is the result of close, patient, quick-witted observation. Yet Nature will often elude one for all his pains and alertness. Thoreau, as revealed in his journal, was for years trying to settle in his own mind what was the first thing that stirred in spring, after the severe New England winter,—in what was the first sign or pulse of returning life manifest; and he never seems to have been quite sure. . . . Nature will not be cornered, yet she does many things in a corner and surreptitiously. She is all things to all men; she has whole truths, half truths, and quarter truths, if not still smaller fractions" (26–28). Like nature itself, the observer of nature exists only in fractions, "in fragments, a trait here and a trait there.

Figure 9. Flight of the Birds, from "Signs and Seasons" (*Century* 25 [March 1883]: 673).

Each person sees what it concerns him to see" (33). For Burroughs, the best observer is ultimately the person, whether poet or naturalist, most concerned to see and understand the "hints and half truths" of nature, for "before a fact can become poetry, it must pass through the heart or the imagination of the poet; before it can become science, it must pass through the understanding of the scientist" (36–37).

As if to seal the power of culture in interpreting the real, Burroughs adds the following passage to the end of "A Sharp Lookout":

> Or one may say, it is with the thoughts and half thoughts that the walker gathers in the woods and fields, as with the common weeds and coarser wild flowers which he plucks for a bouquet,—wild carrot, purple aster, moth mullein, sedge, grass, etc.: they look common and uninteresting enough there in the fields, but the moment he separates them from the tangled mass, and brings them indoors, and places them in a vase, say of some choice glass, amid artificial things,—behold, how beautiful! They have an added charm and significance at once; they are defined and identified, and what was common and familiar becomes unexpectedly attractive. The writer's style, the quality of mind he brings, is the vase in which his commonplace impressions and incidents are made to appear so beautiful and significant. (*Writings* 7:37)

This added passage clearly runs counter to Emerson's "Each and All" and to Whitman's "Standard of the Universal Natural." Only by bringing the common, wild flowers ("half thoughts") indoors and placing them in the vase of his mind and style can the writer make them more than common. Many modern readers might add, "And less than wild." But Burroughs sees no effect of diminishment; instead, the act of bringing the wild indoors adds charm, significance, and beauty. As he states earlier in the essay, "Nature comes home to one most when he is at home," and "this home feeling, this domestication of nature, is important to the observer" (5). The "home feeling" relies on place, on being at home in a place, but it also relies on the intellectual and artistic culture that defines the place of nature.

Although the nature essays of Burroughs and Muir participate in the dominant literary culture of high realism, they also have much in common with post–Civil War regionalism and antimodernism.[20] Like the regionalist

fiction of writers as diverse as Sarah Orne Jewett and Bret Harte, the nature essay functions within the dominant literary culture by occupying a
particular, delimited place—the place of the minor or subsidiary—rather
than the place of major, "great" works such as the novels of the realists
William Dean Howells and Henry James. As Richard Brodhead astutely
argues, regionalism is both a point of literary access and a point of literary
limitation. [21] Because regionalist fiction focuses on remote, rural, preindustrial settings, it has much in common with nature essays like Burroughs's
"Picturesque Aspects of Farm Life in New York" and Muir's "The Bee
Pastures of California."

The affinity between nature writers and antimodernism is equally strong.
Indeed, much regionalist writing could be seen as antimodernist, even
though it is most often written with a modern urban reader in mind.
Glazener concisely defines the movement of antimodernism as "a therapeutic ideal of individual wellness and authentic experience that people
pursued in a number of ways: through obsessive concerns with their health,
through regenerating holidays spent out of doors, through hobbies that allowed them scope for craftsmanship, and through vicarious participation
in earlier, more heroic eras, especially the Middle Ages." [22] Burroughs and
Muir are clearly antimodern in their focus on the "tonic" of nature and the
health of the individual who learns to observe and interpret nature through
direct experience. Both routinely disparage the quality of life in cities and
represent nature as existing outside the borders of the city, in a preindustrial, technologically simple, morally innocent place. Burroughs's lament
in his 1916 journal about the magazine writer's problem of addressing
"the moving-picture brain," for example, is distinctly antimodern in tone
and content. The journal entry expresses Burroughs's sense of displacement from the modern world, but it expresses a characteristic ambivalence
toward modern American culture at the close of the nineteenth century.

The work of historian Jackson Lears strongly argues against viewing antimodernism as a regressive, nostalgic movement of a dwindling intellectual elite. Lears shows that antimodernism was pervasive, widespread, and
mixed with a strong belief in social and material progress and market capitalism. Antimodernism was one part of the social changes that ushered

America into modernity at the turn of the century. In Lears's terms, the late nineteenth century underwent a crisis in cultural authority, and the antimodernists pushed American culture in the direction of a therapeutic worldview. If the malaise of the 1890s betrayed a peculiar sense of helplessness and weightlessness, then the antimodernists wished to provide something like a cure. For Burroughs and Muir as for many other figures in the "back to nature" movement of the 1890s, nature should be a place for revitalizing and restoring American culture.[23]

The Writer's Place

In order for nature to function as a place of refuge and restoration, it has to be protected and preserved. For that reason, the *Century* became the site of the most important environmental advocacy at the turn of the twentieth century. Once again, too, the illustrations in the magazine played a major role in the cultural authority wielded by writers like Muir and Burroughs. The relationship between Muir and Robert Underwood Johnson, associate editor of the *Century* and editor-in-chief after Gilder's death in 1909, was central to the environmental movement of establishing national parks and national forests. Burroughs never committed himself to a public, political role, but his work was nonetheless influential in raising the culture's consciousness of the fragility and dignity of nature.

Burroughs's influence widened as the century drew to a close. His essays in the *Century*, combined with his appearance in other periodicals and the steady publication of collections by Houghton Mifflin Company, made him one of the best known writers of the day. In addition, his work began to reach a new, younger audience as of 1887. In that year, Mary E. Burt, a schoolteacher in Chicago, won approval from her board of education to teach Burroughs's *Pepacton* to her thirty-six pupils. The publisher, Oscar Houghton, visited her class, was impressed by what he witnessed, and asked Burt to edit a small volume of essays by Burroughs. The result was a popular pair of collections edited by Burt—*Birds and Bees* (1887) and *Sharp Eyes* (1890). A rough tally of the sales of these two volumes by Houghton Mifflin shows that *Birds and Bees* had its greatest sales in 1902 (17,596 copies) and that *Sharp Eyes* had its greatest sales in 1906 (16,285 copies). The two volumes averaged between 11,000 and 11,500 copies sold for the period 1904–6. In 1895, with Burroughs's blessing, Burt edited another collection published by the Ginn Company, *Little Nature Studies for Little People*, intended for first-grade students. Given these successes, Burroughs published his own collection of essays for schoolchildren, *Squirrels and Other Fur-Bearers* (1900).[24] Far from retreating into a pastoral or antimodern idealism, Burroughs continually sought to reach new generations of readers.

The basic narrative of the Johnson-Muir collaboration has been told many times and can be sketched quickly. In the spring of 1889, Johnson traveled to California in search of contributors for a *Century* series, "Gold Hunters of California," with the idea of matching the success of the Civil War series. Muir visited Johnson at the Palace Hotel in San Francisco, the first time the two had met face to face. In June, Muir guided Johnson on a trip to Yosemite Valley, the Hetch Hetchy Valley, and Tuolumne Meadows. Johnson claims that he first proposed the project of establishing Yosemite National Park while he and Muir were camped at Soda Springs on the Tuolumne River. The editor convinced the skeptical Muir to write two articles for the *Century*, which would be illustrated by pictures of the wonders of the Yosemite; Johnson would then take the pictures and proofs of Muir's articles to Congress, lobbying his powerful acquaintances for help. Johnson carried out his plan "to the letter," and on October 1, 1890, the Yosemite National Park was established. Johnson immodestly notes in his autobiography that the members of Congress "had never heard of Muir, though they knew of the Muir Glacier," but his presentation of the plan was nonetheless successful.[25]

Muir's two articles, "The Treasures of the Yosemite" and "Features of the Proposed Yosemite National Park," appeared in the August and September 1890 issues of the *Century*.[26] As promised, they were copiously illustrated, and both the texts and the illustrations are rhetorically persuasive in their aims. The first essay, "Treasures," does not focus exclusively on the natural wonders of Yosemite Valley and its surroundings. Instead, from the outset Muir mixes poetic descriptions, narratives, direct addresses to the reader, and guidebook sketches. Likewise, the illustrations include engravings of sublime aesthetic features such as "Mirror View of the Three Brothers," "El Capitan," "Mirror View of Yosemite Falls," "Sentinel Rock," and "Cathedral Rocks," which appear on five successive pages of the article (488–92). But the illustrations also feature "process" reproductions from photographs to show several instances of "Destructive Work in Yosemite Valley." In each case, the caption details the kind of destruction shown, and there is no attempt at aesthetics: "The 'Leidig Meadows' plowed up in October, 1888, to raise hay" (487); "Stump forest, mostly of young pine, in 'State Pasture,' covering some eight acres. Cut in June, 1887, and stumps left standing and perfectly sound. About 2000 trees, or more, felled in this one spot" (493); "Specimen tree trimming done in 1887–88. Much similar work has been done in other parts of the valley" (493). The style of both the captions and the photographs is expository and journalistic. Clearly the two types of illustration heighten the threat of destruction by contrasting the beautiful treasures to environmental disasters.

Muir's writing style likewise heightens the experience of Yosemite as a place. The article begins with an appeal to "the traveler, whether tourist, botanist, geologist, or lover of wilderness pure and simple," to visit Yosemite Valley, and then Muir recalls his own first visit:

One shining morning, at the head of the Pacheco Pass, a landscape was displayed that after all my wanderings still appears as the most divinely beautiful and sublime I have ever beheld. There at my feet lay the great central plain of California, level as a lake, thirty or forty miles wide, four hundred long, one rich furred bed of golden Compositae. And along the eastern shore of this lake of gold rose the mighty Sierra, miles in height, in massive, tranquil grandeur, so gloriously colored and so radiant that it seemed not clothed with light, but wholly composed of it, like the wall of some celestial city. Along the top, and extending a good way down, was a rich pearl-gray belt of snow; then a belt of blue and dark purple, marking the extension of the forests; and stretching along the base of the range a broad belt of rose-purple, where lay the miners' gold and the open foothill gardens—all the colors smoothly blending, making a wall of light clear as crystal and ineffably fine, yet firm as adamant. Then it seemed to me the Sierra should be called, not the Nevada or Snowy Range, but the Range of Light. And after ten years in the midst of it, rejoicing and wondering, seeing the glorious floods of light that fill it,—the sunbursts of morning among the mountain-peaks, the broad noonday radiance on the crystal rocks, the flush of the alpenglow, and the thousand dashing waterfalls with their marvelous abundance of irised spray,—it still seems to me a range of light. But no terrestrial beauty may endure forever. The glory of wildness has already departed from the great central plain. Its bloom is shed, and so in part is the bloom of the mountains. In Yosemite, even under the protection of the Government, all that is perishable is vanishing apace. ("Treasures" 483)

The rhetoric of the final sentences recalls directly Muir's lament for the Central Valley and its flowers in the two-part "Bee Pastures of California" essay, the last article he had published in the *Century* in 1882. Parts of the panoramic description also echo the opening chapter of Muir's *Picturesque California*, published in 1888. But most of the paragraph looks forward to the first chapter of *The Mountains of California*, which Muir would publish for the first time in the 1894 book. The famous description of the Sierra as the "Range of Light" also reappears in "The Yosemite National Park," one of several essays published in the *Atlantic Monthly* and later reprinted in *Our National Parks*.[27] The style emphasizes the divine, celestial colors of the mountains, contrasting that "glory of wildness" to the sadly vanishing "bloom" on the central plain and mountains. Light appears both permanent and evanescent: it forms the wall of the Sierra, "firm as adamant," and yet it vanishes at the end of the paragraph.

Muir stages the tension between permanence and evanescence in other places. For instance, in describing the waterfalls of the Yosemite Valley, he pauses at the Illilouette Fall, one of the least famous of the Yosemite waterfalls, to tell how he once walked up the rugged canyon leading to the falls: "When I reached the fall slant sunbeams were glinting across the head of it, leaving all the rest in shadow; and on the illumined brow a group of yellow spangles were playing, of singular form and beauty, flashing up and dancing in large flame-shaped masses, wavering at times, then steadying, rising and falling in accord with the shifting forms of the water. But the color changed not at all. Nothing in clouds or flowers, on bird-wings or the lips of shells, could rival it in fineness. It was the most divinely beautiful mass of yellow light I ever beheld—one of nature's precious sights that come to us but once in a lifetime" (495). In four artfully crafted sentences, Muir transforms the least grand of the Yosemite waterfalls into a place of wonder, captured during one Indian Summer hike. He creates similar effects by describing "lunar spraybows," visible only at night, and then narrating his wild adventure behind Yosemite Fall one moonlit night (496). In a third passage, he describes the spray of the upper Yosemite Fall, freezing in winter and forming a hollow, truncated cone at the base of the fall; then he casually narrates his attempt to climb the ice-hill under the "suffocating blast, half air, half water" (497). In all three passages, description and narration combine to create a sense of unique wonder and marvelous adventure, but the matter-of-fact tone makes sublime beauty seem ordinary and readily available.

Muir alters the tone in the last movement of the "Treasures" essay in order to seal the effect of wonder and awe. He describes in telling detail the onset of a rainstorm during December 1871, which ultimately creates "Yosemite in full bloom of flood" (498).[28] The waterfalls and streams burst into "a grand jubilee," eventually creating an enormous flood of water, wind, and sound. Typically, Muir is eager to "get into the midst of the show," and his descriptions create the sharp sense of being physically present within an extraordinary natural spectacle. He estimates at one point that the flood creates more than a hundred cascades and falls, and he describes intricate cloud movements accompanying the waters (499–500). Finally, he notes that the "measureless extravagance of storm" goes on for two days and nights, but "mostly without spectators, at least of a terrestrial kind. I saw nobody out—bird, bear, squirrel, or man." The essay closes, however, with the mental image of the same "sublime waterfall flood" occurring in the other "mountain temples" such as Tuolumne Canyon, Hetch Hetchy Valley, King's Canyon, and out across the five hundred miles of the entire Sierra Nevada: "What a psalm was that!" Muir's comprehensive vision gestures toward the unity of the entire mountain range in winter flood, but the grandeur of the spectacle depends, ultimately, on Muir himself as the single spectator and reporter. The Sierra becomes a place of psalm, but Muir is truly the imaginative psalmist.[29]

Muir's cultural power as a celebrity author can be seen in the editorial pages of the *Century*, especially when we consider the orchestrating role of Robert Underwood Johnson. Even before the Yosemite articles appeared, Johnson published an "Open Letter" in the January 1890 issue, recounting his trip to Yosemite with Muir and sketching the arguments that Muir would make in the issues of August and September.[30] Later, Johnson championed related environmental causes such as the recession of Yosemite Valley from state to federal control, the establishment of "forest reservations" or national forests, and—most famously—the fight to preserve the Hetch Hetchy Valley from being dammed. In the 1890s, the pages of the *Century* repeatedly invoked Muir in support of the writer's position. So, for example, George G. Mackenzie's open letter in support of "The Pressing Need of Forest Reservation in the Sierra" begins by noting Muir's November 1891 article about "the wonderful King's River Canyon," which closely follows the pattern of the two Yosemite articles in combining text and illustration. In an April 1893 "Topics of the Time" editorial, Johnson places Muir's King's Canyon article in the service of his larger praise for extensive mountain forest preserves established by John W. Noble, Secretary of the Interior in the Harrison administration. In an April 1896 editorial, Johnson quotes Muir at length regarding the destruction of the Yosemite Valley by uncontrolled fire and grazing and joins him in calling for the recession of the valley to the federal government.[31]

Johnson employs the strategy of orchestration in arguing for the establishment of national forests. In a long open letter of September 1893, the travel writer Eliza Ruhamah Scidmore, best known for her guide to the Inside Passage of Alaska, details the location and status of the fifteen national forests, totaling some thirteen million acres including more than four million acres in the Sierra Nevada of California. In the February 1895 issue, the *Century* publishes responses to the forest preservation plan proposed by Charles S. Sargent, professor of biology at Harvard University, specifically to the idea of military control of the national forests. Among a dozen letters are favorable responses from Frederick Law Olmsted, Theodore Roosevelt, Gifford Pinchot, B. E. Fernow, and John Muir. In a "Topics of the Time" editorial, Johnson himself calls for a National Forest Commission to be appointed by

President Cleveland. By 1896, Sargent would arrange for the commission to be appointed by the National Academy of Sciences on the request of the secretary of the interior, and Johnson would arrange for funding of twenty-five thousand dollars by the Appropriations Committee of Congress. [32]

The strategy of literary and cultural orchestration is familiar to students of celebrity authors. In the antebellum United States, for instance, publisher Robert Bonner advertised the salary and success of the author Fanny Fern in order to make her advice columns and books into best sellers. A firm like Harper's used *Harper's Monthly* to publish its own in-house authors and thereby promote their books. The celebrity novelist Harriet Beecher Stowe toured England after the publication of *Uncle Tom's Cabin* and was met by thousands of adoring fans. After the Civil War, the production of Thoreau's literary reputation in the pages of the *Atlantic Monthly* and the *Century* was part of the same process. In that regard, Burroughs contributed to Thoreau's reputation by publishing his feature article, "Henry D. Thoreau," in the July 1882 *Century*, the same issue that printed Muir's second "Bee Pastures of California" article. [33]

Both Muir and Burroughs benefited greatly from the strategies of orchestrated promotion. In June 1893, Muir traveled to New York City for the first time, on his way to Europe with his friend William Keith, the painter. Writing to his wife Louie Strentzel Muir on June 13, Muir recounted his first meeting with John Burroughs, the editor Richard Watson Gilder, and a host of other literary figures. He writes, "Almost every day in town here I have been called out to lunch and dinner at the clubs and soon have a crowd of notables about me. I had no idea I was so well known, considering how little I have written" (*Life and Letters of John Muir* 2:266). But Muir is surprisingly naïve. In addition to the Yosemite and King's Canyon articles, the *Century* had just published John Swett's feature biographical article on Muir and his work. [34] The article opens with an engraving of Muir, depicting him as if he has just returned from the trail (see figure 10). His hair is uncombed, his beard bushy. He is wearing a cotton flannel shirt and thick coat, and the leather strap of his knapsack lies across his chest. The essay does not present any remarkable insight into Muir's character or the character of his writing, though Swett's biography is quite detailed.

Figure 10. John Muir
(*Century* 46 [May 1893]: 120).

Rather than interpreting Muir's life and work, Swett dramatizes them. He opens the essay by recounting Emerson's visit to Yosemite in 1872, claiming that "Muir was his guide for a week." Upon his return, says Swett, Emerson remarked of Muir, "He is more wonderful than Thoreau." Swett also dramatizes the ten years of exploration that Muir conducted in the high Sierra, painting a vivid portrait of Muir in the 1870s:

> His outfit on one of his ten-day excursions was the lightest possible. It consisted of a pocket aneroid [barometer], chronometer, and thermometer, a note-book and pencil, a few pounds of bread and oatmeal, a little tea and sugar, and a small tin can. After climbing a summit during the day, he descended at night to the timber-line, built a fire, made a can of tea, ate his bread, and lay down by the side of his camp-fire, with no other covering than that which he had worn during the day. . . . Bears never molested him, and other animals were his companions. In this manner for years he studied the channels of ancient glaciers, pushed through the wildest canyons, and noted the forest-covered moraines. (122)

Muir becomes a larger-than-life figure in Swett's description, a combination of scientist, mountaineer, ascetic, and shaman. No wonder the savvy editors of the *Century* decided not to publish the bibliography of Muir's articles that Swett sent them to "fill out the article"; after all, a scholarly addendum would reduce Muir to human proportions. [35]

Burroughs's reputation is also orchestrated in the pages of the *Century*, though his literary celebrity is not used for environmental advocacy. In the January 1877 issue of *Scribner's Monthly*, for example, Joel Benton published a critical survey of Burroughs's published works, including both the literary criticism and the nature essays. The article begins with an engraving of Burroughs, but in this case the figure is well groomed, in coat, tie, collar, and waistcoat. Without appearing stiff, Burroughs is the very picture of the forty-year-old man of letters. Benton stresses his alertness and attention to minute details, his racy, lively writing style, and his "subtle psychic, if not fully understood, affinity" with birds. He finds Burroughs's "predominant gift" to be his "clear and powerful eye," and he claims that his books "do not so much spur you to read and write, as make you observe for yourself, and go tramping about with a pocketful of apples." Although Burroughs is figured as the "more available, and more sociable Thoreau" (Benton quotes James's words approvingly), he is also "our Prophet of Outdoordom" who has "won the well-recognized position, which no one has held so well since Thoreau's death." In effect, Burroughs is a "more available, and more sociable" Muir. He is not associated with wilderness or with the extremes of mountaineering, but his essays still bear "the unmistakable imprint of authenticity," for they spur the reader to participate in "Outdoordom" by making the outdoors available, even sociable. [36]

Burroughs's authenticity marks the feature article on him by the literary critic and editor Hamilton Wright Mabie in the August 1897 *Century*. [37] The only illustration is a plain portrait of the seated, sixty-year-old writer, not unlike the illustration from twenty years before (see figure 11). The direct, composed quality of the portrait evokes the literary and moral quality Mabie finds in Burroughs. Mabie frames the essay with a literary historical discussion of Dante and Petrarch, and then he leaps to the present situation in America. Burroughs's powers of higher observation bring nature and

Figure 11. John Burroughs (*Century* 54 [August 1897]: 560).

humanity into "easy and normal relations," and the result is "a new kind of literature." Like James and Benton, Mabie directly connects Burroughs to Thoreau, but he finds Burroughs more sensitive and susceptible to his own day than Thoreau ever was to his. Burroughs is no less attached to place than Thoreau; Mabie characterizes Burroughs's style as creating a "domesticity of nature; one is aware at all times of the simple, natural background of American life." The quality of "homeliness" and the role of nature as a "home-maker for man" give his essays a "farm-bred" tone, but Burroughs's love of nature takes him into even more intimate relations with it. In domesticity Mabie finds deep harmony and unity between Burroughs and nature. At the same time, he portrays Burroughs as a man of culture, a deeply educated reader of literature. The value of Burroughs's literary criticism is as much in what it reveals of his "intellectual and spiritual character" as in the comprehension of literature itself. In writing about both nature and literature, Burroughs reveals "a search for simplicity, directness, absence of any kind of formalism, love of everything that concerns or contains life, a broad, sane, homely conception of man and his surroundings."[38]

The sense of Burroughs's individual, authentic character appears in the essay "Glimpses of Wild Life about My Cabin," published in the August 1899 issue of the *Century*. The illustrations by Bruce Horsfall have the offhand quality of pen-and-ink sketches, and they point toward the personal qualities of Burroughs and his local place. The initial illustration of Burroughs, lounging and loafing as easily as the poet in "Song of Myself," contrasts sharply with the more formal indoor portraits in the Benton and Mabie articles, and it is even more casual than the Muir portrait in the Swett article (see figure 12). Burroughs's essay focuses on his cabin, Slabsides, which he built in 1895. By 1899, Slabsides was fast becoming a shrine to be visited by nature-loving readers and writers, and the illustrated *Century* article plays a clear role in the development.

The essay opens by explaining why Burroughs would build yet another writer's retreat, which his friends consider a retreat "into the wilderness." Burroughs answers casually, "Well, I do not call it a retreat; I call it a withdrawal, a retirement, the taking up of a new position to renew the attack, it may be, more vigorously than ever."[39] Within the casual response,

Figure 12. John Burroughs, from "Glimpses of Wild Life about my Cabin" (*Century* 58 [August 1899]: 500).

Burroughs hides a militant metaphor—he withdraws in order to attack the culture of inauthenticity and artificiality. As he describes Slabsides, his language echoes the terms used by Hamilton Mabie. He longs for "something more homely, private, and secluded," and he seeks "a more humble and secluded nook or corner, which you can fill and warm with your domestic and home instincts and affections" (*Writings* 13:131). The place is "shut off from the vain and noisy world of railroads, steamboats, and yachts by a wooded, precipitous mountain," so it is here that Burroughs mounts his quiet, pastoral attack (132). But it *is* an attack—not a retreat.

Although Slabsides affords him a writer's solitude, like Thoreau's Walden cabin it abounds in visitors, both human and animal. The essay describes the "visits" of a wide variety of birds, both resident and migratory, and it also records for the first time "a lot of Vassar girls" who come to walk with him in the woods (137). Burroughs revisits some of his favorite birds in the essay, describing with easy charm the thrushes—robin, veery, hermit thrush, wood thrush, water thrush. But he reserves the best visitor for last. The bald eagle, or "bird of Jove," perches in a blasted pine near the cabin, and Burroughs dwells on the circling, soaring bird as a spiritual messenger: "The lift or range of those great wings has passed into my thought" (155). He delivers his own environmental message, deploring any attempt to collect the eagle's eggs or shoot and stuff the bird for a specimen. The eagle is the noble, spiritual image of a soaring solitude:

> He draws great lines across the sky; he sees the forests like a carpet beneath him, he sees the hills and valleys as folds and wrinkles in a many-colored tapestry; he sees the river as a silver belt connecting remote horizons. We climb mountain-peaks to get a glimpse of the spectacle that is hourly spread out beneath him. Dignity, elevation, repose are his. I would have my thoughts take as wide a sweep. I would be as far removed from the petty cares and turmoils of this noisy and blustering world. (156)

The expansive closure to the essay weaves the landscape into an artful tapestry, with its vision of intersecting lines. It is equally effective in developing the paradox of retreat. The retreat becomes a place of attack, just as the homely and humble seclusion is transformed, in this final imaginative passage, into great dignity and elevation, the commanding and powerful vision of a soaring eagle. That is implicitly to claim an equal authority for the writer's imaginative vision, which reaches near to the eagle's eye. Burroughs imagines the writer's place as the intersection of culture and nature, but the place of nature allows him to soar above the mountain peaks.

4 *Landscapes Beginning to Be Born*

Alaska and the Pictorial Imagination

Burroughs and Muir in Alaska

In an apparent aside in the late essay "Emerson and His Journals," Burroughs combines three of his most important influences: "A remark of Emerson's upon Thoreau calls up the image of John Muir to me" (*Writings* 23:23). Burroughs quotes Emerson's journal entry, a perception repeated in his 1862 eulogy—"If I knew only Thoreau, I should think cooperation of good men impossible. Must we always talk for victory, and never once for truth, for comfort, and joy?" Despite Emerson's thorough admiration of Thoreau, he finds his younger friend's paradoxical temperament and oppositional temper unfriendly. As he puts it in the eulogy, "It cost him nothing to say No; indeed he found it much easier than to say Yes."[1] Burroughs associates his good friend Muir with Thoreau because Muir "belonged to the sayers of No. Contradiction was the breath of his nostrils" (23). Burroughs's sudden eulogy for Muir, who had died in 1914, continues for several more telling sentences. He remarks that "writing was irksome to Muir" but that "in monologue, in an attentive company, he shone" (23). He judges him to have been no great thinker but to have displayed "a mind strongly characteristic," a "moral fiber . . . very strong," and a "wit ready and keen" (24).

Burroughs's eulogy draws telling parallels between Thoreau and Muir, on the one hand, and between Emerson and Burroughs himself, on the other. Muir's power of contradictory, witty monologue clearly charmed Emerson, who met Muir in Yosemite in 1871 and afterward listed him in his journal as one of "My Men."[2] As Burroughs notes, "Emerson found him deeply read in nature lore and with some suggestion about his look

and manner of the wild and rugged solitude in which he lived so much"
(*Writings* 23:24). Burroughs mythologizes Muir by mythologizing the encounter between Muir and Emerson, rendering Emerson's response to a
wild, rugged, and solitary Muir. But the paragraph moves between the perspectives of Burroughs and Emerson. In addition to the line about writing
being irksome to Muir, it is clearly Burroughs who says that Muir's "philosophy rarely rose above that of the Sunday school" (24). In Burroughs's view,
Emerson emerges as the best of the three influences because he is best able
to appreciate both Thoreau and Muir, despite their limitations. As the only
living writer among the four figures, moreover, Burroughs accords himself
a privileged status. He appreciates Emerson's sensitivity, his ability to be
"alive to everything around him," and he contrasts that "active, expectant
interest" to the nay-saying contrariness of Thoreau and Muir.

Burroughs's strategically limiting account of Muir figures him as akin
to Thoreau, Burroughs's biggest rival in nature writing. There are good
reasons to believe Burroughs's assertion that Muir did not enjoy writing.
Muir failed to write most of the books he had planned to complete. His first
book, *The Mountains of California* (1894), was published when he was fifty-
six years old. Over the next twenty years, Muir managed to finish five more
books: *Our National Parks* (1901), *Stickeen* (1909), *My First Summer in the
Sierra* (1911), *The Yosemite* (1912), and *The Story of My Boyhood and Youth*
(1913). On his deathbed, he was revising his account of his many trips to
Alaska, focusing on the three trips of 1879, 1880, and 1890. This would become the posthumous book *Travels in Alaska*, published in 1915 under the
direction of his literary executor William Frederic Badè, who shepherded
several more posthumous books through the press: *A Thousand-Mile Walk
to the Gulf* (1916), *The Cruise of the Corwin* (1917), *Steep Trails* (1918),
and *The Life and Letters of John Muir* (1924). Because Burroughs was
writing the Emerson essay in these very years between 1917 and 1920, it is
tempting to see his digression on Muir as an aggressive criticism of a rival.
In the nearly one hundred years since Muir's death, he has outstripped
Burroughs in literary reputation and general fame. Modern editors have
added to his list of publications, using Muir's many journals, letters, and

newspaper articles to create coherent books and enlarge Muir's cultural role in the twenty-first century.[3]

Burroughs figures Muir as a prodigious talker, and that image accords with the impression he gained over their twenty-year friendship. On Christmas Day, 1914, Burroughs wrote in his journal, "News comes of John Muir's death—an event I have been expecting & dreading for more than a year. A unique character—greater as a talker than as writer—loved personal combat, & shone in it. He hated writing & composed with difficulty, tho' his books have charm of style, but his talk came easily & showed him at his best. I shall greatly miss him, tho' I saw him so rarely" (Vassar Folder 4.11). That summary, clearly the source of the eulogy in "Emerson and His Journals," is already forecast in Burroughs's journal for June 22, 1896, when Muir visited him at Slabsides:

> John Muir came last night. J[ulian] & I met him at Hyde Park. A very interesting man, a little prolix at times, you must not be in a hurry, or have any pressing duty, when you start his stream of talk & adventure. Ask him to tell you his famous dog story (almost equal to Rab & his friends) & you get the whole theory of glaciation &c. thrown in. He is a poet, & almost a seer; something ancient & far away in the look of his eyes. He could not sit down in a corner of the landscape as Thoreau did; he must have a continent for his play ground. He starts off for a walk, after graduation, & walks from Wisconsin to Florida, & is not back home in 18 years. In Cal. he starts out one morning for a stroll: his landlady asks him if he will be back to dinner; probably not he says; he is back in 7 days, walks 100 miles around Mt Shasta, & goes 2½ days without food. He ought to be put into a book: doubtful if he ever puts himself into one. He has done many foolish, foolhardy things, I think: that is, throws away his strength without proper return. I fear now he is on the verge of physical bankruptcy in consequence. Probably the truest lover of nature as she appears in woods, mountains & glaciers, we have yet had. (Vassar Folder 3.8)

As in the Emerson essay, Burroughs mythologizes Muir in this journal entry, but he creates a figure that is both larger than life and smaller than expected. Muir is a poet and seer, an amazing adventurer, mountaineer, and storyteller, but his strength is unwisely thrown away in far-flung talk and travel, without being husbanded in literary form. To be a writer, Burroughs implies, one must "sit down in a corner of the landscape as Thoreau did." Burroughs clearly admires his new friend, but he does not seek to emulate him. Thoreau is Burroughs's vexing model, which suggests that the parallel he draws between Muir and Thoreau in "Emerson and His Journals" further limits both Thoreau and Muir.

A mixture of sincere friendship and combative rivalry marked the relationship between Muir and Burroughs from the outset. The two first met in New York City on June 1, 1893, and neither was wholly enthusiastic about the new acquaintance. In his June 13 letter to his wife, Muir established a pattern he would follow for the next two decades. He describes Burroughs as suffering a "headache" from a Whitman memorial dinner the night before: "So he seemed tired, and gave no sign of his fine qualities. I chatted an hour with him and tried to make him go to Europe with me. The 'Century' men offered him five hundred dollars for some articles on our trip as an inducement, but he answered to-day by letter that he could not go, he must be free when he went, that he would above all things like to go with me, etc., but circumstances would not allow it. The 'circumstances' barring the way are his wife. I can hardly say I have seen him at all" (*Life and Letters of John Muir* 2:265). Burroughs's account of the hour is so brief as to be cryptic: "Charming day. Spend it in the city. Meet John Muir, an interesting man, with the western look upon him, not quite enough penetration in his eyes" (Vassar Folder 3.4). The two writers met one another between literary dinners, and the penetrating vision of each writer found limits in the other, but the two accounts create the sense of a mutual lack of recognition.

Muir and Burroughs came into their closest, longest, and most important contact during the Harriman Alaska expedition, which took place between May 23 and July 30, 1899. Organized and completely financed by the railroad magnate E. H. Harriman, the expedition brought together some 126 members, including twenty-five members of the "scientific party," three visual artists, and two professional photographers. Harriman assembled most of the group in New York City on May 23, took a private train across the country to Seattle, and there joined Muir, the California poet Charles

Keeler, and other westerners. The millionaire chartered the steamship *George W. Elder* from the Pacific Coast Steamship Company and had it completely refurbished and outfitted for the two-month voyage from Seattle to Siberia and back.

Many of the professionals were luminaries in their fields. Included in the scientific party, Burroughs and Muir were the most renowned literary naturalists of the day, while George Bird Grinnell was cofounder, with Theodore Roosevelt, of the Boone and Crockett Club and editor of *Forest and Stream* magazine. The scientists were equally distinguished. William H. Dall, paleontologist with the U.S. Geological Survey, was a respected expert on Alaska. Daniel G. Elliot was curator of zoology at the Field Columbian Museum in Chicago. B. E. Fernow was dean of the School of Forestry at Cornell University. Henry Gannett was chief geographer of the U.S. Geological Survey and editor of *National Geographic* magazine. G. K. Gilbert, geologist at the USGS, was an expert on glaciers and glaciation. C. Hart Merriam, in charge of the scientific party, was chief of the Biological Survey of the U.S. Department of Agriculture and eventually editor-in-chief of the 13-volume report, *Harriman Alaska Series*. Robert Ridgway was curator of ornithology at the Smithsonian Institution and author of *A Manual of North American Birds* (1887).[4]

The artists included two well-known magazine illustrators and two young artists who would become famous after the expedition. R. Swain Gifford and Fred S. Dellenbaugh were accomplished New York City painters and illustrators; Gifford's work appeared regularly in the pages of the *Century*. Louis Agassiz Fuertes, an unknown painter listed in the expedition manifest as "Bird Artist," would illustrate many magazine articles and books for Burroughs and other literary naturalists. Edward S. Curtis, owner of a photography studio in Seattle, was already becoming known for his mountaineering pictures of Mount Rainier and for his article "The Rush to the Klondike over the Mountain Passes" in the March 1898 issue of the *Century*. Eventually, Curtis devoted his distinguished career to the masterful set of illustrated volumes known as *The North American Indian* (1907–30).[5]

The Harriman Alaska expedition is important for a number of reasons, not least for establishing the friendship between Muir and Burroughs.

Taking place at the end of the nineteenth century, the expedition was a quintessential project of the genteel tradition, combining scientific exploration, big-game hunting, and sightseeing in a peculiarly American version of cultural pilgrimage. Muir captures this multifarious sense of the expedition in an August 1899 letter to the four girls of the Harriman family: "On the Elder, I found not only the fields I liked best to study, but a hotel, a club, and a home, together with a floating University in which I enjoyed the instruction and companionship of a lot of the best fellows imaginable, culled and arranged like a well-balanced bouquet, or like a band of glaciers flowing smoothly together, each in its own channel, or perhaps at times like a lot of round boulders merrily swirling and chafing against each other in a glacier pothole" (*Life and Letters of John Muir* 2:330). Muir's letter metaphorically combines cultural institutions and natural landscapes, creating a mixed figurative place that also includes both the pastoral "well-balanced bouquet" and the wild "glacier pothole."

The thirteen-volume *Harriman Alaska Series* presents a similarly rich mixture of cultural representations. The first volume, published in 1901, combines Burroughs's "Narrative of the Expedition," Muir's "Notes on the Pacific Coast Glaciers," and Grinnell's "Natives of the Alaska Coast Region." The second volume, published in 1902, presents eight nontechnical essays on subjects ranging from Charles Keeler's "Days among Alaska Birds" to Fernow's "The Forests of Alaska." In the beginning of the first volume, the editor-in-chief Merriam lists forty colored halftone plates of landscapes, birds, mammals, and flowers, most taken from paintings by Dellenbaugh, Gifford, and Fuertes. Next comes a list of over eighty photogravure plates, reproducing sharp halftones of photographs taken by Curtis, Merriam, Gilbert, and a few others. The list of textual figures—process line drawings made from photographs—runs to well over two hundred titles. Louise M. Keeler and W. E. Spader were the principal artists, and the illustrations recall precisely the wood engravings and New School process engravings in the *Century*. The remaining volumes of the series employ illustrations to varying degrees. Volume 3, G. K. Gilbert's *Glaciers and Glaciation* (1904), for instance, prints eighteen halftones and more than a hundred line drawings as textual figures, while volume 4, *Geology and Paleontology* (1904), reproduces only thirty-three halftones of fossils and eighteen textual figures. These two volumes also feature extended commentary on the illustrations; Gilbert's explanations of the plates and figures are especially interesting and are as informative as his general essays. More than a simple report, the thirteen volumes of the *Harriman Alaska Series* present a richly varied array of scientific, literary, and artistic representations of Alaska.[6]

Muir's Alaska

"What's in Alaska?" drone the disaffected stoners in Raymond Carver's short story of the same title, and the point of the story is that the characters can barely remember the question, much less answer it. That would require focused attention, sense of purpose, and desire for knowledge and experience. John Muir never suffered such lack of penetration, despite Burroughs's impression after their initial meeting. By the time the two found themselves together on the Harriman Alaska expedition, Muir had already explored the new territory on six separate expeditions. His knowledge of Glacier Bay was particularly deep, for he was credited with its "discovery" in 1879, and he had returned to study and explore the six surrounding glaciers in 1880 and 1890. The focus of his explorations was Muir Glacier—named, along with the bay, by Captain Lester A. Beardslee of the U.S. Navy in 1880, after Muir supplied him with a detailed map of the bay and its glaciers.[7] Muir thus had every reason to be personally and professionally drawn to the Harriman expedition, since he had the most direct experience of the place. But by the time the two-month voyage was winding to a close, Muir was himself curiously disaffected, if only temporarily. Even though he described the *Elder* as a delightful "floating University," his journal from July 19, 1899, gives a very different impression. Writing after a lecture and discussion, Muir denigrates the importance of the expedition and its future report: "Had long talk on book-making, much twaddle about grand scientific monument, etc. J B will probably write narrative. Much ado about little. Game hunting, mostly missions unsuccessful, the chief aim.

The rest mere reconnaissance." The entry fairly bristles with scorn, both for the "game fellows" who seek "the pleasure of making the hole in the animals" and for "grand scientific monuments."[8]

Part of Muir's scornful tone may be the result of professional jealousy, since the first part of the "monument" would indeed be John Burroughs's narrative of the expedition. But it is more likely that the scorn is fueled by resentment, turning on the very notion of "book-making" as a grand ado. By 1899, Muir had "made" only two books, fashioning *The Mountains of California* (1894) out of previously published articles and editing the mammoth *Picturesque California* (1888). Burroughs, on the other hand, had published a dozen books, with more than another dozen in store. And what, Muir might well wonder, would a book about Alaska contain, since the Harriman expedition was no more than "mere reconnaissance." Muir's disdain comes very close to the language used by G. K. Gilbert, who calls the expedition a "reconnaissance" three times in the first two pages of his volume *Glaciers and Glaciation* (HAS 3:1–2). Indeed, the professional geologist may be a third source of Muir's resentment. After all, why write a book about the glaciers in Alaska when the professional scientist was already doing so?

Muir's journal entry records a sense of displacement based on questions of authority. The questions pertain most directly to the ethics of hunting, which Muir sees as taking pleasure in inflicting pain and death on fellow creatures. But the problem of authority extends to the cultural function of the author—scientific or literary—in creating knowledge and representing experience: what constitutes knowledge and truthful representation of Alaska? This is to ask not only what's *in* Alaska, since Alaska is not merely a repository of big game or a blank space to be filled in and developed. It is to ask what Alaska *is* as a place. Muir's journal entry thus opens crucial, large questions about the relationship of culture to nature, human power and authority over the environment, and ways of knowing and representing place. The scale of these questions, moreover, reduces any literary jealousy to the level of twaddle.

The large questions occupied a major part of Muir's mature years as a writer and explorer. Several times over the years, he used his status as a correspondent for the San Francisco *Daily Evening Bulletin* to finance his wilderness journeys, and the first three trips to Alaska resulted in a copious series of journals, sketchbooks, and newspaper dispatches. The first trip, June 1879 to January 1880, was by far the longest and richest in the sense of discovery. The second, July to September 1880, was rich in incident, including the adventure of Muir and the dog Stickeen on the Davidson Glacier. In these first two journeys, Muir and the Presbyterian missionary S. Hall Young explored southeast Alaska from Fort Wrangell to Skagway and Glacier Bay. The third, May to October 1881, was spent aboard the revenue steamship *Corwin*, which in addition to its regular duties was searching for the missing whaling ship *Jeannette* and traveled beyond the Arctic Circle as far as Wrangell Land, off the northern coast of Siberia.

After 1881, the nearly decade-long hiatus in Muir's literary career intervened, though during that time he did write an article on Alaska for his two-volume *Picturesque California*. In the 1890s, however, Muir gathered steam. During the summer of 1890, he returned to Glacier Bay and made his two-week sled trip on Muir Glacier. In January 1895, he began revising his Alaska journals, clearly thinking in terms of "book-making" on the heels of publishing *The Mountains of California*. In June 1895, he published "The Discovery of Glacier Bay" in the *Century*. In August 1896, he spent three weeks in Alaska with Henry Fairfield Osborn, director of the Natural History Museum in New York City. In August and September 1897, he spent five weeks in the Canadian Rockies and Alaska with his friend Charles S. Sargent, the Harvard University botanist who led the U.S. Forest Commission in 1896. While he was on the Sargent expedition, the *Century* published his essay "The Alaska Trip," in which Muir used several passages from the "Alaska" essay in *Picturesque California*. [9]

As topic and text, Alaska is a place of vast resources. Muir's journals from 1879, 1880, 1881, 1890, and 1899 are especially important, for they record his immediate responses to the landscapes of Alaska and present the hundreds of sketches he made of the glaciers, trees, and Indian artifacts he encountered. A complete account of these journals and sketchbooks remains to be given, and this is only a first step in that direction. Muir's published texts also are important and numerous: the dispatches to the San Francisco *Daily Evening Bulletin*, the "Alaska" essay in *Picturesque*

California, the "Alaska" essay in the May 1893 issue of *American Geologist*, the two *Century* articles, "Notes on the Pacific Coast Glaciers" in the *Harriman Alaska Series*, the article "Glaciers" in the 1904 edition of the *Encyclopedia Americana*, and the posthumous publications *Travels in Alaska* and *The Cruise of the Corwin*. The relationships among these published works are equally numerous and extremely complex, since Muir would often take parts of a previously published dispatch or essay and revise them for another publication. Muir returned to his original Alaska journals in November 1912, hiring Mrs. Marion Randall Parsons as a typist and working in earnest to produce his long-delayed Alaska book. The manuscript sheets of the book were spread about him on the hospital bed when he died (*Life and Letters of John Muir* 2:389–91). All of this evidence indicates that Alaska remained a deeply important place in Muir's mature imagination and that he sought to represent Alaska as a place of nature, akin to Yosemite and the Sierra Nevada.

Given the wealth of material and the duration of Muir's fascination with Alaska, the "Notes on Pacific Coast Glaciers" essay in the *Harriman Alaska Series* volume is curiously brief. Muir begins with a panoramic overview of the Pacific coast, from the Sierra Nevada of California to "the Iceland of Alaska, the region of greatest glacial abundance on the west side of the continent" (*HAS* 1:120). He then suggests a rough taxonomy of glaciers, one that he will repeat in the 1904 encyclopedia article. Those of the "first class" are "complete . . . flowing out into deep ocean water and, of course, discharging bergs" (122). Those of "the second class, flowing down nearly to the sea but not entering it" (121), are "decadent" (123) and silent, "with no ice to spare for bergs" (126). The distinction is hierarchical and value-laden: Muir characterizes the glaciers of the first class as truly noble, active, motion-filled rivers of ice. For that reason, perhaps, he enjoys a third class, the "cascading glaciers" of Port Wells Fiord, "the finest and wildest of their kind, looking, as they come bounding down a smooth mountain side through the midst of lush flowery gardens and goat pastures, like tremendous leaping, dancing cataracts in prime of flood" (127). Muir does not develop or explain the taxonomy; instead, he follows the coast from southeast to northwest, noting the most active glaciers along the way. The essay in effect follows the path of the expedition and provides a simple inventory of glaciers. Thus the final paragraph summarizes the return voyage and the best scenery of the trip, but it does not have anything directly to do with glaciers: "The sail down the coast from St. Elias along the magnificent Fairweather Range, when every mountain stood transfigured in divine light, was the crowning grace and glory of the trip and must be immortal in the remembrance of every soul of us" (135). While this sentence contains many of Muir's characteristic descriptive terms, it does not effectively conclude the account of Pacific coast glaciers. The conclusion is part of a larger problem, for Muir never settles on a structure and does not develop a distinctive argument or point of view. The essay remains, in effect, a "mere reconnaissance."

The tension between a pseudoscientific taxonomy and a full-fledged narrative mars the 1899 essay, but in earlier essays on Alaska Muir is firmly in control of structure, purpose, viewpoint, and audience. The 1879 newspaper dispatches develop both narrative and thematic structures; each letter is under two thousand words in length, so Muir maintains a coherent, focused view.[10] In the fifth dispatch, for example, Baird Glacier is the focus of Muir's description, and even though he asserts that "no written words, however bonded together, can convey anything like an adequate conception of its sublime grandeur," the essay effectively presents what Muir calls a "picture" of the glacier and "a Yosemite Valley in process of formation":

> There is the water foreground of a pale, milky-blue color, from the suspended rock-mud issuing from beneath the grinding glacier, one smooth sheet sweeping back five or six miles like one of the lower reaches of a great river. At the head the water is bounded by a barrier wall of bluish-white ice, from five to six hundred feet high, a few mountain tops crowned with snow appearing beyond it. On either hand stretches a series of majestic granite rocks from three to four thousand feet high, in some places bare, in some forested, and all well patched with yellow-green chaparral and flowery gardens, especially about half-way up from the top to bottom, and the whole built together in a general, varied way into walls, like those of Yosemite Valley, extending far beyond the

ice-barrier, one immense brow appearing beyond the other, while their bases
are buried in the glacier. (*Letters from Alaska* 30)

The essay also emphasizes concrete details through narrative action, describing how S. Hall Young, Reverend Sheldon Jackson, and Muir are "ferried" over the moraine on the backs of Indians and how Young and Muir use axes to chop their way up onto the back of the glacier itself. For Muir, the thesis of the essay emerges clearly: "One easily learns that the world, though made, is yet being made. That this is still the morning of creation . . . that in very foundational truth we had been to church and had seen God" (*Letters from Alaska* 31–32).

Muir's skill as a writer of travel narrative is equally clear in the *Century* articles of 1895 and 1897. In "The Discovery of Glacier Bay," he creates an exciting adventure story about the trip in a thirty-five-foot red-cedar dugout canoe with Young and four Indians from October 9 to November 21, 1879. The focus of the article is apparent from the title, but the essay includes more than the narrative of the 1879 adventure. The bare bones of that story are exciting and colorful in their own right, as can be seen in the version published in the May 1893 issue of *American Geologist*.[11] The stormy, cold rain, low clouds, snow, and darkness; the fear of the Indians regarding both the wilderness and the "Ice Chief" Muir, who "must be a witch to seek knowledge in such a place;" Muir's leadership and eloquent speech, in which he tells the crew "good luck followed me always, though for many years I had wandered in higher mountains than these, and in far wilder storms; that Heaven cared for us and guided us more than we knew, etc."—in all of these details, Muir shows his deep talent as a storyteller. The *Century* article includes all of this, revising it to develop Muir's own viewpoint:

> They seemed to be losing heart with every howl of the storm, and fearing that
> they might fail me now that I was in the midst of so grand a congregation of
> glaciers, which possibly I might not see again, I made haste to reassure them,
> telling them that for ten years I had wandered alone among mountains and
> storms, and that good luck always followed me; that with me, therefore, they
> need fear nothing; that the storm would soon cease, and the sun would shine;

and that Heaven cared for us, and guided us all the time, whether we knew it
or not: but that only brave men had a right to look for Heaven's care, therefore
all childish fear must be put away. This little speech did good. Kadechan, with
some show of enthusiasm, said he liked to travel with good-luck people; and
dignified old Toyatte declared that now his heart was strong again, and he
would venture on with me as far as I liked, for my "wawa" was "delait" (my
talk was very good). The old warrior even became a little sentimental, and said
that if the canoe were crushed he would not greatly care, because on the way
to the other world he would have pleasant companions. (*Century* 50:237)

Muir abounds in what we nowadays call "hard and soft leadership skills."
To his crew he communicates confidence, experience, eloquence, and
faith. To the reader, in addition, he communicates modesty and humor.
Rather than heighten the drama of the situation, he works to undercut the
dramatic quality. But that is the real art of the passage, since by doing so
Muir makes the situation even more dramatic and his leadership more
palpable.

In describing the glacial landscapes, Muir gives his religious language
free rein. On the day after delivering his "sermon" to the crew, he climbs
a mountain at the head of Glacier Bay just as the rain stops and the clouds
lift: "These were the highest and whitest of all the white mountains, and
the greatest of all the glaciers I had yet seen. Climbing higher for a still
broader outlook, I made notes and sketched, improving the precious time
while sunshine streamed through the luminous fringes of the clouds, and
fell on the green waters of the fiord, the glittering bergs, the crystal bluffs
of the two vast glaciers, the intensely white, far-spreading fields of ice, and
the ineffably chaste and spiritual heights of the Fairweather Range, which
were now hidden, now partly revealed, the whole making a picture of icy
wildness unspeakably pure and sublime" (*Century* 50:238). The verbal
picture recalls the newspaper dispatch describing Baird Glacier, and in
both passages Muir combines his gifts in bonding words together and in
sketching visual details. The religious tone seems to rise out of the physical
situation Muir depicts, joining spirituality and wildness in the terms of the
northern landscape.

The reader might well agree with Muir that "it was inconceivable that nature could have anything finer to show us," but the dawn brings a yet more sublime vision. Muir rises to find "a red light burning with a strange, unearthly splendor on the topmost peak of the Fairweather Mountains. Instead of vanishing as suddenly as it had appeared, it spread and spread until the whole range down to the level of the glaciers was filled with the celestial fire." Muir develops the description in more detail, adding color and motion and change to the picture until "the mountains themselves were made divine." The entire crew joins in the vision, and finally they turn to sail away, "joining the outgoing bergs, while 'Gloria in excelsis' still seemed to be sounding over all the white landscape, and our burning hearts were ready for any fate, feeling that whatever the future might have in store, the treasures we had gained would enrich our lives forever" (239). The clear, rich echoes of this passage in the conclusion to "Notes on Pacific Coast Glaciers" make the 1899 essay pale in comparison.

In both *Century* articles, Muir practices an art of combination. As in the California essays of the 1870s, he combines different kinds of language to create a variety of tones and effects. In addition, he combines material from different sources. In "The Discovery of Glacier Bay," for instance, he combines the 1879 canoe trip with the September 1880 return trip to Glacier Bay. Muir combines the two trips in the "Discovery" essay because only in 1880 did he explore Muir Glacier, the largest of the Glacier Bay ice fields. The reader rightly expects a sublime vision from above the prairie of ice, but Muir surprisingly combines panoramic viewpoints with the precise, close-up observation of wildflowers:

> The lower summits about the Muir Glacier, like this one, the first that I climbed, are richly adorned and enlivened with beautiful flowers, though they make but a faint show in a general view. Lines and flashes of bright green appear on the lower slopes as one approaches them from the glacier, and a fainter green tinge may be noticed on the subordinate summits at a height of 2000 or 3000 feet. The lower are made mostly by alder bushes, and the topmost by a lavish profusion of flowering plants, chiefly cassiope, vaccinium, pyrola, erigeron, gentiana, campanula, anemone, larkspur, and columbine,

with a few grasses and ferns. Of these cassiope is at once the commonest and the most beautiful and influential. In some places its delicate stems make mattresses on the mountain-tops two feet thick over several acres, while the bloom is so abundant that a single handful plucked at random will contain hundreds of its pale pink bells. The very thought of this, my first Alaskan glacier garden, is an exhilaration. Though it is 2500 feet high, the glacier flowed over its ground as a river flows over a boulder; and since it emerged from the icy sea as from a sepulcher it has been sorely beaten with storms; but from all those deadly, crushing, bitter experiences comes this delicate life and beauty, to teach us that what we in our faithless ignorance and fear call destruction is creation. (244–45)

Muir fashions a wild bouquet, moving from the lofty, sky-dwelling peaks and the miles-wide expanse of Muir Glacier to the delicate profusion of wildflowers. In naming the flowers, he combines scientific and common nomenclature. The viewpoint shifts remarkably from far to near, from unfamiliar sublime to "commonest" pastoral, from terror and destruction to life, beauty, and creation. Thus Muir brings the reader to a deeper discovery in Glacier Bay.

The reader plays an equally large role in the 1897 *Century* essay, "The Alaska Trip," and the article registers a deep sense of change when we compare it to the account of the 1879 canoe trip. Like the "Alaska" essay in *Picturesque California*, "The Alaska Trip" emphasizes the accessibility and nearness of Alaska for the "ordinary traveler" or "lover of wildness." By the time Muir wrote the *Picturesque California* essay in 1888, there was a well-established tourist industry along the Inside Passage of southeastern Alaska, and in both essays he emphasizes that point by taking the reader on a fictional tour of the coastal region. In "The Alaska Trip," Muir notes that "this vast wilderness with its wealth is in great part inaccessible to the streams of careworn people called 'tourists,' who go forth on ships and railroads to seek rest with nature once a year," but "some of the most interesting scenery in the territory has lately been brought within easy reach even of such travelers as these, especially in southeastern Alaska, where are to be found the finest of the forests, the highest mountains, and the largest glaciers" (*Century* 54:514). Muir Glacier proves the assertion, for "it is the one to which tourists are taken and allowed to go ashore for a few hours, to climb about its crystal cliffs and watch the huge icebergs as with tremendous, thundering roar they plunge and rise from the majestic frontal sea-wall in which the glacier terminates" (523).[12]

Although the organizing trope of the steamship tour works well, "The Alaska Trip" suffers from a lack of action, mainly on the level of language. The essay begins with a remarkable paragraph on the accessibility of wildness, but then much of the subsequent writing directly echoes the "Alaska" essay in *Picturesque California*. Indeed, Muir even uses passages from "The Discovery of Glacier Bay" in the sections "The Birth of the Icebergs" and "Glacial Nights" in "The Alaska Trip." It is as if Muir Glacier has become too accessible, rendering Muir speechless. That suspicion is confirmed by comparing "The Alaska Trip" to "Notes on Pacific Coast Glaciers," in which Muir devotes one sentence to the Muir Glacier (*HAS* 1:126). In the 1899 description of Taku Inlet and the Taku Glacier, moreover, Muir directly copies the parallel passage from "The Alaska Trip" (520). Similarly, the opening of the "Notes on the Pacific Coast Glaciers," in which Muir ranges from the Sierras to Prince William Sound, directly copies a passage from "The Alaska Trip" (522–23). Even the concluding paragraphs in the two essays are disturbingly similar, leaving the tourist "rich in wildness forevermore" (526), as the Harriman expedition members hold the memory of the Fairweather Range "immortal in the remembrance of every soul of us" (1:135). Muir practices the art of combination in "The Alaska Trip," but the combinations are not as inspired as in "The Discovery of Glacier Bay." It is as if the essay forces Muir to become a tourist himself, to engage in "mere reconnaissance" rather than discovery.

Despite the flaws in "The Alaska Trip" and "Notes on the Pacific Coast Glaciers," Muir does not suffer from a lack of inspiration in his later work. If that were the case, "Notes on the Pacific Coast Glaciers" might be Muir's last Alaska essay, and then we could deduce that the Harriman Alaska expedition sounds the knell of Muir's sense of Alaska as a place of nature. But *Travels in Alaska* surely indicates that the memory of Alaska remains vivid in Muir's imagination after 1899. By returning to the Alaska journals in 1912, Muir recaptures the sense of Alaska as a place of discovery.

Landscapes Beginning to Be Born

Muir's Alaska journals function as a source of inspiration not only because of the vivid, immediate writing but, perhaps more importantly, because of the hundreds of sketches contained in them. As the *Studies in the Sierra* essays suggest, Muir's knowledge of glaciation is closely aligned with his ability to sketch the structures of mountain sculpture, glacial movements, glacial denudation, and postglacial erosion. These are the major topics of the *Studies in the Sierra* series, published in the *Overland Monthly* in 1874–75, and Muir's sketches are crucial both to his own understanding of the processes he explains and to that of his readers. The journals of all seven Alaska trips suggest that sketching is a means of understanding glaciers and the glacial formation of landscape. On a basic level, the sketches allow Muir to identify the glaciers, which in many cases are unnamed and unmapped. But Muir's visual sense takes the drawings beyond that rudimentary level of identification. For Muir, the sketches record how Alaska became a place.

The 1879 journals provide numerous examples of Muir's visual art and its functional role in creating Alaska as a place. The written record and visual record are not coordinated; Muir often wrote his journal account in the margins surrounding images he had already drawn. In other instances, the written and visual records are closely aligned. In addition, the 1879 journals show that Muir made numerous small "studies" of particular aspects of the landscape—trees, icebergs, islands, and kinds of glaciers. Drawings of glaciers dominate the notebooks, but Muir also made many drawings of native villages and artworks, especially graves, totem poles, spirit animals, and abstract designs. The journals from all of the Alaska trips show, moreover, that Muir worked with great care and diligence in his drawings. Often he filled several pages with preliminary sketches of rock formations before he filled in the shading necessary for a panoramic view of the landscape.

No published version of Muir's Alaska writings employs his drawings to make the two activities of writing and sketching work together. The definitive edition of Muir's Alaska work remains to be published. By collating texts and drawings, one can arrive at a far deeper appreciation of both the writing and the sketching. For instance, the texts of the 1879 journals, the dispatches edited in *Letters from Alaska*, "The Discovery of Glacier Bay," and *Travels in Alaska* together show that on October 27, 1879, Muir left the camp near the Pacific Glacier, on the northwest end of Glacier Bay, to climb a mountain and obtain "comprehensive views." Before he reached the height of a thousand feet above the bay, the rain stopped and the clouds lifted, lingering about the mountains of the Fairweather Range to the west. At this point, Muir describes the "picture of icy wildness unspeakably pure and sublime," using the religious language to make a verbal picture of the scene ("Discovery" 238; *Travels* 112). In the next paragraph, he actually develops the "comprehensive view" of the Grand Pacific Glacier:

> Looking southward, a broad ice-sheet was seen extending in a gently undulating plain from the Pacific Fiord in the foreground to the horizon, dotted and ridged here and there with mountains which were as white as the snow-covered ice in which they were half, or more than half, submerged. Several of the great glaciers of the bay flow from this one grand fountain. It is an instructive example of a general glacier covering the hills and dales of a country that is not yet ready to be brought to the light of day—not only covering but creating a landscape with the features it is destined to have when, in the fullness of time, the fashioning ice-sheet shall be lifted by the sun, and the land become warm and fruitful. The view to the westward is bounded and almost filled by the glorious Fairweather Mountains, the highest among them springing aloft in sublime beauty to a height of nearly sixteen thousand feet, while from base to summit every peak and spire and dividing ridge of all the mighty host was spotless white, as if painted. (*Travels* 112)

Like the verbal "picture of icy wildness," this passage depicts a landscape in the act of becoming, and like the September 27, 1879, newspaper dispatch describing Baird Glacier, it focuses on the dynamic creativity of the glacier.

Figure 13. Landscapes Beginning to Be Born, from 1879 Alaska Journal
(John Muir Papers, Holt-Atherton Special Collections, University of the Pacific Library,
© 1984 Muir-Hanna Trust).

In the notebook sketch of the scene, Muir labels the page "Sitideka: Landscape beginning to be born," and he adds at the bottom of the page the colors he witnesses: "Beauty sky dark blue at zenith 4 PM then pale bl[ue] then greenish yel[low]" (see figure 13). The word "Sitideka" is Muir's initial spelling of the Tlingit name for the "Ice Bay," or "Sit-a-da-kay" (*Travels* 108). In the 1879 journals, Muir calls Glacier Bay by the native name, gives numbers and directions for the six glaciers he observes in the head of the bay, and refers to the Pacific Inlet as "Cross Sound" because of the physical topography of the northwest arm of Glacier Bay. All of these aspects of nomenclature create the effect of a dynamic landscape, since in 1879 nearly no parts of it have been named or claimed. Combined with Muir's notes and captions, the journal sketch registers the sense of dynamic landscape formation that the verbal picture of Pacific Glacier refers to as "not only covering but creating a landscape." The second caption adds the changing colors of the afternoon sky to the title of the sketch, as if a painter were making notes for an oil painting. Muir's art of combination includes, along with the overpowering sense of dynamic change, the effect of the observer's quasi-scientific precision. Thus we find this headnote, apparently added later: "1st mer de glace, from mtain 1000 ft near camp in highest NW arm of Gl Bay, Looking S."

The combination of dynamism and precision is fundamental to Muir's visual artistry. A series of three sketches from the 1879 exploration of the Lynn Canal shows the care with which he created the drawings. In the first sketch, Muir focuses on the outlines of the mountains and the surface shape of the glacier (see figure 14). Indeed, his characteristic trope of the glacier as a "river of ice" makes a remarkably apt description of the lines in the first drawing. In the second sketch (see figure 15), the mountains gain definition and relief, and in the third (see figure 16) they are rendered in artful shades of the pencil. The juxtaposition of the three drawings shows how Muir creates perspective in landscapes of vast, imposing, but potentially flat and blank structures. Muir approaches each landscape as a unique place, and his drawings render each place in individualizing shapes and shades.

In the journals and notebooks of 1880, 1881, and 1890, Muir develops his skills as a visual artist and draftsman. Glacial landscapes dominate the work. For instance, a sketch of Herald Island, from the 1881 expedition of the *Corwin*, depicts the sheer granite cliffs, shore ice, and steep ravine, full of icy snow. Muir describes these same details in "First Ascent of Herald Island," chapter 13 of *The Cruise of the Corwin* (1917). In several sketches, Muir includes architectural structures or human figures in the landscape to give a sense of scale and perspective to the immense Arctic horizon. Other sketches venture beyond landscape. When the party killed a trio of polar bears near Wrangell Land, for example, Muir sketched a pair of heads in great detail, noting the texture of the pelage as much as the shape of the skull and quality of the eyes. Natives in Plover Bay and St. Michaels provided him with other subjects, and he devoted his discerning eye to the physiognomy and dress of the Chukchi in Siberia. The 1881 sketches are not as exclusively "glacial" as those of 1879, 1880, and 1890, and in some ways Muir exercises greater freedom in his artistry as a result.

The work Muir produced during the Harriman Alaska expedition, on the contrary, does not consistently reach the level of careful artistry. Muir continued to sketch regularly throughout the two-month journey, but his

Figure 14. Lynn Canal Glacier, First Draft, from 1879 Alaska Journal
(John Muir Papers, Holt-Atherton Special Collections, University of the Pacific Library,
© 1984 Muir-Hanna Trust).

Figure 15. Lynn Canal Glacier, Second Draft, from 1879 Alaska Journal
(John Muir Papers, Holt-Atherton Special Collections, University of the Pacific Library,
© 1984 Muir-Hanna Trust).

Figure 16. Lynn Canal Glacier, Final Draft, from 1879 Alaska Journal
(John Muir Papers, Holt-Atherton Special Collections, University of the Pacific Library,
© 1984 Muir-Hanna Trust).

sketches are not nearly as detailed as the drawings he made in all of his earlier trips to Alaska. In the early part of the expedition, the sketches are finished productions, much like the third state of the Lynn Canal drawing from 1880. After the expedition leaves Prince William Sound, however, the drawings strongly resemble the preliminary sketch of the Lynn Canal glacier: outlines of structures are well drawn, but there is little attention to detail and perspective. An exception is the drawing of a rock face on the coast of St. Matthew Island in the Bering Sea (see figure 17), but it is the only "finished" drawing among the seventy-five sketches in the long second Harriman notebook, and it is one of very few sketches that create a three-dimensional effect of perspective. Most of the drawings are flat and full of blank space, and they add to the effect of blankness created by the end of "Notes on the Pacific Coast Glaciers." It may be that Muir found little of interest once the Harriman expedition left behind the glacial territory of Alaska, but that in itself is a disturbing inference. It seems much more likely that the host of Kodak-carrying scientists, artists, and photographers contributed to a sense of the expedition as a glorified tourist cruise,

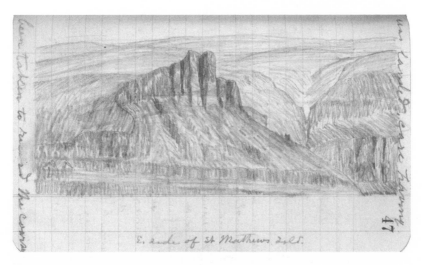

Figure 17. East Side, St. Matthew Island, from 1899 Harriman Notebook
(John Muir Papers, Holt-Atherton Special Collections, University of the Pacific Library,
© 1984 Muir-Hanna Trust).

undermining Muir's artistry. For Muir as for Burroughs, the sense of place depends on a sense of intimacy and proximity between the individual and nature.

Even the sketches Muir made during the grueling mid-July 1890 sled trip on Muir Glacier show more careful attention to the details of texture and shading than we find in the Harriman sketches. Muir left San Francisco on the steamer *City of Pueblo* on June 14, changed to the tourist steamer *Queen* in Port Townsend, and sailed up the Inside Passage with some 180 other tourist passengers. The ship reached Glacier Bay on June 23, and Muir notes that the entire crowd of tourists eagerly went ashore at Muir Glacier, climbing the front wall and some venturing a mile or two farther (*Travels in Alaska* 205–10). On June 24 the *Queen* departed, and Muir settled into camp. More tourists arrived as the days went by, and on July 1 Professor Harry Fielding Reid and a party of students pitched camp beside Muir's. On the 7th, the *Queen* returned, this time with 230 tourists: "What a show they made with their ribbons and kodaks!" (218). Though Muir is not openly disdainful, he must have felt crowded by the tourists and scientists, for on July 11 he set off across Muir Glacier with a homemade three-foot sled and a sack of hardtack, tea, sugar, and sleeping bag.

The conditions Muir faced in 1890 were horrendous: at the very beginning he was ill with a bronchial cough that had hung on for three months; for ten days he hauled the hundred-pound homemade sled across uneven, often dangerous surfaces; his resoled shoes wore out, and his feet were wet and cold for days; he ate little, heating his tea over a fire of cedar shavings and subsisting only on hardtack; his strength and endurance reached an absolute limit after a week. Finally, writing on July 19, he admits that he is "nearly blind. The light is intolerable and I fear I may be long unfitted for work. I have been lying on my back all day with a snow poultice bound over my eyes. Every object I try to look at seems double; even the distant mountain-ranges are doubled, the upper an exact copy of the lower, though somewhat faint" (*Travels* 230). Ever the careful observer, Muir here observes his own physical exhaustion and impaired vision. It is no wonder, then, that he was unable to make the kind of detailed sketches that fill the 1879 journals. The 1890 sketches are nevertheless full of high quality pencil work. Moreover, the 1890 portion of *Travels in Alaska* abounds in close observations along the surface of Muir Glacier, and Muir's eyes do not prevent him from drawing many inferences concerning glacial actions of snow, ice, and water.

Muir's original sketches now reside in faded notebooks and on microfilm, but they had one other important embodiment in his day. Both of the *Century* articles about Alaska feature New School engravings based on sketches Muir made in 1879, 1880, and 1890. In "The Discovery of Glacier Bay," illustrator John A. Fraser produces close approximations of Muir's compositions in pictures of the Hugh Miller Glacier, the Fairweather Range, and the Grand Pacific Glacier. In addition, Fraser makes illustrations from an 1890 photograph of Muir Glacier by Professor Reid, an anonymous photograph of the fossil forest near Muir Glacier, and a painting by Thomas Hill of Muir Glacier, owned by Muir himself. Fraser also produces a host of illustrations for "The Alaska Trip," most of which are based on Muir's sketches. These include Tlingit totem poles and masks on the title page (from the 1879 journals), as well as landscapes of Davidson

Glacier (from the 1880 journal) and Muir Glacier (from the 1890 journal of the sled trip).

Although Burroughs seems to have been correct when he character-ized his friend as more of a talker than a writer, the evidence also sug-gests that Muir was in fact as visual as he was verbal. The two forms of artistry complement one another, and at their strongest they developed Muir's sense of Alaska as a complex place of dynamic, changing beauty, of landscapes beginning to be born. For Muir, sketching the landscapes and their inhabitants—bergs, trees, animals, people—was a fundamental way of knowing Alaska as a physical place. In the descriptive and narrative writing, as well as in the best drawings, Muir created Alaska as a figurative place, both for his own pictorial imagination and for that of the reader.

Burroughs's Alaska and World-Shaping Forces

Muir's deep knowledge of the Alaska coast, especially Glacier Bay, and his deepening friendship with John Burroughs are two of the principal contri-butions he made to the Harriman Alaska expedition. The two contributions merge in Burroughs's "Narrative of the Expedition," revised and reprinted as "In Green Alaska" in the 1904 volume, *Far and Near*. In both versions, Burroughs creates a detailed literary representation of the expedition and of Alaska as a place. Muir's influence on Burroughs's sense of Alaska as a place is, as Muir might say, foundational.

That influence is both friendly and threatening, Burroughs suggests, be-cause he considers himself an authority: "In John Muir we had an authority on glaciers, and a thorough one—so thorough that he would not allow the rest of the party to have an opinion on the subject. The Indians used to call him the Great Ice Chief" (*HAS* 1:18). The manuscript version is less jaundiced: "John Muir knows the glaciers & hungers for them night & day. He is called by the Indians the Great Ice Chief."[13] But if the difference between these two versions suggests that Burroughs had lost his appetite for Muir's authority, the last version, from "In Green Alaska," is much softer in tone: "In John Muir we had an authority on glaciers, and a thorough one; he looked upon them with the affection and the air of proprietorship with which a shepherd looks upon his flock. The Indians used to call him the Great Ice Chief" (*Writings* 13:22). Here Burroughs combines the shepherd and the Great Ice Chief to create an image of Muir that is both pastoral and wild. By reading all three passages together, we gain a rich sense of Burroughs's response to Muir, which is itself a combination of resistance, irritation, admiration, and affection.

The verbal evidence of Muir's influence takes several forms. In an early passage describing a remarkable sunset, for example, Burroughs evokes the scene in painterly terms: "I had often seen as much color and brilliancy in the sky, but never before such depth and richness of blue and purple upon the mountains and upon the water. Where the sun went down the horizon was low, and but a slender black line of forest separated the sky from the water. All above was crimson and orange and gold, and all below, to the right and left, purple laid upon purple until the whole body of the air between us and the mountains in the distance seemed turned to color" (*HAS* 1:21; *Writings* 13:25). In the notebook version, Burroughs strikes through two telling passages. The first is the phrase "truly glorious," a combination of adverb and adjective that all readers of Muir recognize immediately. The second records a moment on deck: "We tried dropping our heads down so that we saw with vertical instead of horizontal eyes. This seemed to enhance the color effects & make the scene more sensual. It was like an enormous canvass of an impressionist painter." Given the trace of Muir in the first phrase, it is tempting to imagine the "we" as including Muir and Burroughs most prominently. The experimentation with perspective recalls similar moments in Thoreau's *Walden*: learning to walk home in the dark ("The Village"); viewing the landscape with one's head between one's legs ("The Ponds"); scanning the pond through the ice ("The Ponds"). It also recalls Muir's constant search for a new perspective or vantage point from which to view the Alaskan landscape. The image of the sunset as "an enormous canvass of an impressionist painter" directly recalls Muir's descriptions from the previous twenty years. Burroughs avoids the easy influence of Muir's rather vague and predictable phrasing, but he is profoundly influenced by Muir's visual sense of place.

Muir's influence becomes more pronounced when the Harriman expedition reaches Glacier Bay on June 8, 1899. In the "Narrative" Burroughs describes the Muir Glacier as the specific goal of the party, and he carefully creates a verbal picture of the scene:

> The next day finds us in Glacier Bay on our way to the Muir Glacier. Our course is up an arm of the sea, dotted with masses of floating ice, till in the distance we see the great glacier itself. Its front looks gray and dim there twenty miles away, but in the background the mountains that feed it lift up vast masses of snow in the afternoon sun. At five o'clock we drop anchor about two miles from its front, in eighty fathoms of water, abreast of the little cabin on the east shore built by John Muir some years ago. Not till after repeated soundings did we find bottom within reach of our anchor cables. Could the inlet have been emptied of its water for a moment we should have seen before us a palisade of ice nearly 1,000 feet higher and over two miles long, with a turbid river, possibly half a mile wide, boiling up from beneath it. Could we have been here many centuries ago, we should have seen, much further down the valley, a palisade of ice two or three thousand feet high. Many of these Alaska glaciers are rapidly melting and are now but the fragments of their former selves. From observations made here twenty years ago by John Muir, it is known that the position of the front of Muir Glacier at that time was about two miles below its present position, which would indicate a rate of recession of about one mile in ten years. (*HAS* 1:35–36; *Writings* 13:39)

The most imaginative moment in this description comes when Burroughs pictures the inlet emptied of water, and that image comes directly from Muir's descriptions of the glacier in his writings. In *Picturesque California*, for instance, he writes, "If the water and the rock-detritus of the bottom were drained and cleared away, this magnificent wall of pale blue ice would probably be found to be not less than a thousand feet in height" (*Nature Writings* 684). In "The Alaska Trip," and again in chapter 16 of *Travels in Alaska*, Muir recurs to the image in order to describe "a sheer precipice of ice a mile and a half wide and more than a thousand feet in height" (*Century* 54:523; *Travels* 200). Burroughs echoes Muir's language, in all probability, because Muir recited the very same image for him as they looked at the front of the glacier. In addition, Muir appears as a figure in the description, both in the reference to his cabin (from 1890) and in the observations he made "twenty years ago" (1880) that suggest the steady recession of the glacier.

None of these three allusions to Muir occur in Burroughs's journal, which focuses on the glacier as "a sort of congealed Niagara." Burroughs uses the Niagara figure twice more in the journal passage, but in the "Narrative" he omits the "congealed Niagara" phrase in order to stress how the calving of icebergs makes the glacier seem "as active as Niagara." The revision makes the glacier appear dynamic rather than frozen or congealed, and the dynamic image once again suggests Muir's influence. At the very least, it suggests that Burroughs thoroughly appreciates Muir's view of glacial action. Already in the journal entry, as well as in both printed versions, Burroughs describes the calving glacier as "a cataract the like of which we have not before seen, a mighty congealed river."

Muir and Burroughs see the glacier both as a place of imperceptible action, in the apparently motionless river of ice, and as a place of sudden dramatic action, in the Niagara-like downpour of icebergs. The journals and "Narrative" show that Burroughs was utterly fascinated by Muir Glacier, spending by far the longest time of the expedition in exploring it. In a long paragraph that begins with the rocky terminal moraine, Burroughs remarks that "few more strange and impressive spectacles than this glacier affords can be found on the continent. It has a curious fascination. Impending cataclysms are in its look." The provocative calm near the glacier's front becomes the occasion for telling how one afternoon "about half a mile of the front fell at once. The swell which it caused brought grief to our photographers who had ventured too near it. Their boat was filled and their plates were destroyed" (see figures 18 and 19). But Burroughs does not dwell on this adventurous, potentially disastrous moment. Instead, he imagines blue ice crystals in the icebergs that rise up suddenly from the depths, imagines how they "have not seen the light since they fell in snowflakes back amid the mountains generations ago," imagines them breaking loose and "free to career in the air and light as dew or rain or cloud," and then finally imagines them being drawn back "into that cycle of transformation and

Figure 18. Muir Glacier, by Edward S. Curtis (University of Washington Libraries, Special Collections, Harriman 28).

Figure 19. Before the Great Berg Fell, by Edward S. Curtis (University of Washington Libraries, Special Collections, Harriman 30).

caught and bound once more in glacier chains for another century" (*HAS* 1:37; *Writings* 13:42). The writer's imagination is both bound and free, fixed in place by the glacier but moving rapidly from stones to torrents of falling ice to invisible crystals.[14]

Even though Burroughs notes that "we were in the midst of strange scenes, hard to render in words," his descriptions of Glacier Bay and Muir Glacier are masterful: "the miles upon miles of moraines upon either hand, gray, loosely piled, scooped, plowed, channeled, sifted, from fifty to two hundred feet high; the sparkling sea water dotted with blue bergs and loose drift ice; the towering masses of almost naked rock, smoothed, carved, rounded, granite-ribbed, and snow-crowned, that looked down upon us from both sides of the inlet; and the cleft, toppling, staggering front of the great glacier in its terrible labor-throes stretching before us from shore to shore" (*Writings* 13:46). The balanced series of phrases, punctuated and orderly, creates a field of past and present actions in the rush of participles.[15]

Over the next several pages, Burroughs develops his focus on Muir Glacier as a place of dynamic action. He echoes Muir's vision of the "landscape beginning to be born" when he describes how the party "saw the world-shaping forces at work; we scrambled over plains they had built but yesterday." With detailed descriptions, Burroughs specifies the world-shaping forces and their work, maintaining a tension between past and present actions. Thus he places the party "in one of the workshops and laboratories of the elder gods, but only in the glacier's front was there present evidence that they were still at work." The desire for evidence leads him farther into place:

> I wanted to see them [the elder gods] opening crevasses in the ice, dropping the soil and rocks they had transported, polishing the mountains, or blocking the streams, but I could not. They seemed to knock off work when we were watching them. One day I climbed up to the shoulder of a huge granite ridge on the west, against which the glacier pressed and over which it broke. Huge masses of ice had recently toppled over, a great fragment of rock hung on the very edge, ready to be deposited upon the ridge, windrows of soil and gravel and boulders were clinging to the margin of the ice, but while I

stayed not a pebble moved, all was silence and inertia. And I could look down between the glacier and the polished mountain-side; they were not in contact; the hand of the sculptor was raised, as it were, but he did not strike while I was around. In front of me upon the glacier for many miles was a perfect wilderness of crevasses, the ice was ridged and contorted like an angry sea, but not a sound, not a movement anywhere. (*HAS* 1:42–43; *Writings* 13:47)

Burroughs's sense of place, like Muir's, includes startling combinations of contrasting elements. The tone of spiritual awe that begins the passage gives way, for example, to tongue-in-cheek humor with the phrase "knock off work." But the place remains magical in its motionless silence, the magic residing in the ironic contrast between scales of time and perspective. The observer can detect evidence of massive action and change, but not so much as a pebble moves while Burroughs stands in the landscape. The passage places the human labor of observation and understanding within a vast, "perfect wilderness," but Burroughs manages to capture the place in words. He creates a kind of verbal workshop that unites nature and culture, the literal, physical place and a figurative sense of place.

For both Muir and Burroughs, the art of combination includes an expository, empirical sense of place. But Burroughs's journal from the Harriman expedition contains surprisingly little of this kind of prose. In the Glacier Bay section, for instance, he notes that three of the scientific party explored the Morse Glacier, a detached tributary of the Muir, but the published versions expand the note into a five-paragraph account of Muir Glacier, moving from eastern rim to western rim and placing the Morse in relation to the "dead" western part of the larger *mer de glace*. The exposition clearly relies on Muir's understanding of glacial action and the formation of medial and terminal moraines, but it also features Burroughs's descriptive language, as when he compares the rim of the Morse Glacier to "a huge turtle shell" (*HAS* 1:45; *Writings* 13:49).

In place of the language of exposition, Burroughs returns to the language of gods when he describes "one ideal day," Sunday, June 11. Burroughs and Charles Keeler climb Mount Wright, three thousand feet above Muir Glacier, and the elder writer comes back to his sense of the elder gods:

It was indeed a day with the gods; strange gods, the gods of the foreworld, but they had great power over us. The scene we looked upon was for the most part one of desolation,—snow, ice, jagged peaks, naked granite, gray moraines,— but the bright sun and sky over all, the genial warmth and the novelty of the situation, were ample to invest it with a fascinating interest. There was fatigue in crossing the miles of moraine; there was difficulty in making our way along the sharp crests of high gravel-banks; there was peril in climbing the steep boulder-strewn side of the mountain, but there was exhilaration in every step, and there was glory and inspiration at the top. Under a summer sun, with birds singing and flowers blooming, we looked into the face of winter and set our feet upon the edge of his skirts. But the largeness of the view, the elemental ruggedness, and the solitude as of interstellar space were perhaps what took the deepest hold. It seemed as if the old glacier had been there but yesterday. Granite boulders, round and smooth like enormous eggs, sat poised on the rocks or lay scattered about. A child's hand could have started some of them thundering down the awful precipices. When the Muir Glacier rose to that height, which of course it did in no very remote past, what an engine for carving and polishing the mountains it must have been! Its moraines of that period—where are they? Probably along the Pacific coast under hundreds of fathoms of water. (*HAS* 1:46–47; *Writings* 13:51–52)

The description hints at Muir's influence in the simple word "scene," and it makes his influence certain in the phrase "glory and inspiration." Burroughs creates another verbal picture of surprising contrasts, but the turning point in the passage takes place in the unexpected opening of the narrator's perspective. The "largeness of view, the elemental ruggedness, and the solitude as of interstellar space" are three aspects of the scene that Burroughs does not record in his journal. They seem rather to grow out of the description itself, as if the narrator must reflect on the experience to determine "what took deepest hold." The reflection, a mixture of memory and imagination, leads Burroughs to an enormous Muir Glacier of even greater depth and power, the glacier that filled the valley all the way to the top of Mt. Wright. And this sense of the prehistoric glacier, which

Burroughs brings near to us in the phrase "in no very remote past," owes much, if not everything, to Muir.

Burroughs's debts extend beyond the glacial vision of his friend Muir. He opens himself to an unfamiliar and remote place, and in doing so he closes the distance between himself and an alien wilderness. The strategic movement strongly recalls the ways Burroughs reads Whitman in such essays as "Before Genius," "Before Beauty," and "The Flight of the Eagle." In all of those essays, the ultimate source of poetry is the "spirit of nature," and the writer reaches the spirit by "affiliating" with the visible objects of the universe (*Writings* 3:216). For Burroughs, moreover, Whitman's poetry forms a "rugged landscape" of elemental, boundless forces (*Writings* 10:133). Thus the "largeness of view, the elemental ruggedness, and the solitude as of interstellar space" are extremely close to Burroughs's strategies for reading Whitman. As a result, the landscape of Muir Glacier becomes a meeting place, not merely for literary influences but for culture and nature. It becomes a place, moreover, in which Burroughs displays the combined power of his imagination and memory.

In several other parts of the "Narrative of the Expedition," Burroughs exercises his power in relation to the Alaskan landscape, making a place for himself. On the morning of July 1, the *Elder* anchored in Uyak Bay on the north side of Kodiak Island (called Kadiak by all of the expedition). In the "Narrative," Burroughs warns the reader that "we were now about to turn over a new leaf, or indeed to open a new book, and to enter upon an entirely different type of scenery,—the treeless type." In place of the spruce forests and glaciers, the island of Kadiak presents "smooth, treeless, green hills and mountains," and when the expedition reaches the village of Kadiak on the south side of the island, Burroughs notes that "we had stepped from April into June, with the mercury near the seventies, and our spirits rose accordingly." The descriptions of Kadiak create a "pastoral paradise" and "dream of rural beauty and repose." Even the unsettled parts of the island look "as if a landscape gardener might have been employed to grade and shape the ground, and plant it with grass and trees in just the right proportion." Burroughs finds walking paths that lead to "a fine trout brook," and he lovingly describes the flowers and birds inhabiting the "mighty emerald billow that rose from the rear of the village,—we all climbed that, some of us repeatedly" (*HAS* 1:77–83; *Writings* 13:81–88).

The pastoral landscape of Kadiak appeals to Burroughs in familiar ways and on familiar terms. Even though he opens himself to the vast, expansive landscape of Muir Glacier, at Kadiak he experiences a kind of spiritual and aesthetic homecoming. And he imagines that the same is true for the other members of the expedition:

> Kadiak, I think, won a place in the hearts of all of us. Our spirits probably touched the highest point here. If we had other days that were epic, these days were lyric. To me they were certainly more exquisite and thrilling than any before or after. I feel as if I wanted to go back to Kadiak, almost as if I could return there to live,—so secluded, so remote, so peaceful; such a mingling of the domestic, the pastoral, the sylvan, with the wild and the rugged; such emerald heights, such flowery vales, such blue arms and recesses of the sea, and such a vast green solitude stretching away to the west and to the north and to the south. Bewitching Kadiak! the spell of thy summer freshness and placidity is still upon me. (*HAS* 1:86; *Writings* 13:92)

This passage turns upon the many meanings of "place." The first sentence locates place in the hearts of all of the expedition members, the communal "us." That emotional place becomes spiritual in the second sentence, and the image of the "highest point" evokes the mountainous landscapes of the sublime. In the third sentence, Burroughs turns to the literary landscape and maps the distinction between epic and lyric, defining the latter genre in personal terms as "more exquisite and thrilling." If the lyric is Burroughs's literary place, he defines the lyrical landscape as a mixed or "mingling" place, combining the domestic and wild, the pastoral and rugged, the real and ideal, the picturesque and the sublime. In the final apostrophe to Kadiak, moreover, personification imbues the actual place with a sustained magical power. The passage defines place in terms of affiliation, and it multiplies the terms of affiliation in order to create a complex, bewitching sense of place. No wonder, then, that Burroughs retitled the narrative "In

Green Alaska," since the island of Kadiak in effect defines his most inclusive sense of what Alaska is as a place.

If Burroughs were to follow the pattern I have traced in Muir's "Notes on the Pacific Coast Glaciers," we would surely detect a plot of decline in the "Narrative" after Kadiak. In reality, moreover, Burroughs's interest does seem to decline. Both Muir and Charles Keeler tell the story of how Burroughs wished to stay in the village of Dutch Harbor, Unalaska, rather than continue with the expedition across the Bering Sea, and how Muir cajoled Burroughs into remaining aboard the *Elder*. Burroughs himself alludes to this event in the "Narrative": "Unalaska looked quite as interesting as Kadiak, and I longed to spend some days here in the privacy of its green solitudes, following its limpid trout streams, climbing its lofty peaks, and listening to the music of the longspur. I had seen much but had been intimate with little; now if I could only have a few days of that kind of intimacy with this new nature, which the saunterer, the camper-out, the stroller through fields in the summer twilight has, I should be more content; but in the afternoon the ship was off into Bering Sea, headed for the Seal Islands, and I was aboard her, but with wistful and reverted eyes." [16]

The impression Burroughs creates in the "Narrative" is that the experience on the Bering Sea was well worth a bit of regret and seasickness. On Hall and St. Matthew Islands, in particular, Burroughs finds "a land of such unique grace and beauty that the impression it made cannot soon be forgotten,—a thick carpet of moss and many-colored flowers covering an open, smooth, undulating country that faced the sea in dark basaltic cliffs, some of them a thousand feet high" (*HAS* 1:109; *Writings* 13:118). The striking contrast between the flowers and the cliffs recalls the description of Muir Glacier, and Burroughs drives that effect home in his account of a hike on St. Matthew Island:

> The highest point of the island was enveloped most of the time in fog and cloud. While groping my way upon one of these cloud summits, probably a thousand feet above the sea which flowed at its base, I came suddenly upon a deep cleft or chasm, which opened in the moss and flowers at my feet and led down between crumbling rocky walls at a fearful incline to the beach.

Figure 20. "The Two Jonnies [*sic*]" on St. Matthew Island, by Edward S. Curtis (University of Washington Libraries, Special Collections, Harriman 186).

> It gave one a sense of peril that made him pause quickly. The wraiths of fog and mist whirling through and over it enhanced its dreadful mystery and depth. Yet I hovered about it, retreating and returning, quite fascinated by the contrast between the smooth flowery carpet upon which I stood and the terrible yawning chasm. (*HAS* 1:112; *Writings* 13:122)

The passage creates a place of sudden meeting, a place that is both fascinating and dangerous in its combination of the picturesque and the sublime.

The sense of place that Burroughs repeatedly creates in the "Narrative of the Expedition" owes much to Muir's friendly antagonism, just as it owes a profound debt to Muir's affiliation with the wild landscapes of glacial Alaska. But ultimately both Muir and Burroughs are much more than representatives of the wild or the pastoral, the far or the near. Together they define the place of nature as combining these conceptual opposites, just as they find a place for nature within late-nineteenth-century American culture. A final way of seeing them in that place of nature appears in the Edward Curtis photograph of the two men on the beach of St. Matthew Island (figure 20). The landscape is barren, suggesting the icy beach and gray basalt cliffs rising behind the two naturalists. But each of them holds a bouquet of wildflowers in his left hand, no doubt gathered during Burroughs's hike. Along with the flowers and the similar pose and dress of the two writers, the caption to the photograph — "The Two Jonnies [*sic*]" — marks the similarity as much as the contrast. The caption is humorous, too, ironically evoking the slang term for "fashionable young men of idle habits" (*OED*). The photograph appropriately figures the proximity of Muir and Burroughs to one another, and it suggests that the "smooth flowery carpet" occupies virtually the same place as the "terrible yawning chasm." Yet more, the presence of the two naturalists on the beach portrays the meeting of culture and nature. The bouquets are themselves aesthetic creations, bringing humanity's creative force to bear on the barren shores of the island. But the humor of the caption resides equally in the sense of nature's power, as if the "two Jonnies" were offering their bouquets to Nature herself.

5 The "Best of Places"
Roosevelt as Literary Naturalist

Oom John

In a dedicatory letter to John Burroughs, penned at the White House on October 2, 1905, President Theodore Roosevelt opened his fourth book on American hunting, *Outdoor Pastimes of an American Hunter*, by addressing his friend as "Oom John"—Dutch for "Uncle John" —a pet name he had given Burroughs during their trip to Yellowstone National Park in April 1903. Roosevelt's affection and admiration for Burroughs are evident in the letter. "Every lover of outdoor life must feel a sense of affectionate obligation to you," the president writes. "Your writings appeal to all who care for the life of the woods and the fields, whether their tastes keep them in the homely, pleasant farm country or lead them into the wilderness. It is a good thing for our people that you should have lived; and surely no man can wish to have more said of him."[1] The praise is absolute and all-encompassing, and it accords well with Roosevelt's penchant for fearlessly hyperbolic generalizations. He treats "Oom John" as a representative national figure, the avuncular nature sage.

At the time, however, Burroughs was in no way a kindly uncle to other nature writers, at least not to those he found lacking in accuracy and truth. In the long second paragraph of the dedication, Roosevelt congratulates Burroughs on his "warfare against the sham nature-writers" and praises him for illustrating "what can be done by the lover of nature who has trained himself to keen observation, who describes accurately what is thus observed, and who, finally, possesses the additional gift of writing with charm and interest" (390). Roosevelt alludes directly to Burroughs's article, "Real and Sham Natural History," which appeared in the March 1903 issue of the *Atlantic Monthly*.[2] In a series of attacks and counterattacks, Burroughs clashed with nature writers Ernest Thompson Seton and Reverend William J. Long, accusing them of grossly misrepresenting animal psychology and inventing stories to corroborate their aberrant theories. For most of his presidency, Roosevelt kept a lightly guarded silence on the controversy. The dedicatory letter clearly shows that he supported Burroughs wholeheartedly, and his private letters to Burroughs and others show that he did not exaggerate his admiration for Burroughs's nature essays.[3] Eventually, Roosevelt was unable to contain himself, publishing two articles in 1907. He attacked Long, Seton, and Jack London and praised Burroughs along with John Muir, Stewart Edward White, Olive Thorne Miller, C. Hart Merriam, artist Frederic Remington, and a half-dozen others.[4]

The story of Burroughs, President Roosevelt, and the "nature fakers" controversy is a fascinating tale of intellectual debate and the cultural definition of nature. Ralph Lutts has told the story with great detail and clarity, and there is no need to repeat his work here.[5] But an important point still needs to be made: for the first and only time in American history, the president of the United States acts as a literary and cultural critic—specifically, as an ecocritic. When President Roosevelt writes the dedicatory letter to "Oom John," he defines Burroughs as the very embodiment of keen observation, accurate description, and literary skill: "You *in your own person* have illustrated what can be done by the lover of nature who has trained himself to keen observation, who describes accurately what is thus observed, and who, finally, possesses the additional gift of writing with charm and interest" (emphasis added). Burroughs personifies the virtues of the literary naturalist. Moreover, Roosevelt uses "Oom John" to define the place of nature within American culture of the day. Americans should "care for the life of the woods and the fields, whether their tastes keep them in the homely, pleasant farm country or lead them into the wilderness." In Roosevelt's shorthand phrasing, the poles of pastoral and wilderness landscapes stand out sharply, recalling the November 1878 issue of *Scribner's Monthly* and the paired essays "Picturesque Aspects of Farm Life in New York" and "A Wind Storm in the Yuba" (*Scribner's Monthly* 17:41–63). But even in Roosevelt's telegraphic formulation, the "life of the woods and the fields" can range widely and inclusively. In effect, the figure of "Oom John" stands both for and within the complex representations of nature that appear in the pages of such cultural institutions as the *Century Illustrated Monthly Magazine* and the *Harriman Alaska Series*.

Roosevelt's creation of "Oom John" is equally important for what it excludes. As in the pastoral representations of Muir and Burroughs, the realities of urban life and rural labor are absent. Roosevelt glances at farm country, but it is merely homely and pleasant. The "life of the woods and the fields" is a blank generalization—nearly a cliché—that the writer does not pause to fill with any detail. The city does not appear at all, even as the place of industrialized, neurasthenic modernity, but its absence suggests Roosevelt's affinity with antimodernism as defined by Nancy Glazener: "a therapeutic ideal of individual wellness and authentic experience that people pursued in a number of ways: through obsessive concerns with their health, through regenerating holidays spent out of doors, through hobbies that allowed them scope for craftsmanship, and through vicarious participation in earlier, more heroic eras" (*Reading for Realism* 158–59).

Roosevelt's sense of "Oom John" extends yet further, to his own cultural role as a nature writer in turn-of-the-century America. In the last paragraph of the dedicatory letter, he specifically cites the trip that he and Burroughs took to Yellowstone in 1903 and notes that it is "described in this volume." Thus he confidently ends the letter, "I trust that to look over it will recall the pleasant days we spent together." Blandly intimate, the final sentence echoes the "pleasant farm country" of the first paragraph, transferring the adjective to the outdoor holiday the president and the naturalist spent together in the first national park. The blandness conceals President Roosevelt's fierce devotion to a far-reaching conservation program, expanding the national forests by millions of acres, adding five national parks during his term of office, establishing fifty-one wildlife refuges, and creating eighteen national monuments under the Antiquities and National Monuments Act of 1906.[6] But as crucial as Roosevelt's conservation program was for the future of the country and for his reputation as a president, it has led modern readers to neglect his role as a nature writer. Recently, Dan Philippon has argued that Roosevelt's nature writing led to the founding of the Boone and Crockett Club and to the first steps of the environmental movement in America.[7] In this chapter I focus on Roosevelt as a nature writer, both for the sake of the writing itself and for the powerful cultural role it plays. Roosevelt named Burroughs his "Oom John" for literary and cultural reasons, placing himself within the tradition of literary naturalists and ecocritics that reaches back through Muir and Burroughs to Whitman, Thoreau, and Emerson.

Roosevelt's Bad Lands

Roosevelt's nature writing is associated most closely with the Bad Lands of the Dakota Territory, where he owned a cattle ranch from 1883 to 1898. He first visited the Bad Lands in September 1883, on a frustrating but ultimately successful hunt for a buffalo. The impetuous twenty-four-year-old ended the month-long trip by signing a contract with Sylvane Ferris and A. W. Merrifield to place four hundred head of cattle on the Chimney Butte Ranch. In June 1884, Roosevelt returned to the Bad Lands, but he was a changed man. On February 14 his mother and his pregnant young wife, Alice, had died within hours of each other. Roosevelt's diary for the day bears a large cross and the sentence, "The light has gone out of my life."[8] Biographer Edmund Morris evaluates the influence of Alice's death as "so violent that it threatened to destroy him," and Roosevelt's family feared that he would actually "lose his reason." Roosevelt's response was to "set about dislodging Alice Lee from his soul," and in an act of massive repression he mentioned her no more than a handful of times after her funeral.[9]

Roosevelt's grief over the death of his young wife emerges in the descriptions of the Bad Lands in his first nature book, *Hunting Trips of a Ranchman* (1885). In the first panoramic view of the northern plains, Roosevelt emphasizes the transience and vulnerability of life:

> The character of this rolling, broken, plains country is everywhere much the same. It is a high, nearly treeless region, of light rainfall, crossed by streams which are sometimes rapid torrents and sometimes merely strings of shallow

pools. In places, it stretches out into deserts of alkali and sagebrush or into nearly level prairies of short grass, extending many miles without a break; elsewhere there are rolling hills, sometimes of considerable height; and in other places the ground is rent and broken into the most fantastic shapes, partly by volcanic action and partly by the action of water in a dry climate. These latter portions form the famous Bad Lands. Cottonwood-trees fringe the streams or stand in groves on the alluvial bottoms of the rivers; and some of the steep hills and canyon sides are clad with pines or stunted cedars. In the early spring, when the young blades first sprout, the land looks green and bright; but during the rest of the year there is no such appearance of freshness, for the short bunch-grass is almost brown, and the gray-green sage-bush, bitter and withered-looking, abounds everywhere, and gives a peculiarly barren aspect to the landscape. (*Works* 1:3–4)

The prose style is detached and quasi-scientific in its objectivity, but Roosevelt also registers the broken quality of the landscape, its "fantastic shapes," and the reality of barrenness underlying the "appearance of freshness." The Bad Lands are aptly named. As he puts it a few pages later, "And when one is in the Bad Lands he feels as if they somehow *look* just exactly as Poe's tales and poems *sound*" (11). The allusion suggests a landscape of loss and mourning, and we have only to recall such works as "Ligeia," "The Fall of the House of Usher," and "The Raven" to appreciate the force of the landscape for Roosevelt.

In other chapters, Roosevelt recurs to the landscape of the Bad Lands and again creates a complex, mixed sense of place. In the chapter "The Blacktail Deer," for example, he discusses the geological nature of the scoria buttes and the variety of effects wrought by erosion: "The peaks and ridges vary in height from a few feet to several hundred; the sides of the buttes are generally worn down in places so as to be steeply sloping instead of perpendicular. The long washouts and the canyons and canyon-like valleys stretch and branch out in every direction; the dryness of the atmosphere, the extremes of intense heat and bitter cold, and the occasional furious rainstorms keep the edges and angles sharp and jagged, and pile up boulders and masses of loose detritus at the foot of the cliffs and great lonely crags"

(111). The observations are as precise as the descriptive language. Though in a completely different style, Roosevelt's eye for landscape recalls Muir's descriptions of the Sierra Nevada and Alaska.

Roosevelt's Bad Lands are more than geological, for they "grade all the way from those that are almost rolling in character to those that are so fantastically broken in form and so bizarre in color as to seem hardly properly to belong to this earth" (111). In the chapter "A Trip after Mountain-Sheep," Roosevelt once again describes the strange and fantastic shapes of the landscape: "Indeed, it is difficult, in looking at such formations, to get rid of the feeling that their curiously twisted and contorted forms are due to some vast volcanic upheavals or other subterranean forces; yet they are merely caused by the action of the various weathering forces of the dry climate on the different strata of sandstones, clays, and marls" (172). Here the opposition between surface and depth operates to create a sense of uneasiness, as if the writer must convince himself of the "merely" surface actions of erosion. The "subterranean forces" are suitably vague, since the emotion Roosevelt evokes is itself a subterranean apprehension.

If the Bad Lands create an ominous effect, the landscape of the northern plains is in some ways crueler in the sharpness of its definitions. In the chapter "A Trip on the Prairie," Roosevelt narrates a solitary hunting trip he took in June 1884, focusing especially on the "great, seemingly endless stretches of rolling or nearly level prairie" (151). At the beginning of the narrative, Roosevelt describes the fresh, moist air and vivid green vegetation, but he also notes the "sweet, sad songs of the hermit-thrushes," echoing Whitman's "When Lilacs Last in the Dooryard Bloom'd" and Burroughs's *Wake-Robin*. The narrator is hunting pronghorn antelope, but the narrative encompasses much more than a long shot across the prairie:

> Nowhere, not even at sea, does a man feel more lonely than when riding over
> the far-reaching, seemingly never-ending plains; and after a man has lived
> a little while on or near them, their very vastness and loneliness and their
> melancholy monotony have a strong fascination for him. The landscape seems
> always the same, and after the traveler has plodded on for miles and miles he
> gets to feel as if the distance was indeed boundless. As far as the eye can see

there is no break; either the prairie stretches out into perfectly level flats, or else there are gentle, rolling slopes, whose crests mark the divides between the drainage systems of the different creeks; and when one of these is ascended, immediately another precisely like it takes its place in the distance, and so roll succeeds roll in a succession as interminable as that of the waves of the ocean. Nowhere else does one seem so far off from all mankind; the plains stretch out in deathlike and measureless expanse, and as he journeys over them they will for many miles be lacking in all signs of life. (151–52)

The artful variation of nouns, while it may combat the sense of monotony, really adds up to one solitary man who undertakes the trip across the prairie. The landscape reflects the traveler's own situation in its melancholy remoteness and loneliness. And this quintessential landscape of loss and death offers no relief to the perceptions; like the ocean, the prairie is so vast as to be "interminable." Moreover, the place enforces the traveler's sense of isolation, for "nowhere else does one seem so far off from all mankind." It is as if the hunter has been shipwrecked. As he draws the long paragraph to a close, Roosevelt notes that "all objects on the outermost verge of the horizon, even though within the ken of his vision, look unreal and strange," and then he specifies the effect of mirage: "A mile off one can see, through the strange shimmering haze, the shadowy white outlines of something which looms vaguely up till it looks as large as the canvas top of a prairie wagon; but as the horseman comes nearer it shrinks and dwindles and takes clearer form, until at last it changes into the ghastly staring skull of some mighty buffalo, long dead and gone to join the rest of his vanished race" (152). The cruelty lies in Roosevelt's clear-eyed perception of death.

The Bad Lands are more than a boundless landscape of loss, and they evoke more than individual death. The buffalo skull symbolizes a "vanished race" and the fact of extinction, but Roosevelt sees it as a strange sign of consolation. Individual death is subsumed within the larger processes of natural selection, a Darwinian perspective that Roosevelt repeatedly adopts in describing the Bad Lands and their inhabitants. In "The Lordly Buffalo," for example, he creates an objective, dispassionate tone to describe the "melancholy monuments" of bleached buffalo skulls: "The rapid and complete extermination of the buffalo affords an excellent instance of how a race that has thriven and multiplied for ages under conditions of life to which it has slowly fitted itself by a process of natural selection continued for countless generations, may succumb at once when these surrounding conditions are varied by the introduction of one or more new elements, immediately becoming the chief forces with which it has to contend in the struggle for life" (188). Roosevelt's analysis stresses general patterns of causality, rendered in abstract language, and he adamantly refuses to accept such phrases as "to 'harmonize with the environment,' to use the scientific cant of the day" (190). From the perspective of white settlers, the slaughter of the buffalo is a "positive boon," and Roosevelt goes so far as to conclude that "from the standpoint of humanity at large, the extermination of the buffalo has been a blessing. The many have been benefited by it; and I suppose the comparatively few of us who would have preferred the continuance of the old order of things, merely for the sake of our own selfish enjoyment, have no right to complain" (191). Roosevelt's anthropocentrism is thorough and consistent, as is his ethnocentric perspective that white America can stand for "humanity at large."

The phrase "the comparatively few of us" suggests that Roosevelt uses the evolutionary perspective to make sense of his own position and his own losses. In the opening chapter, "Ranching in the Bad Lands," he refuses to lament the settling of the land and the displacement (perhaps "extinction" or "extermination" would be the better word) of Indians and white hunters. Even the ranchman, in Roosevelt's Darwinian perspective, is merely a stage in the evolution of settlement: "For we ourselves and the life that we lead will shortly pass away from the plains as completely as the red and white hunters who have vanished from before our herds. The free, open-air life of the ranchman, the pleasantest and healthiest life in America, is from its very nature ephemeral. The broad and boundless prairies have already been bounded and will soon be made narrow. It is scarcely a figure of speech to say that the tide of white settlement during the last few years has risen over the West like a flood; and the cattlemen are but the spray from the crest of the wave, thrown far in advance, but soon to be overtaken"

(17). Roosevelt's perspective is as "broad and boundless" as the prairies or ocean, and he adopts that viewpoint in order to give his experience a larger significance. He therefore employs "civilization" as the legitimating goal of the processes he describes as evolutionary. The Bad Lands become a meeting ground for nature and culture, a place for Roosevelt to interpret the power that white Americans exert over the landscape of the frontier.

Roosevelt understands the Bad Lands and the relationships they represent in a fundamentally elegiac way. He confronts a landscape of loss and death, but he uses a mixture of scientific and historical theories to move toward acceptance and consolation. Like all effective elegies, however, Roosevelt's nature writings do not belittle the losses and the necessity of mourning. Grief is as important and legitimate as the "struggle for life." In the chapter "Still-Hunting Elk on the Mountains," he celebrates the nobility and power of the elk and then predicts that "the elk is unfortunately one of those animals seemingly doomed to total destruction at no distant date" (209). His analysis focuses on the extermination of elk east of the Mississippi and on the role of market hunters in the West: "Wherever it exists the skin-hunters and meat-butchers wage the most relentless and unceasing war upon it for the sake of its hide and flesh, and their unremitting persecution is thinning out the herds with terrible rapidity" (210). Then the writing becomes yet more emotionally charged:

> The gradual extermination of this, the most stately and beautiful animal of the chase to be found in America, can be looked upon only with unmixed regret by every sportsman and lover of nature. Excepting the moose, it is the largest and, without exception, it is the noblest of the deer tribe. No other species of true deer, in either the Old or the New World, comes up to it in size and in the shape, length, and weight of its mighty antlers; while the grand, proud carriage and lordly bearing of an old bull make it perhaps the most majestic-looking of all the animal creation. The open plains have already lost one of their great attractions, now that we no more see the long lines of elk trotting across them; and it will be a sad day when the lordly, antlered beasts are no longer found in the wild, rocky glens and among the lonely woods of towering pines that cover the great Western mountain chains. (210)

By emphasizing the nobility of the "lordly" elk, Roosevelt increases the sense of endangerment and potential loss. Indeed, he registers the losses that have already occurred, since the plains had at one time teemed with elk in the same way they had teemed with herds of buffalo. The tone is clearly one of "unmixed regret," and the only irony arises, for the modern reader, because elk have in fact survived in the Rocky Mountains. In the passage itself, no larger perspective of natural selection or cultural evolution mitigates the sense of grief.

   Given this elegiac strain in *Hunting Trips of a Ranchman*, it surely strikes a present-day reader as strange to find Roosevelt celebrating the role of the hunter. But Roosevelt's ethical stance is quite consistent, even though it might not measure up to the standards of a twenty-first-century environmentalist. First, he makes no bones about killing individual animals for food, for trophies, and for the pleasure of the chase itself. He never entertains the notion that the killing could be wrong in some a priori fashion or that a wild animal has the same ontological and ethical status as a human being. Rather, Roosevelt distinguishes between the "ideal of a bold and free hunter" (106) and "swinish game-butchers, who hunt for hides and not for sport or actual food, and who murder the gravid doe and the spotted fawn with as little hesitation as they would kill a buck of ten points" (107). The market hunters are condemned not because they kill wildlife but because they kill wildlife in an irresponsible, unthinking way and on an unsustainable scale. In *The Wilderness Hunter* (1893), Roosevelt gives a clear formulation of the principle: "I have never sought to make large bags, for a hunter should not be a game-butcher. It is always lawful to kill dangerous or noxious animals, like the bear, cougar, and wolf; but other game should be shot only when there is need of the meat, or for the sake of an unusually fine trophy. Killing a reasonable number of bulls, bucks, or rams does no harm whatever to the species; to slay half the males of any kind of game would not stop the natural increase, and they yield the best sport, and are the legitimate objects of the chase. Cows, does, and ewes, on the contrary, should only be killed (unless barren) in case of necessity; during my last five years' hunting I have killed but five—one by mischance, and the other four for the table" (*Works* 2:353).

From the first pages of *Hunting Trips of a Ranchman*, Roosevelt specifies his ideal as still-hunting, in which the hunter, dressed in a buckskin suit and moccasins, walks as noiselessly and invisibly as possible through the dusk or dawn (86). In the chapter "The Blacktail Deer," he notes that "the successful still-hunter . . . is indeed well up in the higher forms of hunting craft" and that "to be a successful hunter after anything, a man should be patient, resolute, hardy, and with good judgment; he should have good lungs and stout muscles; he should be able to move with noiseless stealth; and he should be keen-eyed, and a first-rate marksman with the rifle" (105). The skills necessary for hunting particular animals may vary greatly, but ultimately the value of a particular kind of game animal depends upon the "nature of the qualities in the hunter which each particular form of hunting calls into play" (106). The most difficult animal to approach and kill is the bighorn sheep, but in terms of "manly qualities" in the hunter Roosevelt also praises the blacktail (mule) deer and elk. The grizzly bear ranks high in his estimation both because it is powerful and dangerous and because the still-hunter must "put on moccasins and still-hunt it in its own haunts, shooting it at close quarters" (234). The order of chapters in *Hunting Trips of a Ranchman* follows this hierarchy of hunting skill, beginning with waterfowl and prairie fowl and ending with elk and grizzly.[10]

If Roosevelt's hunting ethics are obviously anthropocentric, they are also clearly constructed along lines of gender, race, and class. Of these three interpretive categories, moreover, gender functions most tellingly. Even in the few passages I have quoted, he repeats the phrases "a man" and "manly" like a refrain. In Gail Bederman's analysis, Roosevelt constructs "a virile political persona for himself as a strong but civilized white man" (171), and she reads the early nature writings as intended to establish Roosevelt's identity as a "heroic ranchman" (176). Bederman's argument subtly draws together themes of race, manhood, violence, and imperialism, and her book focuses especially on the many, often contradictory processes of articulation by which "civilization" was defined between 1880 and 1920. Dan Philippon's reading, on the other hand, stresses the mixture of frontier romanticism and scientific realism in *Hunting Trips of a Ranchman*, and he tends to focus on the natural history and experiential knowledge in Roosevelt's writings.[11] These interpretations are not mutually exclusive; indeed, they combine to show how complex and powerful Roosevelt's early writings can be. A good example of competing interpretations is the famous image of Roosevelt in his buckskin suit, which served as the frontispiece of *Hunting Trips of a Ranchman* (figure 21). Bederman notes the lack of eyeglasses, interpreting this and other details as signs of manly civilization mixed with the regressive clothing of savages. Philippon focuses on the functional and documentary aspects of the image, emphasizing the reality of Roosevelt's experience and the fidelity to his role as hunter-naturalist.[12]

The cultural role of the antimodern celebrity author provides a third perspective from which to view the buckskin suit and the frontispiece. Like the images of Muir and Burroughs in the pages of the *Century*, the figure of the young Roosevelt functions as both an advertisement and a mythic portrait. Neither function undercuts the realism of the image. Just as the engraving of John Muir accompanies a verbal portrait that makes the figure into a larger-than-life combination of scientist, mountaineer, ascetic, and shaman, so the frontispiece introduces the reader to a latter-day frontiersman who personifies Roosevelt's ideal of the wilderness still-hunter. In his verbal self-portrait, Roosevelt specifies the rifle as a Winchester 45–75 half-magazine carbine, "stocked and sighted to suit myself" and "by all odds the best weapon I ever had" (27), and he associates the buckskin suit with the long hunting trip "where there will be much rough work, especially in the dry cold of fall and winter. . . . Buckskin is most durable, keeps out wind and cold, and is the best possible color for the hunter—no small point in approaching game. For wet, it is not as good as flannel, and it is hot in warm weather" (28). The voice is authoritative and opinionated, conveying the same sense of resolution and experience one sees in the frontispiece.

Other illustrations in *Hunting Trips of a Ranchman* contribute to this portrait of Roosevelt as still-hunter. In the final chapter, "Old Ephraim," for instance, Roosevelt narrates part of a two-week hunting trip to the Bighorn Mountains, which he took in early September 1884 with his foreman, William Merrifield. "Old Ephraim" is the name given the grizzly bear by mountain men, and the engraving illustrates "Close Quarters with Old Ephraim" (figure 22). The engraving renders a brief confrontation between

Figure 21. Roosevelt as Wilderness Hunter, Frontispiece to
Hunting Trips of a Ranchman, Medora Edition (Special Collections,
Clifton Waller Barrett Library of American Literature, University of
Virginia Library).

Figure 22. Close Quarters with Old Ephraim, from *Hunting Trips of a Ranchman*, Medora Edition (Special Collections, Clifton Waller Barrett Library of American Literature, University of Virginia Library).

the two still-hunters and the bear: "When in the middle of the thicket we crossed what was almost a breastwork of fallen logs, and Merrifield, who was leading, passed by the upright stem of a great pine. As soon as he was by it, he sank suddenly on one knee, turning half round, his face fairly aflame with excitement; and as I strode past him, with my rifle at the ready, there, not ten steps off, was the great bear, slowly rising from his bed among the young spruces" (240). Roosevelt immediately shoots the bear between the eyes, and "the whole thing was over in twenty seconds from the time I caught sight of the game." The shot and the kill are narrated in the briefest manner, whereas the tracking and still-hunting are told in abundant detail. The illustration captures the moment before Roosevelt fires, just as the giant grizzly is dropping down onto all fours. Like the frontispiece, the figure of the still-hunter is a mixture of real and ideal: the engraving portrays an actual event, but in doing so it creates an imagined, idealized place, peopled by three imagined, idealized figures.

A third illustration points away from the "manliness" of the hunter toward the appreciation of the naturalist. In "Bear at Elk Carcass," the hunter peers from behind a ridgepole pine trunk, his rifle held at rest, and the foreground is completely occupied by a large grizzly bear in the act of tearing a fresh elk carcass (see figure 23). The illustration is not completely realistic, since the elk carcass is intact and bloodless, as if it had just fallen. An actual bait carcass would be headless and field-dressed, perhaps skinned, and in all likelihood the tenderloin would already be in camp. But the engraving effectively conveys the power of the bear, caught in a moment that few human beings ever witness, and Roosevelt renders the moment just as effectively in the chapter "Still-Hunting Elk on the Mountains":

> The great pine-clad mountains, their forests studded with open glades, were the best of places for the still-hunter's craft. Going noiselessly through them in our dull-colored buckskin and noiseless moccasins, we kept getting glimpses, as it were, of the inner life of the mountains. Each animal that we saw had its own individuality. Aside from the thrill and tingle that a hunter experiences at the sight of his game, I by degrees grew to feel as if I had a personal interest

Figure 23. Bear at Elk Carcass, from *Hunting Trips of a Ranchman*, Medora Edition
(Special Collections, Clifton Waller Barrett Library of American Literature, University
of Virginia Library).

in the different traits and habits of the wild creatures. The characters of the
animals differed widely, and the differences were typified by their actions;
and it was pleasant to watch them in their own homes, myself unseen, when,
after stealthy, silent progress through the somber and soundless depths of the
woods, I came upon them going about the ordinary business of their lives.
The lumbering, self-confident gait of the bears, their burly strength, and their
half-humorous, half-ferocious look, gave me a real insight into their character;
and I never was more impressed by the exhibition of vast, physical power
than when watching from an ambush a grizzly burying or covering up an elk
carcass. His motions looked awkward, but it was marvelous to see the ease
and absence of effort with which he would scoop out great holes in the earth
or twitch the heavy carcass from side to side. And the proud, graceful, half-
timid, half-defiant bearing of the elk was in its own way quite as noteworthy;
they seemed to glory in their own power and beauty, and yet to be ever on the
watch for foes against whom they knew they might not dare to contend. The
true still-hunter should be a lover of nature as well as of sport, or he will miss
half the pleasure of being in the woods. (223–24)

Roosevelt shows his skill as an observer, but he also shows how well he can describe the act of observation. His focus on perceptions turns the observation of actions into "personal interest in the traits and habits of the wild creatures," and that interest leads to a sense of their individuality. Roosevelt surely recalls Burroughs when he notes that it was "pleasant to watch them in their own homes, myself unseen." The observer is invisible, or nearly so, and the engraving captures that quality by minimizing the role of the still-hunter figure in the illustration. The creatures are wild, and the engraving seems particularly taken with the ferocity of the grizzly. But the wild animals still have "homes," a word that evokes the domestic pastoralism of Burroughs's essays. The entire passage creates the "best of places," both for the craft of the still-hunter and for the craft of the literary naturalist.

Visual Place

The illustrations for *Hunting Trips of a Ranchman* suggest that some of the same cultural forces we have seen in the nature essays of Muir and Burroughs are operating in Roosevelt's nature writing. Indeed, in some cases the illustrators themselves work for all three of the writers. Thus R. Swain Gifford, a *Century* artist who made the watercolor landscape paintings for the Harriman Alaska expedition, is responsible for four luxurious etchings in the limited edition of *Hunting Trips*, presenting aesthetic renderings of landscape in "Sunset on Plateau" and "A Night in the Open" (figures 24 and 25). These "India-Proof Impressions" give the effect of pen-and-ink drawings, and they capture precise moments in the fleeting, action-filled life of the cattle ranch. In addition, the Gifford etchings render ranch life in a dark, impressionistic way, effectively evoking the gloomy beauty of the Bad Lands. Other illustrators include Henry Sandham, J. C. Beard, A. B. Frost, and Fannie E. Gifford; ten different artists produced the engravings in the Medora edition of *Hunting Trips of a Ranchman*. In the October 1885 *Atlantic Monthly*, the reviewer notes that the book is "a model of fine book-making" and that "the illustrations are very numerous, and form an important feature of the work."[13]

Figure 24. Sunset on Plateau, from *Hunting Trips of a Ranchman*, Medora Edition (Special Collections, Clifton Waller Barrett Library of American Literature, University of Virginia Library).

Figure 25. A Night in the Open, from *Hunting Trips of a Ranchman*, Medora Edition (Special Collections, Clifton Waller Barrett Library of American Literature, University of Virginia Library).

Both the number and significance of illustrations grow in Roosevelt's second Western nature book, *Ranch Life and the Hunting Trail* (1888). The title suggests the dual focus of the book, and eight of the twelve chapters are devoted to the work of cattle ranching in the Dakotas. The book brings together six articles that Roosevelt published in the *Century* in 1888, illustrated copiously and exclusively by Frederic Remington.[14] By bringing together Roosevelt and Remington, *Ranch Life* recurs to some of the themes in *Hunting Trips of a Ranchman*, but it also explores new territory in representing the place of nature.

True to its dual title, *Ranch Life and the Hunting Trail* combines nostalgic pastoralism and hard-nosed realism. In the opening chapter, "The Cattle Country of the Far West," Roosevelt presents a panoramic view of the "one gigantic, unbroken pasture" that lies between the Bad Lands and the Rockies (*Works* 1:269), recounting the exploration and sparse settlement by stockmen and bringing the history of the place down to the present: "Civilization seems as remote as if we were living in an age long past. The whole existence is patriarchal in character: it is the life of men who live in the open, who tend their herds on horseback, who go armed and ready to guard their lives by their own prowess, whose wants are very simple, and who call no man master. Ranching is an occupation like those of vigorous, primitive pastoral peoples, having little in common with the humdrum, workaday business world of the nineteenth century; and the free ranchman in his manner of life shows more kinship to an Arab sheik than to a sleek city merchant or tradesman" (274). Roosevelt's brand of antimodernism reaches back toward the savage or primitive pastoralism of a preindustrial world, and in that sense the place of nature resembles the remoteness of Muir's glacial wilderness or Burroughs's Hudson Valley farm. But Roosevelt's description also compares the ranchman to "an Arab sheik," giving the Bad Lands an exotic, unfamiliar distance. The distance is also gendered: like the rhetoric of *Hunting Trips of a Ranchman*, Roosevelt's style is resolutely masculine—or, as he aptly puts it, "patriarchal." The ranchman is a figure of primal maleness, remote from the "humdrum, workaday business world" and its constraining, neurasthenic culture. Roosevelt shares the therapeutic ideal of nature with Muir and

Burroughs, but the figuration is specifically tied to the Bad Lands and to "ranch life."

Roosevelt's Darwinian perspective concerning ranch life and the use of land figures as strongly as it did in *Hunting Trips of a Ranchman.* Like the opening chapter in the earlier book, the first two chapters of *Ranch Life and the Hunting Trail* celebrate the open range, but Roosevelt repeatedly warns against overstocking and concludes that "the best days of ranching are over" and "in its present form stock-raising on the plains is doomed." The details of ranch life are "barbarous, picturesque, and curiously fascinating," but the ranches "mark a primitive stage of existence as surely as do the great tracts of primeval forests and, like the latter, must pass away before the onward march of our people" (292). Most striking in this passage is the complete absence of a conservation ethic. Roosevelt assumes that the "onward march" must trample open plains and primeval forests into extinction, but his response to the relentless evolution is elegiac: "we who have felt the charm of the life, and have exulted in its abounding vigor and its bold, restless freedom, will not only regret its passing for our own sakes, but must also feel real sorrow that those who come after us are not to see, as we have seen, what is perhaps the pleasantest, healthiest, and most exciting phase of American existence" (292–93).

Remington's illustrations for the *Century* articles accord with the elegiac tone of Roosevelt's writing. In the February 1888 article, ten engravings present a combination of accuracy and embellishment. The full-page "An Episode in the Opening Up of a Cattle Country" (figure 26) represents a pitched battle between cowboys and Plains Indians, and it appears to be keyed to one sentence in Roosevelt's text: "Both the necessity and the chance for long wanderings were especially great when the final overthrow of the northern Horse Indians opened the whole upper Missouri basin at one sweep to the stockmen" (271).[15] The style is characteristic of Remington's illustrations for Roosevelt's articles. Based on Roosevelt's abstract historical generalization, the engraving represents a dramatic, action-filled episode. The physicality of horses and men expresses the excitement and danger of the frontier life, and the foregrounding of the circle suggests the centrality of the white explorers, who open the country for "the onward march of our people." The figures themselves seem completely accurate, though they are also typical—to the point of becoming stereotypical.

Remington's illustrations are hardly secondary to Roosevelt's writing; rather, they create a visual place for a reader's imagination, filling in Roosevelt's sweeping narrative with episodic detail. This symbiotic relationship between verbal and visual texts could be illustrated repeatedly with Remington's images, but one more from the February 1888 article will suffice. "Bronco Busters Saddling" (figure 27) is photographic in its clarity and physical detail, and it surely gains from the technology of photoxylography developed by *Century* illustrators. Remington illustrates a paragraph on riding, in which Roosevelt notes that the "flash riders, or horse-breakers, always called 'bronco-busters,' can perform really marvelous feats, riding with ease the most vicious and unbroken beasts, that no ordinary cowboy would dare to tackle. . . . But their method of breaking is very rough, consisting only in saddling and bridling a beast by main force and then riding him, also by main force, until he is exhausted, when he is turned over as 'broken'" (285). If Remington were to confine himself to Roosevelt's words, the illustration would present the broncobusters in the saddle. But the image instead presents the moment before a cowboy might mount the animal. The two cowboys are employing all of their "main force" in holding the bucking bronco, allowing him to tire himself to the point of exhaustion. The scene is classic in its triangulated figures, but the triangle is formed by opposing vectors of force and physical power, not by a harmony of calm repose.

Roosevelt and Remington are alike in representing the cattle country as a male domain, but they differ from Muir and Burroughs by moving away from the solitary figure of the mountaineer, the naturalist, or the still-hunter. The engravings and articles create a homosocial world, and it is most fundamentally a world of work. Unlike the pastorals of Muir's "Bee Pasture" essays or Burroughs's "Glimpses of Wild Life about My Cabin," Roosevelt's *Ranch Life* repeatedly delivers scenes of working cowboys in order to develop a consistent theme of the difficulties of the ranching life. Remington's engravings often bear titles that suggest the action of repeated

Figure 26. An Episode in the Opening Up of a Cattle Country, by Frederic Remington (*Century* 35 [February 1888]: 497).

Figure 27. Bronco Busters Saddling, by Frederic Remington (*Century* 35 [February 1888]: 508).

chores, such as "Roping in a Horse-Corral," "Cruising for Stock," and "Line Riding in Winter." The illustrations thus present emblematic episodes and characters, especially portraying the cowboys as "the typical men of the plains" (356). In chapter 4, "The Round-Up," Roosevelt notes that the cowboy's difficult life leads to a high moral tone: "There is a high regard for truthfulness and keeping one's word, intense contempt for any kind of hypocrisy, and a hearty dislike for a man who shirks his work. Many of the men gamble and drink, but many do neither; and the conversation is not worse than in most bodies composed wholly of male human beings. A cowboy will not submit tamely to an insult, and is ever ready to avenge his own wrongs; nor has he an overwrought fear of shedding blood. He possesses, in fact, few of the emasculated, milk-and-water moralities admired by the pseudophilanthropists; but he does possess, to a very high degree, the stern, manly qualities that are invaluable to a nation" (325–26).

In Roosevelt's shifting representations, the "stern, manly qualities" seem valuable both in themselves and in their consequences. In the chapter "Frontier Types," originally published in the October 1888 *Century*, he praises the "old-time hunters" as wild and free, and he finds "very much good about the men themselves" (349–51). But the hunters and trappers form an impermanent stage of existence, giving way to the ranchmen and cowboys at the beginning of the nineteenth century. When Roosevelt narrates his own encounters with "old-style hunters," it is as if he has discovered a living fossil. Even the cowboys are vanishing, and like the hunter and trapper, the cowboy functions as "the grim pioneer of our race; he prepares the way for the civilization before which he must himself disappear" (369). Although Roosevelt tends to represent ranch life by focusing on groups of men at work, he ends the chapter—and the series of *Century* articles— with an image of vanishing solitude: "He lives in the lonely lands where mighty rivers twist in long reaches between the barren bluffs; where the prairies stretch out into billowy plains of waving grass, girt only by the blue horizon—plains across whose endless breadth he can steer his course for days and weeks and see neither man to speak to nor hill to break the level; where the glory and the burning splendor of the sunset kindle the blue vault of heaven and the level brown earth till they merge together in an ocean of flaming fire" (369).

Two articles in the *Century* series focus on a figure we have seen in articles by Muir and Burroughs: the celebrity writer. Though Roosevelt is actually quite modest in his self-representations, always noting his flaws as a horseman, cowboy, and rifleman, the Remington illustrations tend to present him as a hero in a Western adventure. In the May 1888 article "Sheriff's Work on a Ranch," which would become chapters 7 and 8 in *Ranch Life and the Hunting Trail*, Remington repeatedly draws Roosevelt in his buckskin suit. "Standing off Indians" resembles "An Episode in the Opening Up of a Cattle Country" and echoes the titles of typical chores, as if the confrontation with Indians were a characteristic piece of ranch work. Indeed, in chapter 7, "Red and White on the Border," Roosevelt describes his "very mild" adventure with a band of "four or five Indians," then follows it with a scene on the Powder River that could directly describe Remington's "Episode" (371–74). The authenticity of the second story depends on the authority with which Roosevelt tells it, since there is no other source for it than "the men who related the incident to me" (373).

The main narrative of "Sheriff's Work on a Ranch" is the true story of Roosevelt's pursuit and capture of three boat thieves in late March 1886. While most of the illustrations are generic, the climactic "Hands Up!" (figure 28) features Roosevelt in the buckskin shirt and fur cap of the hunter-naturalist. But instead of observing or taking aim at a wild animal, the still-hunter enforces human law. Despite his understated narration of the pursuit and capture of the outlaws, Roosevelt becomes the central figure in the drama because Remington depicts him in that way. Remington's illustrations may evoke the kind of dime cowboy novels that Roosevelt finds among the thieves' belongings: "They had quite a stock of books, some of a rather unexpected kind. Dime novels and the inevitable 'History of the James Brothers'—a book that, together with the *Police Gazette*, is to be found in the hands of every professed or putative ruffian in the West— seemed perfectly in place; but it was somewhat surprising to find that a large number of more or less drearily silly 'society' novels, ranging from Ouida's to

Figure 28. "Hands Up!"—The Capture of Finnigan (*Century* 36 [May 1888]: 46).

those of The Duchess and Augusta J. Evans, were most greedily devoured. As for me, I had brought with me *Anna Karenina*, and my surroundings were quite grey enough to harmonize well with Tolstoi" (395–96). Locating himself on the border between East and West, culture and nature, Roosevelt employs his celebrity to speak with a voice of discriminating authority, whether the topic is legal or literary.

The June 1888 issue of *Century* returns the reader to a familiar place. Roosevelt's article, "The Ranchman's Rifle on Crag and Prairie," is the core of three chapters in *Ranch Life and the Hunting Trail*. The best of the three chapters is the last, "The Game of the High Peaks: The White Goat," which narrates a two-week hunting trip to the Rockies in the fall of 1886. The actual shooting of the white goat is by far the least important aspect of the narrative. Roosevelt devotes the bulk of the chapter to the natural history of the white goat, to the difficult mountaineering necessary to stalk it, and to the physical endurance necessary to pursue it over two weeks. On one page of the *Century* article, Remington portrays "The First Shot" and "The Last Shot" of the mountain hunter. Roosevelt was clearly the model, and the figure of the still-hunter in "The First Shot" accords with Roosevelt's tone of authority and authenticity. But the juxtaposition of the two images and titles is ultimately ironic, perhaps even subversive. Although Roosevelt appears as an athletic, "manly" hunter in "The First Shot," the title of the second illustration refers to the last *image* of the hunter, an image shot by the camera and rendered as a magazine illustration: "Early next morning I came back with my two men to where the goats were lying, taking along the camera. Having taken their photographs and skinned them we went back to camp, hunted up the ponies and mules, who had been shifting for themselves during the past few days, packed up our tent, trophies, and other belongings, and set off for the settlements, well pleased with our trip" (458). The *Century* articles portray Roosevelt as the quintessential hypermasculine frontiersman, embodying the combination of civilized and natural laws. In addition, they serve as advertisements for the writer of *Ranch Life and the Hunting Trail*, since the book publication follows directly on the heels of the serialization.

Both Remington and Roosevelt evoke an evanescent place of nature, making that place more real and seemingly present than the urban reader's own environment. But at the same time, both artists focus unrelentingly on the passing of the place, the change that will exterminate the place as they represent it. Despite their clear yearning for the place and for its preservation by pen and pencil, both artists also participate in the culture that determines the place of nature, and both recognize their role in the culture. For that reason, we can find such ironies as "The Last Shot." The illustration is like a snapshot—ironic word! It renders the details of the two hunters and the white goat with sharp clarity, making the captured moment more real than reality. At the same time, it marks the evanescence of the moment, a moment that centers both on death and on joy. The elegiac blending of realism and pastoralism creates a place of nature, but its effectiveness ironically depends upon the disappearance of the place.

Hunter and Naturalist

In the 1890s and 1900s, Roosevelt's sense of place shifts in several important ways. First, the experience of the Bad Lands in the 1880s expands to include other types of frontier or border landscapes, and the earlier concept of "frontier" becomes a consistent idea of "wilderness." Second, the elegiac landscape of the Bad Lands leads Roosevelt to a focused sense of the American wilderness as endangered and in need of protection. Third, the overwhelming sense of endangerment leads Roosevelt to promote wilderness and wildlife reserves, both in his writings and in his role as president. Fourth, as the twentieth century opens, Roosevelt's writing becomes less anthropocentric and less concerned with the manliness of the hunt. Last, and by no means least, Roosevelt associates the place of nature in American culture with the figure of John Burroughs. Although this final point may seem separate from the first four, the five changes are intimately bound up with one another.

The Wilderness Hunter (1893) announces its serious intentions from the very first page of the opening chapter, "The American Wilderness: Wilderness Hunters and Wilderness Game." The perspective is panoramic, the narrative sweeping and grand, and in many respects Roosevelt's history of wilderness matches exactly the Darwinian history of frontier settlement he gives in *Hunting Trips of a Ranchman*. The narrative emphasizes wilderness hunters as a stage in the inevitable process of civilizing the country (2:7–12), but toward the end of the narrative Roosevelt injects three different accounts of the fifteen-year "war" against the huge bison herds of the western plains (2:10–11, 12–13), ultimately noting that the "seething myriads" are now "on the point of extinction." The loss of the bison is felt not only by those who face a similar extinction. Whereas in *Hunting Trips of a Ranchman* Roosevelt calls cattlemen "the spray from the crest of the wave" of white settlement (1:17), in 1893 he writes that the bison "is truly a grand and noble beast, and his loss from our prairies and forests is as keenly regretted by the lover of nature and of wild life as by the hunter" (2:13).

The opening chapter of *The Wilderness Hunter* suggests a broadening on several fronts. The audience addressed includes the "lover of nature and of wild life" just as much as the hunter or "manly" sportsman. The idea of wilderness also broadens the place of nature. Rather than being found only at the western border between settlements and Bad Lands, wilderness is manifold in its shapes and locations. But wilderness is still marked by the loss of grand and noble fauna. In the final pages of the chapter, Roosevelt lists the big game of the American wilderness according to a mixed taxonomy of size, abundance, and range: bison, moose, wapiti (elk), woodland caribou, whitetail deer, blacktail or mule deer, pronghorn antelope, bighorn sheep, white goat, cougar, wolf, black bear, grizzly bear, peccary (13–16). Noting the diminished numbers and range of the wildlife, he locates the finest wilderness "hunting-ground" in "the mountainous region of western Montana and northwestern Wyoming" because almost all of the species he lists are to be found there in relative plenty (16). The specificity may suggest that Roosevelt sees the Rocky Mountains as the last wilderness, but in fact Roosevelt focuses on them because they contain the greatest variety of large mammals and require of the hunter the most "hardihood, self-reliance, and resolution needed for effectively grappling with his wild surroundings" (17).[16]

While the broadening does not mean that Roosevelt abandons his anthropocentric perspective, it does suggest that the power of the hunter is no longer the main focus of his writing. In the preface, Roosevelt claims that "the finding and killing of the game is after all but a part of the whole" (xxix), and while that cliché of hunting magazines may ring somewhat hollow, much of *The Wilderness Hunter* supports the idea. In the chapter "On the Cattle Ranges; the Pronghorn Antelope," for example, Roosevelt describes the work of riding all day across the plains and Bad Lands, joining a roundup and taking part in all of its work, then hunting pronghorn to feed the crew. But he also notes, at considerable length, the singing of the western meadowlark and plains skylark, developing several paragraphs on how bird songs are associated with place and our love of place (52–56). Along the way, he praises the larks, the thrushes—especially "the serene, ethereal beauty of the hermit's song, rising and falling through the still evening under the archways of hoary mountain forests that have endured from time everlasting" (53)—and the mockingbird, which he recalls hearing near

Nashville, "singing the livelong spring night, under the full moon, in the magnolia tree" (54). This is not merely a five-page digression. Later, in the chapter "Hunting Lore," Roosevelt notes that he has become aware of "a piece of indebtedness" to the writings of John Burroughs: "In my chapter on the prongbuck there is a paragraph which will at once suggest to any lover of Burroughs some sentences in his essay on 'Birds and Poets'" (357). In fact, in "Birds and Poets" Burroughs discusses the very birds Roosevelt does. He describes the western skylark or Sprague's pipit as an "excelsior songster, which from far up in the transparent blue rains down its notes for many minutes together" (*Writings* 3:22). He spends several pages on the mockingbird as a night singer or "*our* nightingale," quoting Whitman's "Out of the Cradle Endlessly Rocking" at great length (10–16). And he of course discusses the hermit thrush in relation to "When Lilacs Last in the Dooryard Bloom'd" (46–47). While none of these sentences seems related to a particular paragraph in Roosevelt's chapter, all of them are related to his discussion of bird songs.

Roosevelt's debt to Burroughs runs much deeper than a few sentences or a paragraph. In the "Hunting Lore" chapter, Roosevelt offers the reader possible outdoor sports such as fishing, snowshoeing, and mountaineering, but then he directly connects the love of wilderness to the love of books: "The dweller or sojourner in the wilderness who most keenly loves and appreciates his wild surroundings, and all their sights and sounds, is the man who also loves and appreciates the books which tell of them" (356). By his own standards, Roosevelt is the keenest lover of the wilderness, for he knows the literature of the outdoors as well as anyone. And he puts Burroughs at the very head of the list of necessary writers:

> Foremost of all American writers on outdoor life is John Burroughs; and I
> can scarcely suppose that any man who cares for existence outside the cities
> would willingly be without anything that he has ever written. To the naturalist,
> to the observer and lover of nature, he is of course worth many times more
> than any closet systematist; and though he has not been very much in really
> wild regions, his pages so thrill with the sights and sounds of outdoor life
> that nothing by any writer who is a mere professional scientist or a mere

professional hunter can take their place or do more than supplement them—
for scientist and hunter alike would do well to remember that before a book
can take the highest rank in any particular line it must also rank high in
literature proper. Of course for us Americans Burroughs has a peculiar charm
that he cannot have for others, no matter how much they too may like him;
for what he writes of is our own, and he calls to our minds memories and
associations that are very dear. His books make us homesick when we read
them in foreign lands; for they spring from our soil as truly as "Snowbound"
or "The Biglow Papers."

   As a woodland writer, Thoreau comes second only to Burroughs. (356–57)

The second, one-sentence paragraph must have thrilled Burroughs, but
more important than the "Thoreau charge" is Roosevelt's assessment of the
literary naturalist. He disparages the "closet systematist" because he favors
the field biologist. Indeed, the tendency of science in the late nineteenth
century to be confined to the laboratory is one of the main reasons Roosevelt
decided not to pursue a career in science. In 1893, Roosevelt served on an
outside review committee for the zoology department at Harvard University,
and in his report he concluded that "the highest type of biologist is the
naturalist, who can work both in the laboratory and afield."[17]

   Burroughs models the naturalist who directly encounters the "sights and
sounds of outdoor life," just as he models the writer who ranks "high in
literature proper." In addition, Roosevelt associates Burroughs with place,
in particular with America, giving him a national importance equal to
that of Whittier and Lowell. By saying that Burroughs "calls to our minds
memories and associations that are very dear" and that his "pages so thrill
with the sights and sounds of outdoor life," Roosevelt echoes his earlier
description of the meadowlark's song: "To me it comes forever laden with a
hundred memories and associations; with the sight of dim hills reddening
in the dawn, with the breath of cool morning winds blowing across lonely
plains, with the scent of flowers on the sunlit prairie, with the motion of
fiery horses, with all the strong thrill of eager and buoyant life. I doubt if
any man can judge dispassionately the bird songs of his own country; he
cannot disassociate them from the sights and sounds of the land that is so

dear to him" (52–53). Burroughs creates the love of place, delivered in literary prose, and his writing parallels the meadowlark's song in calling forth the listener's love of place. Thus Roosevelt's poetic description of the Bad Lands, associated with the meadowlark's song, exemplifies his own place-centered identity as a literary naturalist.

The shifts in emphasis in *The Wilderness Hunter* do not mean that Roosevelt abandons his passion for still-hunting big game in the wilderness. Along with descriptions of landscape and nongame fauna, Roosevelt devotes considerable care to the natural history of game species. The chapter in which he describes the bird songs, for example, is largely devoted to the pronghorn antelope, and he treats the hunt separately in the following chapter, "Hunting the Prongbuck; Frost, Fire, and Thirst." That pattern applies as well to paired chapters on the wapiti and the grizzly bear. First he describes the characteristic habitat and behavior of the high-mountain elk; then he narrates "An Elk-Hunt at Two-Ocean Pass." The first chapter on the grizzly, "Old Ephraim, the Grizzly Bear," is followed by "Hunting the Grizzly." The pattern allows Roosevelt to develop his observations from the field in detail, and he takes that opportunity in discussing three of his favorite species. In other cases, Roosevelt combines natural history and hunting narratives within a single chapter. For example, the chapter "Mountain Game; the White Goat" explores the wilderness of Big Hole Basin in western Montana, narrating successful hunts but also describing the habitat and habits of spruce grouse, the pleasures of mountain camping, and characteristic behaviors of the white goat.

The narratives of *The Wilderness Hunter* reveal a literary artist at work. Having published the two outdoor books focusing on the Bad Lands as well as several academic histories and biographies, Roosevelt commands his narratives with skill. He delights in the sweeping historical panorama, as we see in the opening chapter of all three outdoor books, but he also continually peppers *The Wilderness Hunter* with brief anecdotes, short illustrative stories, tales and legends told by other hunters, and lore that borders upon the supernatural. All of these narrative modes complement his most characteristic narrative, the successful stalking of big game by the wilderness still-hunter.

Two chapters give representative samples of Roosevelt's skill as a story-teller. In "An Elk-Hunt at Two-Ocean Pass," Roosevelt narrates the September 1891 hunting trip to the Shoshone Mountains of northwest Wyoming. The journey of the pack train allows the narrator to dwell on the beauty of the mountain landscape and to develop the humor of driving packhorses through thick woods and over mountainous terrain. Beset by fog and cold rain, the expedition eventually reaches "the wild and lonely valley of Two-Ocean Pass, walled in on either hand by rugged mountain chains, their flanks scarred and gashed by precipice and chasm. Beyond, in a wilderness of jagged and barren peaks, stretched the Shoshones" (148). They arrive in rutting season, so Roosevelt describes in detail the sounds and smells of bugling bull elk. He kills nine elk over the two weeks, but during one ten-day stretch he kills "nothing save one cow for meat; and this though I hunted hard every day from morning till night, no matter what the weather" (154). On one clear morning, he locates and stalks a rutting master bull, killing him with four well-placed, rapid shots (149–53). The hunt requires a combination of stealth and athleticism which the narrator calls "stirring, manly, exciting" (160). Roosevelt concludes the chapter by claiming that "in point of success in finding and killing game, in value of trophies pro-cured, and in its alternations of good and bad luck, it may fairly stand as the type of a dozen such hunts I have made" (159).

In the penultimate chapter of the book, "In Cowboy Land," Roosevelt recurs to the scenes of *Ranch Life and the Hunting Trail*, but the focus of the piece is storytelling itself. The narrator dwells on characters—cowboys and hunters he has known—and on the stories they tell. Dialogue is often im-portant to the texture of the stories, as is Roosevelt's indirect reporting. The chapter includes eight distinct tales, ranging from retrieving a stolen pony to fighting a Sioux war party. There is often much humor in the dialogue, characterization, and plot of frontier justice. In a sudden twist, however, the chapter concludes with a wilderness "goblin-story" that is nothing short of masterful. The "goblin" may be a bear that walks on two legs, or it may be "something either half human or half devil," but the tale never allows that much certainty to take hold of the trapper Bauman, who witnesses the strange events leading to the death of his unnamed partner (347–52).

Roosevelt's narrative holds the reader among uncertainties, investing the wilderness with supernatural power.

Both chapters are significant for other reasons. Roosevelt published shorter versions of both as articles in the *Century*. In the magazine version, the "Elk-Hunt" narrative ends with the narrator's final action of arriving at Mammoth Hot Springs; in *The Wilderness Hunter* chapter, Roosevelt appends the discussion of the hunt as the "type" of other hunts he has made, along with three more paragraphs in which he reflects on still-hunting elk in the mountains as one of the most demanding and rewarding wilderness hunts (159–60). The magazine version of "In Cowboy Land" ends with the first of two tales about cavalry fights with Cheyenne Indians. In the book, Roosevelt adds the second tale, told by Lieutenant John Pitcher, who in 1903 would host the president at Yellowstone National Park. He concludes the chapter with the story of Bauman and the "goblin-beast." In both cases, the additions strengthen the chapters and give new dimensions to the writer's experiences.

Surprisingly, the two *Century* articles are sparsely illustrated. Indeed, "An Elk-Hunt at Two-Ocean Pass" is not illustrated at all—a rarity in the pages of the magazine. "In Cowboy Land" features three illustrations by Frederic Remington, but they are not of particular interest or beauty. Perhaps even more surprisingly, *The Wilderness Hunter* contains only twenty-four illustrations, none of great artistry. Prominent illustrators like Arthur B. Frost and Remington provide twenty "process" reproductions of drawings. The frontispiece, "The Death of the Grisly" by Frost, features Roosevelt in buckskin suit and fur cap, the smoke clearing from his barrel as he approaches the giant grizzly he has slain. "A Shot from the Verandah" by Henry Sandham shows Roosevelt in buckskin, surrounded by three sets of elk antlers, shooting a buck from the porch of the Elkhorn ranch house. The two drawings are close kin to the engravings in *Hunting Trips of a Ranchman* and *Ranch Life and the Hunting Trail*, for they create the same kind of celebrity figure we have seen in those two books. Even in the deluxe limited edition, produced to accord with the Medora edition of *Hunting Trips of a Ranchman*, however, the illustrations tend to be two-dimensional, vaguely drawn, and untextured. The only Remington included, "Splitting the Herd," dates from 1885; none of the three magazine illustrations appears in the book. There are four photographs, including one by Roosevelt called "A Successful Shot," which shows a white goat lying dead in the rocks above the viewer, but these give the appearance of amateur snapshots.

The illustrations of *The Wilderness Hunter* exemplify larger movements in the graphic arts of the 1890s. First, the technology of photography improved rapidly toward the close of the century, and as a result amateur photographers could cover a landscape with their handheld Kodaks. Second, photography revolutionized magazine and book illustration in the 1890s. Photographs could be reproduced on a sensitive plate and printed without the use of engraving. The printing became known as the halftone plate, and it was already in use in the 1880s. As shown by the nature essays of Muir and Burroughs, the *Century* was a leader in the new process, but toward the end of the 1890s Richard Watson Gilder lamented the overwhelming role of photographic illustration and the loss of wood engraving.[18] The illustrations of *The Wilderness Hunter* seem flat and untextured precisely because they are halftone reproductions, rather than engravings. The lines are not at all touched up by an engraver, and the technology of photographic reproduction is not yet capable of rendering the image with the sharpness of engraving.

By the time Roosevelt publishes his next outdoor book, *Outdoor Pastimes of an American Hunter* (1905), photography is the sole means of illustrating his text. The book abounds in photographs, most of which are taken by his hunting companions Philip K. Stewart, Alexander Lambert, and W. Sloan Simpson. In the second edition of the book, published in 1908, Roosevelt adds two chapters and some twenty photographs. Between 1901 and 1908, half a dozen chapters appear as articles in *Scribner's Magazine*, and they are all illustrated by the amateur photographs of Roosevelt's friends.[19] While such snapshots convey immediacy and authenticity, they are far removed from the artistry of the *Century* engravings. Roosevelt evokes the rise of photography in chapter 5, "A Shot at a Mountain-Sheep":

In addition to being a true sportsman and not a game-butcher, in addition to being a humane man as well as keen-eyed, strong-limbed, and stout-hearted, the big-game hunter should be a field naturalist. If possible, he should be an adept with the camera; and hunting with the camera will tax his skill far more than hunting with the rifle, while the results in the long run give much greater satisfaction. Wherever possible he should keep a note-book, and should carefully study and record the habits of the wild creatures, especially when in some remote regions to which trained scientific observers but rarely have access. If we could only produce a hunter who would do for American big game what John Burroughs has done for the smaller wild life of hedgerow and orchard, farm and garden and grove, we should indeed be fortunate. Yet even though a man does not possess the literary faculty and the powers of trained observation necessary for such a task, he can do his part toward adding to our information by keeping careful notes of all the important facts which he comes across. Such note-books would show the changed habits of game with the changed seasons, their abundance at different times and different places, the melancholy data of their disappearance, the pleasanter facts as to their change of habits which enable them to continue to exist in the land, and, in short, all their traits. A real and lasting service would thereby be rendered not only to naturalists, but to all who care for nature. (*Works* 3:8–9)

This remarkable paragraph was originally published in the "Introductory" chapter of Roosevelt's *The Deer and Antelope of North America* (1902).[20] It reveals a distinct shift in sensibility and identity, from still-hunter to field naturalist. The rifle is replaced by the camera, and Roosevelt's surprising claim that the camera demands more skill than the rifle rings true.

The paragraph registers the shift toward the field naturalist most personally by invoking the name of John Burroughs. As in the dedicatory letter to "Oom John," Burroughs stands for the literary naturalist *par excellence*. His place is not wilderness but the domesticated, agricultural places of rural America, and his quarry is the "smaller wild life," especially the birds. Roosevelt invokes Burroughs as a model for the writer of hunting essays and stories—that is, a model for himself. For of course Roosevelt is exactly the "hunter who would do for American big game what John Burroughs has done for the smaller wild life," and *Outdoor Pastimes of an American Hunter* is the fourth attempt he makes at "doing" for the charismatic megafauna.

Burroughs models literary writing about nature, featuring photographic accuracy and keen observation. Roosevelt humbly represents himself in the second half of the paragraph, since the keeping of notebooks is one of his own habits, as are the particular facts he tends to record. Both *The Wilderness Hunter* and *Outdoor Pastimes of an American Hunter* are his most ambitious outdoor books, presenting a combination of natural history and hunting narrative for all of the large ungulate and predatory mammals of North America.

Outdoor Pastimes of an American Hunter marks the apex of Roosevelt's growth as a conservationist. While he mentions the national forest reserves in *The Wilderness Hunter* and in Boone and Crockett anthologies such as *American Big-Game Hunting*, the idea of wilderness preservation becomes Roosevelt's major theme in *Outdoor Pastimes*. The book recapitulates Roosevelt's writing in the early twentieth century, and the second half reveals his emergence as a leading voice for conservation. The first three chapters reprint four *Scribner's* articles from 1901 and 1905. Chapters 4–8 focus on ungulates, especially those of the deer family, and they reprint five revised chapters from *The Deer and Antelope of North America*, adding the narrative "A Shot at a Mountain-Sheep." In chapter 9, "Wilderness Reserves; the Yellowstone Park," Roosevelt revises short essays from the Boone and Crockett collections *American Big-Game Hunting* and *Trail and Camp-Fire*, and he adds an important account of his western trip with Burroughs and Muir in 1903. Chapter 10, "Books on Big Game," is similarly a redaction and expansion of earlier work, and again Burroughs and Muir loom large in his discussion. Chapter 11, "At Home," is an original essay, clearly inspired by Burroughs and devoted to the protection and preservation of birds. Chapter 12, "In the Louisiana Cane-Brakes," reprints a *Scribner's* essay of 1908, while chapter 13, "Small Country Neighbors," reprints a *Scribner's* essay of 1907.

The summary of chapters suggests that *Outdoor Pastimes* is principally a compilation of occasional writings by a busy politician, but by bringing together his outdoor essays written between 1893 and 1908, Roosevelt advances the theme of wilderness preservation in an important new way. In addition, he summarizes his own developing ideas of preservation and his shift from hunter to naturalist. Many of the chapters contain references to the need for wildlife refuges, which in the context of hunting he calls "game reserves." For example, in the chapter on the mule deer, Roosevelt notes that "the numbers are diminishing, and this process can be arrested only by better laws and, above all, by a better administration of the law. The national government could do much by establishing its forest reserves as game reserves, and putting in a sufficient number of forest rangers, who should be empowered to prevent all hunting on the reserves. The State governments can do still more" (*Works* 3:38). He continues the paragraph by appealing to citizens' interests. The local economy would benefit from well-enforced game laws and the resulting visits of "men who come from the great cities remote from the mountains in order to get three or four weeks' healthy, manly holiday" (39). In addition, the local ranchers and farmers would be able to hunt, enjoying "the pleasantest and healthiest of all out-of-door pastimes"; otherwise, he warns, the hunt will become the pastime of the wealthy alone.

Roosevelt adds another argument in the chapter on "The Wapiti, or Round-Horned Elk." He appeals to the reader's sense of the elk's nobility and calls the "needless butchery" of the species "criminal" (73). He then notes that "excellent people who protest against all hunting, and consider sportsmen as enemies of wild life, are ignorant of the fact that in reality the genuine sportsman is by all odds the most important factor in keeping the larger and more valuable wild creatures from total extermination." Roosevelt calls for "some middle ground . . . between brutal and senseless slaughter and the unhealthy sentimentalism which would just as surely defeat its own end by bringing about the eventual total extinction of the game. It is impossible to preserve the larger wild animals in regions thoroughly fit for agriculture; and it is perhaps too much to hope that the larger carnivora can be preserved for merely aesthetic reasons. But throughout our country there are large regions entirely unsuited for agriculture, where, if the people only have foresight, they can, through the power of the State, keep the game in perpetuity" (73–74). Thus Roosevelt seeks to reconcile the competing needs of nature and culture by finding a middle ground between ethical extremes.

The somewhat wistful mention of wilderness aesthetics returns at the end of the "Wapiti" chapter, and Roosevelt clearly shows that hunting big game affects the writer's sense of place. Even though some of his best elk hunts took place in the Rocky Mountains, he argues that "all really wild scenery is attractive" and that "the true hunter, the true lover of the wilderness, loves all parts of the wilderness, just as the true lover of nature loves all seasons." Even "the fantastic desolation of the Bad Lands, and the endless sweep of the brown prairies, alike have their fascination for the true lover of nature and lover of the wilderness who goes through them on foot or on horseback." Roosevelt's appositions reflect some distinctions among hunter, lover of wilderness, and lover of nature, but they also suggest that the three terms are nearly synonymous. He reinforces the similarities by describing his own ranch on the Little Missouri:

> As for the broken hill-country in which I followed the wapiti and the mule-deer along the Little Missouri, it would be strange indeed if any one found it otherwise than attractive in the bright, sharp fall weather. Long, grassy valleys wound among the boldly shaped hills. The basins were filled with wind-beaten trees and brush, which generally also ran alongside of the dry watercourses down the middle of each valley. Cedars clustered in the sheer ravines, and here and there groups of elm and ash grew to a considerable height in the more sheltered places. At the first touch of the frost the foliage turned russet or yellow—the Virginia creepers crimson. Under the cloudless blue sky the air was fresh and cool, and as we lay by the camp-fire at night the stars shone with extraordinary brilliancy. (76)

By focusing on the season and its aesthetics, Roosevelt assumes a balanced identity including the hunter, the lover of wilderness, and the lover of nature. Although the place is a "broken hill-country," it reveals its beauties to the patient observer who appreciates its variety of sights. Even the fresh, cool air seems to strike a balance between the extremes of summer and winter.

Roosevelt develops the theme of wilderness preservation most extensively in chapter 9, "Wilderness Reserves; the Yellowstone Park." Originally published in the "Introductory" chapter of *Deer and Antelope of North America*, the first five paragraphs recur to the ideas expressed in the other chapters taken from that work. Still, the opening sentence is itself a remarkable statement: "The most striking and melancholy feature in connection with American big game is the rapidity with which it has vanished" (85). Roosevelt forcefully argues that the process of extinction must be reversed by "every believer in manliness and therefore in manly sport, and every lover of nature, every man who appreciates the majesty and beauty of the wilderness and of wild life" (86). The gendering of the nature lover is obvious, as it is in all of Roosevelt's outdoor books. But more important, especially given the cultural context within which he was writing, is his foresight in arguing for wilderness and wildlife. He broadens the appeal to a larger audience than wilderness hunters, and he likewise broadens the protected species to include "all the living creatures of prairie and woodland and seashore" (86).

The broadening of audience leads Roosevelt to argue that wilderness and wildlife preservation are "essentially a democratic movement." He relates wise game laws and strict enforcement to "the interests of the people as a whole, because it is only through their enactment and enforcement that the people as a whole can preserve the game and can prevent its becoming purely the property of the rich, who are able to create and maintain extensive private reserves" (87). In addition, he argues that the hunting ethic of "true sportsmen" requires that they follow the game laws for seasons and bag limits, practicing moderation and restraint. Finally, he once again points to the market hunter as the worst enemy of wildlife populations.

The five paragraphs, written in 1901, do not stem only from Roosevelt's experiences as a ranchman and hunter, nor are they abstract, philosophical reflections on the place of nature in twentieth-century America. Rather, they both mirror and participate in the larger cultural conversation about the place of nature in a modernizing, urban America. In part they reflect the controversial movement toward establishing national forests, begun in 1891 by the Forest Reserve Act and President Benjamin Harrison's executive order setting aside thirteen million acres of western watersheds, and extended in 1897 by President Grover Cleveland with the executive order setting aside over twenty-one million acres in thirteen western preserves. In addition, they bespeak Roosevelt's two-year tenure as governor of New

York, during which he investigated the state Fisheries, Forest and Game Commission and lobbied the state legislature for stricter enforcement of laws protecting the forests and wildlife.[21] In all likelihood they allude to his acquaintance with the work of John Muir, whose important essays "The American Forests" and "The Wild Parks and Forest Reservations of the West" were published in the *Atlantic* in August 1897 and January 1898 and then reprinted in *Our National Parks* (1901).[22] They certainly reflect his close relationship with Gifford Pinchot, as does the last paragraph in the section on wilderness reserves. There Roosevelt argues that the reserves "are, and should be, created primarily for economic purposes" (89), but he broadens Pinchot's economic utilitarianism by asserting that they should also be kept in a "state of nature . . . for the sake of preserving all its beauties and wonders unspoiled by greedy and short-sighted vandalism" (89–90).

If the first part of "Wilderness Reserves; the Yellowstone Park" shows how Roosevelt's writing actively engages the cultural discourses of the day, the second part openly avows his debt to Burroughs. He calls the Yellowstone Park "the best possible object-lesson as to the desirability and practicability of establishing such wilderness reserves" (90) and then proceeds to narrate his April 1903 journey to Yellowstone with Burroughs. The narrative runs more than fifteen pages, and the clear purpose is to represent the great wealth of wildlife inhabiting the park. A band of several hundred pronghorn antelope occupy the border area, "almost literally in the streets" of Gardiner, Montana. Mule deer, whitetail deer, and bighorn sheep are likewise numerous and "tame," allowing the president to ride his horse or walk within eighty yards of them. A few days later, the president and Burroughs spend four hours counting great herds of elk, estimating that they have some three thousand in sight at one time (95). Roosevelt recounts how he would run up to the herds on horseback: "One band in particular I practically rounded up for John Burroughs, finally getting them to stand in a huddle while he and I sat on our horses less than fifty yards off" (96). In addition to the abundance of ungulates, Roosevelt notes the presence of predators like the coyote, cougar, and golden eagle. He also describes the many songbirds, especially the western meadowlark and the water ouzel (American dipper). The birds allow him to pass on compliments to his elders: "No bird escaped John Burroughs's eye; no bird note escaped his ear. . . . John Muir's description comes nearest doing [the water ouzel] justice" (102). He treats the stories of brazen park bears in humorous fashion (104–6), concluding that some literary naturalist should spend a year at Yellowstone and study the habits of the wildlife there: "A man able to do this, and to write down accurately and interestingly what he has seen, would make a contribution of permanent value to our nature literature" (106).

Burroughs appears in three other chapters of *Outdoor Pastimes of an American Hunter.* In "Books on Big Game," he is once again the model of literary skill in nature writing. Roosevelt laments that the books by big-game hunters "have not produced a White or Burroughs" and then exclaims, "What could not Burroughs have done if only he had cared for adventure and for the rifle, and had roamed across the great plains and the Rockies and through the dim forests, as he has wandered along the banks of the Hudson and the Potomac!" (111). Toward the end of the chapter, he writes this one-sentence paragraph: "Though not hunting books, John Burroughs's writings and John Muir's volumes on the Sierras should be in the hands of every lover of outdoor life, and therefore in the hands of every hunter who is a nature-lover, and not a mere game-butcher" (120). Burroughs ranks as America's principal literary naturalist, with Muir close beside him.

In the chapter "At Home," Roosevelt attempts to emulate Burroughs by writing about nature that is near at hand and available. He focuses on the birds of Long Island and Washington, D.C., noting the changes in the birds of the capital since Burroughs first wrote about them in *Wake-Robin* (128–30). Nature occupies a familiar domestic place, featuring seashore and woods walks with the family, a shooting range at Sagamore Hill, ponies and horses for the children, and a pet badger named Josiah. Of course, Roosevelt promotes the manly, soldierly virtues, claiming that such pastimes as riding and shooting counteract the "rather overcivilized, modern industrial life" and are a matter of "national ethics" (137). The final chapter of the second edition, "Small Country Neighbors," is similar in focusing on the birds and small mammals of Sagamore Hill, the White House, and the Roosevelts' retreat at Pine Knot in Albemarle County, Virginia. Burroughs visits Roosevelt at all three places, serving as a standard by which

Roosevelt measures his birding abilities.[23] Finally, in both chapters Burroughs is the implied standard for Roosevelt's descriptions of nature in his home places.

If "Oom John" is Roosevelt's exemplary literary naturalist, in the slim volume *Camping and Tramping with Roosevelt* (1907), Burroughs portrays President Roosevelt as a preternaturally energetic literary naturalist, combining diverse interests and abilities.[24] The first section of the book reprints the pamphlet *Camping with President Roosevelt*, originally published in 1906. Burroughs narrates the journey to Wyoming and the two-week camping expedition with Roosevelt in the spring of 1903. Along the way, he tells some of the same stories Roosevelt recounts in *Outdoor Pastimes of an American Hunter*. For example, he tells of the elk roundup and of viewing the three thousand elk across an open landscape near Tower Falls (42–45). But where Roosevelt summarizes, Burroughs expands for humorous and human effect. In narrating the round-up, the sixty-six-year-old tenderfoot becomes the object of laughter: "Now and then the President, looking back and seeing what slow progress I was making, would beckon to me impatiently, and I could fancy him saying, 'If I had a rope around him, he would come faster than that!'"

Burroughs takes care to represent the president as a naturalist rather than a hunter. Twice Roosevelt leaves camp to spend a day alone in the wilderness, stalking elk and mountain sheep so as to "feel the old sportsman's thrill without the use of firearms" (50). Early in the essay, Burroughs scornfully notes the newspaper reports that Roosevelt intended to hunt in the Yellowstone Park, but he quotes him directly on the matter: "The President said, 'I will not fire a gun in the Park; then I shall have no explanations to make.' Yet once I did hear him say in the wilderness, 'I feel as if I ought to keep the camp in meat. I always have.' I regretted that he could not do so on this occasion" (6–7). As the premier literary naturalist of the day, Burroughs exercises his authority in defending the president's hunting trips, citing his roles as a naturalist, preservationist, and writer (7). In addition, he details the mutual interest the two men take in birding. Episodes involving the Townsend's solitaire and the pygmy owl demonstrate the president's enthusiasm for identifying a new species, and Burroughs notes that "I think the

President was as pleased as if we had bagged some big game. He had never seen the bird before" (40).

In the second section of the book, "President Roosevelt as a Nature-Lover and Observer," Burroughs represents Roosevelt as a "rare combination of the sportsman and the naturalist" (80). He details his visit to Sagamore Hill and the identification of a black-throated green warbler (81–82), and that anecdote leads him to discuss other difficult warblers and vireos that Roosevelt identifies at the White House and Pine Knot. He uses such anecdotes to show how the discriminating Roosevelt notes the similarities between the calls of a catbird and the western chewink (85), the yellow-billed and black-billed cuckoos (86), and the night heron and little green heron (87–88). Sight is as important as sound. Inspecting the ground nest of a sparrow, Roosevelt corrects his earlier identification:

> "That is not the nest of the grasshopper sparrow, after all; those are the eggs of the song sparrow, though the nest is more like that of the vesper sparrow. The eggs of the grasshopper sparrow are much lighter in color—almost white, with brown specks." For my part, I had quite forgotten for the moment how the eggs of the little sparrow looked or differed in color from those of the song sparrow. But the President has so little to remember that he forgets none of these minor things! His bird-lore and wood-lore seem as fresh as if just learned. (93)

Although Burroughs is America's recognized authority on bird lore, he becomes a modest student to the president.

The reversal of roles applies most readily to the subject of big game. Burroughs receives a book from the president in which "he had referred to himself as my pupil. Now I was to be his pupil" (94). Roosevelt instructs Burroughs by using artworks that are misrepresentations of nature. First, he shows him a small bronze elephant by the French sculptor Antoine-Louis Barye, asking him if he sees anything wrong with it. By comparing it with another sculpture, by a Japanese artist, Roosevelt demonstrates that the French sculptor misrepresents the movement of the animal, which paces rather than trots (95). Second, he shows Burroughs an error in Remington's drawing of a pronghorn antelope, "Bringing Home the Game," which

illustrates chapter 9 of *Ranch Life and the Hunting Trail*. Remington mis-
places the eye of the animal, and Roosevelt demonstrates the mistake by
comparing the drawing to a mounted head (96–97).[25] Taking down a copy
of *The Deer Family* (1902), Roosevelt shows two captions that misidentify
the illustrated animals (98). In two other sly asides, Burroughs notes that
Roosevelt has ready evidence that the nature fakers, especially Reverend
William Long, are laughable frauds (98, 103–4).

Burroughs's fundamental strategy in *Camping and Tramping with Roosevelt* is to present the president as an exemplar of accurate observation,
truthful reporting, and sympathetic affiliation. In all of these ways, Roosevelt becomes a version of Burroughs himself. Just as important as the
mutual admiration, however, is the way in which the two writers fashion a
place of nature. "Oom John" and "the President" become celebrity naturalists, supporting one another in their writings and instructing their readers
in ways of knowing nature. They stand against the nature fakers, but they
also stand together, occupying a specific and powerful place in American
culture during Roosevelt's presidency. In their essays and books, they follow
the strategy of orchestrated promotion employed by the *Century* and other
magazines. In closing *Camping and Tramping with Roosevelt*, Burroughs
compares the president's nature writing to a bird song "in volume and
continuity, in tuneful, voluble, rapid outpouring and ardor, above all in
skillful and intricate variation of theme" (110). The description blends
culture and nature, to be sure, but it is more remarkable for blending the
sounds of Roosevelt, Burroughs, and the birds. If Burroughs gives Roosevelt
a way of developing his nature writing beyond the confines of the hunting
narrative, Roosevelt opens the aging Burroughs to an exuberant, masculine encounter with wilderness. For both, the literal and figurative place of
nature takes on heightened significance, becoming that "best of places."

6 *The Divine Abyss*
Burroughs and Muir in the New Century

Three Celebrities

  In an editorial titled "The President's Trip and the Forests," Robert Underwood Johnson reflected on President Roosevelt's famous tour of the western wonders in the spring of 1903: "The President's trip is also likely to induce more of his countrymen to see the magnificent scenery of the West. He was happy in his choice, among his companions, of two such lovers and interpreters of nature as John Burroughs and John Muir, writers whose preaching of the gospel of outdoor life is one of the sanest influences of our berated times" (*Century* 66:635). Burroughs accompanied the president for two weeks in Yellowstone National Park, but the text of *Camping and Tramping with Roosevelt* does not fully record Burroughs's sense of the journey to the West. In long "journal-letters" to his literary confidante, Clara Barrus, Burroughs expands on his experiences, a principal aspect of which is his own astonishing celebrity. From the first, he seems genuinely astounded by observing his proximity to greatness: "Think of me, the Henpecked, riding down Pennsylvania Avenue in a carriage beside the President of the U.S., and treated by him as a friend and equal! When I lived in Washington I saw, a few times, the President in his carriage, but in my wildest dreams I never saw myself beside our chief magistrate. Nearly all the honors I have had in the world have been thrust upon me, and have been a surprise" (*Life and Letters* 2:60). At the University of Chicago, Burroughs was amazed to hear professors describe his visit as "an honor to the University," leading him to exclaim, "How strange and absurd it all seems to me—no honor at home, and overwhelmed with it abroad!"

Despite the self-deprecating tone, Burroughs was clearly pleased to find himself a prophet with honor in the West. In St. Paul, Minnesota, for instance, he occupied the presidential carriage alongside Roosevelt, claiming that "in his presence my light is invisible to the crowd," but then "at one point, as we were moving slowly along, I saw a big banner borne by some girls, with this inscription, 'The John Burroughs Society.' The girls pushed their way through the crowd and timidly and hurriedly handed me a big bouquet." The incident pleased Burroughs so much that he included it in the 1906 volume *Camping with President Roosevelt*, specifically admitting to negligence on his part: "I fear I have not to this day thanked the Monroe School of St. Paul for that pretty attention" (11). In another aside to Barrus, he writes that a man at the Minneapolis dinner sat down by him and said that Burroughs "had probably given more pleasure to more people in that gathering than had Roosevelt" (*Life and Letters* 2:62).

Much of Burroughs's celebrity was owing to the marketing of his works by Houghton Mifflin Company. A key moment in this strategy appears to have occurred in 1887, when Oscar Houghton visited Mary E. Burt's classroom in Chicago and observed her teaching Burroughs's *Pepacton* to thirty-six enthusiastic pupils (*Life and Letters* 1:285). As Eric Lupfer has shown, the firm established several institutional programs for building readerships, especially targeting schools. Collections of Burroughs's essays were created specifically for the Riverside Literature Series and the Riverside School Library, titles that were never part of the Riverby edition. Mary Burt's editions called *Birds and Bees* (1887) and *Sharp Eyes* (1888), for instance, sold well over two hundred thousand copies between 1896 and 1907.[1] In a August 20, 1907, letter to the editors of Houghton Mifflin, Burroughs asks if his "nature faker" rival, Reverend William J. Long, is a serious rival in the schools: "Is there any truth in the assertion of Wm J. Long that his books have crowded mine out of the schools? I should like to know the exact facts." The editors apparently replied with a comparison between the two, for the archive contains a rough tally of sales pasted to Burroughs's letter: *Birds and Bees* had its greatest sales in 1902, a total of 17,596, averaging 11,000 copies sold annually for 1904–6; *Sharp Eyes* had its greatest sales in 1906, a total of 16,285, averaging 11,500 copies sold annually for 1904–6.[2]

Burroughs himself edited a third volume, *Squirrels and Other Fur-Bearers*, which was published by the Riverside Press in 1900 as one of their "Outdoor Books."[3] A fourth volume, *Studies in Nature and Literature*, appeared in 1908 in the Riverside Literature Series, edited by Ada L. F. Snell.[4] In addition to the Houghton Mifflin books, Burroughs allowed Burt to edit *Little Nature Studies for Little People from John Burroughs*, published by Ginn and Company in 1895.[5]

In addition to these specific titles by Burroughs, the Houghton Mifflin Company records indicate that several anthologies designed for use in public schools were available in the early twentieth century. In a letter to Burroughs dated September 25, 1912, for example, the editorial staff writes that "in the Seventh Reader that we now have under way we are planning to make a special study of your writings and of you as an author. We expect to have a full page portrait of yourself, a biographical sketch, and several of the best selections from your writings for children of this grade. In this group of selections we should like very much to have a letter from you addressed to the school children of the country, which will tend to arouse greater interest in nature. If you will kindly accommodate us by writing such a letter, we believe that it would give a great deal of pleasure and would be very much appreciated by the thousands of school children who will use the book."[6] Another successful anthology, *In American Fields and Forests* (1909), included works by Thoreau, Burroughs, Muir, Olive Thorne Miller, Dallas Lore Sharp, and Bradford Torrey, selling thousands of copies in the Ohio Teachers' Reading Circle and other continuing education courses ("Reading Nature Writing" 37–58). The anonymous writer of the preface to *In American Fields and Forests* claims, with some justification, that the book is "something more than a collection of essays. It represents both the literary outcome and the literary inspiration of an important movement in American life, — that which has come to be known as the Nature Movement" (vi). In addition, the preface asserts that Burroughs is "the man who probably more than any other one writer is responsible for the present interest in nature-study" (v). The cumulative evidence suggests, then, that Burroughs enjoyed enormous popularity and exercised considerable influence in American schools from the 1880s through the first decade of the twentieth century. As Ralph Lutts puts it, "the children who tossed flowers at John Burroughs on his way to Yellowstone represented a legion" (*Nature Fakers* 29).

As we saw in the previous chapter, a significant aspect of the Yellowstone trip is how Roosevelt employs Burroughs's celebrity status as "Oom John" to sanction his own role as a naturalist. Burroughs confides in the journal-letter of April 1 that Roosevelt's secretary, William Loeb, "says that it was his suggestion that my going with the President be made public when it was, so as to check the idea that it was to be a hunting trip; and that the news had that effect with the newspapers. The yellow journals so exaggerate his hunting trips, and make so much capital out of them, that the President is greatly annoyed. But I have disarmed the yellow journals, so you see I have been of some use already" (*Life and Letters* 2:60). Loeb's concerns were no doubt well founded, but Roosevelt had already enjoyed some fortuitous ill fortune as a hunter in November 1902. His efforts to kill a black bear in Mississippi ended in his refusal to shoot a 235-pound runt tied to a tree, and eventually the work of *Washington Post* cartoonist Clifford Berryman led to the ubiquitously cuddly teddy bear.[7]

Roosevelt's trip to Yellowstone effectively places him on Burroughs's side in the nature-fakers dispute. Burroughs had published the controversial article "Real and Sham Natural History" in the March 1903 *Atlantic*, and the polemical tone of the essay aroused considerable commentary. In a private letter to George Bird Grinnell, whose *Forest and Stream* had attacked Burroughs, Roosevelt takes his Boone and Crockett friend to task: "I am closing a most pleasant holiday which I have spent with John Burroughs here in the Yellowstone. We have been watching the game and the birds. We have been riding and walking and going on snowshoes. No man with any knowledge of the woods or outdoor life can be with him and not be struck by the accuracy of his observations and by the extreme care he takes not to put down as a matter of fact anything of which he is not sure (with some of his matters of opinion quite apart from matters of fact any man of course may differ, which I do). Tomorrow I go back to the political world, to fight about trusts and the Monroe Doctrine and the Philippines and the Indians and the Tariff; but today I allow myself the luxury of calling your attention to this attack in the *F&S* upon one of the Americans to whom good Americans owe a debt, an attack which I am sure you would not have permitted in the paper if you had been fully aware of what it contained."[8] Roosevelt easily negotiates between presidential concerns and literary debates, applying to both his sense of authoritative certitude and proving himself as useful to Burroughs as Burroughs was to him.

The trip to Yellowstone cemented the relationship between Roosevelt and Burroughs, so that ever after the elder writer functioned as Roosevelt's "Oom John." But even though the two writers supported one another throughout the nature-fakers controversy, the debate ultimately had an adverse effect on Burroughs's writing. To be sure, Burroughs had always been interested in the truthful and accurate representation of nature in his literary criticism, and he had often taken poets and writers to task for their inaccurate or fanciful recording of the natural world. Already in the 1873 essay "Birds and Poets," for example, Burroughs discriminates between accurate and inaccurate literary representations of birds and their songs (*Writings* 3:3–48). During the nature-fakers dispute, however, Burroughs becomes intensely dogmatic, one-sided, and negative in treating questions of accurate observation and animal psychology, and his polemics cause him to become more and more mechanistic and deterministic in his representations of wildlife. In *Ways of Nature* (1905), for instance, Burroughs devotes an entire book to questions of the literary treatment of nature. But that does not satisfy him. As the August 20, 1907, letter to Houghton Mifflin implies, he feels he must answer every response, opinion, or claim that differs somewhat from his own. The volume *Leaf and Tendril* (1908) features several essays on observation and true perception, but in the middle of the book Burroughs includes four essays, filling over a third of the volume, that rehash the nature-fakers debate. "Straight Seeing and Thinking" (*Writings* 15:101–23) takes several newspaper editors to task for disagreeing with him, while "Human Traits in the Animals" (125–53) softens some of his most mechanistic arguments concerning the behavior of animals. At the beginning of the fourth essay, "The Reasonable but Unreasoning Animals," Burroughs addresses the reader, "There is to me a perennial interest in this question of animal instinct *versus* intelligence, and I trust my readers will pardon me if I again take the question up" (177). But by 1908, when Jack London attacked the "unholy alliance" of Roosevelt and Burroughs in the pages of *Collier's Weekly*, most readers would hardly wish to indulge Burroughs in his savaging of Reverend Long and the other nature fakers.[9]

Roosevelt's friendship had an adverse effect upon Burroughs and his writing. That is not to cast blame upon Roosevelt, though it is the case that during his presidency he maintained a constant correspondence with Burroughs concerning the nature fakers, in essence making Burroughs into his stalking-horse, since he did not feel that the president should engage in such a public debate. The friendship itself, however, encouraged Burroughs to assume a very public role as the self-appointed defender of truthful writing among literary naturalists. On the trip to Yellowstone, moreover, Burroughs gained the full sense of his own celebrity and therefore took on the full role of cultural authority. Roosevelt enabled him in this perception.

These subtle entanglements come out clearly in a May 5, 1903, letter that Burroughs wrote to Roosevelt. The two had parted company on April 25, Roosevelt heading for the Grand Canyon and Yosemite, Burroughs for Spokane, Washington. Burroughs's long letter from Spokane recapitulates several aspects of the relationship between himself and the president. First, he remarks that "the schools here have shown me much attention" and that "my books are much better known and appreciated than I had expected." Then he moves directly to the topic most of his admirers want to hear about:

> The people are never tired of hearing me talk about you and our trip into the Park, and I am never tired of talking of these subjects. Indeed, I am beginning to suspect that they think I can talk of little else. The fact is, the people everywhere are eager to have a near and full view of a public man who has the qualities of heart and head with which you are so richly endowed. I think it quite certain that no president of this generation has touched the real American mind so closely. And you are going to continue to touch it, and to win it, because you are not playing a game in politics, but are seriously doing the work of the nation. (*Life and Letters* 2:66–67)

Burroughs links his own celebrity to Yellowstone and Roosevelt, and he portrays himself as the privileged insider who can represent the unseen virtues of the "public man," offering his listeners a "near and full view" of Roosevelt's inner qualities. That is precisely the stance Burroughs takes in narrating the Yellowstone trip in *Camping and Tramping with Roosevelt*. Here, we see him discovering the viewpoint and trying it on for size.

The size is large, as is the public man. In the very next paragraph of the letter, Burroughs connects Roosevelt to another great friend who gave the young writer a "near and full view" of larger-than-life personality:

> How I wish Whitman could have witnessed your career! Whitman wrote with his eye upon the West—its larger standards, its greater candor and charity and optimism, its robust manliness, and fervent Americanism; and in you, I think, he would have seen the type of the man he sung and predicted,—a man who can meet the highest on equal terms, and does not hold himself above the humblest. (67)

The irony of the passage lies in the large perspective Burroughs takes. Like Whitman, he has his eye on the West, and in that respect Roosevelt resembles both of his predecessors. But largeness is not the quality Burroughs's eye exhibits over the next five years. Instead, his vision narrows, becomes savagely polemical, and applies overexacting standards. Still, Roosevelt certainly inspires him with a profound belief in the larger standards of the West and the future. The president embodies Whitman's "Standard of the Natural Universal," announced in Burroughs's first book, *Notes on Walt Whitman, as Poet and Person*. Like that standard, the Whitmanian "type" is large, vital, and orbic, analogous to the Earth. In addition, the public man creates a corresponsiveness between himself and the common people, for he can meet the highest or the humblest as an equal.

As if to seal the analogy between the president and the poet, Burroughs apologizes to Roosevelt for writing so directly: "In saying these things to you, Mr. President, I have no purpose of praising you to your face—I am only putting down upon paper my daily thought about you. I hear everywhere the expressions of personal affection for, and solicitude about, you such as I have never before heard expressed toward any president save Lincoln" (67). By invoking Lincoln, Whitman's ideal public man, Burroughs makes Roosevelt into his own modern ideal. Even though he represents himself as the simple scribe of his "daily thought," Burroughs exercises a large literary power in naming Whitman and Lincoln as the proper analogies for Roosevelt's "type." All three are associated with the West as a place of "larger standards," and Burroughs especially focuses on the democratic and generous-spirited "robust manliness" favored by Roosevelt in his ranching and hunting books.

The missing name in this illustrious list is, of course, John Muir. It is a commonplace of Muir criticism that Roosevelt's three-day camping trip with him in Yosemite was instrumental in giving Roosevelt the "quickened conviction that vigorous action must be taken speedily, ere it should be too late" (*Life and Letters of John Muir* 2:411). The story goes that Muir successfully separated Roosevelt from his political entourage and spent three days doing "forest good in talking freely around the campfire."[10] Robert Underwood Johnson even claims that Muir taught the president to "get beyond the boyishness of killing things" (*Remembered Yesterdays* 388). Roosevelt's accomplishments in the presidency are not in question; by the time he left office in 1909, he had set aside some 148 million acres of land in national forests and created eighteen national monuments, including the North Sigillaria Petrified Forest (December 8, 1906), Grand Canyon (January 11, 1908), and Muir Woods (January 9, 1908). But Muir's influence on Roosevelt's presidential decisions should not be exaggerated.[11]

Neither Roosevelt nor Muir provides anything like a detailed account of their time together. Roosevelt includes one paragraph on the visit in his *Autobiography*, sketching the itinerary and two nights outdoors, praising Muir along with the natural beauty of the Sierras, and noting that Muir knew little about the birds beyond the water ouzel (*Autobiography* 321–22). In a May 19 letter to his wife Louie, Muir says that he "had a perfectly glorious time with the President & the mountains" and that he "never before had so interesting hearty & manly a companion." The letter to Louie, along with Roosevelt's May 19 letter to Muir, shows that the two men camped three nights together, in the Mariposa grove of sequoias, in a snowstorm among silver firs near Glacier Point, and in the valley by Bridal Veil Falls.[12]

The skeleton account gains some flesh in another of Burroughs's journal-letters to Barrus. On July 10, 1903, President and Mrs. Roosevelt visited

Burroughs for several hours at Slabsides, and Burroughs summarizes the president's remarks as they walked, "talking vigorously," from the West Park dock on the Hudson River to the writer's retreat: "He complained that Muir could not help him with the birds; that he hardly knew the most common ones. And then he told me frankly, rubbing up against me as he spoke, that he found Muir and his books less charming than he found me and my books. I think I could see where the rub was—both are great talkers, and two great talkers, you know, seldom get on well together. Now he finds me an appreciative listener, and that suits him better" (*Life and Letters* 2:69). Though somewhat self-serving, Burroughs's remark regarding Muir's lack of knowledge about the birds rings true. As for books, Muir had published only two volumes by 1903. But Burroughs is clearly offering his own interpretation when he conjectures that the two talkers did not "get on well together." The passage bespeaks the combination of friendship and rivalry that marked the relationship between Muir and Burroughs from the very beginning.[13]

The Divine Abyss

Although Roosevelt plays a significant role for both Muir and Burroughs during his presidency, the two writers are even more significant for one another in the early twentieth century. Muir introduces Burroughs to three important geological places of the West in 1909: the North Sigillaria Petrified Forest, the Grand Canyon, and Yosemite Valley. The result is as fundamental to Burroughs's late writing as Roosevelt's covert support of his nature-fakers polemics, but Muir's influence is much more profound and salutary than Roosevelt's. Clara Barrus narrates the story of Burroughs's 1909 trip out west in two articles, "With John o' the Birds and John o' the Mountains" in the *Century* of August 1910, and "In the Yosemite with John Muir" in *The Craftsman* of December 1912. She repeats the narrative in chapter 24, "Journeying with Muir," in *Life and Letters of John Burroughs*.[14] At the end of February, Burroughs met Muir at Adamana, Arizona, in company with Barrus and her friend Harriet Ashley. On February 26–27, the party toured the North Sigillaria Petrified Forest, discovered by Muir in

1906, and described by Burroughs as "ruins of a foreworld. One could not look without emotion upon these silicified trunks of trees that had been growing millions of years ago" (*Life and Letters* 2:119). A train took them to the Grand Canyon, where they stayed several days and descended the Bright Angel Trail by mule. In early March, Muir returned to Martinez, while the Burroughs party moved into a bungalow in Pasadena, California. In late April, Muir took the group to Yosemite for a five-day visit. He tried to convince them to stay longer, but they had free passage to Hawaii, provided by the Hawaiian Promotion Committee, and left California in early May.[15]

From first to last, Muir delighted in teasing Burroughs. When the party arrived at Adamana on the night train, Burroughs called out, "I'm here, with two women in my wake. Are you surprised?" To which Muir replied, "Surprised, mon, that there are only two. There were a dozen or two hovering round in Alaska, tucking him up with rugs, running to him with a flower or a bird-song. Oh, two is a very modest number, Johnnie—but we will worry through with them somehow" (*Life and Letters* 2:118). Muir clearly directed part of his response to Barrus and Ashley, rather than to Burroughs, and it seems that he often exaggerated his hectoring style for the ladies' entertainment. In another episode, Muir noticed Burroughs writing during lunch in the Petrified Forest. "By Jove!" he jibed, "A chile's amang us takin' notes. I'll have to mind how I discoorse!" (*Century* 80:524). In a third episode, the group arrived at the Grand Canyon in the morning, and Muir jeered at the easterners for wanting to breakfast before viewing the divine abyss. When they finally approached the south rim, Muir turned and waved his arms toward the canyon, shouting, "There! Empty your heads of all vanity, and look!" (*Century* 80:525).

In person and on paper, Muir always delights in lording it over Burroughs. He teases him, bullies him, argues with him, contradicts him, and dismisses him. His tone ranges from good-natured to spiteful, and the topics run from glaciation to Burroughs's appetite for uncooked wafers. The serious subject, however, is always geology, and at times Muir's bullying seems quite serious. When Burroughs asks Muir about the petrified trees, and how they managed not to decay and disappear, Muir replies, "Oh, get a primer of geology, Johnnie!" (*Life and Letters* 2:119). In Yosemite, Burroughs asks

Muir honest questions about glaciation and erosion, and Muir responds, "Aw, Johnnie, ye may tak' all your geology and tie it in a bundle and cast it into the sea, and it wouldna' mak' a ripple!" (*Craftsman* 23:326). No wonder, then, that when Barrus remarks to Ashley, "To think of having the Grand Canyon, and John Burroughs and John Muir thrown in!" Burroughs retorts, "I wish Muir *was* thrown in, sometimes, when he gets between me and the canyon" (*Life and Letters* 2:122).

Though Muir could seem like an obstacle, Burroughs continually sought his advice and approval as he drafted the essays inspired by the western trip. He began writing "The Divine Abyss," his essay on the Grand Canyon, while the group took up residence in Pasadena, California, in March 1909 (2:124). By September 3, 1909, Burroughs had submitted the essay to the *Century*, and he wrote Muir that he had also "nearly finished a short sketch of Yosemite." "Don't wrinkle your nose now," he adds, "I am only trying to give my readers the impressions these grand scenes made upon me. I have at least one advantage over you in the matter; these scenes have become almost commonplace to you, while we saw them with fresh wondering eyes" (Muir Papers Reel 18). In his response on September 23, Muir takes exception to the idea that Yosemite would ever be "commonplace" in his eyes: "Yosemite commonplace because one has learned something about it! Why Johnnie, Johnnie, Johnnie! You must come again and get rid of such atheism." In November, Muir writes that he will gladly read Burroughs's Yosemite article, but he warns him that Burroughs has "not studied it—only glanced at it." Two weeks later, on November 26, Muir writes Burroughs that he has read the Yosemite manuscript "and can make nothing of it. You saw so little of the Valley, I think you had better say little or nothing of its origin. Leave it all out is my advice. It can do no good to yourself or others to try to tell what you have had no chance to know." He advises Burroughs to avoid "this haphazard brazen ignorance," and tells him, "You must be growing daft." Burroughs responds in kind, though more gently: "I really think, dear Muir, that your Scotch pig-headedness stands as much in your way in the pursuit of truth, as my 'brazen ignorance' stands in my way." In the rest of the letter, Burroughs takes issue with Muir's insistence on the primary role of glaciers in forming Yosemite, and more broadly he asks if it is not possible that other forces, such as water and wind, might have been at work both before and after the Ice Age. Muir writes back on December 14, insisting that Burroughs return to Yosemite for further studies, since "only long plodding observation in the field yields anything worth while, at least to poor dreamy wanderers as dull as I." He tells his friend, "I'd be delighted to have you in spite of your rank Scotch stubbornness; and you might perhaps learn to endure or ignore my glacial behavior and airs." Two weeks later, Burroughs replies, thanking Muir for his letters and telling him, "You are a dear anyway, Scotch obstinacy and all, and I love you, though at times I want to punch you or thrash the ground with you."

By March 31, 1910, Burroughs had consulted with Bailey Willis of the U.S. Geological Survey and revised his Yosemite article, and he writes to Muir that he has "cut out much of the matter that displeased you." He mentions that Robert Underwood Johnson of the *Century* has deleted much of the geology from "The Divine Abyss," too, though Johnson's reasons were editorial rather than scientific. Finally, he tells Muir that he has yet a third paper, "Through the Eyes of the Geologist," that will appear in the May issue of the *Atlantic*. For the third or fourth time, moreover, Burroughs invites Muir to come stay with him, so that they may "make excursions to the Catskills and to the Shawangunk and study the Silurian and Devonian rocks."[16] Despite the sore-headed exchanges, the two old writers remain fast friends.

The correspondence shows that Muir treats Burroughs in much the same way Burroughs treats the nature fakers. That is, the authoritative "professor" condescends to the ignorant, misinformed, somewhat obtuse student. Both Muir and Burroughs are really amateurs, no matter how much they know about mountains and birds. Neither one can truly claim absolute knowledge and authority for the way he interprets nature. So Burroughs's response to Muir's condescending authority is instructive: he does not bow down to Muir and accept his view; instead, he takes it as the opening for further studies on his own. Muir had told him to get a primer of geology, and that is precisely what Burroughs did. In an October 20, 1909, letter to Clara Barrus, Burroughs hints at the ways in which Muir's influence can be measured:

I have had the luck to find Muir's Sierra studies (1874) in the Overland
Monthly. . . . They are real studies and worthy of preservation in book form.
Muir's humor crops out here and there—the Muir we know. Their thorough-
ness, and their searching logic surprise me; but he rides his ice hobby till the
tongue of the poor beast hangs out and he is ready to lie down and give up
the ghost. It is like the work of a great detective working up an obscure case.
It has modified some of my own views, and I have re-written the last part of
my [Yosemite] paper, and will send it to you to copy after a while. I think I
will write Muir and state my objection to his views. (*Life and Letters* 2:134)

Here Burroughs generously acknowledges the scientific and literary value
of Muir's earliest essays on the Sierra, but he also recognizes the "ice hobby"
as a unitary explanation for all geological phenomena. The passage balances admiration and resistance, but Burroughs is willing to revise his own
work in the light of his friend's earlier studies. Most profoundly, Muir makes
Burroughs into a student of nature again, enabling him to escape his own
authority in relation to the nature fakers and questions of animal reason
versus animal instinct.

Muir's skills as a teacher certainly leave much to be desired, and ultimately Burroughs finds Muir more a Thoreauvian goad than an Emersonian sage. Still, Muir and the three western sites combine to inspire
Burroughs in the years from 1909 to 1912. The thirteen essays of *Time and
Change* provide ample evidence of Muir's influence and the profound
response Burroughs had to the science of geology. Even before the 1909
trip, in fact, Burroughs had turned toward the themes of geology for new
material.

Leaf and Tendril

In the preface to *Leaf and Tendril* (1908), Burroughs compares the tendril
to the papers "in which I have groped my way in some of the great problems,
seeking some law or truth to cling to." The "law or truth" does not refer
to Burroughs's strict standards for "Straight Seeing and Straight Thinking"
or "The Reasonable but Unreasoning Animals." The first nine essays in

the volume are associated with the "leaf" of the title, which symbolizes Burroughs's nature sketches. The "tendril," on the other hand, refers to the last four essays in the volume: "The Grist of the Gods," "The Divine Soil," "An Outlook upon Life," and "'All's Right with the World.'"[17] In these four speculative essays, Burroughs broaches the philosophical theme of creative energy and the immanent God of nature, a theme that occupies him in much of his remaining career. Rather than focus on the materialism and mechanism of animal instincts, the elderly writer turns to a broader view of the universe as vitalistic, charged with the energy of Whitmanian transformation and promotion that he associates with the theory of evolution.

In "The Grist of the Gods" (*Writings* 15:199–213), Burroughs looks at the soil underfoot and, like Whitman, finds that it is divine. He begins the essay by meditating on the common dust and our common sayings about it—"earth to earth, and dust to dust" and "as common as dust." Characteristically, Burroughs sees the commonplace reality of the earth as most vital and significant, for "the common, the universal, is always our mainstay in this world" (199). The soil may be lowly and common, but "it is the grist out of which our bread of life is made, the grist which the mills of the gods, the slow patient gods of Erosion, have been so long grinding—grinding probably more millions of years than we have any idea of" (200). The process of erosion figures a universe of vital change, and the synecdoche allows Burroughs to exclaim, "The soil underfoot, or that we turn with our plow, how it thrills with life or the potencies of life!" (203). Because Burroughs's evolutionary perspective embraces geologic time in the essay, he imagines that "much of our soil has lived and died many times, and has been charged more and more during the geologic ages or eternities with the potencies of life" (207). Science, especially the science of geology, leads him to see "the vitality, spirituality, oneness, and immanence of the universe" (211). Despite our limited powers of perception—limits that may in fact be for our own good—we are immersed in divinity, so that Burroughs exults, "The babe in its mother's womb is not nearer its mother than we are to the invisible sustaining and mothering powers of the universe, and to its spiritual entities, every moment of our lives" (212).

The language and imaginative power of "The Grist of the Gods" owe much to Whitman's poetry. Toward the end of the essay, Burroughs quotes from section 3 of "Song of Myself":

> There was never any more inception than there is now,
> Nor any more youth or age than there is now,
> And will never be any more perfection than there is now,
> Nor any more heaven or hell than there is now. (40–43)

This passage leads Whitman to celebrate the "procreant urge of the world" (45), and that is clearly the vitalistic sense of the common dust that Burroughs, too, celebrates. In addition to the quotation, he alludes several other times to Whitman's poems, including the "perpetual transfers and promotions" from section 49 of "Song of Myself" and finding "underfoot the divine soil" from "Starting from Paumanok" (21). But in addition to the direct influence, Whitman's earthy spirituality affects Burroughs's vision, in which "gross matter seems ever ready to vanish into the transcendental" (209).

In "The Divine Soil" (15:215–40), Burroughs begins with the title from Whitman, and at the end of the first section he quotes a long evolutionary passage from section 44 of "Song of Myself," beginning with the line "I am an acme of things accomplish'd, and I an encloser of things to be" (1148–69). But in addition to Whitman, other thinkers exercise an important influence on Burroughs's thinking. Carlyle's contempt for the "gospel of dirt," Darwin's theory of the origin of humankind, Thomas Huxley's polemical defense of Darwinism, and Charles Lyell's *Principles of Geology* (1835) combine to bolster Burroughs's vision of "the creative energy" (215–19). In seven more sections of the essay, he considers the vitalism of the universe as a hierarchical and orderly evolutionary process, and he always roots the abstract and cosmic in a concrete and local sense of place: "Every place is under the stars, every place is the center of the world. Stand in your own dooryard and you have eight thousand miles of solid ground beneath you, and all the sidereal splendors overhead" (224). Burroughs's understanding of evolution is rudimentary, but his questions and concerns are profound. In the final section of the essay, he faces his own limits as a questioner: "I know I am trying to say the unsayable. I would fain indicate how human and hopeless is our question, 'What for?' when asked of the totality of things" (239). Human limits do not apply to the universe, which he renames "the Infinite." Burroughs's cosmic sense of nature as embodying the ineffable is Emersonian in its paradoxes, for the Infinite cannot be defined as merely one thing. For the writer, the figure of speech rings clear: "The Unspeakable will not be spoken" (240).

Given the indeterminacy of Burroughs's resolution in "The Divine Soil," we might expect as much despair as hope in his old-age writings. That expectation is partly met, but in many respects Burroughs maintains a sense of humility and reverence for the unspeakable mysteries he confronts. The last two essays of *Leaf and Tendril* express a limited optimism. In "An Outlook upon Life," for instance, the old man practices his own call for "natural humility of spirit" (241) and finds that "we share in the slow optimistic tendency of the universe, that we have life and health and wholeness on the same terms as the trees, the flowers, the grass, the animals have, and pay the same price for our well being, in struggle and effort, that they pay" (245). Speaking from his own experience, he praises the simple life "because I have lived it and found it good" (260). Such a life brings us closer to the everyday, common, and near-at-hand, and that proximity leads Burroughs, in "All's Right with the World," to conclude, "It is only by regarding man as a part of nature, as the outcome of the same vital forces underfoot and overhead that the plants and the animals are, that we can find God in the world" (267). Science, moreover, "has showed man that he is not an alien in the universe . . . but that he is the product of the forces that surround him" (280). For Burroughs, science and the evolutionary power of nature replace traditional religious belief and the power of creeds.

Reading Time and Place

The essays of *Leaf and Tendril* suggest that Burroughs, past seventy, was preparing to open a new chapter in his writing career. Just at that point, moreover, he opened himself to the West in a new way, making himself available to the influence of his voluble and argumentative friend, John Muir. Goaded in large measure by Muir, Burroughs opened himself to a large new perspective on the natural world and humanity's place in it. And this imaginative opening leads to some of his finest essays in *Time and Change* (1912).

Muir's role is most important in "The Divine Abyss" and "The Spell of the Yosemite," the two essays Burroughs submitted to the Scotsman's criticism. In contrast to Muir's insistence on the primary role of glaciation in forming the earth's surface, Burroughs argues that the "gentle and beneficent forces" of erosion by streams, rivers, rainfall, wind, and sun are fundamental to forming both the Grand Canyon and Yosemite Valley. In both cases, these gentle forces cause the place to have "a certain friendly and familiar look" ("Divine Abyss" 57). Likewise, Burroughs's own Catskills reveal the gentle forces, despite the effects of the ice age: "The great ice sheet rubbed us and ploughed us, but our contours were gentle and rounded aeons before that event" (65). The argument runs directly counter to Muir's theory of "the universality of the ice sheet."[18] Burroughs's language, moreover, suggests that his own cosmic geological vision is closely related to the kind of pastoral landscapes he favors in his other essays. The last ice sheet pulled back from the mountains of New York and New England some twelve thousand years ago, but Burroughs is looking back far beyond that date. His view reaches back millions of years, and as it does so it becomes a vision of domesticity and fertility: "It seems to take millions of years to tame a mountain, to curb its rude, savage power, to soften its outlines, and bring fertility out of the elemental crudeness and barrenness. But time and the gentle rains of heaven will do it, as they have done it in the East, and as they are fast doing it in the West" (59).

From the first paragraph of "The Divine Abyss," Burroughs figures the landscape of the Southwest as a geological textbook, "crying aloud to be read," and a knowledge of geology as necessary for the visitor: "The book of earthly revelation, as shown by the great science, lies wide open in that land, as it does in few places on the globe. Its leaves fairly flutter in the wind, and the print is so large that he who runs on the California Limited may read it. Not being able to read it at all, or not taking any interest in it, is like going to Rome or Egypt or Jerusalem, knowing nothing of the history of those lands" (39). Even though the trope of the "book of nature" is commonplace,

Burroughs owes Muir's *Studies in the Sierra* a debt in his use of the figure. In "The Origin of Yosemite Valleys," for instance, Muir remarks that "the greatest obstacle in the way of reading the history of Yosemite valleys is not its complexity or obscurity, but simply the *magnitude of the characters* in which it is written" (Gifford 1:410). In "Ancient Glaciers and Their Pathways," he notes that the history of the gigantic glaciers of the Sierra is "indelibly recorded in characters of rock, mountain, canyon, and forest; and, although other hieroglyphics are being incessantly engraved over these, 'line upon line,' the glacial characters are so enormously emphasized that they rise free and unconfused in sublime relief, through every after inscription, whether of the torrent, the avalanche, or the restless heaving atmosphere" (420). In "Glacial Denudation," Muir argues that "the ice-sheet of the glacial period, like an immense sponge, wiped the Sierra bare of all pre-glacial surface inscriptions, and wrote its own history upon the ample page" (436–37), and he begins "Post-Glacial Denudation" by stating, "When Nature lifted the ice-sheet from the mountains she may well be said not to have turned a new leaf, but to have made a new one of the old" (445).

Muir's particular turn on the "book of nature" trope is the palimpsest, and he employs that figure repeatedly in his essays on glaciers. The earliest example occurs in "Yosemite Glaciers," the article he published in the *New York Daily Tribune* on December 5, 1871. In that specific instance, he figures Yosemite as a "great open book" whose "granite pages have been torn and blurred." Like a castaway book that he finds under the snow, the Yosemite landscape presents outer pages that are "mealy and crumbly" and inner pages that are "well preserved" and "easily readable." As he develops the figure in the *Overland Monthly* articles on the Sierra Nevada, the landscape-text is constantly being overwritten, so that the geologist must become adept at reading the inner pages or subtext, the nearly invisible record of the past. Thus "we may read the letter-pages of friends when written over and over, if we are intimately acquainted with their handwriting, and under the same conditions we may read Nature's writings on the stone pages of the mountains" ("Glacial Denudation" 437). Burroughs's opening paragraph in "The Divine Abyss" echoes Muir by suggesting that in the Southwest the "book of earthly revelation . . . lies wide open in that land," whereas in the landscapes of the East "the books are closed and sealed, as it were, by the enormous lapse of time" (39). For both Muir and Burroughs, geology is the science of reading landscapes, and for both the landscape of the West is an open book. But there are significant differences in their interpretations of the figures they hold in common.

Burroughs's allusion to the Bible, in the "Divine Abyss," indicates that he considers the landscape-text relatively easy to interpret. The original verse appears in the prophetic book of Habakkuk: "And the Lord answered me: 'Write the vision; make it plain upon tablets, so he may run who reads it" (2:2). Burroughs turns the biblical source in two ways. By including the "California Limited" train, he gives the ancient verse a humorous modernity in the industrial twentieth century, and by reversing the main and subordinate clauses of the Bible verse, he emphasizes the fundamental and necessary speed with which the modern reader moves through the landscape.

Muir's palimpsest, on the other hand, stresses the difficulty of reading the landscape and the necessary patience of the reader. Even in Yosemite, the landscape is difficult to read, not because of complexity and obscurity but because of the grand scale of the characters, and Muir notes that he has spent "five years' observation in the Sierra" in order to interpret the landscape-text (Gifford *Life and Letters* 1:410). Through most of the Sierra except the high summits, external agents such as torrents, earthquakes, avalanches, forests, and fields have combined to dim, erase, cover, and confuse the geological record, and only the "laborious student can decipher even the most emphasized passages of the original manuscript" (437).

Muir's sense of the time and labor necessary for reading the geological text may well account for his bullying attitude toward Burroughs during the 1909 tour. Muir begins his essay "The Grand Cañon of the Colorado," published in the *Century* in November 1902, by meditating on the conditions of the modern tourist:

Happy nowadays is the tourist, with earth's wonders, new and old, spread invitingly open before him, and a host of able workers as his slaves making everything easy, padding plush about him, grading roads for him, boring tunnels, moving hills out of his way, eager, like the devil, to show him all the kingdoms of the world and their glory and foolishness, spiritualizing travel for him with lightning and steam, abolishing space and time and almost everything else. Little children and tender, pulpy people, as well as storm-seasoned explorers, may now go almost everywhere in smooth comfort, cross oceans and deserts scarce accessible to fishes and birds, and, dragged by steel horses, go up high mountains, riding gloriously beneath starry showers of sparks, ascending like Elijah in a whirlwind and chariot of fire.[19]

This paragraph fairly drips with sarcasm, directed most bitingly at the modern tourist who insists first of all on comfort and speed. Muir's religious language is at its most Calvinistic here, and it tellingly echoes Hawthorne's satirical sketch, "The Celestial Railroad," in depicting the devilish ease with which industrialized Americans attain a "spiritualized" access to nature.

Muir's scorn springs from his fear that the railroads will change the wilderness. He sees "loss as well as gain" in the extension of the railroads into great natural places such as Yosemite, the sequoia groves, Yellowstone, Alaska, and the Grand Canyon. But even though he mounts a prophetic sermon of fear, he finds consolation in the very size of "a few big places beyond man's power to spoil—the ocean, the two icy ends of the globe, and the Grand Cañon" (790). The irony of Muir's list is devastating to us today; our power to spoil the few big places appears limitless. In his own day, however, he can look at "those trains crawling along through the pines of the Cocanini Forest and close up to the brink of the chasm at Bright Angel" and be "glad to discover that in the presence of such stupendous scenery they are nothing. The locomotives and trains are mere beetles and caterpillars, and the noise they make is as little disturbing as the hooting of an owl in the lonely woods" (790–91). The key to his optimistic perspective is scale: the Grand Canyon reduces human power to the level of insects; the vastness of the place swallows industrial noise, reducing it to the faint hooting of an owl.

Tourists thus embody a double threat. Without any power of their own, they bespeak the industrial might of American culture and symbolize the potential of culture to convert big places into "belts of desolation." In addition, they lead toward the "disenchantment" of the wilderness by making it too accessible, too easy, too "smooth" (790). In "The Divine Abyss," Burroughs also catches the threat of tourism at the very moment he describes the canyon for the first time: "A friend of mine who took a lively interest in my Western trip wrote me that he wished he could have been present with his kodak when we first looked upon the Grand Cañon. Did he think he could have got a picture of our souls? His camera would have shown him only our silent, motionless forms as we stood transfixed by that first view of the stupendous spectacle. Words do not come readily to one's lips, or gestures to one's body, in the presence of such a scene" (47). The friend's "kodak" figures the tourist's mechanically framed view of the Grand Canyon, a view that is as interested in the spectators as in the spectacle. Burroughs contrasts his own silent, motionless reverence to "the smoking and joking tourists sauntering along in apparent indifference, or sitting with their backs to the great geologic drama" (47). Though the rhyme belittles the tourists, Burroughs does not dwell on their inability to appreciate the wonder of the "glorious spectacle" (47), preferring to enumerate the proper responses of other visitors—tears, terror, joy, awe. He focuses on the sublime aesthetic dimensions of the place, and his essay expresses the limited, disenchanting power of the tourist, not the larger threat of industrial culture.

Burroughs and Muir are most alike in their sense of time and change, which exert far more power than any human forces. Both writers dwell upon the magnitude of the Grand Canyon, its architectural forms, and the opulence of its color effects. Both describe being there as a spiritual experience. Burroughs calls the canyon "some greater Jerusalem . . . like a vision, so foreign is it to all other terrestrial spectacles, and so surpassingly beautiful" (48). Muir praises the "wild architecture" of the place and names it "nature's own capital city" (794), and as he describes the vast gulf of the divine abyss he employs his favorite metaphor: "It seems a gigantic statement for even nature to make, all in one mighty stone word, apprehended at once like a burst of light, celestial color its natural vesture, coming in glory to mind and heart as to a home prepared for it from the very beginning. Wildness so godful, cosmic, primeval, bestows a new sense of earth's beauty and size. Not even from high mountains does the world seem so wide, so like a star in glory of light on its way through the heavens" (796).

Burroughs's descriptions are ultimately more measured than Muir's, less given to hyperbole and purplish glory. After narrating the group's descent into the canyon along the Bright Angel Trail, he offers a characteristically meditative summary:

> It is always worth while to sit or kneel at the feet of grandeur, to look up
> into the placid faces of the earth gods and feel their power, and the tourist
> who goes down into the cañon certainly has this privilege. We did not bring
> back in our hands, or in our hats, the glory that had lured us from the top,
> but we seemed to have been nearer its sources, and to have brought back
> a deepened sense of the magnitude of the forms, and of the depth of the
> chasm which we had heretofore gazed upon from a distance. Also we had
> plucked the flower of safety from the nettle danger, always an exhilarating
> enterprise. (69)

Burroughs's appreciation depends upon proximity, upon coming nearer to the sources of glory. The strategy of the description differs markedly from Muir's, which builds its hyperbolic gigantism through repetition and panoramic vision. Burroughs does not expand his perspective toward the planetary, in which the earth becomes "like a star in glory of light on its way through the heavens." Instead, his eye is sharpened and deepened, his ear awakened, leading in the final paragraph to three pastoral discoveries: "We had left plenty of ice and snow at the top, but in the bottom we found the early spring flowers blooming, and a settler at what is called the Indian Gardens was planting his garden. Here I heard the song of the cañon wren, a new and very pleasing bird-song to me. I think our dreams were somewhat disturbed that night by the impressions of the day, but our day-dreams since that time have at least been sweeter and more comforting, and I am sure that the remainder of our lives will be the richer for our having seen the Grand Cañon" (70). Like Muir, Burroughs finds in the divine abyss a new sense of death, for death certainly haunts his dreams. Burroughs embraces the danger of this new sense, but finally he plucks the flower of safety from the nettle.

If Burroughs's insistent pastoralism leads inexorably to that final statement of safe and certain riches, we must insistently recall Muir's final palimpsest in the closing paragraph of "The Grand Cañon of the Colorado." The landscape of the Grand Canyon leads him to reflect on "the natural beauty of death," for the place inseparably combines destruction and creation. The wild landscapes are "derived from other landscapes," and "each wonder in sight becomes a window through which other wonders come to view." Muir brings the potentially bewildering series of openings — a geological *mise en abime* — to a close, and the closure is as conventionally pastoral as Burroughs's final sentence. Likening the whole canyon and adjacent plateau to "a grand geological library — a collection of stone books covering thousands of miles of shelving tier on tier conveniently arranged for the student," Muir plunges into the contents of the library: "And with what wonderful scriptures are their pages filled — myriad forms of successive floras and faunas, lavishly illustrated with colored drawings, carrying us back into the midst of the life of a past infinitely remote. And as we go on and on, studying this old, old life in the light of the life beating warmly about us, we enrich and lengthen our own" (808–9). The layers of fossil records reveal "a past infinitely remote," and they are constantly being eroded as the canyon grows wider and deeper. But this vision of death and destruction leads Muir to celebrate the life of both the remote past and the near present, and it ultimately leads him to the continuing enrichment and lengthening of our own lives.

In "The Spell of the Yosemite," Burroughs steps directly into Muir's home territory, but his pastoral strategies make claims of their own. Rather than open the essay with geology, Burroughs focuses on a robin, "the first I had seen since leaving home." The bird "struck the right note, he brought the scene home to me, he supplied the link of association. . . . Where the robin is at home, there at home am I" (71). The image recalls that of the canyon wren with which Burroughs closes "The Divine Abyss," and in both cases the bird domesticates a potentially foreign wildness. Thus the opening paragraph of "The Spell of the Yosemite" strikes a balance between the wild and the domestic, the sublime and the pastoral: "But many other things helped to win my heart to the Yosemite — the whole character of the scene, not only its beauty and sublimity, but the air of peace and protection, and of homelike seclusion that pervades it; the charm of a nook, a retreat, combined with the power and grandeur of nature in her sternest moods" (71). As in "Wild Life about My Cabin," from *Far and Near* (1904), Burroughs's ideal place is a combination, "a tract of wild land, barely a mile from home, that contained a secluded nook and a few acres of level, fertile land shut off from the vain and noisy world of railroads, steamboats, and yachts by a wooded, precipitous mountain" (*Writings* 13:132).

This mixed landscape differs strongly from Muir's way of reading Yosemite in the two *Century* articles of August–September 1890. As we saw in chapter 3, in "The Treasures of the Yosemite," Muir repeatedly describes the sublime beauty of Yosemite Valley in order to stage the tension between permanence and evanescence, portraying the place as endangered rather than protected. That is also the way Muir describes the Sierra Nevada as the Range of Light—in the "Treasures" article, in the first chapter of *The Mountains of California* (1894), and in the third chapter of *Our National Parks* (1901). But when he describes Yosemite Valley in *Our National Parks*, Muir sounds remarkably like the Burroughs of 1909:

Nowhere will you see the majestic operations of nature more clearly revealed beside the frailest, most gentle and peaceful things. Nearly all the park is a profound solitude. Yet it is full of charming company, full of God's thoughts, a place of peace and safety amid the most exalted grandeur and eager enthusiastic action, a new song, a place of beginnings abounding in first lessons on life, mountain-building, eternal, invincible, unbreakable order; with sermons in stones, storms, trees, flowers, and animals brimful of humanity. During the last glacial period, just past, the former features of the range were rubbed off as a chalk sketch from a blackboard, and a new beginning was made. Hence the wonderful clearness and freshness of the rocky pages.[20]

In this passage Yosemite presents a mixed landscape, but it is not Muir's characteristic palimpsest. The valley is a spiritual retreat, exhibiting the "unbreakable order" of nature. The glacial text is clear and fresh, easy to read. Complications arise from the play of solitude and "charming company," a phrase that could refer to "God's thoughts," to the wildlife and mountains, or to the many tourists. As Dan Philippon argues, the essays of *Our National Parks* bring together Muir's dual concerns of conservation and tourism, and Yosemite is clearly the central place for combining the two.[21] Thus Muir opens the volume by asserting that "the tendency nowadays to wander in wildernesses is delightful to see. Thousands of tired, nerve-shaken, over-civilized people are beginning to find out that going to the mountains is going home; that wildness is a necessity; and that mountain parks and reservations are useful not only as fountains of timber and irrigating rivers, but as fountains of life" (1). Like Burroughs, Muir mingles wildness and domesticity in a subtle representation of a pastoral landscape. And Muir manages to control his sarcasm as he considers the "charming company" of tourists: "Even the scenery habit in its most artificial forms, mixed with spectacles, silliness, and kodaks; its devotees arrayed more gorgeously than scarlet tanagers, frightening the wild game with red umbrellas, — even this is encouraging, and may well be regarded as a hopeful sign of the times" (2). The "new song" of Yosemite describes both the place and Muir's representation of it.

Burroughs's descriptions of Yosemite Valley echo Muir in several ways. He figures the valley as "some vast house or hall carved out of the mountains" (71), and the place casts a "spell of the brooding calm and sheltered seclusion." Passing the tumult of the Merced River and tumble of boulders, the visitor enters "the ordered, the tranquil, the restful, which seems enhanced by the power and grandeur that encompass them about." For Burroughs, Yosemite Valley is marked by a "gentle rural and sylvan character," and the landscape repeatedly evokes peace, seclusion, privacy, and enchantment (72). In contrast to the "touch of the sylvan and pastoral" in Yosemite, the Grand Canyon is "like a vision of some strange colossal city uncovered from the depth of geologic time" (75–76). "I do not think," remarks Burroughs, "one could ever feel at home in or near the Grand Cañon."

As in his description of the Grand Canyon, Burroughs sees Yosemite Valley as enacting a "great geologic drama" (79), but when he considers the geology of Yosemite, he directly contradicts Muir's glacial doctrines. In *Our National Parks*, Muir remarks that "no other mountain chain on the globe, as far as I know, is so rich as the Sierra in bold, striking, well-preserved glacial monuments, easily understood by anybody capable of patient observation," and Yosemite is "the brightest and clearest of all" (84). But even though Burroughs notes in his October 20, 1909, letter to Barrus that Muir's research is "like the work of a great detective working up an obscure case" and that "it has modified some of my own views, and I have re-written the last part of my paper" (*Life and Letters* 2:134), he does not embrace the glacial explanation. He argues that "the Sierra lies beyond the southern limit of the great continental ice-sheet of late Tertiary times, but it nursed and reared many local glaciers, and to the eroding power of these its Yosemites are partly due. But water was at work here long before the ice — eating down into the granite and laying open the mountain for the ice to begin its work. Ice may come, and ice may go, says the river, but I go on forever" (81). Burroughs gives Muir's glaciers partial credit, but he reserves the major force for "the still, small voice of the rain and the winds, of the frost and the snow, — the gentle forces now and here active all about us, carving the valleys and reducing the mountains, and changing the courses of rivers" (82). He ends the Yosemite essay by alluding to Bailey Willis, citing the authority of "the geologists of our day," who ascribe the main role in the formation of the landscape to water rather than to ice (82–83).

Despite these clear differences, Burroughs and Muir share a profound vision of time and change. Muir's glacial theory paradoxically leads to his sense of dynamic, vital change. At the close of the third chapter of *Our National Parks*, for example, he imagines an observer stationed atop Red Mountain or Mount Dana during the glacial period:

> An observer stationed here, in the glacial period, would have overlooked a wrinkled mantle of ice as continuous as that which now covers the continent of Greenland; and of all the vast landscape now shining in the sun, he would have seen only the tops of the summit peaks, rising darkly like storm-beaten islands, lifeless and hopeless, above rock-encumbered ice waves. If among the agents that nature has employed in making these mountains there be one that above all others deserves the name of Destroyer, it is the glacier. But we quickly learn that destruction is creation. During the dreary centuries through

which the Sierra lay in darkness, crushed beneath the ice folds of the glacial winter, there was a steady invincible advance toward the warm life and beauty of to-day; and it is just where the glaciers crushed most destructively that the greatest amount of beauty is made manifest. But as these landscapes have succeeded the preglacial landscapes, so they in turn are giving place to others already planned and foreseen. The granite domes and pavements, apparently imperishable, we take as symbols of permanence, while these crumbling peaks, down whose frosty gullies avalanches are ever falling, are symbols of change and decay. Yet all alike, fast or slow, are surely vanishing away. (96–97)

Like the close of "The Grand Cañon of the Colorado," this paragraph stresses the combination of destruction and creation—what Muir calls in the earlier essay "the natural beauty of death." Even though Muir imagines the "lifeless and hopeless" landscape of the Ice Ages, he also imagines "a steady invincible advance toward the warm life and beauty of to-day." As he gazes into the future, moreover, he confidently predicts that "Nature is ever at work building and pulling down, creating and destroying, keeping everything whirling and flowing, allowing no rest but in rhythmical motion, chasing everything in endless song out of one beautiful form into another" (97).

Burroughs could readily accept Muir's vitalistic sense of an evolving natural world. After all, he had already proposed just such a vision of time and change in the last essays of *Leaf and Tendril*. More important is the way in which Muir influences Burroughs to accept, in however qualified a manner, a spiritual dimension to the processes of nature. The geological scale of time leads Burroughs to meditate on cosmic forces, relating human life to processes on a much vaster scale, and this in turn leads him to write several short essays in *Time and Change*—"The Old Ice-Flood," "The Friendly Soil," "Primal Energies," and "Scientific Faith."

In all four of these essays, Burroughs develops the concept he calls the "scientific imagination." The first three essays might be called exercises in the geological imagination he first encountered in Muir. In "The Old Ice-Flood," for example, he notes that the idea of the prehistoric glaciers "so vastly transcends all our experience with ice and snow, or the experience of the race since the dawn of history, that only the scientific imagination and faith are equal to it. The belief in it rests on indubitable evidence, its record is written all over our landscape, but it requires, I say, the scientific imagination to put the facts together and make a continuous history" (*Writings* 16:161). He illustrates the point by telling how he shows Vassar undergraduates a boulder near Slabsides, clearly polished by a glacier, and explains to them that "the ice was at one time two or three thousand feet thick above the place where they now stand" (162). To the students it sounds "like a dream or a fable," because the vast scale of global time and change extends "quite beyond our horizon—beyond the reach of our mental apprehension" (163). Like Muir in Glacier Bay, Burroughs adopts a perspective that unites scientific knowledge and the imagination. In the second part of the essay, he uses the example of a glacial erratic, placed as a family monument at a neighboring farmer's house, in order to imagine "the flowing or the creeping of this old ice-sheet, so that it could transport large boulders hundreds of miles" (164), and he ends the essay with an image of a "river of ice" that could easily appear in Muir's glacial writings: "The old ice-sheet, or ice sea, flowed around and over mountains as a river flows around and over rocks. Where a mountain rose above the glacier, the ice divided and flowed round it, and reunited again beyond it. One may see all this in Alaska at the present time" (165).

The scientific imagination does not reduce nature to a mechanistic system; instead, as Burroughs puts it in "Scientific Faith," it "enhances the value or significance of everything about us that we are wont to treat as cheap or vulgar, and it discounts the value of the things far off upon which we have laid such stress." The scientific imagination focuses on the near-at-hand, tying us to the earth and making the "revolutionary revelation" that "the creative energy is working now and here underfoot, the same as in the ages of myth and miracle; in other words, that God is really immanent in his universe, and inseparable from it; that we have been in heaven and under the celestial laws all our lives, and knew it not" (179). Thus the concrete theme of the essay is the evolutionary "origin of man from some lower form" and the lingering inability of the "ordinary mind" to exercise "such a plunge into the past, and such a faith in the transforming power of the biological laws, and in the divinity that lurks in the soil underfoot and streams from the orbs overhead" (175).

In "Scientific Faith" and other essays in *Time and Change*, Burroughs shows that his is no ordinary mind. The idea of "creative energy" runs through meditations on the forces of erosion and the "evolution of the landscape, the evolution of the animal and vegetable kingdoms, the evolution of the suns and planets" (186). In "'The Worm Striving to Be Man'" and "'The Phantoms Behind Us,'" Burroughs imagines evolution as a mental and spiritual process, "the spiritualization of matter" (187). As the titles suggest, Emerson and Whitman provide the literary sensibility for Burroughs's scientific imagination, and his own sense of "the divinity that hedges us about" results from his perception of "the creative energy inherent and active in the ground underfoot not less than in the stars and nebulae overhead" (198–99). For Burroughs, that is to open his mind to "miracle in the new scientific sense" (211). His imagination stops only at the most vexing questions of origins: "What can we make of it all by way of concrete conception of what actually took place—of the visible, eating, warring, breeding animal forms in whose safekeeping our heritage lay? Nothing. We are not merely at sea, we are in abysmal depths, and the darkness is so thick we can cut it" (222). In "The Hazards of the Past," however, he imagines his previous existence in several different forms and periods, for evolution "gives us an outlook upon the past that is startling, and in some ways forbidding, yet one that ought to be stimulating and inspiring" (228). Burroughs is not sentimental about extinctions. The theme reinforces his wonderment at the fragility of human evolution, and it leads him to reflect on the ultimate fate of the human race—the "slow, insensible failure, through the aging of the planet, of the conditions of life that brought man here" (241).

Burroughs draws an extended set of large conclusions concerning the spirituality of nature in the final essay of the volume, "The Gospel of Nature." He represents nature as both divine and impersonal, hygienic but amoral. And yet nature rewards the balance of knowledge and appreciation: "the way of knowledge of Nature is the way of love and enjoyment, and is more surely found in the open air than in the school-room or the laboratory" (250). This is to be a nature-lover, not a scientific naturalist, though for Burroughs the ideal is to "enjoy understandingly" (251), and he preaches "the gospel of contentment, of appreciation, of heeding simple near-by things—a gospel the burden of which still is love, but love that goes hand in hand with understanding" (262). Nature is composed of "primal sanities, primal honesties, primal attraction," but it also exhibits "primal cruelty, primal blindness, primal wastefulness" (264). Burroughs's gospel is admittedly hard, and he emphasizes the indifference of nature much more than Muir does in his vision of universal destruction and creation, the "natural beauty of death." But if nature is not ultimately benevolent, it is nonetheless just, for it acts on a scale beyond our knowledge or sense of purpose. Thus Burroughs ends the book by relinquishing the conventional view of humanity as the apex of evolution, and in doing so he sounds most like Muir:

> I do not say that he is the end and aim of creation; it would be logical, I
> think, to expect a still higher form. Man has been man but a little while
> comparatively, less than one hour of the twenty-four of the vast geologic day;
> a few hours more and he will be gone; less than another geologic day like the
> past, and no doubt all life from the earth will be gone. What then? The game
> will be played over and over again in other worlds, without approaching any
> nearer the final end than we are now. There is no final end, as there was no
> absolute beginning, and can be none with the infinite. (273)

Burroughs as Literary Model

If John Muir goaded John Burroughs into a new phase of writing, marked by the growth of his scientific imagination, Burroughs also profoundly influenced Muir in the final phase of his writing career. Just as the essays of *Leaf and Tendril* suggest that Burroughs was already primed for Muir's influence, moreover, correspondence between Muir and his editors indicates that he was measuring himself against Burroughs by the time the two traveled to Alaska in 1899.

In the summer and autumn of 1897, Muir found himself in close contact with his friend Robert Underwood Johnson of the *Century* and Walter Hines Page, editor of the *Atlantic*. The correspondence with Johnson involved two essays, "The Alaska Trip" and "An Adventure with a Dog and a Glacier," eventually published in the August and September issues of the *Century*. Johnson made a strategic error by changing the title of the story from "Stickeen" and making cuts in the narrative without asking Muir's permission. In a July 16 letter, Muir agreed to the cuts but noted, "I hope however that in striving for artistic effect you will not blur the story." Johnson failed to notice that Muir was unhappy about his editorial work; after all, the two had plenty upon which they agreed, especially the work of the National Forest Commission.

But it was precisely the work of the commission that led to Muir's contracts with Houghton Mifflin Company. Charles Sprague Sargent became an intermediary between Muir and Walter Hines Page, encouraging the two to cooperate in publishing Muir's work. While Johnson was acting in a rather high-handed manner toward his author, Page was wooing him with charm and grace. Already in June 1897, Sargent helped bring Muir to the pages of the *Atlantic*, where his essay "The American Forests" would appear in August. By September 1897, Page was actively pressing Muir for magazine articles and promoting the plan of gathering the articles in book form for publication with Houghton Mifflin Company. In a letter of September 1, for example, Page uses the connection between the magazine, the book publishers, and John Burroughs as a way of persuading Muir to work with him:

> The greatest single compact body of American literature of permanent value that exists anywhere is put forth by this firm. This single fact gives the firm an advantage that no other one has in putting writings which have sufficient merit first alongside of this compact mass of permanent literature and finally into it—thus bringing about not simply such a sale of a book as can be made so long as it is a new publication, but in addition thereto such a continual nurture of it as a piece of literature as will keep it alive as long as it has any vitality whatever. I believe that Mr. Burroughs, for instance, has found great benefit of this kind by reason of the publication of his works by Messrs. Houghton, Mifflin, and Company. I do not mean of course to make any comparisons, but I cannot help thinking it doubtful whether, if he had pursued a different

course, he now would have the satisfaction of having a beautiful complete edition of his writings such as was issued by us last year.[22]

By the end of October, Muir had agreed to write articles on the parks and reservations for the *Atlantic*, and Page sealed the deal for book publication as well. In addition, he received Muir's verbal agreement to the plan for a book on Alaska. In order to mark the event, Page wrote to Muir on October 29, thanking him "very heartily . . . for the definite promise of these books" and sending him a gift: "The firm sends you, with its compliments, a set of the complete Burroughs, to show something of the excellence of their making of books. As for illustrations, they will be put in in the most artistic and effective fashion." In his final sentence, Page assured his new writer that "the two books on the Parks and on Alaska will not need any special season's sales nor other accidental circumstances: they'll be Literature!"

Muir remained silent about this new arrangement until December 6, when he wrote in reply to Johnson's letter of December 1. Johnson had been importuning Muir to undertake a new exploration of the interior of Alaska, especially the Klondike. But he was shocked to read Muir's words of December 6. The author was friendly but firm: the book rights of his *Atlantic* articles would remain with Houghton Mifflin, and he had also promised them the Alaska book. He complained that the *Century* had held "The Alaska Trip" for three years before finally publishing it, and his last essay on forestry had been rejected. In addition to these delays and rejections, he was very sorry that the story of Stickeen had been given a "vulgar catchy" title. Johnson replied diplomatically on December 14, and Muir did not break completely with the *Century*. Indeed, the magazine published "The Grand Cañon of the Colorado" in November 1902, and Johnson championed the preservation of the Hetch Hetchy Valley by publishing Muir's essay "The Endangered Valley" in January 1909 and *The Yosemite* in April 1912.[23]

Still, there is no doubt that Page was successful in wooing Muir away from the Century Company. The double effect is clear in *Our National Parks*, which compiles ten articles published in the *Atlantic*, beginning with the "American Forests" article of August 1897. In March 1909, Houghton

Mifflin published *Stickeen* as a slim volume; in October 1909, the company brought out an illustrated edition of *Our National Parks*. The first four months of 1911 saw four articles by Muir in the *Atlantic*, collected and published by Houghton Mifflin in June 1911 as *My First Summer in the Sierra*. In the last two months of 1912 and first two months of 1913, Muir once again published four articles in the *Atlantic*, which were collected and published by Houghton Mifflin in March 1913 as *The Story of My Boyhood and Youth*. In addition, the company published selections of Muir's work in its Riverside Literature Series (no. 247), and ultimately it published his posthumous works and several multivolume editions of *The Writings of John Muir*.[24]

Walter Hines Page's letters to Muir suggest strongly that Burroughs provided the model for Muir's late-blooming career: steady magazine publication of articles, followed by collections of essays in book form. Muir and Houghton Mifflin were expert in bringing the two publishing channels together in the work of his last years. Already in the September 3, 1909, letter to Muir, Burroughs himself encouraged his friend to keep working with words: "Are you making headway with your writing? The world wants all that harvest of yours thrashed out and made up into crisp, sweet loaves, such as you know how to make. I salute you in love and comradeship" (*Life and Letters* 2:132). By the time Muir was done, he might have "thrashed" Burroughs more than his own harvest of writing. But the new relationship with Houghton Mifflin was certainly fruitful. In his own lifetime Muir never reached the number of readers that Burroughs commanded, but his posthumous publications and twentieth-century career outstripped Burroughs by a wide margin. At this point, Walter Hines Page seems strangely prescient: by being included in the Library of America series, Muir's work has earned a place in "American literature of permanent value," but Burroughs's "beautiful complete edition" has been out of print for so long that it is difficult to find as a complete set anyplace.

The Place of Elegy

Affiliations

John Burroughs outlived nearly all his friends, and his direct reflections on those who died are often curiously brief, bordering on the perfunctory. On Christmas Day 1914, upon learning of John Muir's death, Burroughs writes telegraphically in his journal that it was "an event I have been expecting and dreading for more than a year." He calls Muir a "unique character—greater as a talker than as a writer" and says, "I shall greatly miss him" (*Life and Letters* 2:214–15). Writing two years later in response to an invitation from the University of Wisconsin, Burroughs expands on his honest sense of Muir:

> My affection and admiration for Muir were deep and genuine. When in his
> company I used to chafe a good deal under his biting Scotch wit and love of
> contradiction. He loved a verbal contest, which was, with him, only another
> form of the trial of grit which in his school days he used to cheerfully submit
> to when the boys, armed with whips, used to stand up before each other
> and lay on till one of them cried enough. As I never had that kind of Scotch
> discipline, I did not keenly enjoy this sort of diversion. But his heart was all
> right, only he liked too well to mask its real kindliness in this way.
>
> He was a genuine student and lover of nature, and he brought to us the
> message of the mountains as no other man has.
>
> In recently reading Emerson's Journals I was struck and pleased with the
> fact that he places John Muir in the list of what he called 'My men.' In this
> list the first is Thomas Carlyle, whom he first met in 1833, and the last is John
> Muir, whom he met in 1871. Muir's nature lore, and his striking characteris-
> tics were bound to make an impression upon Emerson. He met no 'mush of
> concession' when he met Muir. (*Life and Letters* 2:241)

Much of this letter seems written for possible quotation, as if Burroughs were hoping to be cited during the memorial service at Muir's alma mater. The first paragraph alludes to chapter 1 of Muir's autobiography, *The Story of My Boyhood and Youth* (1913), with its tales of the "fighting school" in Scotland. It also recalls Burroughs's struggles with Muir from 1899 to 1909, both in person and in letters. The second paragraph is a quotable one-liner. But the third paragraph runs deeply, for it is a rough draft for the digression on Muir in "Emerson and His Journals," the first essay in Burroughs's projected volume on Emerson and Thoreau.

Published posthumously as *The Last Harvest*, the Emerson-Thoreau book is Burroughs's last farewell to the "great neighbors" who came before him. By including Muir among them, he in effect includes him as one of *his* men. That is the sense of his final statements on Muir: "His philosophy rarely rose above that of the Sunday school, but his moral fiber was very strong, and his wit ready and keen. In conversation and in daily intercourse he was a man not easily put aside. Emerson found him deeply read in nature lore and with some suggestion about his look and manner of the wild and rugged solitude in which he lived so much" (*Writings* 23:24). This final assessment seems eminently intelligent and fair in several respects. It is true, for instance, that Muir's philosophy is not original or particularly deep, and as a writer he is often content to evoke the glory of God in nature. But his moral perspective regarding wilderness and its inhabitants is profound, and his writing style is often as witty as his speech. Moreover, Muir is tenacious, as any of his political opponents in the Hetch Hetchy fight would acknowledge. Muir is a student and lover of nature, converting the field observations of botany and geology into literary "lore." Most important, he translates "the wild and rugged solitude" into his own "look and manner." This last point is Burroughs's deepest: Muir is most himself because of the wild places he has inhabited. More than any of the other characteristic traits that Burroughs catalogs, the identification of Muir with places of "wild and rugged solitude" makes Muir into Muir.

Burroughs pays his best tribute by bringing person and place together in the practice of elegy. Muir does not merely occupy the "wild and rugged solitude"; he inhabits it, and it inhabits him. The elegiac mode enacts the reciprocal affiliation of human being and place. Another brief example of this kind of writing occurs in a letter written soon after Muir's death: Burroughs declares that "the death of John Muir has made California seem very dark and deserted" (*Life and Letters* 2:215). A more extended instance is the creation of "Whitman Land" in the preliminary essay to *Whitman: A Study* (*Writings* 10:3–5). In that case, the landscape surrounding Slabsides becomes the very embodiment of the dead poet and the occasion for beginning the book about him. A final telling example occurs in the January 1919 issue of *Natural History*, devoted to Roosevelt. Burroughs's elegiac essay leads the volume. Burroughs first associates Roosevelt with several specific places, including Yellowstone National Park, the Pine Knot presidential retreat in Virginia, the Roosevelt home at Oyster Bay, the White House, and Slabsides. In all of these places, Burroughs says, he felt "the arousing and stimulating impact of his wonderful personality. When he came into the room it was as if a strong wind had blown the door open. You felt his radiant energy before he got halfway up the stairs."[1] Although the essay has moments of radiance, it is for the most part rather vague in memorializing the dead president. Only at the very end does the style tentatively rise to create an elegiac place marked by absence, much like the dark and deserted California without John Muir: "A pall seems to settle upon the very sky. The world is bleaker and colder for his absence from it. We shall not look upon his like again. Farewell! great Soul, farewell!" (7).

Bidding Perpetual Farewell

Between age seventy-five and his death in 1921, just a few days before his eighty-fourth birthday, Burroughs published five more books and wrote enough additional material to fill two posthumous volumes. Despite the somber tone of many of these works, the last volumes show that Burroughs's "vital currents, like mountain streams, tend to rejuvenate themselves as they flow" (*Writings* 17:v). In *The Summit of the Years* (1913), Burroughs seems quite aware that his eye for the beauty and wonder of the world depends upon the elegiac perspective of an old man facing his own death: "How these things come home to me as life draws near the end! I am like the man who makes a voyage and falls so much in love with the ship and the sea that he thinks of little else and is not curious about the new lands before him. I suppose if my mind had dwelt much upon the other world toward which we are headed, and which is the main concern with so many passengers, I should have found less to absorb and instruct me in this" (*Writings* 17:14). In the last section of the title essay, Burroughs meditates on the "voyage we are making on this planet" (21), focusing especially on the night as "the revelation or the apocalypse of the darkness" (22). Even though he declares that he is "a creature of the day," belonging to "the open, cheerful, optimistic day," Burroughs devotes himself to the night, "the not-day, the great shadow which is a telescope through which we see the Infinite" (23). Thus "The Summit of the Years" creates a balanced place of elegy, one that allows Burroughs to look back over his life "as a traveler might look back over his course from a mountain-top" (4). The perspective depends upon his sense of his own mortality.

Other essays in *The Summit of the Years* evoke a strong sense of place in relation to Burroughs's retrospective, elegiac vision of his life and death. The place of elegy is perhaps strongest in the paired meditations "The Bow in the Clouds" and "The Round World," which act in many ways like prose poems. The first essay explores the paradox that the rainbow is of the earth but beyond it: "Born of the familiar and universal elements, the sun and the rain, it is yet as elusive and spectral and surmising as if it were a revelation from some other sphere" (212). In just four pages, Burroughs turns the rainbow to scientific and poetic account, ultimately declaring that he will employ it for his own purposes:

> The rainbow shall stand to me for the heaven-born in nature and in life—
> the unexpected beauty and perfection that is linked with the eternal cosmic
> laws. Nature is not all solids and fluids and gases, she is not all of this earth;
> she is of the heavens as well. She is of the remote and the phenomenal; seen
> through man's eyes she is touched by a light that never was on sea or land.
> Neither is life all of the material, the tangible, the demonstrable; the witchery
> of the ideal, the spiritual, at times hangs the bow of promise against the darkest
> hours. (215–16)

The rainbow promises that the spiritual is also real, and that is an important moment of elegiac consolation for Burroughs, who is typically given
to the darkest hours regarding human mortality. Similarly, in "The Round
World," he entertains the paradoxes of our limited perspective, in which
"to our senses the bullet-like speed of the earth through space amounts to
absolute rest" and "all is fixed, yet all is in motion" (221). Science corrects
the errors of our senses, but we can never "penetrate the final mystery of
things, because behind every mystery is another mystery." For Burroughs,
"we are prisoners of the sphere on which we live, and its bewildering contradictions are reflected in our mental lives as well" (222). The place of elegy
connects human beings to the environment, but it does so in order to show
us both our limited perceptions and our momentary insights. Burroughs
attaches himself and his readers to place, and the place of elegy functions
most often as a pastoral refuge or momentary stay against the confusion of
death. But the place of elegy is not only surrounded by displacement, loss,
and death; it also depends upon them for its vital power.

In the last volumes, Burroughs pairs his own death with the death of
religion and literature at the hands of scientific materialism. The opening sentence in *The Breath of Life* (1915), for example, notes that "as life
nears its end with me, I find myself meditating more and more upon the
mystery of its nature and origin" (*Writings* 18:v). Burroughs acknowledges
the truths of modern science, but he resists the complete abandonment of
metaphysics. Thus he argues for a vitalistic theory of life, basing much of
his thinking on Henri Bergson's *Creative Evolution* (1911), but he does not
wish to fall into simpleminded anthropomorphism. As he says in "The Naturalist's View of Life," Burroughs adopts "the point of view of naturalism;
not strictly the scientific view which aims to explain all life phenomena
in terms of exact experimental science, but the larger, freer view of the
open-air naturalist and literary philosopher" (18:257). The larger, freer
perspective combats Burroughs's claustrophobic sense of death as a return
to inert matter.

Burroughs associates the largeness of perspective with literature, religion,
and philosophy. In *Under the Apple-Trees* (1916), he specifically cites Emerson, Whitman, and Bergson as "world-openers," and the "world-opening" is

"almost a sacrament; it implies a spiritual illumination and exaltation that does not and cannot come to every mind. It means the opening of a door that our logical faculties cannot open" (*Writings* 19:205). In *Field and Study* (1919), Burroughs practices the old art of "world-opening" by focusing on the near and common, especially songbirds and small mammals, but he reflects on the art in essays like "Literature," "Science," "Evolution," and "Nature and Natural History." The incessant, blind vitalism of nature is fascinating but chilling, and Burroughs constantly schools himself to interpret it in a consoling way. So the final sentence of the volume can stand for the whole: "The caterpillar hurriedly crawling about my porch, going this way and that way, changing its course every second or two, lifting up its head and feeling right and left as if searching for some particular object, crossing and recrossing the porch floor, feeling into the cracks, climbing up the vines and creeping to the pendant end of one of the shoots, and then hanging by the tip of its body, then feeling out in all directions, and finally letting go its hold and falling to the floor, where it again begins to search till it at last mounts my leg as I sit writing, and appears upon my knee, furnishes a good sample of blind, pushing Nature, radiating in all directions in order to be sure to hit a mark that lies only in one particular direction—in this case, a suitable place or corner in which the insect may weave the shroud in which it is to undergo its metamorphosis, and emerge a winged creature" (*Writings* 20:318–19).

In *Accepting the Universe* (1920), Burroughs faces the large philosophical implications of his elegiac vision. Nature is vast and beneficent, but it is also completely indifferent and merciless: "The universe is not a schoolroom on the Montessori lines, nor a benevolent institution run on the most modern improved plan. It is a work-a-day field where we learn from hard knocks, and where the harvest, not too sure, waits upon our own right arm" (*Writings* 21:18). He admits that the scientific perspective delivers a "cosmic chill" (104), and that religions are "so many diverse attempts to clothe the spirit against the cosmic chill of the vast, unhoused, unsanctified, immeasurable out-of-doors of the universe" (256). But Burroughs insists that the Darwinian "struggle for life" is "only the struggle of the chick to get out of the shell, or of the flower to burst its bud, or of the root to penetrate the soil. It is not the struggle of battle and hate" (123). In a brief essay called "Death," part of the fifteen-section "Soundings," he uses a similar image of enclosure, but for a different point: "We look upon death as an evil because we look upon it from the happy fields of life, and see ourselves as alive in our graves and lamenting that we are shut off from all the light and love and movement of the world" (292). Burroughs delivers a provisional sense of acceptance, but the large imagination must accept its own limitations.

Most often in the last volumes, Burroughs evokes the figure of Whitman when he contemplates the place of elegy. He ends *Accepting the Universe* with "The Poet of the Cosmos" because Whitman offers a hopeful vision of the struggle for life and the inevitability of death. Burroughs recurs to his earliest work on Whitman, dating back nearly sixty years, to draw the affiliation between the poet and nature: "Who before Whitman ever drew his poetic, his aesthetic, and ethical standards from the earth, from the sexuality, from the impartiality of the earth, or his laws for creations from the earth?" (319). Most important is the poet's largeness and vitality: "With Whitman we saunter on the hills, or inhale the salt air of the seashore, or our minds open under the spread of the midnight skies—always the large, the elemental, the processional, the modern" (323). In clear echoes of *Notes on Walt Whitman as Poet and Person*, Burroughs refashions Whitman as a cosmic philosopher and prophet. But the figure of Whitman expresses, perhaps most deeply, Burroughs's own affiliation with the poet and his own reading of the poet as bespeaking a universal natural standard. In that sense, Burroughs paints a partial portrait, but it delivers a larger-than-life sense of the writer's place:

> I do not wonder that Whitman gave such a shock to the reading public sixty years ago. This return, in a sense, to aboriginal Nature, this sudden plunge into the great ocean of primal energies, this discarding of all ornamentation and studied external effects of polish and elaboration, gave the readers of poetry a chill from which they are not yet wholly recovered. The fireside, the library corner, the seat in the garden, the nook in the woods: each and all have their charm and their healing power, but do not look for them in

Walt Whitman. Rather expect the mountain-tops, the surf-drenched beach, and the open prairies. A poet of the cosmos, fortified and emboldened by the tremendous discoveries and deductions of modern science, he takes the whole of Nature for his province and dominates it, is at home with it, affiliates with it through his towering personality and almost superhuman breadth of sympathy. (327)

NOTES

Introduction. The Power of Place

1. Love, *Practical Ecocriticism*, 13–36. Love uses the metaphor of "embrace" in the heading "Can Humanism Embrace the Nonhuman?" (23).

2. Rosendale, *The Greening of Literary Scholarship*; Branch and Slovic, *The ISLE Reader*.

3. Casey, *The Fate of Place*, xi.

4. Casey, *Getting Back into Place*, 252–53. See also Berry, *Home Economics*, 12–14.

5. For a fine survey of Tuan's work, from the seminal 1976 article "Humanistic Geography" to the present, see Entrikin, "Geographer as Humanist." Entrikin employs an epigraph from Heidegger to structure the essay. The volume in which this essay appears, Adams, Hoelscher, and Till, *Textures of Place: Exploring Humanist Geographies*, is an excellent collection of twenty-six essays dedicated to Tuan and showing the influence of his thinking on current geography. The most telling literary piece is Howarth, "Reading the Wetlands."

6. A more recent work by Tuan, *Cosmos and Hearth* (1996), expands on the themes of *Topophilia* and *Space and Place* and deepens the discussion of place. The last seven essays in Adams, Hoelscher, and Till, *Textures of Place*, are devoted to the theme of Cosmos versus Hearth. Tuan's introduction to the section notes that the polarized terms are intended not to describe the world but to clarify his arguments. In his essay "Body, Self, and Landscape," Edward Casey argues for a phenomenological understanding of Tuan's concepts.

7. Sack, *Homo Geographicus*, chapters 1–5.

8. The loops and circuits become important in chapters 4, 7, and 8 of Sack's argument, though I have not attempted to apply this part of the model to my thinking about place. See *Homo Geographicus*.

9. Cohen, "Blues in the Green," 30. The entire article is essential reading for students and teachers of environmental literature and history.

One. Great Neighbors

1. See bMS Am 1925 (300), Houghton Mifflin Archives, Houghton Library, Harvard University. My reconstruction of the dialogue between Burroughs and Greenslet is

incomplete, but it suggests that Burroughs was under financial and artistic pressure in the last years of his life.

2. There are several versions of Burroughs's *Writings*, none of them complete. The twenty-three-volume Riverby edition is common in libraries, but there is also the Wake-Robin edition. For a useful index to the collected works, see the website for the John Burroughs Association, http://research.amnh.org/burroughs/index.html. I quote from the Riverby edition, using its volume and page numbers in my parenthetical citations.

3. Except where noted otherwise, quotations from Burroughs's journals are my transcriptions of manuscripts contained in the John Burroughs Papers in the Special Collections Department at Vassar College Library. Other printed selections can be found in *The Heart of Burroughs's Journals* and *The Life and Letters of John Burroughs*, both edited by Clara Barrus.

4. "Emerson and His Journals," 72–73. The original appears in Emerson, *Journals and Miscellaneous Notebooks*, 14:258. A useful compendium is Porte, *Emerson in His Journals*. On Emerson as antimentor, see Buell, *Emerson*, 288–334.

5. Lowell, *My Study Window*, 193–209.

6. The interview appears in Johnston, *John Burroughs Talks*, 177.

7. All three notebooks are contained in the Berg Collection of the New York Public Library. I quote the manuscripts unless otherwise noted.

8. *Atlantic Monthly* 6 (November 1860): 572–77.

9. Burroughs's copies of Emerson's *Essays: First Series* (1857) and *Essays: Second Series* (1857) are in the Vassar Special Collections Department. The italicized passage appears on page 264 of *Essays: First Series*; the emphasis is Burroughs's.

10. Emerson, *Nature, Addresses, and Lectures*, 43.

11. Most of the correspondence between Benton and Burroughs is contained in the Berg Collection. The lifelong friendship between the two writers is narrated in *Life and Letters of John Burroughs*. I quote from 1:64. Unfortunately, my efforts to find extant copies of the *New York Leader* articles have failed.

12. Burroughs Papers, Folder 2.1, in Vassar Special Collections; see also *The Heart of Burroughs's Journals* 74–75.

13. *Nation* 22:66.

14. Edward Waldo Emerson (1844–1930) wrote biographies of his father and Thoreau and edited the twelve-volume centenary edition of Emerson's *Complete Works* (1903–4), cited by most scholars until the modern editorial projects at Harvard University began in the 1970s.

15. My transcription is from the Burroughs Papers, Folder 2.3, in Vassar Special Collections; compare Barrus's edited version in *Life and Letters* 1:254, which gives a different sense to the passage.

16. For a clear account of Thoreau's reputation, both during his lifetime and after his death, see Harding, "Thoreau's Reputation."

17. For an excellent account of the *Journal* in Thoreau's imaginative life and posthumous career, see Witherell, "General Introduction." To date, eight volumes of the *Journal* have been published under the general editorship of John C. Broderick. For critical appraisals of the *Journal*, see Cameron, *Writing Nature*, and Schneider, *Thoreau's Sense of Place*.

Two. Whitman Land

1. A eulogy by Burroughs appears in an April 1892 supplement to the *Conservator*, edited by Horace Traubel and titled *At the Graveside of Walt Whitman*; it includes eulogies by Thomas B. Harned, Daniel G. Brinton, Richard Maurice Bucke, and Robert G. Ingersoll. The December 1891 journal is in the Berg Collection; I quote from *Life and Letters of John Burroughs* 1:318. The details of the friendship are given full play in Renehan, *John Burroughs*, 69–90, 182–202, et passim. The best source for these details is Barrus, *Whitman and Burroughs, Comrades*; Barrus lists the celebrities at the burial and says that the printed eulogy was not written for the occasion (295–96). In his journal for March 30, 1892, Burroughs describes the burial as "very beautiful: a great crowd the scene very impressive: the great tent, perfumed with flowers. Everything goes on in decency & in order. Ingersoll speaks an eloquent & impressive oration. Shall always love him for it, some passages in it will last. As he was speaking I heard a blue-bird warble over the tent most joyously. The tomb is very grand & will endure as long as time" (Burroughs Papers, Vassar College Library Special Collections).

2. Miller, *The Correspondence of Walt Whitman*, 3:77; the original is in the Vassar Special Collections. For Burroughs's correspondence with Houghton Mifflin, see bMS Am 1925 (300), Houghton Mifflin Archives. Burroughs proposed several titles to Whitman for the first book of nature essays, and Whitman immediately chose *Wake-Robin* and "held me to that one" (*Life and Letters* 1:128).

3. Renehan, *John Burroughs*, 84–85. See *Life and Letters* 1:126–29 for the exchange of letters Burroughs had with a pseudonymous correspondent in 1920 on the question of Whitman's role in the first book.

4. Whitman, *Leaves of Grass*, 1:259. All quotations from Whitman's poetry refer to this edition and are cited parenthetically by line number.

5. In the letter of April 1, 1875, Whitman criticizes the essays as "a good deal too diffuse, and too Emersony in themselves—I should select about one third of the MS. as *first rate* (including the opening part). My opinion is that you had perhaps better work it all over, and leave out at least half" (Miller, *Correspondence*, 2:327).

6. "Before Genius," *Galaxy* 5 (April 1868): 421–26; "What Makes the Poet?" *Galaxy* 22 (July 1876): 55–60; the passages in the latter that reappear in "Before Beauty" include a long paragraph on cellular and crystalline form. Burroughs revised the piece in interesting ways, such as omitting direct references to Emerson but including a comparison between Wordsworth and Tennyson (173–75).

7. "Before Genius" 424–25. Whitman's *Democratic Vistas* (1871) is a compilation of three essays: "Democracy" and "Personalism," from the two *Galaxy* issues, and a third, un-published essay called "Orbic Literature." See my *Walt Whitman's Language Experiment* 109–21.

8. See Renehan, *John Burroughs*, 187 and Barrus, *Whitman and Burroughs, Comrades*, 293–331.

9. Renehan, *John Burroughs*, 184.

10. Buell notes this fact in *The Environmental Imagination*, 490 n. 21. See also Barrus, *Whitman and Burroughs, Comrades*, 24 and Renehan, *John Burroughs*, 82–83. The song of the hermit thrush runs throughout Burroughs's first book, *Wake-Robin*, most of which was composed between 1863 and 1868.

11. Renehan, *John Burroughs*, 138–39; Barrus, *Whitman and Burroughs, Comrades*, xxiv, 169–70.

12. The first passage is quoted from an unnamed Danish critic; the second is taken from the Scottish poet Robert Buchanan, who defended Whitman in a March 1876 essay in the *London Daily News*; see Allen, *The Solitary Singer*, 470–71.

13. Burroughs wrote to Myron Benton in September 1865 that Whitman "is deeply interested in what I tell him of the Hermit Thrush, and says he has used largely the information I have given him in one of his principal poems" (Barrus, *Whitman and Burroughs, Comrades*, 24).

14. See Renehan, *John Burroughs*, 98–104. For two months in the fall of 1871, Bur-roughs was traveling as part of a Treasury Department mission to convey fifteen million dollars in United States bonds to an English bank and supervise the destruction of the old bonds.

Three. Pastoral Illustration

1. *Life and Letters of John Burroughs* 1:313. Burroughs was not the only reader to criticize the illustrations and article in the February 1891 *Century*. Clare de Graffenried's "The Georgia Cracker in the Cotton Mills" (*Century* 41:483–98) excited cries of slander and mendacity in the South, and the *Atlanta Constitution* called Kemble's illustrations "libelous." See John, *The Best Years of the Century*, 204. John's study is invaluable for its objective and detailed narrative.

2. The most important source of information on American magazines is Mott, *A History of American Magazines*. I have used volumes 3 (1865–85) and 4 (1885–1905) extensively in researching this chapter. In both volumes, the supplemental "Sketches of Certain Important Magazines which Flourished" give extremely helpful insights into readership, business arrangements, circulation, and literary achievement.

3. See Sedgwick, *The Atlantic Monthly, 1857–1909*, 38–40, for the contrast between the two audiences. The quotation is taken from an advertisement for *Harper's Monthly*, quoted by Sedgwick on p. 38.

4. The list of articles can be found at the University of Michigan website for the *Making of America* editorial project: http://moa.umdl.umich.edu/. For an excellent account of the founding of the magazine and its imitation of the *Atlantic Monthly* and *Lippincott's*, see Mott, *A History of American Magazines*, 3:402–9.

5. A helpful omnibus volume that includes the seven "Studies in the Sierra" essays, along with much other useful material, is *John Muir: His "Life and Letters" and Other Writings*, edited by Terry Gifford. Another useful anthology of Muir's writings is John Muir, *Nature Writings* (New York: Library of America, 1997), which includes "Yosemite Valley in Flood" and other early essays, as well as four of his best-known books.

6. *Overland Monthly* 9:547–49; *Harper's New Monthly Magazine* 51:769–76.

7. Scholnick, "*Scribner's Monthly* and the 'Pictorial Representation of Life and Truth' in Post–Civil War America," focuses especially on Holland's purposes of reaching even nonreaders with the illustrated monthly and engaging controversial issues in his "Topics of the Time" columns. See also John, *The Best Years of the Century*, 76–91 for an excellent discussion of the role of illustrations in the larger cultural mission of the magazine.

8. See John, *The Best Years of the Century*, 181–97, 233–39; Mott, *A History of American Magazines*, 3:187–90, 457–80. For a contemporary critical view of this "process" illustration and the New School, see Linton, *The History of Wood-Engraving in America*. By the 1890s, the halftone process would replace the New School techniques of photoxylography, effectively rendering wood engraving obsolete. The halftone process employs a diamond-ruled screen interposed between the light-sensitive plate and photographic negative of the original artwork, producing dots of varying sizes on the plate; for a concise description and history, see Reed, *The Popular Magazine in Britain and the United States, 1880–1960*, 27–34.

9. The table of contents to each issue gives specific credit to artists for illustrations. Foote was a novelist as well as a capable artist (John, *The Best Years of the Century*, 155, 160); in his *History*, Linton praises her as "the best of our designers on the wood" (33) and faults engravers like Timothy Cole for marring her work (51).

10. See Raymond Williams's seminal work, *The Country and the City*, especially chapters 2–4, where Williams develops the pastoral nostalgia as a "problem of perspective" and notes the tendency of pastoral to erase labor (9–45).

11. *Scribner's Monthly* 17:55. The essay appears in slightly revised form as chapter 10, "A Wind-Storm in the Forests," in Muir's first book, *The Mountains of California*. Four other essays in the "Studies in the Sierra" series appear in volume 17 of *Scribner's Monthly* and are revised as chapters of *The Mountains of California*: "The Douglass Squirrel of California" (December 1878: 260–66); "Mountain Lakes of California" (January 1879: 411–21); "The Glacier Meadows of the Sierra" (February 1879: 478–83); "The Passes of the Sierra" (March 1879: 644–52). Two good modern editions of the book are Edward Hoagland's Penguin Nature Classics paperback, which prints the illustrations from *Scribner's* and the *Century* (New York: Penguin, 1997), and the Library of America *Nature Writings*, 311–547; editor William Cronon gives the account of the eighteen essays Muir used to make *Mountains of California* (850–51). I quote from the Penguin paperback because of its convenience for readers.

12. *Century* 24:222–29 and 388–96. Both parts are generously illustrated, especially the longer second part. The Penguin edition of *Mountains of California* omits one illustration of sheep herds that appears with the first part, but otherwise the illustrations are complete.

13. The silence came about because of Muir's work at the family ranch in Martinez and the birth of his two daughters, Helen and Wanda. On the gap between the early career and the later career, see Cohen, *The Pathless Way*. Johnson went to California in 1889 to explore the possibilities of a series of articles on the "Gold-Hunters," but he met Muir in San Francisco and later visited Yosemite Valley with him. See Johnson's memoir, *Remembered Yesterdays*, 278–89.

14. See Glazener, *Reading for Realism*, especially 1–50 and 257–66.

15. On the development of taste and cultural hierarchy, Glazener relies on Bourdieu, *Distinction*, but for the sense of cultural authority exercised by the magazines she uses Althusser's classic essay, "Ideology and Ideological State Apparatuses." Glazener's most powerful theoretical inflections are her own.

16. For a clear discussion of this role, see John, *The Best Years of the Century*, 146–80. The pervasive power of the genial and genteel led later commentators to polemical dismissals of the "Genteel Tradition." See Santayana, *The Genteel Tradition*. Glazener discusses Santayana and later commentators in her conclusion and in excellent notes (239–55, 336 n.10).

17. See also Brodhead's more recent study, *Cultures of Letters*.

18. For a rough but interesting content analysis of major magazines of the period, see Reed, *The Popular Magazine in Britain and the United States, 1880–1960*, 236–46. On the first decade of the *Century* under Gilder's editorship, see John, *The Best Years of the Century*, 125–45.

19. The essay appears in *Century* 25:672–83. Retitled "A Sharp Lookout," it is the lead essay in the volume *Signs and Seasons* (*Writings* 7:3–37), from which I quote.

20. Glazener's chapters on these two topics have been crucial for my discussion. See *Reading for Realism*, chapters 4 and 5.

21. The point is particularly applicable to the work of Sarah Orne Jewett. See Brodhead, *Cultures of Letters*, 107–76.

22. Glazener's definition (158–59) summarizes the work of Lears, *No Place of Grace*. One part of Lears's argument that Glazener does not directly mention is the "martial ideal" as the source of the cult of experience. See chapter 5 for this aspect of antimodernism in Theodore Roosevelt's representations of nature.

23. Lears, *No Place of Grace*, 4–58. For the "back to nature" movement and the legion of participants, see Schmitt, *Back to Nature*.

24. The statistics are joined to a August 20, 1907, letter from Burroughs to Houghton Mifflin, asking the editors if the works of William J. Long have crowded his out of the schools; their response shows that Burroughs's work was overwhelmingly popular. The letter and tally are in bMS Am 1925 (300), Houghton Mifflin Archives. The correspondence between Burroughs and Houghton Mifflin also shows that the author was always concerned with his sales. He defends his plan to work with Burt for the Ginn and Company collection in a letter of September 21, 1893, citing his sense that "a man's life work ought to bring him more than $500 a year. One successful school book would do much better than that." The story of Burt, *Pepacton*, and Oscar Houghton is told in *Life and Letters of John Burroughs* 1:285. For a brief, informative essay on this topic, see Lutz, "The Influence of John Burroughs on Education."

25. Johnson, *Remembered Yesterdays*, 279–91; both quotations appear on 288.

26. *Century* 40.4 (August 1890): 483–500; 40.5 (September 1890): 656–67. The "Treasures" essay appears in revised form as chapters 1 and 2 of *The Yosemite* (1912); the "Features" essay appears in revised form in chapters 12 and 14 of *The Yosemite*.

27. "The Yosemite National Park," *Atlantic Monthly* 84 (August 1899): 145–52; Muir, *Our National Parks* (1901), reprints nine essays that appeared in the *Atlantic Monthly* between August 1897 and April 1901. Terry Gifford reprints the chapters of *Picturesque California* and the two *Century* essays in his *Life and Letters* omnibus volume (513–614).

28. An earlier version of the passage appears as "Yosemite Valley in Flood," *Overland Monthly* 8 (April 1872): 347–50, reprinted in *Nature Writings* 587–91.

29. The second article, "Features of the Proposed Yosemite National Park," takes the form of a guided tour, focusing especially on the Tuolumne Meadows area and the Hetch Hetchy Valley. Muir details excursions from the Soda Springs campgrounds to surrounding peaks such as Mount Dana and Mount Lyell and guides a reader through the Tuolumne Canyon to Hetch Hetchy. Unlike the "Treasures" essay, the article gives no narratives, no extraordinary adventures, and very little of the lyrical description that marks

Muir's best writing. The one exception may be the brief account of the ascent of Mount Dana, with the description of the glacial tarn below Dana Glacier. The illustrations, however, are better than the text. The description of the Lyell Glacier is unremarkable, but William Fraser's landscape presents the scene vividly. Muir describes the Big Tuolumne Canyon in cursory fashion, though he also asserts that the eighteen-mile descent requires mountaineering skill; Thomas Moran captures the sense of cascading water and the half dome formation. The most prominent feature of Hetch Hetchy, the rock Kolana, comes to life under Moran's hand. Although Muir does not match the intense artistry of the "Treasures" essay, the illustrations rescue the "Features" article from a kind of perfunctory, guidebook quality. Indeed, the article exemplifies a tendency in the later *Century* to subordinate text to illustration, though in this case illustrations function as part of the magazine's cultural authority. Mott, *A History of American Magazines*, quotes the *Philistine* from June 1895: "The *Century*, it is said, will insert a page or two of reading matter between the Italian art and the ads" (3:475).

30. *Century* 39:477–78. Johnson's pictorial sense comes out in a passage like this one: "In walking and driving over the valley, one's feelings of awe at the unspoilable monuments of nature are often marred by the intrusion of the work of unskillful hands upon the foreground of the picture" (478).

31. *Century* 39 (January 1890): 477–78; 44 (June 1892): 318–19; 45 (April 1893): 950–52; 51 (April 1896): 950–51. Johnson recounts many of these fights in *Remembered Yesterdays*, 289–313.

32. *Century* 46 (September 1893): 792–97; 49 (February 1895): 626–34. Johnson tells how he worked with Sargent to establish and fund the commission in *Remembered Yesterdays* 296–300.

33. The best studies of antebellum celebrity authors are Kelley, *Private Woman, Public Stage*; Tompkins, *Sensational Designs*; and Brodhead, *School of Hawthorne* and *Cultures of Letters*. In a recent paper, delivered at the 2003 ASLE conference, Eric Lupfer argued that Thoreau's reputation was the direct creation of post–Civil War nature writers, thus reversing the usual sense of influence.

34. John Swett, "John Muir," *Century* 46 (May 1893): 120–23. Swett was City Superintendent of Education for San Francisco and met Muir through William Keith in 1874. Muir boarded with the Swett family for months at a time in the years 1875 to 1879, while he worked on his articles for the *Overland Monthly*; see *Kindred and Related Spirits: The Letters of John Muir and Jeanne C. Carr*, edited by Bonnie Johanna Gisel, 233–70.

35. John Swett, "John Muir," *Century* 46 (May 1893): 120–23. Swett's cover letter and typed bibliography are in Box 99 of the Century Collection, Manuscripts and Archives Division, New York Public Library.

36. *Scribner's Monthly* 13 (January 1877): 336–41. Benton was the cousin of Burroughs's best friend, Myron Benton.

37. Mabie was associate editor of the *Outlook* from 1884 to 1916. For the history of the journal and Theodore Roosevelt's later association with it, see Mott 3:422–35.

38. *Century* 54 (August 1897): 560–68.

39. *Century* 58 (August 1899): 500–511; the essay is reprinted, with the revised title "Wild Life about My Cabin," in *Far and Near* (1904) and in *Writings* volume 13, from which I quote.

Four. Landscapes Beginning to Be Born

1. Emerson, *Essays and Poems*, 1011.

2. For Emerson's list, see *JMN* 16:188. Muir biographer Linnie Marsh Wolfe recounts the Yosemite meeting in *Son of the Wilderness*, 143–51. She asserts that Burroughs was the first to note Emerson's inclusion of Muir in the list (151). Muir wrote a deep appreciation of Emerson in his manuscript essay, "Emerson" (*John Muir Papers, 1858–1957*, reel 43). For my work in the Muir Papers, I have consulted the 51 microfilm reels and 53 microfiche cards, edited by Ronald H. Limbaugh and Kirsten E. Lewis. See their *Guide and Index to the Microform Edition of the John Muir Papers, 1858–1957*. The Muir Papers are held by Holt-Atherton Library, University of the Pacific, Stockton, California. For a fine account of Muir's relationship to Emerson and to American Romanticism, see Branch, "Telling Nature's Story."

3. The two most recent examples are *Kindred and Related Spirits*, edited by Bonnie Johanna Gisel, and *John Muir's Last Journey*, edited by Michael P. Branch. Other notable editions are *John of the Mountains*, edited by Linnie Marsh Wolfe; *To Yosemite and Beyond*, edited by Robert Engberg and Donald Wesling; and *Letters from Alaska*, edited by Robert Engberg and Bruce Merrell, which prints fourteen of the eighteen "newspaper letters" that Muir published in the *San Francisco Daily Evening Bulletin* in 1879–80.

4. The best published account of the Harriman Alaska expedition is Goetzmann and Sloan, *Looking Far North*. A recent article by Ken Chowder, "North to Alaska," is a useful introduction. A deeply interesting meditation on the journey is Lord, *Green Alaska*. For an excellent website on the television special "Harriman Expedition Retraced," see www.pbs.org/harriman/index.html.

5. Biographical sketches of the four artists appear on the "Harriman Expedition Re-traced" website, under "1899 Expedition, Original Participants." Gifford (1840–1905) was the oldest of the four and the most distinguished at the time, having illustrated many articles in the *Century* and having taught for years at the Cooper Union; his work can still be seen in the permanent collections of major museums in the Northeast. Dellen-baugh (1853–1935) was well known for having been chosen, at age eighteen, for the second Powell expedition down the Colorado River; he continued to illustrate and write about landscapes in the western United States. Fuertes (1874–1927) was only twenty-five

when Merriam invited him to join the expedition, but his exacting work became the modern standard in the field. Curtis (1868–1952) was to become the most famous of the four artists, mainly because of his photographs of Native Americans. For an excellent account of Curtis's career, see Gidley, *Edward S. Curtis and the North American Indian, Incorporated.*

6. The publication history of the *Harriman Alaska Series* is somewhat complicated. From 1901 to 1905, the volumes were privately printed by Doubleday, Page and Company and copyrighted to E. H. Harriman. After Harriman's death in 1909, Mrs. Harriman transferred the publication to the Smithsonian Institution, which reissued all of the published volumes with new title pages. The last of the volumes to be published appeared in two parts in 1914, financed by Mrs. Harriman. Volumes 6 and 7 were never completed. I quote from the 1910 reissue of the first four volumes, citing volume and page number parenthetically. For publication history, see Goetzmann and Sloan, *Looking Far North*, 193–200; Goetzmann and Sloan refer to the volumes as "one of the most lavish publications of the age" (200).

7. See Kimes and Kimes, *John Muir*, nos. 144A–D.

8. This is my transcription from the third manuscript journal of the Harriman trip, *John Muir Papers*, reel 29. My transcription differs slightly from Wolfe's edition, which regularizes grammar and punctuation (*John of the Mountains* 413).

9. The most detailed chronology of Muir's travels appears in the *Guide and Index to the Microform Edition*, pp. 20–31, and much of these two paragraphs draws on the information there. The *Century* articles appear as follows: "The Discovery of Glacier Bay," *Century* 50 (June 1895): 234–47; "The Alaska Trip," *Century* 54 (August 1897): 513–26.

10. A selection of dispatches from 1879 and 1880 appears in *Letters from Alaska*, edited by Robert Engberg and Bruce Merrell. The introduction, notes, and bibliography to this edition are invaluable. My comparison of the dispatches to the descriptions in the *Reading Bibliography* (nos. 89–99) has led me to number them somewhat differently from the editors. The fifth dispatch appears on pages 28–32. Compare the parallel passages in *Picturesque California* (*Nature Writings* 676–77) and chapter 5 of *Travels in Alaska*, 51. The revisions are minor, but they show Muir's careful attention to style and suggest that *Travels in Alaska* should be considered the pinnacle of Muir's Alaska writings. See also the parallels and revisions in the concluding passage on the "morning of creation" (*Nature Writings* 679; *Travels in Alaska* 53–54).

11. For the portion dealing with the discovery of Glacier Bay, see *Letters from Alaska* 44–51.

12. For a clear account of the tourist industry in Alaska, see Hinckley, "The Inside Passage." A popular guidebook of the day was Scidmore, *The Guide-Book to Alaska and the Northwest Coast* (1893). Travelogues were also popular. Good examples are Scidmore,

Alaska: Its Southern Coast and the Sitkan Archipelago (1885), and Woodman, *Picturesque Alaska* (1889), both of which describe steamer trips to Muir Glacier.

13. Burroughs's two notebooks from the Harriman Alaska expedition are in the Huntington Library. I quote from my transcription of the manuscript, HM 33770.

14. The two photographs by Curtis appear on a single page, with the captions "Edge of Muir Glacier" (figure 18) and "Front of Muir Glacier. Just after this was taken, a huge berg fell off, the wave almost swamping the canoe and washing overboard a series of very large negatives of the glacier front" (*HAS* 1:38). My reproductions are from the Curtis Collection at the University of Washington Library. A link to this collection can be found at the "Harriman Expedition Retraced" website.

15. Compare the punctuation in *HAS* (1:42), in which Burroughs uses no colon/semicolon structure to balance the sentence. Many of the revisions for the "In Green Alaska" version are of this type.

16. Compare *HAS* 1:93, which has the erroneous reading "limpid torrent streams." Muir's journal account is terse: "We kept John Burroughs on the ship" (*John of the Mountains*, 405). Charles Keeler is the source for the "complete" story (*John of the Mountains*, 405 n. 1). Keeler's typescript *Friends Bearing Torches* is contained in the Charles Keeler Papers at the Huntington Library. Much of the chapter on Muir is given to Keeler's narrative of the Harriman Alaska expedition. Keeler's account of Burroughs and Muir stresses "an instinctive feeling of superiority on the part of Muir, the dour champion of the wilderness in its sublimest aspects" (66). Muir and Burroughs traded doggerel jabs concerning the episode. See Muir's poem "The True Story of J. B. and Behring Sea" (*John of the Mountains* 422–26) and Burroughs's "revenge" poem, "Snapping, snarling Bering Sea" and these salient lines: "Had not John Muir put in his lip, / Thou hadst not found me in this ship" (*Life and Letters of John Burroughs* 1:381–82).

Five. The "Best of Places"

1. *The Works of Theodore Roosevelt* 2:390. All references to Roosevelt's works are to this edition, unless otherwise noted.

2. *Atlantic Monthly* 91:298–309.

3. In a letter of June 8, 1903, for example, Roosevelt thanks Burroughs for the set of his works that has just arrived at the White House, plans a visit to Slabsides for July, recounts some of the birds he saw in California, and promises to send Burroughs a copy of *Ranch Life and the Hunting Trail* (Clifton Waller Barrett Collection). In an April 24, 1903, letter to George Bird Grinnell, editor of *Forest and Stream* and Roosevelt's cofounder of the Boone and Crockett Club, the president blasts a negative editorial by a writer called "Hermit" who has dared to attack Burroughs in the controversy, assuring the editor that there is "no writer of Mr. Burroughs' type who is in Mr. Burroughs' class" and that he is

"one of the Americans to whom good Americans owe a debt" (*The Letters of Theodore Roosevelt* 3:468, 470).

4. The first was in the form of an interview by Edward B. Clark, "Roosevelt on the Nature Fakirs," *Everybody's Magazine* 16 (June 1907): 770–74, reprinted as "Men Who Misinterpret Nature" (*Works* 5:367–74); the second was an essay, "Nature-Fakers," which appeared along with Clark's article, "Real Naturalists on Nature Faking," in *Everybody's Magazine* 17 (September 1907): 423–30, and is reprinted in the National edition (*Works* 5:375–83).

5. See Lutts, *The Nature Fakers*.

6. See Paul Russell Cutright, *Theodore Roosevelt*, 210–37.

7. Daniel J. Philippon, *Conserving Words*, 33–71.

8. The best account of Roosevelt's prepresidential years is Edmund Morris, *The Rise of Theodore Roosevelt*. For the death of his mother and wife, see 237–45; for the diary quotation, see 241; for the ranching years, see 270–341. Another informative narrative of the period is Michael Collins, *That Damned Cowboy*.

9. Morris, *Rise of Theodore Roosevelt* 243–45.

10. Dan Philippon interprets this structure as a "hierarchy of species" based on scientific description and argues that it shows Roosevelt's zoological, taxonomic interests (*Conserving Words* 48).

11. While I would disagree with Philippon's characterization of Bederman as "cynical" about Roosevelt's self-representations, he is certainly correct to stress the role of natural history and experience in the early writings. Philippon's analysis of Roosevelt's writing in fact accords well with Bederman's focus on issues of race, class, and gender. Both analyses owe much to the work of Richard Slotkin. See his "Nostalgia and Progress"; *The Fatal Environment*; and *Gunfighter Nation*.

12. Bederman 176–77; Philippon 44–46.

13. *Atlantic Monthly* 56:565. Only five hundred copies of the Medora edition were published by Putnam's Sons in June 1885. Gifford's etchings are called "most striking and vigorous," and that is true of the other two illustrations as well: "Within Doors" renders the dark, barren interior of the ranch house; "Geese on Sand Bar" is a gorgeous silhouette.

14. The *Century* serialization was Remington's first major commission as a magazine illustrator, and Roosevelt specifically chose him for the work. The six articles featured sixty-four illustrations, and the first edition of the book contained eighty-four illustrations, all by Remington. See Aloysius A. Norton, *Theodore Roosevelt* (Boston: Twayne, 1980) 94, and Atwood Manley and Margaret Manley Mangum, *Frederic Remington and the North Country* (New York: E. P. Dutton, 1988) 94–98. For a cultural interpretation of Remington's paintings and sculptures, see Alexander Nemerov, *Frederic Remington and Turn-of-the-Century America* (New Haven: Yale University Press, 1995). The original

edition of *Ranch Life and the Hunting Trail* (New York: The Century Company, 1888) did not include chapter 11, "The Bighorn Sheep," which according to Hermann Hagedorn appeared for the first time in the Memorial edition (*Works* 1:250).

15. The lightly revised *Century* article forms the first two chapters of *Ranch Life and the Hunting Trail*. I quote Roosevelt's book but use the *Century* illustrations. See *Century* 35:495–511. The episode that the illustration in fact relates is told in the chapter "Red and White on the Border" (373–74).

16. In addition, the Rockies were the site of Roosevelt's six wilderness hunting trips between 1884 and 1891: Big Horn Mountains of Wyoming in 1884; Coeur d'Alenes of Idaho in 1886; Selkirks of British Columbia in 1888; Bitterroots of Wyoming and Idaho in 1889; Yellowstone National Park in 1890; Shoshone Mountains in Wyoming in 1891 (Philippon 59).

17. The report is quoted in Cutright 190. For the entire review and C. Hart Merriam's support of Roosevelt's report, see 188–91. For Roosevelt's undergraduate education in zoology, see 103–6, 118–30. For his decision not to pursue a scientific career, see *Autobiography* 24–25.

18. See Mott 4:148–54.

19. The articles appear in the following order: "With the Cougar Hounds. First Paper," *Scribner's* 30 (October 1901): 417–35; "With the Cougar Hounds. Second Paper," *Scribner's* 30 (November 1901): 545–64; "A Colorado Bear Hunt," *Scribner's* 38 (October 1905): 386–405; "A Wolf Hunt in Oklahoma," *Scribner's* 38 (November 1905): 513–32; "Small Country Neighbors," *Scribner's* 42 (October 1907): 385–95; "In the Louisiana Canebrakes," *Scribner's* 43 (January 1908): 47–60. The six articles are illustrated by seventy-three photographs.

20. Roosevelt's five-chapter work appears in *The Deer Family*, edited by Caspar Whitney. The bulk of the five chapters appears in chapters 4, 6, 7, 8, and 9 of *Outdoor Pastimes of an American Hunter*. Writing from the "Vice-President's Room, Washington, D.C., June, 1901," Roosevelt provides the one-sentence foreword to *The Deer Family*: "This volume is meant for the lover of the wild, free, lonely life of the wilderness, and of the hardy pastimes known to the sojourners therein."

21. Michael Cohen recounts the complex situation clearly in *The Pathless Way* 286–97. On Roosevelt's governorship see Cutright 199–209 and chapter 8 of *Autobiography*, especially appendix A, "Conservation" (313–15).

22. "The American Forests" appears in *Atlantic* 80 (August 1897): 147–57 and is reprinted as the final chapter of *Our National Parks*. "The Wild Parks and Forest Reservations of the West" appears in *Atlantic* 81 (January 1898): 15–28 and is reprinted as the first chapter of *Our National Parks*. In his discussion (298–316), Turner adds a third essay, "Forest Reservations and National Parks," *Harper's Weekly*, June 5, 1897. See also Wolfe, *Son of the Wilderness*, 268–74, and Cohen 297–301.

23. The essay only relates the visit to Sagamore Hill in June 1907 (164). For the visits to the White House and Pine Knot, see Renehan 249–50.

24. The first section reprints *Camping with President Roosevelt*; the second reprints the article "President Roosevelt as Nature Lover and Observer," *Outlook* (13 July 1907): 547–53. The book is not included in Burroughs's *Writings*.

25. *Ranch Life and the Hunting Trail*, 135. Roosevelt also points out that Remington makes the tails of elk and pronghorn too long (130–31).

Six. The Divine Abyss

1. Eric Lupfer, "Reading Nature Writing," 55. Lupfer's research in the Houghton Mifflin Archives is extremely important for setting an economic and social structure for the emergence of nature writing as a genre in the late nineteenth and early twentieth centuries. Two of Burroughs's collections, *Riverby* (1894) and *Signs and Seasons* (1886) were assigned in the Ohio Teachers' course for 1895–96 and 1900–1901, respectively.

2. bMS Am 1925 (300), Houghton Mifflin Archives. Reverend Long's titles were far less popular than Burroughs's, averaging 3,800 annual copies and 850 annual copies for the same period.

3. I do not have sales records for this book, but copies are available in most research collections. The copy I have examined is held at Vassar College Special Collections Department. The book contains fifteen brief, charming accounts of mammals, with accompanying illustrations, and it would seem to be designed for use in the schools. The advertisement at the end of the volume includes many of the same titles discussed by Eric Lupfer, "Before Nature Writing."

4. Only 112 pages long, this pocket-sized book features a brief preface by Snell, who calls Burroughs "our greatest literary naturalist," and nine essays selected from Burroughs's fifteen volumes published by that time.

5. Neither Burt nor Burroughs was ever satisfied with their publishers. Writing on May 20, 1908, Burt rails against all publishers, none of whom has taken adequate pain in producing Burroughs's books, notes that he is legally due 5 percent per annum from sales of *Little Nature Studies*, and then proposes producing yet another anthology of his work for schoolchildren (Vassar Folder 68.10). In another letter, Burt comments, "Oh yes, I love Mr. Ginn. If I were a man I'd kick him." In a letter of September 21, 1893, to Houghton Mifflin, Burroughs defends the Ginn contract because "a man's life work ought to bring him more than $500 a year. One successful school book would do much better than that" (bMS Am 1925 [300], Houghton Mifflin Archives). Ralph Lutts adds yet another title in his discussion—*A Bunch of Herbs and Other Papers*—but without publication information (*The Nature Fakers* 29).

6. bMS Am 1925 (300), Houghton Mifflin Archives. I have not been able to identify the Seventh Reader by title.

7. Morris, *Theodore Rex*, 171–74.

8. The letter runs to six typed pages and contains a host of detailed criticisms of the original letter by "Hermit." For the quoted passage, see *Letters of Theodore Roosevelt* 3:470; for a good account of the debate with "Hermit" (Mason A. Walton), see Lutts 50–55. Burroughs's article appears in *Atlantic Monthly* 78 (1903): 293–309.

9. See Lutts 101–38 for an excellent account of these years and the Roosevelt-Burroughs connection. In responding to London's article, Roosevelt noted to *Collier's* editor Mark Sullivan that he in fact differed from Burroughs in his conception of animal intelligence (*Letters of Theodore Roosevelt* 6:1220–23). The London article appears in *Collier's Weekly* 41 (September 5, 1908): 10–11, 25–26.

10. The phrase appears in Muir's March 12, 1903, letter to Charles Sprague Sargent, with whom he was planning a botanical trip through Russia and Asia (Muir Papers reel 13). The full sentence gives the context: "Now, I am anxious to know the date of sailing, and whether without deranging your plans the date might be in say the first week in June instead of last of May, as in one of your letters you proposed, because an influential man from Wash[ington] wants to make a trip into the Sierra with me, and I might be able to do some forest good in talking freely around the campfire."

11. Cutright's account is judicious (*Making of a Conservationist* 238–70); Turner's version less so (*Rediscovering America* 327–28).

12. Muir Papers reel 13.

13. For more on this friendship, see chapter 4. The correspondence between Muir and Roosevelt lapsed during Muir's round-the-world tour, but when it was taken up again in November 1904, the two were on very friendly terms (Muir Papers reel 14).

14. *Century* 80:521–28; *Craftsman* 23:324–35; *Life and Letters* 2:118–32.

15. Muir may have put Burroughs in contact with the Hawaii Promotion Committee, since they had written him on May 14, 1908, thanking him for accepting their invitation to visit the islands at his earliest convenience (Muir Papers reel 17).

16. The exchange of letters appears in *Life and Letters* 2:135–38 and in Muir Papers reels 18 and 19. Three letters from Bailey Willis to Burroughs are contained in the Burroughs Papers at Vassar College Special Collections. Willis wrote on December 21 and 31, 1909, and on January 5, 1910. Far from dismissing Burroughs's views of the origins of Yosemite, he urges him to avoid theories of faulting and to focus on the "slow process of erosion." He also points out that Yosemite is more the work of rivers than of glaciers, though he urges caution in all such theorizing.

17. At one point Burroughs contemplated combining the first and second essays to form a long two-part essay, "Mother Earth." In a January 22, 1908, letter to Houghton

Mifflin, he decides against the idea and restores the two essays to present form (bMS am 1925 [300], Houghton Mifflin Archives).

18. "Mountain Sculpture," in Gifford's *Life and Letters*, 1:395. Modern geologists posit a succession of ice sheets, numbering from nine to twelve, rather than one universal event.

19. *Century* 65 (November 1902): 107–16. The essay is reprinted in the Library of America edition of *Nature Writings* (790–809), from which I quote.

20. Boston: Houghton Mifflin, 1901. The passage appears on 78–79 of this edition. All further citations refer to this first edition. The book is included in Gifford, *The Eight Wilderness-Discovery Books*, 456–605. The ten chapters were first published as articles in the *Atlantic* between August 1897 and September 1901. See Kimes no. 237.

21. *Conserving Words* 136–55.

22. All of the materials for this discussion are taken from Muir Papers reel 9.

23. "The Endangered Valley. The Hetch Hetchy Valley in the Yosemite National Park," *Century* 77:464–69; *The Yosemite* reprints material from *The Mountains of California* and *Our National Parks*, but it also includes a long chapter on the Hetch Hetchy. The book is dedicated to Johnson. See Kimes nos. 265 and 308.

24. For the book publications, see Kimes nos. 281, 286, 299, 315, 316, 333, 339, and 341–44.

Conclusion. The Place of Elegy

1. *Natural History* 19 (January 1919): 5. The editor notes that the article was read, in part, before the Roosevelt Memorial Meeting at the Century Club, New York City, on February 9, by Major George Haven Putnam. In remaining personally undelivered, the essay recalls Burroughs's eulogy for Whitman.

BIBLIOGRAPHY

Manuscript Materials

Burroughs, John. Papers. Albert Berg Collection, New York Public Library.

Burroughs, John. Papers. Huntington Library, San Marino, California.

Burroughs, John. Papers. Special Collections, Vassar College Library.

Century Collection. Manuscript and Archives Division, New York Public Library.

Clifton Waller Barrett Collection. Alderman Library, University of Virginia.

Houghton Mifflin Archives. Houghton Library, Harvard University.

Keeler, Charles. Papers. Huntington Library, San Marino, California.

Muir, John. Papers. Holt-Atherton Library, University of the Pacific.

Theodore Roosevelt Collection. Houghton and Widener Libraries, Harvard University.

Primary Printed Sources

WORKS BY JOHN BURROUGHS

Accepting the Universe. Boston: Houghton Mifflin, 1920.

Birds and Poets. Boston: Hurd and Houghton, 1877.

The Breath of Life. Boston: Houghton Mifflin, 1915.

Camping and Tramping with Roosevelt. Boston: Houghton Mifflin, 1907.

Camping with President Roosevelt. Boston: Houghton Mifflin, 1906.

Far and Near. Boston: Houghton Mifflin, 1904.

Field and Study. Boston: Houghton Mifflin, 1919.

Fresh Fields. Boston: Houghton Mifflin, 1884.

The Heart of Burroughs's Journals. Ed. Clara Barrus. Boston: Houghton Mifflin, 1928.

Indoor Studies. Boston: Houghton Mifflin, 1889.

John James Audubon. Boston: Small, Maynard, 1902.

The Last Harvest. Boston: Houghton Mifflin, 1922.

Leaf and Tendril. Boston: Houghton Mifflin, 1908.

Life and Letters of John Burroughs. Ed. Clara Barrus. 2 vols. Boston: Houghton Mifflin, 1925.

The Light of Day. Boston: Houghton Mifflin, 1900.

Literary Values. Boston: Houghton Mifflin, 1902.

Little Nature Studies for Little People from John Burroughs. Boston: Ginn and Company, 1895.

Locusts and Wild Honey. Boston: Houghton, Osgood, 1879.

"Narrative of the Expedition." In *Harriman Alaska Series,* 13 vols., edited by C. Hart Merriam, 1:1–118. New York: Doubleday, Page, 1901–1910.

Notes on Walt Whitman as Poet and Person. New York: American News, 1867.

Pepacton. Boston: Houghton Mifflin, 1881.

"Real and Sham Natural History," *Atlantic Monthly* 91 (1903): 298–309.

Riverby. Boston: Houghton Mifflin, 1894.

Signs and Seasons. Boston: Houghton Mifflin, 1886.

Squirrels and Other Fur-Bearers. Boston: Houghton Mifflin, 1900.

The Summit of the Years. Boston: Houghton Mifflin, 1913.

Time and Change. Boston: Houghton Mifflin, 1912.

Under the Apple-Trees. Boston: Houghton Mifflin, 1916.

Under the Maples. Boston: Houghton Mifflin, 1921.

Wake-Robin. Boston: Hurd and Houghton, 1871.

Ways of Nature. Boston: Houghton Mifflin, 1905.

Whitman: A Study. Boston: Houghton Mifflin, 1896.

Winter Sunshine. Boston: Hurd and Houghton, 1875.

Writings of John Burroughs, Riverby Edition. 23 vols. Boston: Houghton Mifflin, 1905–1922.

WORKS BY RALPH WALDO EMERSON

Essays: First Series. Boston: Phillips, Sampson, 1857.

Essays: Second Series. Boston: Phillips, Sampson, 1857.

Essays and Poems. New York: Library of America College Edition, 1996.

Journals and Miscellaneous Notebooks. 16 vols. Ed. William H. Gilman. Cambridge: Harvard University Press, 1960–82.

Nature, Addresses, and Lectures. Vol. 1, *The Collected Works of Ralph Waldo Emerson.* 5 vols. to date. Ed. Robert E. Spiller. Cambridge: Harvard University Press, 1971– .

WORKS BY JOHN MUIR

The Cruise of the Corwin: Journal of the Arctic Expedition of 1881 in Search of De Long and the Jeanette. Ed. William Frederick Badè. Boston: Houghton Mifflin, 1917.

Edward Henry Harriman. New York: Doubleday, Page, 1911.

John Muir: His "Life and Letters" and Other Writings. Ed. Terry Gifford. Seattle: The Mountaineers, 1996.

John Muir: The Eight Wilderness-Discovery Books. Ed. Terry Gifford. Seattle: The Mountaineers, 1992.

John Muir's Last Journey. Ed. Michael P. Branch. Washington, D.C.: Island, 2001.

John of the Mountains: The Unpublished Journals of John Muir. Ed. Linnie Marsh Wolfe. Boston: Houghton Mifflin, 1938.

Kindred and Related Spirits: The Letters of John Muir and Jeanne C. Carr. Ed. Bonnie Johanna Gisel. Salt Lake City: University of Utah Press, 2001.

Letters from Alaska. Ed. Robert Engberg and Bruce Merrell. Madison: University of Wisconsin Press, 1993.

Life and Letters of John Muir. Ed. William Frederick Badè. 2 vols. Boston: Houghton Mifflin, 1924.

The Mountains of California. New York: Century, 1894. Reprint, New York: Penguin, 1997. Page references are to the Penguin edition.

"Notes on the Pacific Coast Glaciers." In *Harriman Alaska Series,* 13 vols., edited by C. Hart Merriam, 1:119–35. New York: Doubleday, Page, 1901–10.

Our National Parks. Boston: Houghton Mifflin, 1901.

Picturesque California and the Region West of the Rocky Mountains, from Alaska to Mexico. (Edited by Muir.) 2 vols. San Francisco: J. Dewing, 1888.

Stickeen. Boston: Houghton Mifflin, 1909.

The Story of My Boyhood and Youth. Boston: Houghton Mifflin, 1913.

To Yosemite and Beyond: Writings from the Years 1863 to 1875. Ed. Robert Engberg and Donald Wesling. Madison: University of Wisconsin Press, 1980.

Travels in Alaska. Boston: Houghton Mifflin, 1915.

The Yosemite. New York: Century, 1912.

WORKS BY THEODORE ROOSEVELT

An Autobiography. New York: Scribner's, 1913.

The Deer Family. Ed. Caspar Whitney. New York: Macmillan, 1902.

Hunting Trips of a Ranchman. New York: Putnam's, 1885.

The Letters of Theodore Roosevelt. Ed. E. Elting Morison. 8 vols. Cambridge: Harvard University Press. 1951.

Outdoor Pastimes of an American Hunter. New York: Scribner's, 1905.

Ranch Life and the Hunting Trail. New York: Century, 1888.

The Wilderness Hunter. New York: Putnam's, 1893.

The Works of Theodore Roosevelt. National Edition. Ed. Hermann Hagedorn. 11 vols. New York: Charles Scribner's Sons, 1926.

Secondary Sources

Allen, Gay Wilson. *The Solitary Singer.* New York: Macmillan, 1955.

Althusser, Louis. "Ideology and Ideological State Apparatuses (Notes towards an Investigation)." In *"Lenin and Philosophy" and Other Essays,* translated by Ben Brewster. New York: Monthly Review Press, 1971.

Barrus, Clara. *Whitman and Burroughs, Comrades.* Boston: Houghton Mifflin, 1931.

Bederman, Gail. *Manliness and Civilization: A Cultural History of Gender and Race in the United States, 1880–1917.* Chicago: University of Chicago Press, 1995.

Berry, Wendell. *Home Economics.* New York: North Point Press, 1987.

Bourdieu, Pierre. *Distinction: A Social Critique of the Judgment of Taste.* Trans. Richard Nice. Cambridge: Harvard University Press, 1984.

Branch, Michael P. "Telling Nature's Story: John Muir and the Decentering of the Romantic Self." In *John Muir in Historical Perspective,* edited by Sally M. Miller. New York: Peter Lang, 1999.

Branch, Michael P., and Scott Slovic, eds. *The ISLE Reader: Ecocriticism, 1993–2003.* Athens: University of Georgia Press, 2003.

Brodhead, Richard. *Cultures of Letters: Scenes of Reading and Writing in Nineteenth-Century America.* Chicago: University of Chicago Press, 1993.

———. *School of Hawthorne.* New York: Oxford University Press, 1986.

Buell, Lawrence. *Emerson.* Cambridge: Harvard University Press, 2004.

———. *The Environmental Imagination: Thoreau, Nature Writing, and the Formation of American Culture.* Cambridge: Harvard University Press, 1995.

———. *Writing for an Endangered World: Literature, Culture, and Environment in the U.S. and Beyond.* Cambridge: Harvard University Press, 2001.

Cameron, Sharon. *Writing Nature: Henry Thoreau's Journal.* New York: Oxford University Press, 1985.

Casey, Edward S. "Body, Self, and Landscape: A Geophilosophical Inquiry into the Place-World." In *Textures of Place: Exploring Humanist Geographies,* edited by Paul C. Adams, Steven Hoelscher, and Karen E. Till. Minneapolis: University of Minnesota Press, 2001.

———. *The Fate of Place: A Philosophical History.* Berkeley: University of California Press, 1997.

———. *Getting Back into Place: Toward a Renewed Understanding of the Place-World.* Bloomington: Indiana University Press, 1993.

Chowder, Ken. "North to Alaska." *Smithsonian* 34 (June 2003): 91–101.

Cohen, Michael P. "Blues in the Green: Ecocriticism under Critique." *Environmental History* 9 (January 2004): 9–37.

———. *The Pathless Way: John Muir and American Wilderness.* Madison: University of Wisconsin Press, 1984.

Collins, Michael. *That Damned Cowboy: Theodore Roosevelt and the American West, 1883–1898.* New York: Peter Lang, 1989.

Cutright, Paul Russell. *Theodore Roosevelt: The Making of a Conservationist.* Urbana: University of Illinois Press, 1985.

Entrikin, J. Nicholas. "Geographer as Humanist." In *Textures of Place: Exploring Hu-*

manist Geographies, edited by Paul C. Adams, Steven Hoelscher, and Karen E. Till. Minneapolis: University of Minnesota Press, 2001.

Gidley, Mick. *Edward S. Curtis and the North American Indian, Incorporated.* Cambridge: Cambridge University Press, 1998.

Glazener, Nancy. *Reading for Realism: The History of a U.S. Literary Institution, 1850–1910.* Durham: Duke University Press, 1997.

Goetzmann, William H., and Kay Sloan. *Looking Far North: The Harriman Expedition to Alaska 1899.* New York: Viking, 1982.

Harding, Walter. "Thoreau's Reputation." In *The Cambridge Companion to Henry David Thoreau.* Cambridge: Cambridge University Press, 1995.

Harriman Expedition Retraced. Public Broadcasting System. http://www.pbs.org/harriman/.

Hinckley, Ted C. "The Inside Passage: A Popular Gilded Age Tour." *Pacific Northwest Quarterly* 56 (1965): 67–74.

Howarth, William. "Reading the Wetlands." In *Textures of Place: Exploring Humanist Geographies*, edited by Paul C. Adams, Steven Hoelscher, and Karen E. Till. Minneapolis: University of Minnesota Press, 2001.

John, Arthur. *The Best Years of the Century: Richard Watson Gilder, Scribner's Monthly, and the Century Magazine, 1870–1909.* Urbana: University of Illinois Press, 1981.

Johnson, Robert Underwood. *Remembered Yesterdays.* Boston: Little, Brown, 1923.

Johnston, Clifton, ed. *John Burroughs Talks.* Boston: Houghton Mifflin, 1922.

Kanze, Edward. *The World of John Burroughs.* New York: H. N. Abrams, 1993.

Kelley, Mary. *Private Woman, Public Stage: Literary Domesticity in Nineteenth-Century America.* Oxford: Oxford University Press, 1984.

Kimes, William F., and Maymie B. Kimes, eds. *John Muir: A Reading Bibliography.* Fresno: Panorama West Books, 1986.

Lears, T. J. Jackson. *No Place of Grace: Antimodernism and the Transformation of American Culture, 1880–1920.* New York: Pantheon, 1981.

Limbaugh, Ronald H., and Kirsten E. Lewis, eds. *Guide and Index to the Microform Edition of the John Muir Papers, 1858–1957.* Alexandria, VA: Chadwyck-Healey, 1986.

Linton, William J. *The History of Wood-Engraving in America.* Boston: Estes and Lauriat, 1882.

Lord, Nancy. *Green Alaska: Dreams from the Far Coast.* Washington, D.C.: Counterpoint, 1999.

Love, Glen. *Practical Ecocriticism.* Charlottesville: University of Virginia Press, 2003.

Lowell, James Russell. *My Study Window.* Boston: Houghton, Mifflin, 1871.

Lupfer, Eric. "Before Nature Writing: Houghton, Mifflin and Company and the Invention of the Outdoor Book, 1800–1900," *Book History* 4 (2001): 177–204.

———. "Reading Nature Writing: Houghton Mifflin Company, the Ohio Teachers'

Reading Circle, and *In American Fields and Forests* (1909)." *Harvard Library Bulletin* 13 (Spring 2002): 37–58.

Lutts, Ralph H. *The Nature Fakers: Wildlife, Science and Sentiment.* Golden, CO: Fulcrum, 1990. Reprint, Charlottesville: University Press of Virginia, 2001.

Lutz, John E. "The Influence of John Burroughs on Education." In *Sharp Eyes: John Burroughs and American Nature Writing*, edited by Charlotte Zoe Walker. Syracuse: Syracuse University Press, 2000.

Making of America. Cornell University. http://moa.cit.cornell.edu/moa/.

Making of America. University of Michigan. http://www.hti.umich.edu/m/moagrp/.

Manley, Atwood, and Margaret Manley Mangum. *Frederic Remington and the North Country.* New York: E. P. Dutton, 1988.

Marshall, Ian. *Peak Experiences: Walking Meditations on Literature, Nature, and Need.* Charlottesville: University of Virginia Press, 2003.

———. *Story Line: Exploring the Literature of the Appalachian Trail.* Charlottesville: University of Virginia Press, 1998.

Merriam, C. Hart, ed. *Harriman Alaska Series.* 13 vols. New York: Doubleday, Page, 1901–10.

Miller, Edwin Haviland, ed. *The Correspondence of Walt Whitman.* 6 vols. New York: New York University Press, 1961–77.

Morris, Edmund. *The Rise of Theodore Roosevelt.* New York: Coward, McCann and Geoghegan, 1979.

Mott, Frank Luther. *A History of American Magazines.* 5 vols. Cambridge: Harvard University Press, 1939–68.

Nemerov, Alexander. *Frederic Remington and Turn-of-the-Century America.* New Haven: Yale University Press, 1995.

Norton, Aloysius A. *Theodore Roosevelt.* Boston: Twayne, 1980.

Philippon, Daniel J. *Conserving Words: How American Nature Writers Shaped the Environmental Movement.* Athens: University of Georgia Press, 2004.

Porte, Joel, ed. *Emerson in His Journals.* Cambridge: Harvard University Press, 1982.

Reed, David. *The Popular Magazine in Britain and the United States, 1880–1960.* Toronto: University of Toronto Press, 1997.

Renehan, Edward. *John Burroughs: An American Naturalist.* Post Mills, VT: Chelsea Green, 1992.

Rosendale, Steven, ed. *The Greening of Literary Scholarship: Literature, Theory, and the Environment.* Iowa City: University of Iowa Press, 2002.

Ryden, Kent C. *Landscape with Figures: Nature and Culture in New England.* Iowa City: University of Iowa Press, 2001.

———. *Mapping the Invisible Landscape: Folklore, Writing, and the Sense of Place.* Iowa City: University of Iowa Press, 1993.

Sack, Robert David. *Homo Geographicus: A Framework for Action, Awareness, and Moral Concern.* Baltimore: Johns Hopkins University Press, 1997.

Santayana, George. *The Genteel Tradition: Nine Essays by George Santayana.* Cambridge: Harvard University Press, 1967.

Schmitt, Peter J. *Back to Nature: The Arcadian Myth in Urban Nature.* New York: Oxford University Press, 1969.

Schneider, Richard J., ed. *Thoreau's Sense of Place.* Iowa City: University of Iowa Press, 2000.

Scholnick, Robert. "*Scribner's Monthly* and the 'Pictorial Representation of Life and Truth' in Post–Civil War America." *American Periodicals* 1.1 (1991): 46–69.

Scidmore, Eliza Ruhama. *Alaska: Its Southern Coast and the Sitkan Archipelago.* Boston: D. Lothrop, 1885.

———. *The Guide-Book to Alaska and the Northwest Coast.* London: William Heinemann, 1893.

Sedgwick, Ellery. *The Atlantic Monthly, 1857–1909: Yankee Humanism at High Tide and Ebb.* Amherst: University of Massachusetts Press, 1994.

Slotkin, Richard. *The Fatal Environment: The Myth of the Frontier in the Age of Industrialization, 1800–1890.* New York: Atheneum, 1985.

———. *Gunfighter Nation: The Myth of the Frontier in Twentieth-Century America.* New York: Atheneum, 1992.

———. "Nostalgia and Progress: Theodore Roosevelt's Myth of the Frontier." *American Quarterly* 33 (Winter 1981): 608–37.

Tompkins, Jane. *Sensational Designs: The Cultural Work of American Fiction, 1790–1860.* Oxford: Oxford University Press, 1985.

Tuan, Yi-Fu. *Cosmos and Hearth: A Cosmopolite's Viewpoint.* Minneapolis: University of Minnesota Press, 1996.

———. *Space and Place: The Perspective of Experience.* Minneapolis: University of Minnesota Press, 1977.

———. *Topophilia: A Study of Environmental Perception, Attitudes, and Values.* New York: Columbia University Press, 1974.

Turner, Frederick. *John Muir: Rediscovering America.* Cambridge MA: Perseus, 2000.

Walker, Charlotte Zoe, ed. *Sharp Eyes: John Burroughs and American Nature Writing.* Syracuse: Syracuse University Press, 2000.

Warren, James Perrin. *Walt Whitman's Language Experiment.* University Park: Pennsylvania State University Press, 1990.

Westbrook, Perry. *John Burroughs.* New York: Twayne, 1974.

Whitman, Walt. *Leaves of Grass: Comprehensive Reader's Edition.* Ed. Harold Blodgett and Sculley Bradley. New York: New York University Press, 1965.

Williams, Raymond. *The Country and the City.* Oxford: Oxford University Press, 1973.

Witherell, Elizabeth Hall, ed. "General Introduction." *Journal*. Vol. 1. Henry D. Thoreau. Princeton: Princeton University Press, 1981.

Wolfe, Linnie Marsh. *Son of the Wilderness: The Life of John Muir.* New York: Alfred Knopf, 1945.

Woodman, Abby Johnson. *Picturesque Alaska*. Boston: Houghton, Mifflin, 1889.

INDEX

aesthetics, 18; ecocentric, 42, 49, 50
Alaska: Baird Glacier, 123, 124, 130;
 Davidson Glacier, 121, 136–37; Dutch
 Harbor, Unalaska, 147; Fairweather
 Range, 125–26, 128, 130, 136; Glacier
 Bay, 119, 121, 125, 126–27, 130, 131,
 137, 139, 142; Glacier Point, 201;
 Grand Pacific Glacier, 130, 136; Hall
 Island, 147; Hugh Miller Glacier, 136;
 Kadiak (Kodiak) Island, 145–47; Lynn
 Canal, 132; Morse Glacier, 143; Mount
 Wright, 143–44; and Muir, 114, 119,
 121, 122, 135–36, 137; Muir Glacier,
 100, 119, 121, 126–27, 128, 135–46
 passim; Pacific Glacier, 130, 131; Plover
 Bay, 132; St. Matthew Island, 147–49;
 St. Michaels, 132; Taku Glacier, 128;
 Taku Inlet, 128; tourism in, 127, 135
analogy, 24; agricultural, 55
antimodernism, 97, 98–99, 100
Antiquities and National Monuments Act,
 152
Aristotle, 4, 6, 13
Arnold, Matthew, 32

Bad Lands (of Dakota territory): landscape
 of, 153–55; significance of, for
 Roosevelt, 156–59
Badè, William Frederic, 114
Barrus, Clara, 1, 16, 202–3; as Burroughs's
 editor, 14; correspondence between
 Burroughs and, 194, 195, 201, 205, 219

Beardslee, Lester A., 119
beauty, 48, 60
Benton, Joel, 107
Benton, Myron, 27–28
Bergson, Henri, 231
Berry, Wendell, 4, 7
Berryman, Clifford, 197
Bible, 54, 64–65, 212
birds: as subject for Burroughs, 2, 33,
 48, 58–59, 71, 94, 111, 216; as subject
 for Roosevelt, 177–78, 179, 190–91;
 watching, 64, 111, 191
books, as tools, 11–13
Boone and Crockett Club, 117, 153, 197
Burroughs, John: aesthetics of, 48, 49, 50,
 51; catalogues in works of, 53; death
 of, 1; as dogmatic, 198–99; early life
 of, 1, 22, 46; editions of writings of,
 236n2; elegiac mode of, 1, 227–34;
 as Emersonian, 23–24, 27, 43, 71,
 209; on England, 70; on experiential
 knowledge, 66; farm life of, 1, 46,
 85; and geology, 203–6, 207, 210–12,
 218–21; as literary critic, 2, 18, 51, 60,
 61, 62; as literary naturalist, 15, 44,
 52–54, 58, 62–63, 72, 151, 231; and
 modernity, 1, 15, 98–99; and "nature
 fakers" controversy, 150–51, 193, 195,
 197, 198–99; on the past, 16–17;
 perceptive style of, 64, 95, 97, 198;
 and the picturesque/pastoral, 84, 85,
 216; popularity of, 11, 14, 15, 99–100,

Burroughs, John (*continued*)
107, 194, 196; on relationship between nature and art, 63; on relationship between nature and culture, 2–3, 15, 61–62, 66–71, 97, 99, 112, 145; on religion, 232; rhetoric of domestication in writings of, 48, 52, 109; rhetoric of sources in writings of, 52–53, 54; and science, 3, 207, 209, 231, 232; and "scientific imagination," 220; sense of nature of, 3, 17, 23–24, 30, 193, 207–9, 221–22, 232–33; sense of place of, 13, 31–32, 49, 70–71, 143, 146, 148–49; on standards of literary value, 61, 63, 198; teaching of, to children, 99–100, 195–97; and theory of evolution, 207–9, 221–23, 232–33; on tourism, 214; on United States, 70

Burroughs, John, works of: *Accepting the Universe*, 232–34; "The Adirondacks," 66; "All's Right with the World," 207, 209; "Another Word on Emerson," 28, 32; "Another Word on Thoreau," 15, 19–22, 67; "Arnold's View of Emerson and Carlyle," 28, 31; "Before Beauty," 50; "Before Genius," 34, 50, 51; "Birch Browsings," 66, 67; "A Bird Medley," 71; *Birds and Bees*, 99, 195; "Birds and Poets," 29, 178, 198; *Birds and Poets*, 2, 28, 29, 34, 42, 50, 52, 63, 71; "The Bow in the Clouds," 230; *Camping and Tramping with Roosevelt*, 191, 200; *Camping with President Roosevelt*, 195; "Death," 233; "The Divine Abyss," 204–5, 210–12, 214, 215; "The Divine Soil," 207, 208–9; "An Egotistical Chapter," 22, 26, 35; "Emerson," 28, 29–30, 52; "Emerson and His Journals," 15, 17–19, 21, 228;

"The Exhilarations of the Road," 33, 34, 68; "Expression," 23–27; *Far and Near*, 137, 217; *Field and Study*, 232; "Flies in Amber," 15, 16–17; "The Flight of the Eagle," 52; *Fresh Fields*, 28; "From the Back Country," 27; "Glimpses of Wild Life about My Cabin," 109–12, 217; "The Gospel of Nature," 222; "Grist of the Gods," 207–8; "The Hazards of the Past," 222; "Henry D. Thoreau," 36, 105; "Human Traits in the Animals," 198; "In Green Alaska," 137, 146–47; "In the Hemlocks," 64–66; *Indoor Studies*, 28, 36; journals, 15, 33, 35, 115, 140, 143, 144; *The Last Harvest*, 33, 228; *Leaf and Tendril*, 198, 206, 220; *The Light of Day*, 3; *Literary Studies*, 28; *Literary Values*, 29, 39; *Little Nature Studies for Little People*, 100, 196; "Narrative of the Expedition," 118, 137, 139, 140–48; "The Naturalist's View of Life," 231; *Notes on Walt Whitman, as Poet and Person*, 42–46, 48–50; "An October Abroad," 70; "The Old Ice-Flood," 220, 221; "An Outlook upon Life," 207, 209; *Pepacton*, 99, 195; "The Phantoms Behind Us," 222; "Picturesque Aspects of Farm Life in New York," 82–85, 93, 98, 151; "The Poet of the Cosmos," 233; "Real and Sham Natural History," 150, 197; "The Reasonable but Unreasoning Animals," 198; *Recent Phases of Criticism*, 29; *Riverby*, 58; "The Round World," 230, 231; *Science and the Poets*, 31–32; "Scientific Faith," 221–22; *Sharp Eyes*, 99–100, 195; "A Sharp Lookout," 97; "Signs and Seasons," 94; *Signs and Seasons*, 29, 84; "The

Spell of the Yosemite," 210, 216–17, 218; "A Spray of Pine," 29; "Spring at the Capital," 67–68; *Squirrels and Other Fur-Bearers*, 100, 196; "Straight Seeing and Thinking," 198; "Style and the Man," 29; "The Summit of the Years," 230; *The Summit of the Years*, 229–31; "A Sunday in Cheyne Row," 28; "Thoreau's Wildness," 39–41; *Time and Change*, 206, 210, 220–23; "Touches of Nature," 2, 71; *Under the Apple-Trees*, 231; *Under the Maples*, 14; *Wake-Robin*, 42, 63–68, 155, 190; *Ways of Nature*, 198; "What Makes the Poet?" 50; *Whitman: A Study*, 56–62; *Winter Sunshine*, 34, 63, 68–71; "The Worm Striving to Be Man," 222

Burt, Mary E., 99–100, 195, 196

California, 89–90, 100; Mount Ritter, 76
Catskills, 1, 66, 67, 210
Century Illustrated Monthly Magazine (originally *Scribner's Monthly*), 35, 73–112 passim; cultural influence of, 74, 81–82, 152; and environmental advocacy, 99
Cleveland, Grover, 188
common, the: value of, for Burroughs, 25, 27, 35, 48–49, 55, 69, 207; value of, for Emerson, 24, 25–26
Concord, MA, 17, 22, 35
concrete, the, 2, 17, 25, 26, 30, 35, 208; in form of object-world, 44, 53
Corwin (steamship), 121, 132
Creative Evolution (Bergson), 231
culture, relationship between nature and, 2–3, 7, 8–9, 12–13, 88; Burroughs on, 2–3, 15, 61–62, 66–71, 97, 99, 112, 145;

Muir on, 120; Roosevelt on, 151, 175, 176, 186, 188; Whitman on, 44, 61
Curtis, Edward S., 117, 118

Darwin, Charles, 207, 208
de Graffenreid, Clare, 73–74
Dellenbaugh, Fred S., 117, 118
discipleship, 18, 47
duality, 24–26

ecocriticism, 3–4, 11; Burroughs and, 2, 44, 49, 54, 62, 72; Burroughs's works of, 29, 58, 60; Roosevelt and, 151, 153; Whitman and, 44
elegy, 58
Emerson, Edward Waldo, 35
Emerson, Ralph Waldo, 2, 12, 13, 15, 106; Burroughs's opinion of, 114, 231; environmental aesthetics of, 49; influence of, on Burroughs, 22–27, 28, 51, 62–63; influence of, on culture, 16, 18, 19, 52; as New Englander, 29–30; poetry of, 29–30; remoteness of, 32; reputation of, 16, 18, 31; science as interest of, 32; sense of division of, 17; sense of limitation of, 17–18, 24, 31; sense of nature of, 17, 23–26; on the soul, 17, 24, 25
Emerson, Ralph Waldo, works of: "Each and All," 49; *Essays: First Series*, 24; *Essays: Second Series*, 24; *Nature*, 24, 25, 69; "The Over-Soul," 24; "The Poet," 24
essay, nature, genre of, 74–75, 81, 82, 93, 98

farm life: of Burroughs, 1, 46, 85; as subject, 82–85
Foote, Mary Hallock, 82

Forest and Stream, 117, 197
Forest Reserve Act, 188
forests, national, 99, 104–5, 188, 201
formalism, classical, 32
Fraser, John A., 136
Frost, Arthur B., 166, 182
Fuertes, Louis Agassiz, 117, 118

geography, 7–8; literary, 22, 29, 52, 63
George W. Elder (steamship), 117
Georgia "cracker," 73
Gifford, R. Swain, 117, 118, 166
Gilbert, G. K., 117, 118, 119, 120
Gilder, Richard Watson, 35, 73, 82, 105
Ginn Company, 100, 196
Glaciers and Glaciation (Gilbert), 118,
   120
God, 17–18, 24, 64, 65
Grand Canyon, 199, 201–4, 210
Greenslet, Ferris, 14
Grinnell, George Bird, 117, 118, 197

Harper's New Monthly Magazine, 74
Harriman, E. H., 116; family of, 118
Harriman Alaska expedition, 116, 121–35
   passim; importance of, 117–19; Muir's
   opinion of, 119–20
Harriman Alaska Series, 117, 118–19,
   122–49 passim; importance of, 119, 152
Harte, Bret, 75, 98
Hawthorne, Nathaniel, 213
Heidegger, Martin, 7
Herald Island, Russia, 132
Hetch Hetchy Valley, 100, 103, 104, 225
Holland, Josiah Gilbert, 74, 81
Horsfall, Bruce, 109
Houghton, Oscar, 99, 195
Houghton Mifflin: and Burroughs, 14, 42,
   99, 195, 196; and Muir, 224–26

illustration: effect of, with essays, 76–81;
   half-tone plates, 82; New School
   process of (photoxylography), 82, 84,
   118, 136, 170; photography, 183–84;
   wood engravings, traditional, 76, 118
In American Fields and Forests, 196
Indians: and Muir, 124, 137; and
   Roosevelt, 157, 169, 173, 182

Jackson, Sheldon, 124
James, Henry, 34, 37, 70–71, 98
Johnson, Robert Underwood: and Muir,
   89, 99, 100, 104–5, 205, 223–24, 225;
   on Roosevelt's travels, 194

Keeler, Charles, 116–17, 118, 143, 147
Keeler, Louise M., 118
Keith, William, 105
Kemble, E. W., 73–74
Kingsley, Elbridge, 95

language, Burroughs's sense of, 24, 25, 26,
   63
Last Harvest, The, 14
Lincoln, Abraham, 200
Linton, W. J., 84
Loeb, William, 197
London, Jack, 151, 199
Long, William J., 151, 193, 195, 199
Lowell, James Russell, 19, 23

Mabie, Hamilton Wright, 107
Mackenzie, George G., 104
magazines, illustrated: cultural influence
   of, 12, 90, 93; and the nature essay,
   74–75, 81–82
Merriam, C. Hart, 117, 118, 151
Merrifield, A. W., 153, 161
Montana, 180, 189

movies, Burroughs on, 15

Muir, John, 11, 74, 75, 104–7, 196; Alaska trips of, 114, 119, 121; Alaska's significance for, 122, 137; art of combination used by, 126, 128, 131, 143; Burroughs's opinion of, 113–14, 115, 201, 227, 228; celebrity of, 104–7; and conservation, 218; death of, 227; Emerson and, 113–14; Emerson's opinion of, 227, 228; and geology, 212, 216; on hunting, 120; as illustrator, 75–76, 78–81, 85–87, 121, 129–30, 131, 132–137; influence of, on Burroughs, 137–45, 148, 202, 205–6, 209–10, 220; influence of Burroughs on, 223–26; journals of, 115, 119, 121, 129, 130, 131; leadership skills of, 125; as nature writer, 11, 89, 113, 114; newspaper dispatches of, 121, 123; papers of, 121–22; on railroads, 213–14; relationship of Burroughs and, 12, 82, 113–16, 137, 202, 203–5; religious language of, 125–26, 130, 213, 228; sense of nature of, 78, 81, 88, 99, 220; sense of place of, 138, 143; sled trip on Muir Glacier of, 135–36; temperament of, 113, 114, 203, 205, 227; on tourism, 212–14, 218; as travel writer, 124

Muir, John, works of: "An Adventure with a Dog and a Glacier," 224; "Alaska" in *American Geologist*, 122; "Alaska" in *Picturesque California*, 121, 127, 129; "The Alaska Trip," 121, 127–28, 136, 139, 224; "The American Forests," 189, 224, 225; "The Bee Pastures of California," 89–90, 98, 105; *The Cruise of the Corwin*, 114, 122, 132; "The Discovery of Glacier Bay," 121, 124–27, 128, 130, 136; "The Endangered Valley," 225; "Features of the Proposed Yosemite National Park," 89, 100; "Glaciers," 122; "The Grand Cañon of the Colorado," 212–16, 225; *Letters from Alaska*, 123–24, 130; *The Mountains of California*, 89, 114, 120, 121; *My First Summer in the Sierra*, 114, 226; "Notes on the Pacific Coast Glaciers," 118, 122–23, 128, 134; *Our National Parks*, 102, 114, 189, 217–20, 225, 226; *Picturesque California*, 120, 121, 127, 129; *Steep Trails*, 114; *Stickeen*, 114; *The Story of My Boyhood and Youth*, 114, 226, 228; "Studies in the Sierra," 75, 76, 129, 211; *A Thousand-Mile Walk to the Gulf*, 114; *Travels in Alaska*, 114, 122, 128, 130, 139; "The Treasures of the Yosemite," 89, 100–103, 217; "The Wild Parks and Forest Reservations of the West," 189; "A Wind Storm in the Forests of the Yuba," 82, 85–88, 151; *The Writings of John Muir*, 226; *The Yosemite*, 114, 225; "Yosemite Glaciers," 211

Muir, Louie Strentzel, 105, 116, 201

Nation, 34, 90

National Forest Commission, 224

Natural History, 229

nature: and culture 8–9, 12–13, 151; representations of, 12, 152; "second," 20; spiritual quality of, 65, 145; as standard for judging art, 44

nature essay. *See* essay, nature, genre of

New School. *See under* illustration

New York (state), 84, 89

New York City, 85, 105, 116

New York Leader, 28

Noble, John W., 104

North American Indian, The (Curtis), 117
North Sigillaria Petrified Forest, 201, 202

Ohio Teachers' Reading Circle, 196
Osborn, Henry Fairfield, 121
Overland Monthly, 75, 76, 87, 129

Page, Walter Hines, 223–26
Parsons, Marion Randall, 122
pastoralism: Burroughs's use of, 58–60,
    62; elegy, 58; imagery of, 52; tradition
    of, 21, 59–60, 63, 85
periodicals, 74–75, 82
Pinchot, Gifford, 189
Pitcher, John, 182
place: concept of, as critical tool, 20, 22,
    33, 36, 63; as metaphor, 4–5; power of,
    5–6
Poe, Edgar Allan, 154
poetry, 24, 29, 55; as place, 56
power, 18, 24, 53, 55; as source of beauty,
    52
Principles of Geology (Lyell), 208

realism, genre of, 93, 97
regionalism, 97, 98
Remington, Frederic, 151, 168–72, 173,
    182, 192
Riverby, 85
Rock Creek, 67–68
Rocky Mountains, 174, 177
Roosevelt, Alice, 153
Roosevelt, Theodore, 5, 11, 104, 117;
    anthropocentrism of, 157, 160, 177;
    antimodernism of, 152, 161, 168, 190;
    on Bad Lands landscape, 153–58; on
    Burroughs, 150–52, 153, 176, 178–79,
    190–91, 197; Burroughs on, 191–93,
    199–200, 229; celebrity of, 161, 173–74,

175, 182; and conservation, 152, 169,
    176, 185–86, 187–89, 201; Darwinian
    perspective of, 156, 169; effect of wife's
    death on, 153; elegiac mode of, 158,
    169, 175; ethnocentric perspective
    of, 157; as governor of New York,
    188–89; hunting ethics of, 158–60,
    186, 188; images in works of, 161–66,
    169–72, 173, 182–83; influence of,
    on Burroughs, 193, 199; influence
    of Burroughs on, 178, 189, 193; as
    inspiration for teddy bear, 197; journals
    of, 153; and masculinity, 168, 170, 172,
    188; and Muir, 151, 189, 190, 194, 201;
    as naturalist, 164, 179, 184, 186, 191,
    197; on "nature fakers," 150–51, 193,
    197, 199; as nature writer, 152–53, 158,
    166, 180, 187; and observation, 150,
    151, 166, 184, 185; and pastoralism,
    168, 175; on plains landscape, 155–56;
    and ranching, 157, 168–73; realism of,
    160, 168, 175; relationship between
    Burroughs and, 12, 150, 192–93, 198;
    romanticism of, 160; sense of nature
    of, 151–52, 168, 175, 176, 177, 193;
    sense of place of, 176, 180, 187; as
    still-hunter, 160–66, 175; as storyteller,
    181–82; on Thoreau, 179; tours western
    wonders, 194; Virginia retreat of, 190;
    as Whitmanian ideal, 200; on wildlife,
    157–59, 176–77, 180, 188
Roosevelt, Theodore, works of: *An
    Autobiography*, 201; *The Deer and
    Antelope of North America*, 185, 187;
    The Deer Family, 193; *Hunting Trips of
    a Ranchman*, 153–67; *Outdoor Pastimes
    of an American Hunter*, 150, 183,
    184–91; *Ranch Life and the Hunting
    Trail*, 168, 170, 172; "The Ranchman's

Life and the Hunting Trail," 174; "Sheriff's Work on a Ranch," 173; *The Wilderness Hunter*, 159, 176–83, 185

Sargent, Charles S., 104, 105, 121, 224
Scidmore, Eliza Ruhamah, 104
Scribner's Monthly. See *Century Illustrated Monthly Magazine*
self-reliance, 17, 18
Seton, Ernest Thompson, 151
sexuality, 55
Shoshone Mountains, 181
Siberia, 117, 121, 132
Sierra Nevada, 75–78, 89, 101–3, 201, 211–12, 219
Slabsides, 56–62, 109, 111, 115, 202, 221, 229
Spader, W. E., 118
St. Paul, Minn., 195
Stickeen, 121
Swett, John, 105–7

Thoreau, Henry David, 2, 12, 15, 196; as azad, 39; Burroughs's opinion of, 19–22, 38, 39–40, 95; and the concrete, 40, 49; and Emerson, 19, 36, 113; fractiousness of, 21, 113, 114; idealism of, 21; influence of, on Burroughs, 33–34, 35, 62–63; literary contribution of, 22; as naturalist, 21, 38–39; reputation of, 19, 105; rhetoric of, 21, 55; as seeker of truth, 40; sense of place of, 37–39; solitude of, 19–20; style of, 38; as supernaturalist, 21, 38; wildness of, 37–38, 39, 40
Thoreau, Henry David, works of: *The Maine Woods*, 66; *Walden*, 19, 34, 39, 70; "Walking," 20, 34
Trail and Campfire, 185

transcendentalism, 22, 23, 30
truth, natural, 18
Tuolumne Meadows, 100

University of Chicago, Burroughs visit to, 194

Vassar College, 111, 221

Walden Pond, 20, 22, 35, 38
walking, as means of experiencing landscape, 68–70
Washington, D.C., 42, 67, 190, 194
West Park, NY, 1
Whitman, Walt, 2, 12; Burroughs on, 54, 200, 231, 233–34; catalogue style of, 55; concept of nature of, 44–45; contributions of, to Burroughs's work, 44–48; correspondence of, 43, 50; death of, 58; ecocentric aesthetics of, 49; as editor of Burroughs's work, 42, 50; emotion in works of, 52; evolution in works of, 55–56; as foil to Emerson, 52; the ideal in works of, 56; influence of, on Burroughs, 25, 42, 43, 51, 62–63, 208; as modern, 55; rhetoric of, 45; on role of nature in criticism, 44–46; role of nature in work of, 44–45, 61; spirituality of, 56; on writer-reader relationship, 45–46
Whitman, Walt, works of: "The Dalliance of the Eagles," 58; *Leaves of Grass*, 50, 60; "Out of the Cradle Endlessly Rocking," 54, 178; "Song of Myself," 49, 208; *Specimen Days & Collect*, 43; "Standard of the Natural Universal," 44–45, 200; "Starting from Paumanok," 208; "There Was a Child Went Forth," 54; "When Lilacs Last in the Door-yard Bloom'd," 58, 155, 178

Whitman Land. *See* Slabsides
wildness, 21, 37, 39
Willis, Bailey, 205, 219
Wordsworth, William, 20, 21, 47–48, 59,
    60, 70
Wyoming, 181, 191

Yellowstone National Park: Roosevelt in,
    182; trip of Burroughs and Roosevelt to,
    150, 152, 189, 194, 197, 199
Yi-Fu Tuan, 7–8
Yosemite, 75, 100–104, 106, 199, 201–5
    passim, 210, 212, 219
Young, S. Hall, 121, 124

Kurt Weill
An Illustrated Biography

Kurt Weill

An Illustrated Biography

Douglas Jarman

The Sidney B. Coulter Library
Onondaga Community College
Rte. 173, Onondaga Hill
Syracuse, New York 13215

Orbis Publishing
London

First published in Great Britain
by Orbis Publishing Limited, London 1982

© Douglas Jarman 1982

All rights reserved. No part of this
publication may be reproduced, in any
form, or by any means, electronic,
mechanical, photocopying, recording or
otherwise, without the prior permission of
the publishers. Such permission, if
granted, is subject to a fee depending on
the nature of use.

Printed in Great Britain by William Collins Sons & Co Ltd., Glasgow

ISBN 0-85613-326-4

Contents

Introduction 7

Part One
The Man and His Times

Chapter 1 **The Early Years** 13

Chapter 2 **Weill's Berlin** 22

Chapter 3 **1926-1929** 39

Chapter 4 **1930-1935** 54

Chapter 5 **The American Years** 71

Part Two
Assessing the Music

Chapter 6 **The Early Instrumental and Vocal Music** 87

Chapter 7 **The European Dramatic and Vocal Works** 96

Chapter 8 **The American Works** 132

Chronological List of Works 144

Discography 147

Bibliography 148

Notes 150

Acknowledgements 157

Index 158

Introduction

The output of most composers can be seen, at least in retrospect, as falling into a number of different 'periods' corresponding to the different stages in their musical development. This division into periods is simply a convenient method of categorizing the music: an 'early' period, which demonstrates the composer's gradual mastery of his technical resources and the development of an individual style, a 'middle' period in which the style and the technical problems which it raises are explored to the full, and a 'late' period in which the composer moves beyond the confines of his earlier style into new and uncharted areas of music. The different stages are rarely marked by clearly defined breaks.

Weill stands as a curious, problematic and, in some respects, unique figure in the history of music since his output falls into three periods which seem, at first glance, to have nothing in common with one another. Weill, perhaps alone amongst composers, built for himself not one successful career but three quite separate ones, writing three quite distinct types of music. Such a course of development presents the commentator with a number of musical problems, not least in attempting to define anything that can be described as a recognizable 'Weill style', and with the necessity of also attempting to deal with various autobiographical and psychological problems.

Thanks to individual numbers such as the 'Alabama Song', 'Surabaya Johnny', 'September Song' and, above all, the 'Moritat' of *The Threepenny Opera* (a song which has become better known as 'Mack the Knife') Weill is one of the few twentieth-century composers whose music has achieved a really popular success. Weill's songs are known, and sung, by people who would not regard themselves as lovers of 'serious' music and who, perhaps, do not even know Weill's name. Yet only a small part of his output is known, even by professional musicians. Ignorance of the works of Weill's first, pre-Brecht, period is understandable since, with the exception of a few pieces such as the First Symphony and the Violin Concerto, most of the scores of this period remain unpublished and unperformed. The works of Weill's last, American, period are periodically revived in the United States but are almost totally unknown in Europe where, having gained a reputation for being inferior to the European works (a reputation gained largely, one suspects, because these American works are Broadway musicals rather than because their critics are acquainted with the music) they are dismissed out of hand. However, as I shall try to show, some knowledge of the music of these two outer periods is vital to an understanding of Weill himself and also his aims and intentions in the better-known European works.

At the moment, Weill's reputation rests almost entirely on works written during the eight years between 1927–35 – correctly so, in that the music of this period represents his most important and original achievement; incorrectly so in that, even within this short period, only a tiny handful of works are well known while many, including some of his most ambitious and substantial pieces, remain ignored.

Weill's musical language is so different from that of most 'serious' twentieth-century music and so far removed from what has become the most important line of musical development that it is easy for many musicians and music lovers – already, perhaps, ill at ease and confused by the more obviously 'popular' elements of his style – to regard him as a 'peripheral' composer of little importance. I shall later discuss the extent to which Weill's reputation has been affected by the various fluctuations of intellectual and social fashion and I shall attempt to argue the musical grounds for regarding Weill as a composer of greater stature than is usually considered.

Although no extra-musical argument can invest a work with an artistic stature that it does not already possess by virtue of its own intrinsic value there are, however, at least two historical reasons for considering Weill worthy of serious attention. Firstly, Weill was one of the first composers to abandon the emotional and dramatic ethos of Wagnerian opera and to cultivate instead, an objective, non-realistic, ritualistic music-theatre. Such a conception of opera has become a feature of many works written since 1950 and Weill has had an inestimable influence on the development of this form of music-theatre. Thanks to his association with Brecht, this kind of music-theatre and the kind of techniques employed in it have come to be called 'Brechtian', although many of the ideas and techniques employed in such a 'Brechtian' theatre were in fact formulated by Weill, and were demonstrated in his scores, some years before the two artists began to collaborate. Secondly, Weill deserves the attention of anyone interested in the general cultural and artistic history of the twentieth century as someone who stands at a particularly important point in the development of modern thought. While no artists live and create in a vacuum, removed from the social and artistic currents of their time, some seem to reflect their age more clearly than others. Living in Germany during the inter-war years, in a Berlin which was, for a short period, the centre of European thought, Weill stands at the point where many of the most important artistic, intellectual, political, social and historical currents of the century meet. Although a minor master, Weill – more than Schoenberg, Stravinsky or the other giants of twentieth-century music – is one of the key figures in the general history of our times.

I have avoided the paraphernalia of footnotes in the following chapters by listing sources by chapter at the end of the book. Although all sources are indicated in this way I must here acknowledge a particular debt to the work of David Drew who, almost alone among musicologists, has championed Weill's cause for many years and whose work provides the most perceptive and often the only source of scholarly information about Weill's output. I have drawn extensively on Mr Drew's editions of writings by and on Weill, on his own published articles and have been deeply influenced in my own view of Weill by his work. My thanks are due to Howard Davies and Pat Carter, who were kind enough to advise me on certain points, to Jonathan Reed, the results of whose picture research form the most fascinating part of what follows, to Caroline Schuck and Alexandra Artley of Orbis Publishing and to Mrs Christine Ratcliffe who typed the manuscript.

My thanks are also due to the librarians and the staff of the Royal Northern College of Music, the Henry Watson Music Library in Manchester and the Hebden Bridge Library for their help and to Mr Eric Forder of Universal Edition, London.

My especial thanks go to Mrs Susan Davies, who translated a number of German texts for me, and, as always, to my long-suffering wife to whom this book is dedicated.

Part One
The Man and His Times

Chapter 1
The Early Years

The Weill family emanated from the Baden area of south-west Germany and had its origins in that large Jewish community which settled on the banks of the Rhine during the fourteenth century. Weill's father, Albert, was the cantor at Dessau and it was here that his fourth child, Kurt, was born on 2 March 1900.

Living within a community that was, by tradition, both politically and culturally liberal in outlook, Weill's parents took a lively interest in the arts. By the late nineteenth century the Jewish communities in Europe, and particularly those in Germany, attached considerable importance to the music used in their religious services and encouraged the use of far more music than was allowed by strict synagogue tradition. As cantor, Albert Weill was a figure of some standing in the community. A composer in his own right, he provided liturgical music for the synagogue at which he was cantor and where he was responsible for the maintenance of musical standards. The artistic interests of Weill's mother Emma, on the other hand, seem to have been mainly literary; through her, the family possessed an extensive and up-to-date library.[1] Although Weill abandoned the Jewish faith early in his adult life,[2] he was brought up as an orthodox Jew; the influence of this upbringing can be seen in almost all his early music and was to reappear, reawakened by the experiences of the early 1930s, in some of his later works.

As a child Weill showed an early aptitude for music and by the age of ten had taught himself to play the piano (he made his first public appearance as a pianist at the age of fifteen) and had attempted to compose. A number of short piano pieces and a song cycle, *Schilflieder*, date from his early teens as does his first attempt at writing an opera.[3]

Recognizing his son's musical gifts, Albert Weill arranged for him to study theory and composition with Albert Bing, the musical director of the Dessau Opera House and a former pupil of Hans Pfitzner. Weill studied with Bing for three years before becoming a full-time student at the Hochschüle für Musik in Berlin in September 1918. While at the Hochschüle Weill studied composition with the director, Engelbert Humperdinck (the composer of *Hansel und Gretel*), conducting with Rudolf Krasselt and harmony and counterpoint with Friedrich Koch. Weill appears to have been an outstandingly successful student during his period at the Hochschüle and not only composed a symphonic poem (based on Rilke's *Die Weise von Liebe und Tod des Cornets Christopher Rilke*) which was thought good enough to be performed by the Hochschüle orchestra, but also succeeded in winning a bursary offered by the Felix Mendelssohn Foundation.[4] However, despite this success, Weill was disillusioned by the Hochschüle and by what he regarded as its 'unsympathetic atmosphere'[5] and left after only one year to become, firstly, *répétiteur* at the opera house at Dessau, under Knappertsbusch and his old teacher Albert Bing, and then, a few months later in December 1919, to become the staff conductor of the opera house in the small Westphalian town of Lüdenscheid. The work at Lüdenscheid provided Weill with a great deal of valuable practical theatre experience but did not hold him for long. Work as a conductor at one of the small, provincial German opera houses was unrewarding, devoted, in the main, to the preparation of rather trivial operettas. Besides which Weill had now realized that he wanted to be a composer. In the autumn of 1920, Busoni, persuaded by his former pupil Leo Kestenberg, who held the post of music director in the Prussian Ministry of Education, returned from Zurich to take charge of the Master Class in composition at the Berlin Academy of Art. Seeing the appointment announced in a newspaper, Weill returned to Berlin in September 1920 with a portfolio of compositions. The portfolio probably contained, among other earlier works, the String Quartet in B minor, which Weill had written shortly after leaving the Hochschüle, the Cello Sonata, a one-act opera *Ninon de Lenclos* based on a play by Ernst Hardt and at least part of, or sketches for, a symphony on which Weill was working and which he completed in December 1920. In any event, Busoni was sufficiently impressed by the portfolio to accept Weill as one of the six pupils in the composition Master Class and, in December 1920, Weill became a pupil at the Berlin Academy of Art. Neither he nor any of Busoni's other composition pupils had to pay tuition fees; Busoni had stipulated, as a condition of his accepting the post, that tuition should be free and the students chosen entirely on merit. Nonetheless, Weill needed money on which to live. He supported himself by playing the piano in a bierkeller at night.

Weill had also completed a third opera, on a text by Hermann Sudermann, before beginning his studies with Busoni (like its predecessors the opera is now lost) and Weill seems to have spent his three years at the Academy working, almost entirely, on non-theatrical music. During the same period, however, Busoni himself was working on *Doktor Faust*, a piece with which Weill must have become acquainted during these three years, and one which had a permanent effect on his own view of music-theatre.

Apart from his work on *Doktor Faust*, teaching seems to have been the only activity to which Busoni was willing to devote himself entirely during these final years of his life. Cosmopolitan in his outlook (Weill called him 'the spiritual European of the future'), passionately interested in people and in new ideas, Busoni seems to have needed his students both to provide human contact and the kind of intellectual stimulation which he required. One of his biographers has observed that Busoni, 'who frequently grudged every moment of his time and strength not devoted to work, and who considered giving concerts an insufferable waste of energy' was, nonetheless, prepared 'to exhaust himself teaching'.[6] In return, Busoni's students were devoted to their teacher, with his volatile Latin temperament, his sudden rages and equally sudden outbursts of volcanic laughter.

A description of Busoni's teaching methods has been left by his official biographer, Edward Dent, who records how, when Busoni was teaching the piano in Weimar in 1900, the class met twice a week:

> those who had prepared a work played it, while the others sat around and listened. After that there would be general discussion, overflowing on to the lawn outside. Busoni seldom discussed matters of pure technique; technique was taken for granted, and he preferred to talk about the music itself . . . his teaching was by no means confined to the hours in the Tempelherrenhaus; his pupils were with him for most of the day and a good part of the night as well. Busoni wanted to know them all intimately and to study the personality of each.[7]

The Berlin composition class seems to have followed a similar pattern. The class was supposed to meet twice a week ('The youngsters come on Monday and Thursdays' wrote Busoni to his wife in July 1921) but, as Weill himself remembered:

> there were no actual lessons, but he allowed us to breathe his aura, which emanated in every sphere but eventually always manifested itself in music. Those hours spent daily in his company are still too recent for me to be able to speak about them. It was a mutual exchange of ideas in the very best sense, with no attempt to force an opinion, no autocracy, and not the slightest sign of envy or malice; and any piece of work that revealed talent and ability was immediately recognised and enthusiastically received.[8]

When Weill first joined the class, in 1920, he remembered Busoni as being 'different from what he had expected: more mature, more controlled – and younger.'[9] By 1922, however, the kidney and heart disease which was to cause his death in 1924, had already begun to affect Busoni's physical appearance. A friend who visited him in December 1922 recorded that 'He was fifty-six and looked an old man; his noble face ravaged by illness, his mouth noticeably pinched, his splendid brow crowned with snow-white hair, already showing signs of his fatal disease.'[10] Although by November 1923, when Weill was about to end his studies, Busoni was 'exhausted and weary; illness and over-work had cast deep shadows over his noble, prematurely aged features'[11] he was still 'keenly interested in all that was going on' and 'to the younger generation of musicians he was always accessible.'[12]

An impression of the young Weill at this time of his life was given by Rudolf Kastner, then music critic of the *Vossischen Zeitung*:

> One afternoon Busoni introduced me to a small, quiet man of about twenty. Two bright eyes flickered behind spectacles. In conversation he revealed himself to be an unusually serious, clearsighted and characterful person. Busoni spoke of him, in his absence, with particular warmth.[13]

Indeed, Weill is reported to have been one of Busoni's favourite pupils. The first work which Weill wrote as a pupil, though not under the direct supervision of Busoni, was what is now called the First Symphony, the earlier Symphony of 1920 having disappeared without

trace. By April and June 1921, when the First Symphony was composed, Weill had become a member of the Novembergrüppe and the
aims of this artistic group (which will be discussed in the following
chapter) are reflected in the socialist and pacifist subtitle which
appeared on the original title page of the Symphony: 'Workers,
Peasants and Soldiers – a People's Awakening to God', a reference to
the title of a play by Johannes Becher. A piano duet arrangement of
the Symphony was played at one of the private concerts which
Busoni held in his house, but, with this exception, the work was never
performed during Weill's lifetime. The score of the work, hidden
away by friends of Weill who wished to protect him (and who also
removed the title page with its incriminatingly socialist subtitle),
disappeared during the Second World War and was only rediscovered
in the late 1950s.[14]

In 1922 Weill composed a large number of works: the ballet *Die
Zaubernacht*, written as a Russian ballet for children, the *Divertimento*
for small orchestra and men's chorus, the *Sinfonia Sacra*, the String
Quartet op 8 and the orchestral *Quodlibet* which Weill arranged from
the music of *Die Zaubernacht*. That year he also started to work on a
setting, for voice and piano, of poems from Rilke's *Book of Poverty and
Death*; the setting was left incomplete and was eventually taken up
again, in 1925, when it became the *Stundenbuch* for voice and orchestra.
More importantly, for an aspiring young composer, the 1922-3 concert
season saw what, for someone who was still a student, was an
extraordinary number of performances: not only the successful
première of *Die Zaubernacht* at the Theater am Kurfürstendam on
18 November 1922, but also premières of all the other works written
during the year. The following year saw the completion of the *Recordare*
for double chorus and the *Frauentanz* for soprano and small instrumental ensemble. The *Frauentanz* was performed with great success
at the Salzburg Festival on 6 August 1924 in a concert that included
the Bax Violin Sonata, Pizzetti's Cello Sonata and Ernst Krenek's
Fourth String Quartet.

By now Weill was attracting a considerable amount of attention
from a small, but influential, group of music lovers and, as a result –
and thanks to Busoni's championship – Universal Edition, the leading
publishers of new music, offered Weill a contract. Hans Heinsheimer,
who worked for Universal Edition at that time, has described how
'Busoni had introduced Weill to Hertzka [the director of U E] and, to
please the great Ferruccio, Hertzka had given Weill a ten years'

contract.'[15] Such contracts were not, however, as good as they at first appeared since they

> put a strict obligation on the composer to submit anything he wrote during the next ten years to the publisher before showing it to anybody else . . . there were no guarantees, no advances or monthly payments and any money the composers were to get was to be earned by royalties.[16]

Weill completed his studies with Busoni in December 1923, seven months before Busoni's death in July 1924.

Despite his moderate success and the large number of performances which his music was receiving, Weill was hardly able to live on the income from performances and commissions. The first Berlin radio station had begun transmitting in October 1923 and, intrigued by the social and artistic possibilities of the new medium, Weill became at first an occasional contributor and then, from April 1925 onwards, the regular music and drama critic and Berlin correspondent for the weekly journal of German radio, *Der Deutsche Rundfunk*. Weill remained the journal's chief critic for over four years until the success of *The Threepenny Opera* finally gave him enough financial security to allow him to resign from the post.[17] At the same time Weill acquired a number of private composition students including Claudio Arrau, Nikos Skalkottas and Maurice Abravanel, who was to become one of Weill's warmest advocates and the conductor of the premières of many of his European and American works.

In 1922 Weill and his fellow students had travelled with Busoni to Dresden to hear the State Opera's production of Busoni's *Arlecchino*. Weill had been introduced to the conductor Fritz Busch who had, in turn, introduced him to the playwright Georg Kaiser. The meeting with Kaiser was one of the most important and fortunate events in Weill's early career. Kaiser was one of the most eminent men in the German theatre, a playwright whose work was performed throughout the country and who was generally considered to be among the most significant and radical dramatists of his time. It must have seemed unlikely that so famous a writer should be prepared to collaborate with a young composer who was still relatively unknown outside specialist music circles. Kaiser was not only willing to work with Weill, however, but (according to Weill himself) actually offered to write something. The first discussions between Kaiser and Weill about a possible project took place in January 1924 and were initially about collaborating on a full-length ballet. It was only after about ten weeks of work and after a considerable part of the music had been written (according to Weill some three-quarters of the ballet, including the Prelude and the whole of the first two acts) that the two collaborators realized that the project would not work: 'We got stuck,' said Weill in his own account of the event, 'We had outgrown the material. The silence of these figures was tormenting us and we had to break the bonds of this pantomime; it had to become an opera.'[18] Abandoning the original subject Kaiser turned to an earlier one-act play, *The Protagonist*, which he had, in any case, originally regarded as a work for the opera stage.

Set in Elizabethan England, the play is concerned with the leader of a troupe of travelling players (the 'Protagonist' of the title); an actor who, using his art as a means of protecting himself from reality, sees his everyday life as a series of imagined theatrical rôles. When he is confronted by unavoidable reality, in the shape of his sister and her young lover, the dividing line between the real exterior world and the private dream-world of his own imagination finally disappears. Retreating into one of his acting rôles the protagonist stabs his sister to death, declaring afterwards that he has now achieved the perfect and ultimate fusion of art and life by reaching a state in which there is 'no longer any difference between real madness and feigned madness'.

While Kaiser reworked his play, during the April and May of 1924, Weill turned his attention elsewhere and wrote a concerto for violin and wind band for the violinist Joseph Szigeti. The work received its first performance at an ISCM (International Society for Contemporary Music) concert on 1 June 1925 where it was played by Marcel Darrieux and conducted by Walter Straram. The first German performance of this concerto took place in Weill's native city of Dessau.

For the rest of 1924 and during the early months of 1925 Weill worked on the score for *The Protagonist*, frequently visiting the Kaisers at their lakeside home at Grünheide. It was on one of these visits that he met, apparently for the second time, a young dancer called Lotte Lenya.

Born Karoline Blaumauer, Lotte Lenya was the daughter of a Viennese coachman and a laundress. During the First World War she had lived with an aunt in Zurich where she had studied ballet and drama and had become a member of the *corps de ballet* at the Stadt Theater. Lenya herself described her initial meeting with Weill:

When my teacher – who was also a director – decided to
move his family to Berlin in 1924, I went along with them.
One day after we arrived there he showed me a notice in
the newspaper about auditions for young singers and
dancers for a ballet called *Zaubernacht*. He took me along
because he was hoping to get the job as director and when
I was called to the stage the producer said, 'Miss Lenya,
I would like to introduce you to our composer Kurt Weill'
and I said, 'Where is he?'. The producer indicated that he
was sitting in the orchestra pit but I couldn't see him.
I only heard a soft voice say, 'Very glad to meet you, Miss
Lenya' but I never actually saw him. And although I did
get the job I didn't take it so I didn't see him again at that
time.[19]

Their second, and more fruitful, meeting took place in the summer of
1924:

I met the playwright Georg Kaiser and visited his home
which was on a lovely lake outside Berlin. One Sunday
morning he said, 'Lenya, there's a young composer coming
– I'm writing a one-act libretto for him . . . would you
mind picking him up at the station?' Well, the shortest
way was to row a boat across the lake. I'll never forget the
way he looked. He had a blue suit but no waistcoat . . . just
a little taller than I, very neat and correct, with very thick
glasses . . . he wore a little bow tie and one of those typical
borsalino musicians hats – at that time very fashionable,
most musician's wore a certain style of black brimmed hat.
I said, 'Are you Mr Weill?' and he said he was and
I invited him to enter the boat. So we sat down and I
rowed – in typical German fashion I rowed him. And
while I was rowing he looked at me and after a while he
said, 'You know, Miss Lenya, we have met before'. I said,
'Oh, really? Where?' And he reminded me of that ballet
audition.[20]

Having completed *The Protagonist* in April 1925, Weill returned to his
abandoned Rilke settings and, in September 1925, to the composition
of the Cantata *Der Neue Orpheus* based on a text of Ivan Goll. Weill's
use of a text by Goll is an indication of the extent to which he was in
touch, and sympathized with the more radical theatrical movements
of his time. Goll, one of the leading expressionist writers, was also a
member of the Dada movement; many of the technical innovations

which were to characterize the theatrical experiments of the later years of the Weimar Republic (and which are discussed in the following chapter) were already anticipated in the works which Goll wrote and produced in the early 1920s. Both Brecht and Piscator admired Goll's surrealistic and fantastic dramas and were influenced by his work.

Itself a strange, surrealistic piece *Der Neue Orpheus* presents the story of an Orpheus, born into a modern industrial world, who meets his Eurydice on a railway station. Having pursued various careers (as a piano teacher, a writer of freedom songs, the conductor of Mahlerian symphony concerts, an international celebrity) and having found that neither the world nor Eurydice listens to him, he shoots himself.

Kurt Weill and Lotte Lenya lived together for two years before they married at the beginning of 1926. Lotte Lenya has given a charming description of the circumstances under which Weill proposed marriage:

> One Sunday afternoon I took him on a boat on the lake.
> He was very near-sighted; he wore thick, thick glasses and
> I did something and hit his glasses and they fell in the lake.
> That was the time he proposed marriage. I said later on,
> 'Kurt, would you have married me with the glasses on?'
> He replied, 'Yes, I think so, yes.'[21]

Weill has himself left a touching memory of the woman who was his wife, the foremost interpreter of his music and the guardian of his legacy:

> She is a terrible housewife but a wonderful actress. She
> can't read a note of music but when she sings it sounds like
> Caruso. (Besides, I feel sorry for those composers whose
> wives can read music.) She doesn't take any notice of my
> work (that is one of her greatest qualities) but she'd be
> very angry if I didn't show an interest in her work.
>   Most of her friends are men, which she attributes to the
> fact that she doesn't get on well with women (but perhaps
> she doesn't get on with women because most of her friends
> are men). She married me because she wanted a taste of
> the horrors – a wish which, she maintains, has been granted
> many times over.
>   My wife is called Lotte Lenya.[22]

Chapter 2
Weill's Berlin

The Berlin in which Weill settled in September 1920 was the scene of an artistic and intellectual upheaval almost unparalleled in the twentieth century; the centre of the intellectual life, not only of Germany but also, for a brief period of some fifteen years, of the whole of Western Europe. At the same time, the legendary 'Golden Twenties' of the Weimar Republic was a period of unceasing political turmoil and violence in which strikes, street fights, revolutions, counter-revolutions and political murder were regular occurrences.

The sudden and unexpected defeat of the German forces at the end of the First World War left many Germans bewildered. In the early months of 1918 a German victory had seemed assured; the army had won the war in the east and, by March 1918, stood within a mere forty miles of Paris. The spectacular collapse of this Western offensive, in the autumn of 1918, came as a complete surprise to the German people. The deprivations which the population had suffered during the war, the sacrifice of nearly two million lives and the wounding of another four million soldiers suddenly seemed to have been utterly pointless. The German people felt betrayed and developed both a deep desire for peace and a profound sense of resentment towards those who had led them during the war.

The general feeling of disillusionment first expressed itself in practical action in October 1918, when the sailors at Kiel and the other North Sea ports mutinied. The Kiel mutiny was the start of the German Revolution. The Allies had already made it clear that they would not negotiate with the Kaiser. On 9 November 1918, with rebellion spreading throughout the Reich, with Bavaria declared a republic, the Kiel sailors in possession of the Royal Palace and the streets of Berlin in turmoil, Kaiser Wilhelm II was forced to abdicate.

In the political vacuum created by the resignation of the Kaiser, only two outcomes seemed possible; the assumption of power by some kind of coalition of the Social Democrat and the Independent parties, or the declaration of a Soviet Republic under the Spartakist leader Karl Liebknecht.

On the afternoon of 9 November the socialist, Philipp Scheidmann, fearing the imminent seizure of power by the left-wing Spartakist group, proclaimed the formation of a Republic under the Social Democrat, Friedrich Ebert.

The new Republic began life with a considerable amount of popular support. Many people saw the formation of the Republic as representing a complete break with those who had led the country into a disastrous war; few regretted the fall of the Kaiser and his discredited imperial regime. Yet many of those elements which would lose the Republic this popular good will, were the consequences of actions taken within the first few days of its formation.

Threatened by the Communist Left, Ebert's government could maintain power only by relying on the army. On 10 November, only one day after the formation of the Republic, Ebert and General Groener agreed that the army would be 'placed at the disposal of the government' and that the government, in return, would help maintain order and discipline within the army. The protection of Ebert's socialist Republic from its left-wing opponents thus rested in the hands of the officers and generals of the old imperial regime.

Nor was the military high command the only remnant of the Kaiser's empire to maintain its power in the new Republic. The imperial judiciary was also retained. With its traditionally strong right-wing bias, the judiciary was not simply out of sympathy with the socialist Republic but was opposed to its most basic principles. As a result, Weimar justice became little more than a mockery. In the first four years of the Republic, for example, right-wing activists were responsible for some 450 political murders; of the twenty-four people convicted for these crimes, none was executed and the average prison sentence was four months. Of the thirty-eight left-wing activists accused during the same period, ten were executed and the others served prison sentences averaging fifteen years.

The hopes which many people had felt for the new Republic soon gave way to a sense of disillusionment. 'It was the same old clique,' wrote Stefan Zweig in his autobiography:

the so-called men of experience who now surpassed the folly of war with their bungling of the peace. To the extent that it was wide-awake the world knew that it had been cheated. Cheated the mothers who had sacrificed their children, cheated the soldiers who came home as beggars, cheated those who had subscribed patriotically to war loans, cheated all who had placed faith in any promise of the state, cheated those of us who had dreamed of a new and better-ordered world and who perceived that the same old gamblers were turning the same old trick in which our existence, our happiness, our time, our fortunes were at stake.[1]

The first clash between the military and the citizens of the Republic, and the first test of the allegiances of the already demoralized and embittered army, came in December 1918, when Ebert called on his forces to free the Chancellery buildings taken over by the sailors of the Kiel mutiny. Some thirty sailors were killed and over a hundred injured in the resulting confrontation. The battle was ended, however, by the intervention of a huge crowd of people, mobilized by the Communists, who feared the start of a military putsch. The army refused to fire on the civilians and withdrew.

Faced with such a volatile political situation, and dependent upon an army which had shown itself to be unreliable, Ebert began to encourage the growth of Freikorps units – armed groups of volunteers drawn from the ranks of demobbed soldiers. Ebert and his war minister, Fritz Noske, seem to have regarded the encouragement of the Freikorps and similar military groups as a means of providing a body of men who could be relied on to protect the Republic against its left-wing enemies. In the event, the growth of the Freikorps simply ensured the continuation of the right wing of the German army and eventually provided Röhm and Hitler with a nucleus around which they could build the SA.

The clashes between the government and the Communists reached a climax in the early months of 1919. In January of that year, an attempt by Noske's Freikorps to crush a Spartakist uprising led to more than a week of savage street fighting, during the course of which over 1000 people were killed. In the aftermath the Spartakist leaders, Karl Liebknecht and Rosa Luxembourg, were arrested and murdered. Luxembourg's body was thrown into the Landwehr Canal where it was discovered four months later. In March 1919, while Ebert was

24

convening the inaugural session of the Assembly of the Republic in Weimar, there was a further confrontation between the Freikorps and the left wing. Some 2000 people were killed and the centre of Berlin devastated.

While what was virtually a civil war was being waged in the streets of Berlin, the Allies were preparing their peace treaty, the terms of which were announced in the summer of 1919. According to the Versailles Treaty, Alsace-Lorraine was to be ceded to France, who would also occupy all German territory west of the Rhine, large sections of German land were to go to Denmark, Poland and Belgium, while the Saar and Germany's African colonies were to become the possession of the League of Nations. In addition, most of Germany's military forces were to be disbanded, reparations were to be imposed and Germany was to accept the burden of guilt for the atrocities, loss and damage which had been inflicted on the Allied powers during the course of the war.

The terms of the peace treaty were bitterly resented by many Germans and were widely regarded as humiliating. The government found itself in an impossible position. Although the war had been ended at the insistence of the German High Command, the military leaders had left the civilian government to assume responsibility for the capitulation. In the eyes of many right-wingers the government had already betrayed Germany by capitulating. The government's eventual agreement to the terms of the Versailles Treaty – an agreement in which it had very little choice – was regarded as a further betrayal and Ebert lost what little right-wing and moderate support remained. In particular, the government lost the support of many ex-soldiers and, in March 1920, a brigade of Freikorps marched on Berlin in an attempted right-wing putsch, the so-called Kapp Putsch. Ebert and his ministers fled and the putsch was prevented from succeeding only by a remarkable display of power by the people of Berlin, who immediately went on strike. The strike was total. The whole city was paralysed – without water, power, transport, schools, shops or administration. Four days later the Freikorps marched out of Berlin defeated.

In addition to the continuing political chaos (a chaos made even worse by the election of June 1919, as a result of which no single party had an overall majority in the Reichstag) the government was faced with ever-increasing social problems and particularly by the problem of spiralling inflation.

The war had been financed by printing money, rather than by increasing taxes, and inflation was already under way before the war ended. With the losing of the war, the economic dislocation caused by the need to change from a war-time to a peace-time economy, the slow recovery of German industry and, perhaps above all, with the Allies' imposition of reparation payments at a level which the Germans were quite unable to meet (the total sum was eventually fixed at 132 billion marks) coupled with the movement of capital investments out of Germany and into countries that were more politically stable, the inflationary spiral began in earnest.

Standing at its traditional 4.20 to the dollar in 1918, the value of the mark had dropped to 75 to the dollar by the summer of 1920. By the summer of 1922 it had dropped to 400 to the dollar and then, with confidence further undermined by both the assassination of the then foreign minister Walter Rathenau and the Allies' continued refusal to declare a moratorium on reparation payments, began a period of rapid decline. By 1 January 1923, the mark had fallen to 7000 to the dollar; by June 1924, following the French occupation of the Ruhr – the industrial area on which, following the loss of Silesia to Poland, depended Germany's only hope of economic recovery – the mark had fallen to 160,000 to the dollar; by 1 August to 1,000,000; by 1 November to 130,000,000; by 14 November to 13,000,000,000,000.

In his autobiography, Bruno Walter describes how, on returning to Germany from America in the spring of 1923, his attention was attracted by a strange notice in shop windows:

> A 'Multiplier' had come into existence. It was the figure by which the normal price of merchandise had to be multiplied in accordance with the progress of inflation. If the figure had been 150,000 in the morning, enabling people to buy a pair of gloves normally worth 2 marks for 300,000, it might be 160,000 in the evening of the same day. The gloves cost 20,000 marks more although the buyer's earnings had, in the meantime, not increased proportionally.[2]

In June 1923 a pound of butter cost 15,000 marks; by November of that year a pound of butter cost a skilled labourer two days' wages. Stefan Zweig remembered how:

> On street-cars one paid in millions, lorries carried the paper money from the Reichsbank to the other banks, and

a fortnight later one found hundred-thousand-mark notes in the gutter; a beggar had thrown them away contemptuously. A pair of shoe laces cost more than a shoe had once cost, no, more than a fashionable store with two thousand pair of shoes had cost before; to repair a broken window more than the whole house had formerly cost, a book more than the printer's works with a hundred presses. For £20 one could buy rows of six-storey houses on Kurfürstendamm, and factories were to be had for the old equivalent of a wheelbarrow. Some adolescent boys, who found a case of soap forgotten in the harbour, disported themselves for months in cars and lived like kings, selling a cake every day, while their parents, formerly well-to-do, slunk about like beggars.[3]

Walter also tells how, when preparing for a concert, the rehearsal had to stop half-way through when the musicians were paid. Orchestral musicians told him that they 'would have to make some kind of purchase immediately: if they waited to do so two hours later the purchasing power of their money would, in the meantime, have shrunk.'[4] Money was invested in any kind of tangible merchandise, no matter how strange. Everybody, remembered Zweig, 'rushed to buy whatever was for sale whether it was something they needed or not. Even a goldfish or an old telescope were "goods" and what people wanted was goods instead of paper.'[5]

One musician told Bruno Walter that he had used his entire wage to buy a bag of salt.

Far from seeking ways in which to curb the inflation, the government seems to have taken a certain pride in the efficiency with which they encouraged it. In 1923 the President of the Reichsbank went before the Reichstag to boast that the bank's presses, operating day and night, were able to print 46 million marks daily.

It is impossible to overestimate the effect which inflation had on German society in the five years from 1918 to 1923 and the extent to which, as Alan Bullock has remarked, it undermined the foundations of that society 'in a way which neither the war, nor the revolution of November 1918 nor the Treaty of Versailles had ever done.'[6] Hunger and illness became a normal part of life. Food, which, according to George Grosz, consisted almost entirely of turnips, became the only popular conversational topic. In Berlin alone, almost a quarter of the children were starving and fifteen thousand children suffered from tuberculosis. As in all times of inflation and economic unrest, there were many who were prepared to exploit the situation. Berlin abounded with black-marketeers, speculators and profiteers like the notorious Hugo Stines who, having persuaded German businessmen to deposit their money in his Dutch bank then used the money to buy German businesses himself. Foreigners, who could live in luxury for next to nothing, flocked to the city.

Above all, inflation attacked the moral basis of society. Berlin was, by tradition, a liberal and cosmopolitan city. The end of austerities and the relaxation of political and moral censorship immediately after the war had already encouraged the growth of more permissive social attitudes. Now in the early 1920s, the political and economic instability encouraged an outburst of frenzied hedonism. Money and the belief in money had been destroyed. Work no longer enabled a person to support himself and his family. The entire savings of the middle classes were wiped out overnight and with them, the traditional middle-class virtues which they represented. Stefan Zweig, commenting on inflation in Austria in the preceding years remarked:

A man who had been saving for forty years and who, furthermore, had patriotically invested his all in war bonds, became a beggar. A man who had debts became free of them. A man who respected the food rationing system starved; only one who disregarded it brazenly could eat his fill. A man schooled in bribery got ahead, if he speculated he profited. If a man sold at cost price he was robbed, if he made careful calculation he yet cheated. Standards and values disappeared during this melting and evaporation of money; there was but one merit: to be clever, shrewd, unscrupulous, and to mount the racing horse rather than be trampled by it.[7]

However, inflation, and its effects on society, were far worse in Germany than in Austria:

All values were changed, and not only material ones; the laws of the State were flouted, no tradition, no moral code was respected. Berlin was transformed into the Babylon of the world.

Bars, amusements parks, red-light houses sprang up like mushrooms. What we had seen in Austria proved to be just a mild and shy prologue to this witches' sabbath; for the Germans introduced all their vehemence and methodical organization into the perversion. Along the entire Kurfürstendamm powdered and rouged young men sauntered and they were not all professionals; every high-school boy wanted to earn some money, and in the dimly lit bars one might see government officials and men of the world of finance tenderly courting drunken sailors without any shame. Even the Rome of Suetonius had never known such orgies as the pervert balls of Berlin, where hundreds of men costumed as women and hundreds of women as men danced under the benevolent eyes of the police. In the collapse of all values a kind of madness gained hold particularly in the bourgeois circles which until then had been unshakable in their probity.[8]

Every extravagant idea that was not subject to regulation reaped a golden harvest: theosophy, occultism, spiritual-ism, somnambulism, anthroposophy, palm-reading, graphology, yoga and Paracelsism. Anything that gave hope of newer and greater thrills, anything in the way of narcotics, morphine, cocaine, heroin found a tremendous market.[9]

The Berlin which Zweig describes, a city of feverish sexuality and hysterical permissiveness, the Berlin of popular imagination, of Christopher Isherwood's novels and Von Sternberg's film *The Blue Angel*, existed alongside the extreme poverty, the political murder and the street violence. Observing the clashes between the Freikorps and the left-wing demonstrators in March 1919 Count Harry Kessler remarked:

The abominations of a merciless civil war are being per-petuated on both sides. Business as usual in the cabarets, bars, theatres and dance halls . . . Berlin has become a nightmare, a carnival of jazz bands and rattling machine guns.[10]

Inflation was eventually brought under control by Hjalmar Schlacht at the end of 1923, simply by ending the printing of money, stopping all credit and announcing the creation of a new 'Rettenmark' which would be backed by all Germany's land and resources. A few months later, as a consequence of the Dawes plan, Germany's reparation payments were reduced and the French left the Ruhr. Deprivation and hardship continued, and even increased for a time as the tightening of the money supply increased unemployment, yet eventually even these began to disappear. Foreign investments began to flow back into the country as confidence was restored; new factories were built, wages rose and unemployment fell.

As social conditions improved so, also, did the chaotic political situation. Political extremists on both the right and left wings seemed to have been controlled and the Nazi Party, in particular, seemed to have disappeared as a political force following the abortive Munich Beer hall putsch of 1923. As Stefan Zweig testified, 'The name of Adolf Hitler all but fell into oblivion. Nobody thought of him as a political factor'.[11] When, following the death of Ebert in 1925, the ageing Hindenburg was made President of the Republic, domestic and international fears about Germany's recovery waned even further, Germany's isolation was gradually ended and a period of relative peace, stability and prosperity followed. From 1923 to 1933, said Zweig, 'Peace at last seemed guaranteed in Europe . . . for a world moment – those ten years – it seemed as if normal life was again in store for our much-tried generation.'[12]

The years from the turn of the century until 1914 were crucial in the development of the arts for it was during this time that the most radical and far-reaching changes took or began to take place as the aesthetics, the theories and the practices of the past were re-examined. The Italian Futurists, dedicated to the establishment – by violence if necessary – of a new art form based on 'the dynamics of modern life', had published their first manifesto in 1909; between 1905 and 1910 Les Fauves in France and Die Brücke in Germany arrived at their own forms of expressionism and prepared the way for the beginnings of abstract art in the pre-war work of Kandinsky (1866-1944), Franz Marc (1880-1916) and a number of French and Russian artists; Picasso (1881-1973) had completed *Les Demoiselles d'Avignon* in 1907 and by 1909 the term 'cubism' had been coined to describe the new style which was emerging; Dadaism, which was to become the basis of much later experimental art, had appeared in America in the early 1910s (Marcel Duchamp's *Nude Descending a Staircase* and his first 'ready-made' appeared in 1912) and in Europe in 1915. Thus, in the visual arts, all the major twentieth-century artistic movements, with the exception of surrealism, had appeared in some form before the First World War. Similarly radical advances were made in literature, theatre and the other arts at the same time. In music, for example, Stravinsky's *The Rite of Spring*, the première of which caused an uproar, was first performed in 1913 by which time Schoenberg, Berg and Webern were already writing 'free' atonal music in which traditional tonal criteria no longer operated.

But although the foundations of modernism had been laid during the first one and a half decades of the century, it was only after 1918 that the consequences of these pre-war developments could be fully explored, consolidated and formalized. In the years before the war, Berlin had been one among many centres of artistic and intellectual experiment. During the inter-war years – the years of the Weimar Republic – Berlin stood at the very centre of European thought. For a period Berlin was, as Lotte Lenya has said, 'the most exciting city in the world . . . for all the arts in general and that includes everything: writers, painters, sculptors, architects.'[13] Among the composers living in Berlin during this period were Hindemith, Krenek, Busoni and later Schoenberg, who took over the composition class at the Academy following Busoni's death in 1925.

Wilhelm Fürtwängler was in charge of the Berlin Philharmonic Orchestra, Otto Klemperer conducted the Kroll Opera, Bruno Walter the new Municipal Opera and Erich Kleiber, who staged the premières of Berg's *Wozzeck* and Janáček's *Jenůfa* in Berlin during these years, was director of the State Opera. Walter Gropius, the director of the Bauhaus in Dessau, Mies van der Rohe and Eric Mendellsohn were all engaged on the designs for new buildings for Berlin or its neighbouring suburbs. Josef von Sternberg, Fritz Lang, F W Murnau and G W Pabst were working at the Universum Film AG studios in Berlin.

In the theatre the dominant figure was Max Reinhardt, who ran the Deutsches Theater and the Kammerspiel, but, as Bruno Walter says in his autobiography, there were many other, equally vital and exciting theatres and directors:

> The Tribüne, under Eugen Robert, was devoted to careful and vivacious performances of French, English and Hungarian comedies. At the State Theatre Leopold Jessner's dramatic experiments caused heated discussion while Karlheinz Martin conducted the destiny of the Volksbühne with a genuine understanding of the artistic popularization of plays and the theatre . . . What the Berlin theatres accomplished in those days could hardly be surpassed in talent, vitality, loftiness of intention and variety.[14]

Anything approaching a complete survey of the culture of the Weimar Republic lies outside the scope of this book. However, many of the artistic developments and attitudes of the period have a direct bearing on Weill's work and some description of these general artistic trends is as relevant to an understanding of Weill's music as is an awareness of the political background against which it was conceived.

German art, before the First World War, had been dominated by expressionism; indeed the term 'expressionist' – signifying a style in which aspects of reality are violently distorted for expressive ends – is now generally used to refer to a specifically German phenomenon. German expressionism embraced all the arts: the paintings of the Dresden-based Die Brücke and the Blaue Reiter artists of Munich, the poetry and the novels of Werfel, Trakl and Kafka, the plays of Kaiser, the architecture of Eric Mendellsohn and the free atonal music of Schoenberg and Berg, are all equally characteristic manifestations of the expressionist movement. Expressionism was still a potent force after the First World War (as is shown by Robert Wiene's film made in 1920, *The Cabinet of Dr Caligari*) yet, in the light of the political, military and social catastrophes of the war, expressionism was beginning to seem a self-indulgence. To many post-war artists, expressionist art seemed to be so centred on the artist's examination of his own subjective response that it had no relevance to the real world and nothing to say about the political and social conditions under which many people lived. Expressionism was regarded as 'a withdrawal, a flight from the hard edgeness of things';[15] it consisted, it was said, of nothing but 'symbolic vagaries and an intentionally indiscriminate jumble of colours, lines, distortions, words and concepts.'[16]

Following the Revolution of 1918, a group of over a hundred German artists formed the Novembergrüppe, a socially conscious artistic body dedicated to the spirit of the Revolution. The group sought to be a 'union of radical artists' which would re-examine the relationship between the arts and the public and would put into effect 'a far reaching programme' which was intended to bring about 'the closest mingling of art and people'.

The Novembergrüppe was too large and too diffuse a collection of individuals for it to hold together as a distinct entity for any length of time and the group gradually petered out in the 1920s. Nonetheless, the ideals and the aesthetics of the Novembergrüppe (and other similar groups, such as Walter Gropius's Arbeitsrat für Kunst)

ABOVE *Kurt Weill and Lotte Lenya, 1929* BELOW LEFT *Weill's teacher Ferruccio Busoni in his Berlin home during the final years of his life. The aesthetic stance which Busoni advocated was to have a lasting effect on Weill's own musical beliefs* BELOW RIGHT *Engelbert Humperdinck (1854-1921), composer of* Hänsel und Gretel *and director of the Hochschüle für Musik in Berlin. Weill studied composition with Humperdinck from September 1918 to the spring of 1919*

ABOVE Toads of Property, *by George Grosz, first appeared in 1921 in a volume of fifty-five political drawings,* The Face of the Ruling Class ABOVE LEFT *The revolution in Berlin, 1918. The protection troops of the newly formed Workers' and Soldiers' Council in Unten den Linden on November 9th, the day on which the Social Democrat Philipp Scheidemann declared Germany a republic* BELOW LEFT *Berlin 1922. As the value of the mark fell, so the value of goods, as opposed to paper money, rose accordingly. Here a poster offers two million marks for a single gold ring*

TOP *A scene from the original production of Brecht's* Drums in the Night *at the Munich Kammerspiele in 1922* ABOVE *The band of the Hotel Adlon in Berlin, 1930. A typically heterogeneous collection of instruments, similar to that employed in many of Weill's works* ABOVE LEFT *Erwin Piscator (left) and Brecht (right) with the actress Carola Neher and Herbert Jhering the critic between them* BELOW LEFT *Still from Robert Wiene's* The Cabinet of Dr Caligari, *Berlin 1920*

ABOVE *Weill in Dresden during the rehearsals for the première of* The Protagonist. *From left to right: Weill, Fritz Busch (who conducted the première), Alfred Rencker and the director Josef Gielen* ABOVE RIGHT *A sketch by Adolph Mahnke for the set of the original production of* The Protagonist *at the Dresden State Opera in 1926* BELOW RIGHT *Brecht's Berlin flat, about 1927. At the time Brecht was working on an (unfinished) biography of the German middle-weight champion boxer, Paul Samson-Körner. From left to right, Samson-Körner (playing the piano), Brecht, Seelenfreund (wearing boxing gloves), Hans Borchardt, Hannes Küpper and, far right, Brecht's collaborator Elisabeth Hauptmann. The painting on the wall is by Caspar Neher*

ABOVE *Baden-Baden 1927, the première of* Mahagonny Songspiel. *Bottom row (left to right): Lotte Lenya, Walter Brügmann and Hannes Küpper; centre row: Brecht and Heinrich Burkhard; top: Weill, Frau Brügmann, and the Mahagonny cast* BELOW *Scene from* Mahagonny Songspiel

underlie much of the art of the Weimar Republic. The belief was that art could help bring about the kind of new society which was regarded as desirable and in order to achieve this end, art must reject the subjectivity, élitism and the discredited aesthetic of nineteenth-century romanticism and renew its links with the people.

The Dadaists were the most violently disruptive in their rejection of previous culture. Dada had begun in Zurich during the war and had, despite its deliberately iconoclastic and provocative intentions, been a relatively light-hearted affair. Transferred to Germany, the movement acquired a more severe tone. In his autobiography Richard Hulsenbeck, one of the co-founders of Berlin Dada, describes the characteristically serious aims of the German Dadaists: 'in Zurich, where there was no rationing, art could not help being all idyllic and frivolous . . . In Berlin, fear gripped the heart and the horizons darkened; there were too many people in mourning.'[17]

In its violently aggressive attack on both social and artistic values, German Dadaism sought to reject everything that German culture represented, and, in so doing, demonstrate its revulsion with the society that had led the country into the horrors of the First World War. Dadaism thus became a form of social protest and it was, perhaps, inevitable that the Dada movement in Germany should have become as much a political as an artistic movement.

The Berlin Dadaists produced little in the way of painting or sculpture and those members of the group who are remembered today are remembered only because their work expanded beyond the limits of pure Dadaism. Nonetheless, the Dadaists had an incalculable effect on both the attitudes and the practical techniques of many artists. In its desire to abolish the mystery and élitism of art, Dada cultivated a deliberately anti-art, anti-romantic attitude, promoting the use of everyday materials, commonplace subjects and activities of a kind that had not previously been regarded as suitable material for artistic treatment. As a result, collage and photo-montage became, for the first time, recognized techniques, new technical means such as film were incorporated into theatrical productions and playwrights began to set their plays in aggressively down-to-earth locations. The boxing-ring setting, the projections and the megaphones of the original production of the Brecht-Weill *Mahagonny Songspiel* are obvious examples of this Dada influence.

By the mid-1920s, the tough, anti-romantic, anti-emotional attitude of the Dadaists had become part of a more general artistic movement towards a cooler, more committed – and often cynical or caricatured – style that had acquired the name of Neue Sachlichkeit or 'New Objectivity', a term invented in 1923 by Gustav Hartlaub, the director of the Mannheim Kunsthalle. Hartlaub defined the style in painting as being marked by a 'new realism bearing a socialistic flavour'. The most important exponents of the Neue Sachlichkeit in painting were George Grosz and Otto Dix. Grosz had been one of the most active members of the Berlin Dada group and the gradual transformation of Dada, from an artistically iconoclastic to a politically conscious movement, can be seen in his bitterly satirical drawings of a Berlin in which self-satisfied, bloated army officers and businessmen indulge themselves against a background of poverty, decay and death. Significantly, the authorities themselves prosecuted Grosz for 'defaming the reputation of the army and defaming public morals by corrupting the inborn sense of shame and the innate virtue of the German people.'

In music, the belief that art should have a social function led to the development of Gebrauchsmusik (a word which meant 'utility music' or 'music for use'), a music written to meet a specific need (such as music written for radio or films) or to provide amateur musicians with new works to perform. Hindemith is said to have coined the term, although he later disowned it. His school opera *Wir bauen eine Stadt* is one of the best known examples of this type of music. Hindemith summed up the social beliefs behind such music by saying:

> A composer should write today only if he knows for what purpose he is writing. The days of composing for the sake of composing are perhaps gone forever. On the other hand, the demand for music is so great that the composer and the consumer ought most emphatically to come at least to an understanding.[18]

While the composers of Gebrauchsmusik were attempting to break down the barriers between new music and the public, and thus reach a wider audience, other composers, such as Eisler, advocated a more directly political music, the function of which was to develop 'new methods of musical technique which will make it possible to use music in the class struggle better and more intensively.'[19] To such composers, the 'noncommitted amusement' which was thought to characterize Gebrauchsmusik was an indication that its composers represented 'the vanguard of the bourgeois in collapse'[20]:

> When I hear talk of the 'community-building spirit', through the 'joy in playing' then I become suspicious and immediately wonder what sort of community is going to be built and why these pieces of music, mostly pseudo-baroque, should arouse that joy . . . Baroque style today is escape into music history. Composers in this style believe that they have overcome the refined and certainly over-heated subjectivity of the old avant-garde and have acquired a social conscience.[21]

In the theatre, the new social and political aims of the arts were being developed by many playwrights and directors. By the beginning of the war the new forms to which expressionism had given rise in the theatre had become over-ripe; expressionistic theatre, with what Brecht called 'its escapism and screaming' had become self-centred and isolationist. As John Willett has observed, 'incoherence and exaggeration started to rank as virtues; presented in the name of Mankind, self-dramatisation and self-pity were inflated into a pretentious vogue'; what was needed was 'a gritty, tough, less blowsily egotistical style'.[22]

The foremost of those directors trying to fashion this tough style, and the most important as far as the development of Brecht's own dramatic ideas were concerned, was Erwin Piscator. In Germany the theatre had always been regarded as a means of presenting serious moral and social criticism; in the hands of Piscator theatre became an openly political and revolutionary art form. The purpose of the theatre, according to Piscator, was to explain, analyse and demonstrate topical issues – 'to portray the conditions of life truthfully would be enough to condemn the society that had created them'[23] and thus 'to kindle the flame of revolt among the workers'.[24] It was only by becoming overtly propagandistic, argued Piscator, that theatres could achieve perfection: 'Pure art is not possible in the context of the present times. But the art which consciously serves a political cause, as long as it never compromises, will ultimately reveal itself as the only one possible and thus as the pure art of our time.'[25] In order to create such a form of theatre, the function of the actor, the relationship between the play and the audience, the methods of staging and design and every aspect of the dramatic experience had to be re-examined.

When Brecht arrived in Berlin in 1924, Piscator had just taken over the large and influential Volksbühne; three years later he set up his own independent company, the Piscator-Bühne, at the Theater am Nollendorfplatz. C D Innes has remarked that 'the five years between his appointment to the Volksbühne and the closing of the Piscator-Bühne was the most fruitful period of Piscator's career'.[26] It was a period during which Piscator exploited many techniques that have had a permanent effect on the modern theatre.

One of Piscator's chief concerns was to develop a method of staging which, by breaking away from the naturalistic tradition, allowed the action to operate on different levels in such a way that the specific event could be set against a larger historical context and the play could thus comment upon and criticize itself. If art was to portray life truthfully, then the artistic process had to be de-mystified; the machinery not only of society but of art itself had to be exposed. To this end Piscator devised complex mechanical sets which freed the action from the temporal and physical restraints of the naturalistic theatre (sets which included stages at different levels and such devices as the double treadmill built for *The Good Soldier Schweyk*), exploited the artificiality of the theatrical situation (by employing puppets, by masking the actors and by having the actors step outside their rôles to explain or comment upon the action), placed actors within the audience, and employed film, projection, newspaper headlines, statistics, placards and signs.

Piscator's technical innovations were not entirely without precedent. Leopold Jessner, whose revolutionary production of Schiller's *Wilhelm Tell* at the State Theatre in 1919 produced one of Germany's first great theatre riots, was working along similar lines. In the early 1920s Ivan Goll, the author of the texts of two of Weill's works, had used films, placards, newspaper cuttings and masks in two of his productions. Even Max Reinhardt, though for reasons quite different from those of Piscator, had attempted to create a 'total theatre' which would involve and dazzle the audience. However, perhaps the most important influence on Piscator and his German contemporaries was the cinematic and theatrical experiments taking place in post-revolutionary Russia.

Eisenstein's film *Battleship Potemkin* was first shown in Berlin in 1925 and had an immediate and overwhelming effect on all who saw it. As C D Innes has pointed out, the influence of the Russian cinema, and of *Potemkin* in particular, 'can be seen not only in Piscator's use of film, his adaptations of cinematic techniques and his adoption of montage as an organizing principle, but also in the staging of specific productions.'[27] Similarly, Meyerhold, the most inventive and influential of the Russian theatre directors, had already anticipated many of Piscator's most characteristic techniques (the use of film, of machinery, of placards and of agitprop methods of production) in his work of the early 1920s, at a time when 'Piscator had not developed any but the most rudimentary of his techniques'.[28]

The importance of Meyerhold and his Russian contemporaries, as far as the development of the German theatre was concerned, lay less in their prophetic use of specific stage devices (Meyerhold's company appeared in Berlin for the first time in 1930 and Piscator almost certainly had little knowledge of his work until that time) than in their being the first people to attempt to develop a modern theatre which could deal directly with topical, social and political themes.

Meyerhold and Piscator shared a similar aim and a similar viewpoint; both developed, apparently independently, similar techniques as a means of achieving their aims. Thus, Meyerhold is reported to have believed that 'a performance is good theatre when the spectator does not forget for a moment that he is in the theatre'.[29] Piscator similarly remarked that the purpose of theatre was 'to teach how to think rather than how to feel'. Both observations are precise statements of the beliefs which underlie Bertolt Brecht's theories and techniques.

Brecht worked with Piscator on a number of productions and acknowledged Piscator's influence in a letter, saying: 'No one in the whole of my productive period was as valuable for my artistic development as yourself.'[30] Ernst Busch, one of Brecht's leading actors, later declared that 'everything that distinguishes Brecht's style he got from Piscator'.[31] But perhaps the most important of the politically orientated art forms of the period, and one which exerted an enormous influence on the other arts, was the political cabaret. The popular image of the Berlin cabaret is either that of the seedy establishment depicted in Von Sternberg's *The Blue Angel* or of the kind of pornographic cabaret which sprang up in the inter-war years to cater for the needs of wealthy businessmen, speculators and profiteers. Alongside such 'Amusierenkabaret', however, there still existed the original form of cabaret which had been introduced into Germany from France in about 1900. Literary, aggressive and socially conscious from its inception, this cabaret became, during the years of the Republic, the most politically articulate and telling of all the art forms.

Always to the left socially, cabaret tended to adopt left-wing political attitudes as well, although few cabarets – and perhaps only that of the *Kuka* or *Kunstler Cafe*, where the leading writer was the Communist poet Erich Weinert – were completely dedicated to revolutionary politics. Many of the most important cabaret writers, such as Kurt Tucholsky, Walter Mehring, Eric Müsham, Klabund and Eric Kästner, had pronounced left-wing sympathies and most were associated with the weekly paper *Die Weltbühne*, the principal and most prestigious outlet for radical political and cultural thought. The cabaret writers in Berlin, and elsewhere in Germany, also contributed to a variety of satirical papers – notably *Jugend* and the Munich-based *Simpizissimus* – but their real sphere of influence came from the cabaret stage. Mixing sentimental and satirical ballads with social criticism and broad humour, the whole held together by the topical comments of the *conférencier* (the compère of the cabaret), cabarets such as Rosa Valetti's *Grössenwahn* and Trude Hesterberg's *Wild Stage* exerted enormous influence on popular opinion. The strength of such cabarets lay in the fact that they were, above all, popular entertainments, reaching people that the other arts – even those, such as Piscator's Proletarian Theatre, that were specifically designed to 'serve as a catalyst for the cultural will of the proletariat'[32] – could not reach.

Chapter 3
1926-1929

Kurt Weill and Lotte Lenya were married on 28 January 1926, two months before *The Protagonist* received its première at the Dresden State Opera. To have an opera performed in Dresden was a singular honour for a young composer since the famous opera house there was the 'birthplace of most operas by Richard Strauss . . . to have an opening night on the same stage where *Der Rosenkavalier* had made its first bow was quite something.'[1]

Conducted by Fritz Busch, whom Weill had met at the Dresden performance of Busoni's *Arlecchino*, and directed by Josef Gielen, the première of *The Protagonist* on 27 March 1925 marked a turning point in Weill's career and immediately established him as one of the leading theatre composers of the day. Writing in *La Revue Musicale*, Maurice Abravanel described the piece as placing Weill 'in the first ranks of theatre composers' and observed:

> I have only once before – at the performance of *The Rite of Spring* – seen the German public allow itself to be overwhelmed by the immediate power of a work whose musical substance could, after all, hardly be immediately comprehended.[2]

This sudden change in Weill's critical standing did not go unnoticed by his publishers. Hans Heinsheimer, who worked for Universal Edition, remembers how, on the day following the première of *The Protagonist*, he and the great Emil Hertzka, the director of Universal Edition, met Weill for lunch in the Bellevue Hotel:

> The Bellevue offered two luncheons: a simple two marks one and a fancier one, including fish as well as meat in the

fare, for three marks. All these days before the première we
had shared lunch with Kurt, and every day Hertzka had
ordered three luncheons without fish . . . This time, however, Hertzka called the waiter, asked for the menu and
handed it smilingly to Kurt Weill. 'What would you like to
eat, Mr Weill?', he asked. Then I knew that Kurt Weill
was a composer to be reckoned with in the future.[3]

The enthusiastic reception of *The Protagonist* created an immediate
interest in Weill's music and both the one-act ballet-opera *Royal
Palace*, completed in January 1926, and the cantata *Der Neue Orpheus*,
written the previous September, were scheduled for performance at
the State Opera in the coming 1926-7 season. Weill also received his
first radio commission. He was asked to produce a score, for chorus
and orchestra, for a production by the Berlin Funke-Stunde of
Grabbe's *Herzog von Gothland*.

At the same time Weill began work on a full-length opera entitled
Na und . . . (So What . . .). He spent almost eighteen months working
on *Na und* . . ., at the end of which he found himself with a completely
unwanted work. Heinsheimer describes Weill's initial attempts to
interest Universal Edition in the piece:

> He played the whole opera, softly singing with his veiled
> voice and went on quite undisturbed while Hertzka and
> I were following this unheralded entry of 'So What . . .'
> into the world. After Kurt had finished we felt that there
> was only one thing to do: to make this first performance of
> 'So What . . .' under all circumstances the last . . . I got up
> from my chair . . . went over to the piano. 'Kurt', I said,
> 'tonight you are going back to Berlin. Shortly after the
> train leaves Vienna it crosses the Danube. When you are
> in the middle of the bridge, open the window, take your
> score and just drop it in the river'. Kurt looked back.
> He did not say anything. He just took his music, put it in
> his brief case and walked out of the room.[4]

The opera was never performed and, with the exception of a few
sketches, *Na und* . . ., which may well have been one of the key works
in Weill's development during this crucial period of his creative
career, has disappeared without trace. Weill later wrote to Universal
Edition describing the piece as 'a transitional work, linking the
period of Busoni-influenced classical writing to a very different kind
of music I feel is slowly growing within me.'[5]

With *Na und* . . . completed, Weill turned again to Georg Kaiser for the libretto of a one-act comic opera, *Der Zar lässt sich photographieren (The Tsar has his Photograph Taken)*, which would be a companion piece to *The Protagonist*. *Der Zar*, a political satire, tells the story of an attempt by a band of anarchists to assassinate the Tsar while he is on a visit to Paris. The Tsar is persuaded to have his photograph taken at the studio of Angèle, a well-known lady photographer. On arriving at the studio he finds an impostor – the false Angèle, a member of the anarchist group, waiting for him. Showering her with compliments and even persuading her to let him take her photograph, the Tsar reduces the situation to such a level of absurdity that the anarchist conspirators are forced to abandon their plan and escape.

Weill began work on *Der Zar* in March 1927. At the same time (on 2 March), *Royal Palace* received its première under Kleiber at the State Opera, where it formed half of a double bill with Falla's *Master Peter's Puppet Show*. The work was coolly received and ran for only seven performances. It was produced only once more during Weill's lifetime, at Essen in 1929.

But a more momentous event took place in March 1927, for it was in that month that Weill first began his collaboration with Bertolt Brecht. The results of this collaboration have now assumed such legendary proportions that the circumstances of the original meeting have become almost buried beneath a number of imaginative additions and fictional memories. Lotte Lenya recalls that the two men, brought together by mutual friends, first met:

> in a very famous theatre restaurant in Berlin called 'Schlichter' . . . from that point on Kurt and Brecht visited each other quite often and started discussing what they could do together. I think Kurt suggested at that time that he would like to set the five *Mahagonny-Gesänge* and, in that way, the *Little Mahagonny* came to life.[6]

In his essay, *On the Use of Music in an Epic Theatre*, Brecht claimed that he approached Weill and asked him to set the *Mahagonny* verses which had just been published:

> This type of song was created on the occasion of the Baden-Baden Music Festival of 1927, where one-act operas were to be performed, when I asked Weill simply to write new settings for half-a-dozen already existing songs.[7]

In fact, Weill and Brecht probably met when Weill attended the rehearsals for a radio performance of Brecht's *Mann ist Mann* on 18 March 1927. Through this, and subsequent meetings, there developed the idea not, initially, of setting the five *Mahagonny Songs* from Brecht's *Hauspostille*, but of doing the full-scale *Mahagonny* opera. According to a letter from Weill to his publishers, the outline plan of the *Mahagonny* opera must have been written during March and April 1927. From March to August 1927 Weill was hard at work on the score of *Der Zar lässt sich photographieren* (a one-act opera on a libretto by Georg Kaiser) and it was while engaged on this, and simultaneously planning *Der Aufstieg und Fall der Stadt Mahagonny (The Rise and Fall of the City of Mahagonny)*, that he received a commission from the committee of the Baden-Baden Festival of German Chamber Music to write a short one-act opera. Having considered a number of possible subjects, Weill decided to set the five *Mahagonny Songs* from the *Hauspostille*, using the Baden-Baden commission as a preliminary study for the opera. The decision to set the *Mahagonny Songs* thus came from Weill, not Brecht, and was made at a time when the full-length opera *The Rise and Fall of the City of Mahagonny* was already planned. In his own 1930 *Notes on Mahagonny*, Weill says that he saw the setting of the *Mahagonny Songs* as a 'way of moving the project forward' and as a chance of exploring a musical style on which he 'had an idea but needed to try it out'.[8]

The resulting *Mahagonny Songspiel* was written in May 1927. According to Lotte Lenya, the 'Alabama Song' was originally written for her own, untrained, voice.[9]

According to David Drew, the *Songspiel*, like the later *Mahagonny* opera, was written for professional singers and it was only later that Weill decided that one of the two female rôles should be sung by his wife, Lotte Lenya (the other was sung by Irene Eden).[10]

At all events, Brecht agreed that Lenya should sing the part. His only comment after hearing her sing the 'Alabama Song' for the first time was to ask her to make her gestures 'not so Egyptian'.[11]

The *Mahagonny Songspiel* had its première at the Baden-Baden Festival on 18 July 1927 as part of a programme of short chamber operas. The rest of the programme consisted of Milhaud's *The Rape of Europe*, Ernst Toch's *The Princess and the Pea* and Hindemith's *Hin und Zurück*. Caspar Neher, an old friend of Brecht's from his childhood days in Augsburg, had designed a set which consisted of a boxing ring and a screen onto which slides were projected. The *Songspiel* created a sensation. As Lotte Lenya remembers:

Our little *Mahagonny* was preceded and followed by the most austere forms of modern chamber music, mostly atonal.

But that sophisticated international audience stared in bewilderment when the stage hands began to set up a boxing ring on the stage. The buzz increased as the singers, dressed as the worst hoodlums and 'frails' climbed through the ropes, a giant Caspar Neher projection flashed on the screen hung behind the ring and *Mahagonny* began – with a real, an unmistakable tune. The demonstration began as we were singing the last song, and waving placards – mine said 'For Weill' – with the whole audience on its feet cheering and booing and whistling. Brecht had thoughtfully provided us with whistles of our own, so we stood there defiantly whistling back. Later I walked into the lobby of the fashionable hotel where most of the audience went for drinks after the performance, and found a frenzied discussion in progress. Suddenly I felt a slap on the back, accompanied by a booming laugh: 'Is here no telephone?' (a line from one of the songs). It was Otto Klemperer. With that the whole room was singing the 'Benares Song' and I knew that the battle was won.[12]

Back in Berlin after the Baden-Baden Festival, Weill and Brecht continued their work on the *Mahagonny* opera, meeting almost daily during the late summer and autumn of 1927. While still working on the details of the *Mahagonny* libretto, Weill was also busy with other projects including the incidental music for productions of Strindberg's *Gustav II* and for Arnolt Bronnen's *Katalaunische Schlacht* (to be directed by Leopold Jessner at the State Theatre), a setting of another Brecht poem from the *Hauspostille* collection and, in April 1928, the composition of the incidental music for a production by Erwin Piscator. The Brecht setting, *Vom Tod im Wald* for bass and orchestra, had its first performance at a concert given by the Berlin Philharmonic with the solo part sung by Heinrich Hermanns, on 23 November 1927. The Piscator production (of *Konjunktur*, Leo Lania's 'comedy of economics') opened at Piscator's new Theater am Nollendorfplatz, where it played 'for four weeks to dwindling houses'.[13]

Other, more important, projects now interrupted Weill's work on the *Mahagonny* opera. It was through the impresario Ernst Robert Aufricht, who had started life in the theatre as an actor in Dresden, that Weill came to be involved in these other schemes. As the son of a wealthy father, Aufricht had attempted to further his acting career in Berlin by contributing money to 'Die Truppe', a repertory company run by Berthold Viertel, the director upon whom Christopher Isherwood based the figure of the director in *Prater Violet*. However, Aufricht remained an unsuccessful actor and, having failed in his original career, began afresh as an impresario and theatre administrator by buying and restoring the old Theater am Schiffbauerdamm. Aufricht then needed a new play with which to open his new theatre:

> We went to Toller, to Feuchtwanger and others but none had a piece ready. Finally we could only turn to the artists in the Schwannecke and the Schlichter. We went to the Schlichter in the Lutherstrasse – and there in the second room sat Brecht.[14]

Brecht was already working on an adaptation of *The Beggars' Opera*, an eighteenth-century play by John Gay, when Aufricht approached him. *The Beggars' Opera* had recently been revived, with great success, at the Lyric Theatre in London where it had run for two years. Elisabeth Hauptmann, Brecht's collaborator and amanuensis, had drawn his attention to the piece and he had sketched out six scenes of a possible German version.

In Brecht's final version, which became known as *Die Dreigroschenoper (The Threepenny Opera)*, the opera begins with the hurdy-gurdy man singing the famous 'Moritat' about Mack the Knife (Macheath). Act I introduces Mr Peachum, who makes a living out of hiring costumes (designed to elicit sympathy and, thus, money) to the various beggars and thieves who ply their trade in Soho. Meanwhile Polly, Peachum's daughter, is marrying Mack the Knife, the leader of one of Soho's gangs. The wedding is attended not only by Mack's gang but also by his friend Tiger Brown, the Commissioner of Police. The Peachums are furious about their daughter's marriage and arrange for Mack to be caught, bribing the prostitute Jenny to betray his whereabouts to the police. Mack is betrayed and taken to jail, only to escape again thanks to the help of Lucy, Tiger Brown's daughter, to whom he is also married. Peachum, beside himself with rage, threatens to flood the streets of London with his beggars, and thus disrupt the coming coronation, if the police do not catch Mack again. Arrested once more, Mack is reprieved a few seconds before his execution by the arrival of a Royal Messenger with a pardon, a knighthood and a pension from the Queen.

The day after the meeting, Fischer, Aufricht's assistant, went to Brecht's furnished room in the Spichternstrasse and collected the preliminary sketches. It was on the basis of these sketches that *The Threepenny Opera* was commissioned.

Brecht had already decided that Weill should write the music for the work and, having informed Aufricht of this decision, Brecht and Weill left for the French Riviera where they had hired a house for themselves and their wives for the summer. According to Lotte Lenya, 'The two men wrote and re-wrote furiously night and day, with hurried swims between. I recall Brecht wading out, trousers rolled up, cap on head, cigar in mouth.'[15] *The Threepenny Opera* was, nevertheless, completed by the time the two men returned to Berlin at the end of July.

Meanwhile Aufricht, who was unfamiliar with Weill's work, had been to the Charlottenburg opera where *Der Zar* and *The Protagonist* were being performed. Horrified by what he heard, Aufricht asked Theo Mackeben, who would eventually conduct the première of *The Threepenny Opera*, secretly to prepare a version of the original Pepusch score as a safeguard. Aufricht finally heard, and was converted to, Weill's music on the second day of rehearsals.

Rehearsals began on 1 August and the opening night was to be 31 August. The rehearsal period was fraught with difficulties. Carola Neher, who was playing the part of Polly, did not return from her holiday in St Moritz where she was tending her husband, the cabaret poet Klabund, who was ill with tuberculosis. Peter Lorre, who was to have played Mr Peachum, fell ill and had to be replaced. Helene Weigel, Brecht's wife, who was playing the brothel madam, developed appendicitis. Harald Paulsen, playing Macheath, thought his rôle too small (legend has it that Weill and Brecht wrote the famous 'Moritat', the ballad about Macheath which opens the piece and has since become the best-known number from it, overnight to satisfy Paulsen). The backers objected to Lotte Lenya, a relatively unknown actress, taking the rôle of Jenny. Above all, Brecht was continually changing things and arguing with the director, Erich Engel, about the way in which the songs were to be performed. It was soon generally agreed among those in the Berlin theatre world that the show would be a disaster.[16]

The omens looked even less propitious on 31 August, the opening day. Hans Heinsheimer arrived at the Theater am Schiffbauerdamm at midnight to find:

> the stage filled with shouting people wildly gesticulating, yelling at each other and only making common cause in threatening the director, who outshouted everybody else . . . smoke filled the air, crumpled papers, empty bottles and broken coffee cups littered the floor.[17]

New problems and arguments arose as the dress rehearsal proceeded. It seems that Rosa Valetti, the great cabaret artist who was playing the rôle of Mrs Peachum, had signed a contract with the Kabarett der Komiker which was due to take effect from the day after the première. Erich Ponto, who had taken over Peter Lorre's rôle of Mr Peachum, objected to the proposed shortening of his part (it had been decided that the piece was three-quarters of an hour too long and had to be cut) and packed his bags ready to return to Dresden. The actor playing the small part of Filch threatened to stop the première unless his pay was trebled. New arguments began between Aufricht and Caspar Neher about the sets, between Aufricht and Brecht about the horse on which the King's messenger was to appear, between Paulsen and everyone else about the tie which he, as Macheath, insisted on wearing.

The dress rehearsal lasted until six in the morning at which point, when everyone was exhausted and distraught, the actors and stage hands were sent home; 'many people fell asleep in their dressing room or backstage on a pile of clothes or just on the scenery or stage.'[18] Brecht, Aufricht and Weill stayed at the theatre and worked on the text; 'the brothel scene', remembers Lenya, 'was torn apart, begun over again and still didn't work'.[19] The three men were surrounded 'by theatrical people, writers, musicians, actors, critics whose opinion was ùnanimous: "For heaven's sake, call it off".'[20]

The cast reassembled at noon, new changes were announced and a final rehearsal began. The reworked brothel scene was not rehearsed until five o'clock on the day of the première. Lotte Lenya recalls that the cast heard that 'Aufricht was out front asking people if they knew where he could find a new play in a hurry.'[21]

Throughout most of this turmoil Weill had remained calm. When Heinsheimer had arrived at the theatre he had found Weill quietly sitting in the middle of the pandemonium, 'his mocking smile on his lips, as unconcerned as if he were just a disinterested outsider, calmly enjoying the débâcle of a crowd of strangers.'[22] 'Weill', commented Heinsheimer 'is a cold-blooded fish . . . he has no artistic temperament, no outbreaks, no breakdowns.'[23] Finally, however, the innately retiring

Weill lost his temper, 'for the first and only time in his theatrical career,'[24] when he discovered that Lotte Lenya's name had been omitted from the programme. It was only after considerable argument that he was persuaded to let her go on and the curtain finally rose to a packed house that included such distinguished figures as Otto Klemperer, Erwin Piscator, Karl Kraus, the great Viennese satirist, and Fritz Korner, the leading actor at the State Theatre.

Some idea of what the production was like on the first night can be gathered from the review which appeared in *The Times* on 25 September 1928. Noting the influence of the 'Communistic Herr Piscator' (and somewhat confused about the author whom it calls 'Kurt Brecht'), *The Times* observed that:

> The production is deliberately crude. Adopting the idea that it should be a 'Threepenny Opera', which fits in well with the tendencies now in the dramatic air, the producers have provided a dirty cream-colour curtain about 10 feet high, worked by a primitive arrangement of strings, such as might be used in amateur theatricals. Across the curtain is painted, in crooked letters *Die Dreigroschenoper*. For the stable scene, in which Macheath and Polly celebrate their wedding breakfast, there is provided only a wooden wall a few feet high and a door. The rest of the stable is indicated by means of the cinematograph. There is the occasional Expressionistic touch, such as the sudden letting down of a placard by ropes from above.

The production, remarked *The Times*, illustrates:

> the progress of a movement towards freeing music, acting and cinematograph from the ruts of Italian Opera, Wagnerian music drama, drawing-room comedy and Hollywood and creating something new.

In his essay, *On the Use of Music in an Epic Theatre*, Brecht called the production of *The Threepenny Opera*, 'the most successful demonstration of the epic theatre' and described the way in which the musical numbers had been staged:

> This was the first use of theatrical music in accordance with a new point of view. Its most striking innovation lay in the strict separation of the music from all the other elements of entertainment offered. Even superficially this was evident from the fact that the small orchestra was

47

installed visibly on the stage. For the singing of the songs a special change of lighting was arranged: the orchestra was lit up; the titles of the various numbers were projected on the screens at the back, for instance, 'Song concerning the insufficiency of human endeavour' or 'A short song allows Miss Polly Peachum to confess to her horrified parents that she is wedded to the murderer Macheath'; and the actors changed their positions before the numbers began.[25]

The initial reaction to the piece is best described by Lotte Lenya herself:

> The play opened on time and from the start there was complete silence in the audience . . . it seemed cold and apathetic, as though convinced that it had come to a certain flop . . . until we came to the 'Kannonen-Song'. Then, all of a sudden, something happened to the audience, because by that time they must have caught on to the fact that something new was happening there. From that point it was wonderfully, intoxicatingly clear that the public was with us.[26]

Again, Universal Edition was quick to appreciate the effect of this success on Weill's standing and on his commercial prospects. Two days after the première of *The Threepenny Opera*, Emil Hertzka arrived in Berlin and took Weill and Lotte Lenya to lunch. During the meal

> Hertzka did something that nobody would ever have expected from him or any other music publisher in the world. He searched in his pockets and brought out at last a large sheet of cream-coloured paper. He put it on the table. It was the ten-year contract he had signed with Kurt Weill six years ago.
> 'This is our contract, Mr Weill', Hertzka said. 'As you know it has four more years to run.'
> 'I know', said Weill. The mocking smile had disappeared. He seemed tense and hostile.
> Hertzka took the document and tore it into shreds.
> 'I think it is about time that we made a new contract', he said.[27]

The immense success of *The Threepenny Opera* gave Weill both financial security and popularity. According to Heinsheimer, the piece was performed more than ten times every day during its first year, achieving some 42,000 performances during one single year.

Other commissions still prevented Weill from concentrating solely on the score of *The Rise and Fall of the City of Mahagonny*. Towards the end of 1928 he was offered another radio commission from Frankfurt Radio. Turning again to the *Hauspostille* and other texts by Brecht, Weill wrote the *Berlin Requiem* in November and December 1928. The piece underwent a number of changes, both before and after its first performance (Weill had originally intended to include the setting of *Vom Tod im Wald*) but the real problems were political rather than artistic and, when submitted to Frankfurt Radio, the committee responsible for censoring programme material had various objections. Writing about this 'secular requiem' in 1929, Weill hinted at some of the problems he had with the Frankfurt committee, observing that the work's intentions had been questioned 'by some particularly powerful censors' who showed 'a frightening lack of knowledge about the artistic needs of that group of people who form the largest part of the radio public'.[28] The *Berlin Requiem* was finally broadcast, after numerous postponements, on 22 May 1929. The performance was given by the Frankfurt Radio Orchestra conducted by Ludwig Rotterburg with Hans Grahl (tenor), Johannes Willy (baritone) and Jean Stern (bass) singing the solo parts.

In early 1929, while still working on the score of the *Mahagonny* opera, Weill also found time to arrange a suite for wind band based on material from *The Threepenny Opera* (the *Kleine Dreigroschenmusik* which had its first performance under Klemperer at the Kroll Opera on 8 February 1928), to compose the songs for a play *(Die Petroleuminseln)* by Lion Feuchtwanger and to work on *Der Flug der Lindberghs (The Lindbergh Flight)*, a short radio cantata commissioned by the Baden-Baden Festival.

The Lindbergh Flight was the first of Brecht's Lehrstücke, didactic plays intended to instruct the performers in moral and political ideas. Writing about the piece, Brecht described it as 'an object of instruction . . . it is valueless unless learned from. It has no value as art which would justify any performance not intended for learning.'[29] Like the later *Der Jasager (The Yes-Sayer)*, *The Lindbergh Flight* was designed to be performed by schoolchildren.

At its first performance, the work had a score by Weill and Hindemith, the two composers having set alternate numbers. A description of the first performance appears in Brecht's essay on the piece entitled 'An Example of Pedagogics':

The employment of *Der Flug der Lindberghs* and the use of the radio in its changed form was shown by the demonstration at the Baden-Baden Festival of 1929. On the left of the platform the radio orchestra was placed with its apparatus and singers, on the right the listener who performed the part of the Flier, i.e. the paedagogical part, with a score in front of him. He read the sections to be spoken without identifying his own feelings with those contained in the text, pausing at the end of each line; in other words in the spirit of an *exercise*. At the back of the platform stood the theory being demonstrated in this same way.[30]

In autumn 1929, after the Festival performance, Weill rewrote the work for choir and orchestra, recomposing the numbers originally set by Hindemith. This new version was given its first performance by Klemperer at the Kroll Opera concert series. In later years Brecht took exception to Charles Lindbergh's political views and the piece was retitled *Der Ozeanflug (The Ocean Flight)*.

Weill always composed quickly and even with these interruptions the full score of *The Rise and Fall of the City of Mahagonny* was completed in April 1929, only two years after he had started working on it. *Mahagonny*, the focal point of the whole Brecht-Weill collaboration, is the most openly political and socially critical of their large-scale works. The opera begins with the arrival of Widow Begbick, Moses and Fatty, all of whom are wanted by the police. The truck on which they are travelling has broken down and, rather than attempt to continue, they decide to stay and found a city – a city which will be devoted to pleasure. The new city soon attracts inhabitants, prostitutes and men from Alaska and the West eager to enjoy the pleasures which the city has to offer. However, these pleasures soon prove inadequate and one of the inhabitants, Jim, complains that the city has too many rules. He is about to leave when it is announced that a hurricane is heading for the city.

The hurricane passes by, leaving the city untouched. In the general rejoicing that follows a new doctrine is announced – from now on everything is to be allowed. The citizens then proceed to indulge in the various pleasures offered: love, eating (a glutton dies asking for more food) and fighting (a man is killed in a boxing match). Jim, who has proposed the new *laissez-faire* doctrine, invites everyone to drink but has no money with which to pay. Deserted by everyone he is bound and led away to trial. The trial is presided over by Widow

Begbick; Moses acts as prosecutor. Jim's case is preceded by a murder trial in which the accused bribes the judge and is released. No-one will lend Jim the money with which to pay his bills, however, and he is found guilty and condemned to death. In the final scenes of the opera Jim is executed and the city is destroyed by fire.

Universal Edition had already seen a synopsis of the *Mahagonny* libretto and had expressed fears about the kind of reception the work might have. On receiving the completed opera, Universal became even more anxious and began to doubt whether the piece could be staged at all in a German opera house. Faced with Universal's objections, Weill agreed to make some optional cuts and to rewrite some of the numbers of the brothel scene in Act III, the scene which most worried his publishers. The so-called 'Crane Duet' between Jim and Jenny was one of the numbers written and inserted into the score at this stage.[31]

As Universal Edition began negotiating with various opera houses for the première of *Mahagonny*, Weill, Brecht and Aufricht turned their attention elsewhere. Hoping for another commercial success with which to follow *The Threepenny Opera*, Aufricht persuaded the two men to begin work on a farcical gangster comedy to be entitled *Happy End*. The plot concerns Lillian Holiday, a lieutenant in the Salvation Army, who falls in love with a gangster boss, Bill Cracker, and is consequently dismissed from the Army. Returning to the gangsters Lillian converts not only Bill but the whole of his gang, all of whom then join the Salvation Army.

The songs were to be only loosely connected with the play (and, indeed, some of the song texts had been written before the idea of the play was conceived).

Weill and Brecht planned to spend the summer of 1929 working on *Happy End* in the South of France, as they had spent that of 1928 working on *The Threepenny Opera*. They left Berlin for France in May but Brecht had an accident *en route* and had to turn back; Weill continued and wrote some of the music in the South of France, while Brecht and Elisabeth Hauptmann were still working on the play, and the rest in July and August while on holiday near Munich.[32]

With a relatively trouble-free rehearsal period, a strong cast – including Carola Neher as Lillian, Helene Weigel as the Lady in Grey, Peter Lorre as Dr Nakamura, Oskar Homolka as Bill and Kurt Gerron as Sam – and the same production team, designer, conductor and instrumentalists as had, just over a year before, mounted *The*

Threepenny Opera, all seemed set for a great success.

Happy End opened at the Theater am Schiffbauerdamm on 2 September 1929. At first, recalls Lotte Lenya, 'everything seemed to be going well. During the second act intermission, people were saying, "Oh, this will be a bigger hit than *The Threepenny Opera*".'[33]

During the period between the writing and the staging of the play, however, Brecht's friends had persuaded him that the work's lack of political commitment suggested that he had capitulated to the bourgeois idea of the theatre as mere 'entertainment'.

The results of this persuasion are described by Lotte Lenya:

> Brecht's wife, Helene Weigel, came out in the third act with a Communist pamphlet and read from it, making a speech to sort of whitewash what had been done in *Happy End* . . . it wasn't part of the original plan to do this and nobody – not Kurt or the producer or anyone – had any idea this was going to happen. Helene just walked out and did it.[34]

The sudden, deliberately provocative, introduction of a political speech in the middle of what had, up to that point, seemed to be a light comedy proved too much for the audience. The première ended in uproar and the police were called in.

Happy End had been announced as a German adaptation by Elisabeth Hauptmann of a magazine story by a certain 'Dorothy Lane'; only the song texts were officially credited to Brecht. No-one was deceived by the credit given to the enigmatic Miss Lane, however, ('the comedy is so slipshod that it can only be by Brecht', wrote one critic) and the drama critics – many of whom welcomed an opportunity of attacking Brecht – wrote savage reviews.[35] A potential success was turned into a resounding flop and the work was withdrawn after a few performances. Brecht never admitted authorship of the piece and even today copies of the script and the score credit the non-existent Dorothy Lane as the source.

By the summer of 1929 the negotiations for the première of *Mahagonny* were finally concluded. Weill's hope that the work would receive its first performance under Klemperer at the Kroll Opera had come to nothing and instead an agreement had been reached with the Leipzig Opera House. The première was scheduled for March 1930 and it had been agreed that Brecht and Weill would attend and supervise the rehearsals.

However, the political and economic situations were to change radically in the six months that elapsed between the première of *Happy End* and the first performance of *The Rise and Fall of the City of Mahagonny*. By the end of the year, as a result of the Wall Street Crash on 29 October 1929, not only the German economy but the economy of the whole of the Western world lay in ruins.

Chapter 4
1930-1935

Although the full extent of the economic depression which followed the Wall Street Crash only became evident towards the end of 1930, some effects began to make themselves felt almost immediately. Bankruptcies and suicides resulting from bankruptcies soon became commonplace; factories began to close and to lay off workers; the number of the unemployed, which had been negligible during the apparently prosperous years of the later 1920s, began to climb steadily again. At the time of the Wall Street Crash, Germany had had 1,320,000 unemployed. By January 1930 the figure had risen to two-and-a-half million and, by September of that year, stood at three million. Within the next two years the number of unemployed would climb still further until, at its highest point, in the early months of both 1932 and 1933, it stood at over six million. Many of the unemployed were also homeless and were driven to settle in one of the many 'tent towns' that sprang up around Berlin. Those people still in work were forced to accept drastic cuts in their wages as a means of staying employed.

The economic crisis inevitably produced a political crisis as the differences between the parties forming the coalition government widened. As the number of those unemployed grew, the payment of unemployment benefits became the particular focus of political argument: the right-wing parties, arguing that the country could not afford such benefits, demanded cuts; the left-wing demanded that the benefits be financed by increasing the taxes paid by employers. Finally, in March 1930, the coalition government collapsed.

A new cabinet under Heinrich Brüning attempted to implement a programme of austerity. On 16 July 1930, the Reichstag refused to agree to such a programme, whereupon Brüning dissolved the Reichstag by presidential decree and announced 14 September as the date of elections for a new Reichstag.

In addition, there remained the problem of the Treaty of Versailles, still the cause of much bitterness and resentment. The question of Germany's reparation payments had never been completely settled and negotiations between the Germans and the Allies had dragged on throughout the late 1920s. When the Young Plan of 1929 finally fixed the total sum of Germany's reparation payments, the right-wing mounted a violent campaign of opposition to the Plan. One of the leaders of this opposition was Alfred Hugenberg, the leader of the National Party. A man of considerable wealth and influence, with financial interests in newspapers, advertising and film companies, Hugenberg needed someone who could gain mass support for his campaign. He turned to Adolf Hitler. With the financial backing of Hugenberg and the publicity offered by Hugenberg's chain of news-papers, Hitler turned himself into a national figure. The Nazi Party (which during the previous period of prosperity had declined to a point at which it had little political significance) had thus re-established itself and had begun to re-emerge as a political force before 1930. With the sudden collapse of the economy following the Wall Street Crash and with the population becoming more and more fearful as the economic depression deepened, the Nazis found them-selves faced with a situation which they were well prepared to exploit. With large numbers of the unemployed rallying to the Nazi cause, Hitler reinforced and reorganized his Stormtroopers and, in 1930, began the first of the series of long and violent campaigns which, three years later, were to bring him to power.

During the spring of 1930, Weill was engaged on the composition of *Der Jasager*, an opera for schools on a text which Brecht had adapted from a Japanese Nō play. Brecht's adaptation is largely identical with Elisabeth Hauptmann's translation of the English version of *Taniko* by Arthur Waley. The sketches of *Der Jasager* were made in January 1930 and the piece was composed between April and May. In the months between the sketching out and the com-position of *Der Jasager*, Weill was busy with the preparations for the Leipzig première and the subsequent Kassel production of *Mahagonny*. Commissioned by the Berlin Neue Musik 1930 Festival, the successor to the Baden-Baden Festival, *Der Jasager* was to be one of a number of works written specifically for children; Hindemith (who contributed

Wir bauen eine Stadt – We Build A City), Dessau and Toch were to be among the other composers represented. Writing about the piece in *Die Szene* in August 1930 Weill said:

> An opera can be an education for a composer or for a generation of composers. Now, when we are trying to find a new basis for 'opera' as a form and to redraw the boundaries within which it operates, it is important that we concern ourselves first and foremost with the content and structure of new kinds of music theatre . . . An opera can also be an education in the interpretation of opera . . . in this sense a school opera can serve as a study for opera schools, helping to train singers to achieve a simplicity and naturalness . . .
>
> In a third sense a 'school opera' is an opera for use in schools – an attempt to create a piece which is not an end in itself but at the service of an institution which needs and values new music . . . For this reason I have written *Der Jasager* in such a way that all the parts (choral, orchestral and solo parts) can be taken by students and that these students can also design the stage set and the costumes. The score is also designed to accommodate the possible instruments in a school orchestra: strings (without violas) and two pianos, and then, at will, three wind instruments (flute, clarinet, saxophone), percussion and plucked instruments.
>
> I do not believe that one should think about the difficulties of the music for a school opera to such an extent that one writes a particularly 'childish', easily learned piece. The music of a school opera must be capable of being studied for a long period of time. It is in the studying of the work that its practical value lies and the performance of such a piece is far less important than the education derived from rehearsing it.[1]

In the event *Der Jasager* was performed outside the Festival. Following an attempt by the Festival committee (which included Hindemith) to censor Brecht's *Die Massnahme*, a Lehrstück which was to have been performed with music by Hans Eisler, (the Festival directorate rejecting the work on the grounds that the text was 'artistically mediocre'), Weill withdrew *Der Jasager* in protest. The piece received its first performance in the studio of Berlin Radio on 24 June 1930.

David Drew has described *Der Jasager* as being Weill's greatest success up to that date, greater than that of *The Threepenny Opera*.[2]

Adopted, and officially encouraged, by the Music Education Department of the Ministry of Culture – the head of which was Leo Kestenberg, a former piano pupil of Busoni – the work was performed by schools throughout Germany. Hans Heinsheimer, who mounted a production with schoolchildren in a poor district of Vienna, remembers the extraordinary success and effect which the work had:

> Never have I seen an audience so deeply moved as by the simple lines and primitive melodies of this score . . . I can still hear the music, the little voice trembling with excitement, the sob of the mother in the audience, the violent storm of applause.[3]

Drew has persuasively argued that this success rested on a misunderstanding of the apparently anti-humanitarian moral of the piece and has pointed out that the work's great popularity (it received over 100 productions in Germany between June 1930 and the end of 1932) itself carried ominous implications, resting, as it did, on the belief that the work sanctioned the submission of the individual will to the demands of a cause.[4] The piece caused much ideological confusion. Some critics saw it as a deeply religious piece; others, such as the critics of *Die Weltbühne*, many of whom were personal friends of Brecht's, denounced it as demonstrating 'all the evil ingredients of reactionary thinking, founded on senseless authority. This "Yes-sayer" reminds us of those during the war.'[5] Brecht responded to such criticism by writing a companion piece, *Der Neinsager (The No-Sayer)*, and said that they should be performed together.

Certainly the moral of *Der Jasager* is ambiguous and can be seen as commending the submission of the individual to the demands of an abstract cause. Neither Brecht nor Weill were likely to have felt much sympathy towards such an interpretation, however, for, by April 1930, when Weill began work on the composition of *Der Jasager*, *Mahagonny* had received its first performance and both poet and composer had had direct experience of the ugliness that can result when individual morality becomes subservient to an overwhelming belief in a cause.

The first performance of *The Rise and Fall of the City of Mahagonny* took place in Leipzig on 9 March 1930. Hans Heinsheimer was in Leipzig for the dress rehearsal on 8 March and was already conscious of 'a strange and unknown tension in the theatre'.[6]

Worried by the tense atmosphere Heinsheimer went to Brecher, the conductor, and warned him, 'I have the feeling that we are playing this opera on a powder keg.'[7] Brecher is reported to have said that, as a musician, his interest was in the score: he knew nothing about politics. On the night of the première Heinsheimer saw:

> crowds of Brown Shirts on the streets (there had already been rumours that the Nazis had bought whole blocks of seats) and the square and the opera house were full of them. They carried banners and placards protesting against the new work by Weill and Brecht. People on the streets, people in uniform, were protesting against an opera before it was even performed.[8]

The first performance began:

> it was not long before demonstrations broke out in the auditorium . . . a little uneasiness at first, a signal perhaps, then noise, shouts, at last screams and roars of protest . . . Some of the actors couldn't stand it any more. They stepped out of their parts, rushed to the rim of the stage and shouted their protests against the intruders.[9]

By the end of the work the demonstrations had developed into a full-scale riot. Lotte Lenya, who was in the audience, has described how:

> by the time the last scene was reached, fist fights had broken out in the aisles, the theatre was a screaming mass of people; soon the riot spread to the stage, panicky spectators were trying to claw their way out and only the arrival of a large police force finally cleared the theatre. The second performance took place with the house lights up and with the theatre walls lined with police.[10]

A further production of *Mahagonny* which opened in Kassel on 12 March proved to be a success, as did one that autumn for the Frankfurt Festival and a further Leipzig production for the Arbeiter-Bildungs-Institut. These last two performances, however, were 'private' ones; public performances were still greeted with the kind of reception that the work had met at its Leipzig première. *Mahagonny* had become the target of a campaign designed to drive it off the stage. The riots at the Leipzig première had been reported in all the newspapers and frightened opera house managers were soon cancelling any planned productions of the work.

It was during the rehearsals for the Leipzig première of *Mahagonny* that the differences between Weill and Brecht first became apparent. Personal and artistic differences between the two men had been present from the start of their collaboration. Lotte Lenya has suggested that, from the outset, Brecht felt some sense of jealousy and competition between himself and Weill, remembering that as early as the 1927 première of the *Mahagonny Songspiel* Brecht had remarked, 'You know, Lenya, Weill must get used to the fact that his name is not on the programme.' Lotte Lenya has also observed that, 'when you look at the book of *The Threepenny Opera* there you see, way up in the corner: collaborators: Elisabeth Hauptmann (first) and Kurt Weill.'[11] However, such jealousies, if they existed, were far less important than the artistic differences between the two men. The relationships and the differences between Brecht's and Weill's artistic ideas will be discussed in detail later but some mention of them is necessary at this point in order to understand why the two men decided to part.

In some ways the differences between Brecht and Weill were simply new manifestations of those arguments about the relative importance of words and music that have dogged opera since its beginnings. But the development of Brecht's theatrical ideas during the late 1920s and early 1930s was such that he not only regarded the music as being subservient to the text, but that he demanded that the music have a specific function. Like the other elements which went to make up Brecht's epic theatre the music had to force people to think, rather than to feel.

In his essay *On the Use of Music in an Epic Theatre* Brecht demanded a 'gestic' music which avoided 'narcotic effects', 'lyricism' and 'expression for its own sake'; the solutions of musical problems were 'to be directed to the clear and intelligible underlining of the political and philosophical meaning of the poem.'[12] Weill could not accept such a restriction and in pieces such as the beautiful 'Crane Duet' in *Mahagonny*, he wrote the kind of music which encouraged the emotional involvement of the listener. In so doing he introduced an emotional ambiguity which obscured the 'political meaning' of the text and thus went against all Brecht's intentions. It is significant that in *On the Use of Music in an Epic Theatre*, although it was published after his partnership with Weill was ended, Brecht could not resist observing (presumably with numbers such as the 'Crane Duet' in mind) that he did not regard Weill's music for *Mahagonny* as being 'purely gestic'.

The production of *Mahagonny*, in which, more than in any other of their joint collaborations, the music played a conspicuously dominant rôle, must have confirmed Brecht in his suspicions that he and Weill had different aims. Both men must have begun to feel that each was simply using the other as a means of furthering his own ends – Brecht feeling that Weill simply wanted someone who could provide words which would act as a vehicle for the music; Weill feeling that Brecht needed only a musical hack.

There were also growing political differences between the two men. During the years from 1929 to 1931 Brecht became more overtly and dogmatically Communist in his political thought. Weill, who had sympathized with the social and ethical aims but had never subscribed to the openly Marxist aims of some sections of the Novembergrüppe, was unwilling to adopt Brecht's political stance. Lotte Lenya has described how:

> Brecht at that time got more political by the minute . . .
> I remember when Brecht came to visit us and we gave him
> a guest room which was quite comfortable with the usual
> furnishings – curtains, a rug and so on. Well, when I came
> up after a few minutes to bring him some towels, I found
> that he had completely transformed the room: the rug was
> shoved under the bed, the picture on the wall had been
> taken down and in its place there was a Chinese scroll, and
> there was a sort of clothes line stretched across the room
> from one window to another with a red star hanging from
> it. Within ten minutes he had completely transformed the
> room with those things which he must have carried with
> him wherever he went . . . Kurt said, 'I'm not interested in
> composing Karl Marx; I like to write music.'[13]

Brecht needed a more politically committed, more emotionally neutral composer; a composer whose political convictions enabled him to accept as necessary the musical restriction of epic theatre. Brecht found such a composer in Hanns Eisler and Eisler's score for *Die Massnahme* in 1930 was the first extensive collaboration and the beginning of a long partnership between the two men.

Finally, and perhaps less important than either the artistic or political differences between Weill and Brecht, there was the fact that Brecht was at that time going through a particularly difficult period in his personal life. The Nero-Film Company which was filming *The Threepenny Opera* with G W Pabst as director, had hired both Brecht and Weill to work on the film. Brecht, in the light of his now whole-hearted commitment to Marxism, insisted on making alterations to the original text. The Nero-Film Company, wanting to make a film of a work which had already proved to be an enormous success on the stage, objected. Brecht had then started a court case against the film company in an attempt to stop the film being made. The case was heard in the courts in October 1930 and created immense interest, becoming for some months one of the great topics of conversation in Berlin society. Brecht lost the case, although Weill won a suit which prevented the Nero-Film Company from altering the musical score.

The most surprising aspect of the Weill-Brecht collaboration is not that it eventually broke up but that it lasted so long and produced so many works. The differences between the two men had been there from the start and it was only their mutual sense of interdependence and their tacit, and perhaps subconscious, recognition of the fact that their own best ends were served by ignoring these differences that enabled them to work together for over three years. Indeed, the unique character and quality of the works produced within these years may be the result of the unspoken artistic tension between the two partners. Brecht's gradual development of his theories of epic theatre and his adoption of a more overtly Marxist political view simply brought these innate tensions to the foreground. Once the differences were openly recognized, the partnership could no longer continue.

By the time *Die Massnahme* was performed, Weill had already begun work on an opera based on a text by Caspar Neher. Caspar Neher was an old school friend and a devoted and passionate admirer of Brecht – even to the extent of wearing, 'as a token of sympathy and approval . . . the steel-rimmed glasses with the leather cap' which were the mark of Brecht's own characteristic mode of dress.[14] In his rôle as designer, Neher had played a vital part in bringing about the successful productions of almost all of Brecht's works, including those which had been written in collaboration with Weill. Neher was not only the finest stage designer of his generation, however, but also a man whose contribution to the development of the theatre during the years of the Weimar Republic extended to many other areas, including direction (he was to be co-director, with Brecht, of the first Berlin production of *Mahagonny*) and the actual writing of plays. John Willett has described how Neher not only designed the sets and the costumes of many of Brecht's plays but 'in dozens of sketches would suggest the action too'.[15] Brecht himself gave an indication of the extent to which Neher contributed to and involved himself in the actual creation of a work when he wrote, in his diary for 2 March 1921: 'In the morning Cas and I worked on the Webb's film *The Rotating Wine Jar*. Cas acted as midwife and took over the groaning too. He get the pains; I get the child.'[16] Little wonder, then, that Brecht regarded Neher as the most important and creatively stimulating of his theatrical partners.

Die Bürgschaft (The Pledge), the three act opera for which Neher provided the libretto, is the story of the relationship between two men, Johann Mattes, a farmer, and his friend the corn dealer David Orth.

In the Prologue to the opera Mattes, who has lost everything gambling, persuades Orth to lend him the necessary money.

In Act I, which takes place six years later, Mattes again goes to his friend for help and persuades Orth to sell him his last two bags of grain. Only afterwards does Orth discover that one of the sacks contained a considerable amount of money which had been hidden there, for safety, by his son. Orth is not worried, since he knows that Mattes will return with the money. Mattes, however, does not return and only much later, when threatened by blackmailers, does he confess and offer Orth his money. Orth refuses, saying that the offer has come too late, and suggests that they allow the courts to decide who is the legal owner of the money.

At the start of Act II the judge decides that the money should be shared between Mattes's daughter and Orth's son. During the course of the act, however, it is announced that the country has been invaded and conquered by a neighbouring power; the land will henceforth be ruled by the laws of money and of force. The humanitarian judge is removed from office and the case of Mattes and Orth re-tried. Both are found guilty and the money is confiscated by the State.

Six years later, when Act III begins, both men have become corrupted by power and by the money which they have made by exploiting the war which rages across the land. Mattes has used the administrative disorganization of the wartime conditions to steal from the people; Orth has deliberately withheld grain from the starving people in order to force up prices. In the final scene of the work Mattes, mobbed by an angry crowd, again turns to Orth for protection. Orth, acting now according to the 'law of money and of force' hands his friend over to the crowd to be killed.

Die Bürgschaft was begun in August 1930 and completed some fourteen months later in October 1931. During these fourteen months, however, the political situation in Germany had become even more dangerous. In the elections of September 1930 the Nazis, who had held a mere twelve seats in the previous Reichstag, won 170 seats. The Nazi vote had risen from 810,000 to six-and-a-half million and they now became the second largest party in the Reichstag. The new parliament opened on 13 October 1930 with Nazi demonstrations inside, and with riots and parades outside the Reichstag buildings. Throughout the following fifteen months the Nazis kept up an unceasing campaign of propaganda and violent activity in the streets. In 1931 the editor of *Die Weltbühne*, the main voice of the left wing, was arrested. SA violence at showings of the American film *All Quiet on the Western Front* forced the government to ban the film on the grounds that it 'endangered Germany's national prestige'. There was, said the British Ambassador to Berlin in July 1931, 'an un-natural silence hanging over the city . . . an atmosphere of extreme tension similar to that which I observed in Berlin in the critical days immediately before the war.'[17]

At the same time the economic situation deteriorated even further as the full effects of the Wall Street Crash made themselves felt. By March 1931 the unemployment figures stood at nearly five million. In July, the banking crisis which had been threatening for two years finally occurred. Towards the end of June one of Germany's largest textile concerns had been forced to declare itself bankrupt. The Darmstadt Bank, which had invested in the concern, lost nearly forty million marks in the collapse and, as unrest spread, the public began to withdraw its money from the bank. With the subsequent collapse of the great Kreditanstalt of Vienna, Austria's largest banking group, the run spread to other banks and the collapse of the whole banking system seemed imminent. The Stock Exchange was closed for more than a month, industrial production and shares fell dramatically, banks closed. The complete collapse of the financial system was narrowly avoided but the crisis seriously undermined the standing of the government, forcing it to demand even greater sacrifices from, and placing further austerities on, the public.

It was against this background that *The Rise and Fall of the City of Mahagonny* finally received its first performance in Berlin. That the performance took place at all was due to the courage of E J Aufricht, the man who had commissioned *The Threepenny Opera* and *Happy End*. Aufricht decided to mount the work, not in the Theater am Schiffbauerdamm, where the earlier pieces had received their premières, but in the larger Theater am Kürfurstendamm, Max Reinhardt's theatre which was hired for the run. Hoping for a financial success on the scale of *The Threepenny Opera*, Aufricht persuaded Weill to agree that the cast should consist of cabaret performers, rather than opera singers, and that the work should be cut to make it more accessible to a popular audience. Weill undertook a further revision of the score, adding new pieces and rewriting or omitting some (such as the 'Crane Duet') that would have been impossible or unsuitable for the voices at his disposal. The work had its Berlin première on 21 December 1931 and was conducted by Alexander von Zemlinsky. The production and set designs were by Caspar Neher. The cast included Harald Paulsen (the original Macheath) as Jimmy Mahoney, Trude Hesterberg (the owner of the famous *Wild Stage* cabaret) as Widow Begbick and Lotte Lenya as Jenny. Surprisingly, perhaps, the piece ran without any of the interruptions which had marred the Leipzig staging of the work as well as subsequent performances. With the Nazi seizure of power less than eighteen months ahead, Berlin maintained its tradition of tolerance and cosmopolitanism. Berlin was the only place left in Germany where the work could still be staged.

The Berlin première of the *Mahagonny* opera was among Weill's last German successes. On 10 March 1932 the State Opera gave the first performance of *Die Bürgschaft* conducted by Fritz Stiedry and produced by Carl Ebert. A few critics reviewed the piece favourably but, on the whole, the work was given only a luke-warm reception. The Nazi press had launched a violent campaign against the work some time before the première. The day before the opening the Nazi *Völkischer Beobachter* had published a notice which declared:

> The State Opera intends to slap the German nation in the face in the first half of March by giving the première of a new opera, *Die Bürgschaft*, by Kurt Weill, the composer who has been shameless enough to offer the German people *The Threepenny Opera*, *The Rise and Fall of the City of Mahagonny* and the other inferior works that he has written. This Jew has yet to realize that the last named piece led to a riot in Leipzig and that his abominable and worthless

Brecht and Weill were rarely photographed together; these photographs are from a series probably taken when they were preparing The Threepenny Opera

ABOVE *Weill's original manuscript of the lovesong from Act 1 of* The Threepenny Opera. *Weill seems to have changed his mind about the disposition of instrumental parts in this number at the last moment* ABOVE RIGHT *Casper Neher's design of the final scene for the original production of* The Threepenny Opera *at the Theater am Schiffbauerdamm, Berlin 1928* BOTTOM RIGHT *The photo-montage by Günter Hirschel-Protsch which formed the backdrop of the only staged version of* Der Ozeanflug *(originally* Der Flug der Lindberghs)*; Breslau 1930*

LEFT *Lotte Lenya as Jenny and Harald Paulsen as Paul Ackermann in the first Berlin production (1931) of* The Rise and Fall of the City of Mahagonny, *which was conducted by Alexander von Zemlinsky (above left) and with sets designed by Casper Neher (above right), who collaborated on most of the Brecht/Weill works* BELOW *Carola Neher as Lillian, Oskar Homolka as Bill and Peter Lorre as Dr Nakamura in the original production of* Happy End *at the Theater am Schiffbauerdamm, Berlin September 1929. Although Brecht was undoubtedly the author of this play, it was attributed to 'Dorothy Lane'*

ABOVE *Rudolf Forster as Macheath and Lotte Lenya as Jenny in the brothel scene from* G W Pabst's *film of* The Threepenny Opera ABOVE RIGHT *A propaganda photograph showing Nazis being cheered by on-lookers as they drive through the streets of Berlin in 1929* BELOW RIGHT *G W Pabst directing Carola Neher (Polly) and Rudolf Forster (Macheath) in the wedding sequence during the shooting of the film version of* The Threepenny Opera BELOW FAR RIGHT *The cover of the programme for the opening night of* Die Bürgschaft

Städtisches Opernhaus-Restaurant

Inhaber Hermann Lindner

Bitte beachten Sie die ausgehängte Speisekarte

Theatersoupers zu zeitgemäßen Preisen
In allen Räumen Bier
Gesellschaftszimmer und Festsäle

Bitte beachten Sie die ausgehängte Speisekarte

Fernsprecher: C 4 Wilhelm 793

Turnus 1

Donnerstag, den 10. März 1932

Uraufführung

Die Bürgschaft

Oper in 3 Akten und einem Vorspiel von **Kurt Weill**

Text von **Caspar Neher**. (Unter Verwendung einer Parabel von Herder)

Musikalische Leitung: **Fritz Stiedry**   Inszenierung: **Carl Ebert**

Bühnenbild: **Caspar Neher**   Chorleitung: **Hermann Lüddecke**

Technische Leitung: **Kurt Hemmerling**

Choreographie: **Lizzie Maudrik**

Kassenöffnung 19 (7) Uhr   Anfang 20 (8) Uhr

Ende gegen 23½ (11½) Uhr

Das Fundbüro der Städt. Oper, Erdgeschoß (Zimmer 23), Eingang Sesenheimer Straße, ist werktags von 10-2 Uhr geöffnet

Eigener Untergrundbahnhof mit direktem Eingang zur Städtischen Oper

ABOVE LEFT *Collecting copies of the works of blacklisted authors for public burning which took place in Berlin in 1933* ABOVE RIGHT *This plaque, calling on all Germans to boycott Jewish businesses was just one example of the antisemitic campaign the Nazis were waging in Berlin by 1932* BELOW *Caspar Neher's sketch of a scene from the original production of* Der Silbersee, *Leipzig February 1933, the last work which Weill wrote in Germany*

Threepenny Opera is rejected everywhere. It is inconceivable that a composer who purveys such totally un-German pieces should again be given the chance to appear at a theatre which is supported by the German tax-payer's money. Let Israel find edification in Weill's new opera.[18]

Those opera houses that had been about to produce the piece quickly changed their plans and the future performances, which the State Opera had already announced for the coming season, never took place. It was no longer safe to bill such a work and it would not be long before any association with Weill's music was a danger. When Ebert was eventually dismissed from his position at the State Opera, his advocacy of *Die Bürgschaft* was cited as one of the reasons. Kestenberg, who, as head of the Music Education Department, had promoted *Der Jasager* was also dismissed. Brecher, who had conducted the Leipzig première of *Mahagonny* and who, in 1930, had denied having any interest in politics, shot his wife and then committed suicide in 1935.

By early 1932 Hindenburg's seven year term of office had expired and a new presidential election became necessary. The presidential campaign of March 1932 was the first of five election campaigns in Germany during that year. The results of the March campaign were inconclusive; although the Nazi vote had risen to 11.4 million, Hindenburg polled seven million votes more than the Nazis. However, Hindenburg had failed by 0.4 per cent to achieve the absolute majority required and another election was needed. In the second election, on 10 April, Hindenburg attained the required majority but the Nazis increased their vote by two million.

A fortnight later the Prussian state elections showed a similar dramatic increase in the Nazi votes when, from having had nine seats, they became the largest party with 162. From that point onwards, the political situation began to gather the momentum that, within six months, would bring Hitler the Chancellorship and the Nazis to power. As Stefan Zweig observed:

> Inflation, unemployment, the political crisis and, not least, the folly of lands abroad, had made the German people restless; a tremendous desire for order animated all circles of the German people, to whom order had always been more important than freedom and justice. And anyone who promised order – even Goethe said that disorder was more distasteful to him than even an injustice – could count on hundreds of thousands of supporters from the start.[19]

Because of various manoeuvres by a number of powerful enemies, and, in particular by General Schleicher, the position of Chancellor Brüning had been so undermined that President Hindenburg no longer regarded him with any confidence and demanded his resignation. The new Chancellor, Franz von Papen, Schleicher's candidate, immediately dismissed the Reichstag and called for a new election on 31 July. He also lifted the ban that had been imposed on the SA. Alan Bullock has described how, 'in the weeks that followed, murder and violence became everyday occurrences in the streets of the big German cities. According to Grzesinski, the Police President of Berlin, there were 461 political riots in Prussia alone betwen June 1st and July 20th 1932.'[20] The fiercest fighting was between the Nazis and the Communists and, as Bullock remarks, the 'impression that events favoured the triumph of one or other form of extremism was strengthened, and helped both parties to win votes at the coming election.'[21]

In July 1932, amidst this political turmoil, Weill began working on what was to be the last work which he would complete in Germany, the incidental music to Georg Kaiser's *Der Silbersee*. Inevitably, perhaps, the piece was concerned with the social problems of economic decline and unemployment.

On 28 January 1933, General Schleicher resigned the Chancellorship and two days later, on 30 January, Adolf Hitler became Chancellor of the German Reich.

Der Silbersee received simultaneous first performances in Leipzig, Erfurt and Magdenburg on 18 February 1933. The *Berlin Tageblatt*, which carried reviews of both the Leipzig and Magdenburg performances, described the success of the work as being 'very great' and said that 'Weill, Sierck [the designer of the Leipzig production], Brecher [the conductor] and the principals had to take many curtain calls' and bemoaned the fact that Berlin was not to see a performance of the piece.[22] The *Leipziger Neuste Nachrichten* of 19 February carried a similarly favourable review. F A Hauptmann, the music critic of the Nazi *Völkischer Beobachter*, however, commented:

> One must distrust an artist who concerns himself with such subjects, who writes 'music' for works which are intended to destroy art and the meaning of true art, especially if this artist is a Jew who is allowed to use the German stage to achieve his goal. The music of *Silbersee* shows that these misgivings are correct.[23]

The second performance of *Der Silbersee* in Magdenburg on 21 February was interrupted by riots organized by the Nazi Kampfbund für Deutsche Kultur.

On 27 February 1933, less than a week after this second Magdenburg performance of *Silbersee*, the Reichstag fire occurred, the event which signalled the beginning of Hitler's purge on his political opponents. On the following day Hitler announced the suspension of the Weimar constitution and declared that there would be imposed 'for the protection of the people and the state, lawful restriction on personal liberty, on the rights of free expression of opinion including the freedom of the press, on the rights of assembly and associations'. In addition, 'violations of the privacy of postal, telegraphic and telephonic communications, warrants for house searches and orders for confiscation as well as restriction of property' were declared 'permissible beyond the legal limits otherwise prescribed'.

Many left-wing sympathizers, writers and artists – including Brecht – left Germany on 28 February, the day after the Reichstag fire. Weill remained in Berlin for another month, until 21 March, the so-called 'Day of Potsdam' when Hitler and Hindenburg publicly sealed their alliance at a ceremony marking the opening of the new Reichstag. The new Reichstag elections had taken place on 4 March when the Nazis had won a bare majority. Learning that he was on the Nazi blacklist, and knowing that many of his acquaintances had been arrested, Weill and his wife Lotte Lenya left Germany by car for France on 21 March 1933. On 10 May 1933, less than two months after Weill had left Germany, the works of Brecht and many other writers were publicly burned. Weill's publisher, Universal Edition, was based in Austria rather than Germany, and his scores therefore remained safe until 1938 when, immediately after the Anschluss, the offices of Universal were raided by the Gestapo and many of the scores held there were destroyed.

The Weills arrived in Paris on 23 March 1933. Weill was already well known in France. A concert performance of *Der Jasager* and the *Mahagonny Songspiel* under Walter Straram in the Salle Gaveau in Paris on 11 December 1932 had been met with rapturous acclaim, affording Weill what David Drew has described as 'the last, and by far the greatest, triumph of his European career'. The French composer Darius Milhaud, a close friend of Weill's in both Europe and America, has described the effect of this Parisian concert in his autobiography as follows:

Thanks to the generosity of the Vicomtesse de Noailles, we were able to present Kurt Weill's *Mahagonny* and *Der Jasager*, for which the soloist Lotte Lenya and the conductor Maurice Abravanel came from Germany as well as a group of children, for *Der Jasager* was written specifically for schools. I was lecturing in Holland at the time the concert was given and, in the train that was bringing us back to Paris, I told Madeline that we should no doubt find that the city had been taken by storm. Little did I know how true this was, for the delirious enthusiasm aroused by these two works lasted for several days. The Montparnasse set used the concert as a pretext for political diatribes; it saw in it an expression of the moral bankruptcy and pessimism of our time. Smart society was as carried away as if it had been the first performance of a Bach Passion.[24]

Reviewing the concert in *Candide* on 15 December 1932, Émile Vuillermoz said: 'It is many years since Paris has become aware of such strong and lofty emotions. Such performances must be offered to the public again'.[25] Marcel More, in *La Politique*, became lyrical in his praise of a score which had 'the consummate skill and lively emotion of an 18th-century master . . . its extraordinary qualities brought forth all the applause. A unique voice speaks to us in these works – despairingly beautiful and tragic, like the long stem of a black rose with spikes and sharp thorns.'[26]

As a result of this success the Princesse Edmonde de Polignac, the great French patroness of new music, had commissioned Weill to write the work that was eventually to become the Second Symphony. Weill had started work on the piece in Berlin in January 1933, after the completion of *Der Silbersee*. Having taken sketches for the Symphony with him when he left Germany, he now continued work on the composition. Within a few weeks of arriving in France, however, his work on the Symphony was interrupted by a more urgent composition for a ballet for 'Les Ballets 1933', a newly formed company directed by the young George Balanchine and Boris Kochno, Diaghilev's secretary. Brecht (who had left Berlin before Weill but had travelled to France via Czechoslovakia, Austria and Switzerland) had just arrived in Paris and Weill turned once more to him for a subject. The resulting 'ballet with songs' – *The Seven Deadly Sins of the Bourgeoisie* – was written during April and May and received its first performance at the Théâtre des Champs Élysées on 7 June 1933.

The ballet tells the story of Anna, a young girl sent out into the world to earn money to build her family a house in Mississippi. Anna is represented by two people – Anna I (the singer) representing the practical realist; Anna II (the dancer) representing the idealistic aspects of the character. During the course of the work the realistic Anna I is gradually shown to have overcome the moral scruples of Anna II. Each scene is set in a different city and in each Anna II is persuaded to avoid one of those virtues which the bourgeoisie regards as deadly sins – for example the sin of sloth (in performing an injustice which would enable one to rise up the social ladder), the sin of lust (which makes a woman go with a man she likes rather than with a man who can pay well), the sin of anger (which encourages one to fight a mean action, even if the fight is against one's own best interests) and so on. Having successfully avoided these 'sins', Anna returns home with enough money to build the family house.

The work had a mixed reception, leaving many critics puzzled by its unusual form. Walter Mehring, the great satirist, found it 'a marvellous evening . . . an élite of celebrated artists and interpreters such as one was used to in ·the days of the great German theatre.'[27] Count Harry Kessler, on the other hand, thought 'the music pretty and original . . . everything much the same as in *The Threepenny Opera*' but noted that 'it had had a bad reception in the press and with the public – in spite of the popularity which Weill enjoys here.'[28] The conductor was Maurice Abravanel; the main dancer was Tilly Loch and the singer Lotte Lenya. The sets were by Caspar Neher, the librettist of *Die Bürgschaft* and the designer for all Brecht's and Weill's previous works. It was the last time that Brecht, Neher and Weill would collaborate.

Weill returned to his work on the Symphony in the late summer of 1933 and completed the piece in the following February, by which time the Weills had acquired a house in the village of Louveciennes. Arno Huth has left a description of the house in which Weill spent his two years in France:

> A simple country house in a charming village outside Paris has become Weill's second home. Here everything breathes an air of serenity – the countryside, the little village, the house. Both the grounds and the architecture of the house itself are unusual. The high hall with its natural wood beams and large chimney remind one that the house was

once a smithy. A wooden step leads from the hall to three bright, friendly rooms, simply furnished with a few beautiful pieces of old furniture.[29]

Here at Louveciennes Weill wrote the music for *Marie Galante*, a musical play based on a novel by Jacques Deval, composed a number of songs on French texts, *Der Kuhhandel* – a political operetta based on a libretto by Robert Vaubery and, in February 1934, completed the Second Symphony.

Marie Galante was first performed at the Théâtre de Paris in Paris on 2 December 1933. In mid-summer 1934 Weill and Lotte Lenya visited England for the première of *Der Kuhhandel* (temporarily entitled *Kingdom for a Cow*) at the Savoy Theatre in London on 28 June. While in London, Lotte Lenya also took part in performances of *The Seven Deadly Sins* and a version of the *Mahagonny Songspiel* at the Savoy. The Second Symphony received its first performance by the Concertgebouw Orchestra under Bruno Walter in Amsterdam on 11 October 1934. The performance received a cool reception and the work remained unpublished until 1966.

In the later summer of 1934 Weill was approached to write the score for a Biblical drama – *Der Weg der Verheissung (The Way of the Promise)* – by Franz Werfel. The work, the idea of which originated with Max Reinhardt, was to be a monumental pageant depicting the development and the fate of the Jewish people. Weill had long since moved away from his orthodox Jewish background and, for many years, had admitted only to being a humanist. Nonetheless, the persecution of the German Jews which he had witnessed, and from which he had suffered, forced him, as it did many others – including Schoenberg – to become more consciously aware of his Jewish ancestry. Weill accepted the commission and, turning to the Jewish music of his youth for his inspiration, worked on the piece from August 1934 until December 1935. The première, scheduled for early 1936, was to take place in New York after which the production would tour the United States. Weill had been invited to conduct the first performance and, in September 1935, he sailed for New York in order to prepare for the première. He was to return to Europe only once during the remaining fifteen years of his life, and then only very briefly.

Chapter 5
The American Years

The Weills sailed into New York on the S S Majestic on 10 September 1935. On arrival they booked in at the St Moritz Hotel, overlooking Central Park, and went to see a film:

> We were ardent readers of people like Hemingway and Scott Fitzgerald, and we saw all the movies. So when we arrived, we dropped our bags and went to Broadway into a movie. We saw *The Dark Angel* with Ronald Coleman and Vilma Blank. That was the first thing and from then on there was really nothing strange or unfamiliar. [1]

Weill had left Europe intending to stay in America for only a few months, until *Der Weg der Verheissung* was produced at the beginning of 1936. However, the work soon ran into trouble and even before rehearsals began, a series of crises had eaten up all the available money. Reinhardt and his designer Norman Bel Geddes (a man who, according to one writer 'despised anything less than ten feet tall'[2]) had visions of a spectacle of the most epic and lavish proportions, with a cast that included forty-three principal actors and scenic designs that at some points operated on three separate levels. One set, for example, was to show a contemporary synagogue on the lowest of the three levels, Moses in the wilderness on the central level and, at the top, a representation of the heavens, complete with angelic chorus.

In order to accommodate the production, the Manhattan Opera House, where the work was to be mounted, had to be radically modified. At an early stage in the preparation it had been decided that the orchestra pit would be needed as part of the stage area; the

71

orchestra would, therefore, have to be moved. Even then the pit was not deep enough to contain the spectacular effects proposed by Reinhardt and Bel Geddes, and the decision was taken to deepen it by drilling down into the bedrock beneath. Unfortunately, the drill hit a spring – sending a spout of water some twenty-one feet (six metres) high into the auditorium – which then had to be capped before work could continue. With such set-backs it was not long before new financial backing was urgently needed. As rehearsals started and as crisis followed crisis, the date of the opening was postponed time and again until Weill found himself having to search for work in order to stay in the United States until the show was finally mounted.

Weill's music was not generally known by the American public at that time, and certainly did not enjoy the kind of reputation which it had in Europe. Of all his works only *The Threepenny Opera* had been staged in America before 1935 and that production, the first English language production of the work, had had a bad critical reception. Opening on 13 April 1933 at the Empire Theatre in New York *The Threepenny Opera* had run for a mere twelve performances. However, Weill's works were known to a number of important musicians and theatre people. George Gershwin, for example, was already an admirer of Weill's music and, a few weeks after Weill's arrival in the United States, had invited him to attend the dress rehearsal for the première of *Porgy and Bess* (which had its first night at the Alvin Theatre on 10 October 1935), while in December 1935 a New York concert of Weill's music was promoted by the influential League of Composers.

Many left-wing theatre groups, aware of Weill's European reputation, had given him a warm welcome and, early in 1936, the Group Theatre of New York commissioned a score for *Johnny Johnson*, a musical play by Paul Green, Professor of drama at the University of North Carolina and a former Pulitzer prize winner. An anti-militaristic satire, *Johnny Johnson* tells the story of a Schweyk-like figure who, involved against his will, manages to disrupt the war by spraying the entire allied High Command with laughing gas. Committed to a mental institution because of this insane act, he and his fellow inmates establish a League of World Republics and he is finally allowed to return to his home village where he devotes himself to selling non-martial toys.

It was the policy of the Group Theatre, a splinter group of the prestigious Theatre Guild, to spend the summer working at a summer camp, where its members could receive 'intensive training in the art of interpretation and ensemble playing'.[3] Weill spent the summer of 1936 at the Group Theatre's summer camp, lecturing and working on the score for Green's play. It was during this same period that he first met Elmer Rice, the dramatist whose Pulitzer prize winner *Street Scene* Weill had seen in Europe. Weill offered to write a score for the play but Rice thought it 'too early for a show of that sort' and the plan was temporarily abandoned.

Directed by Lee Strasberg, *Johnny Johnson* received its première at the Group Theatre's New York base on 44th Street on 19 November 1936, with a cast that included Lee J. Cobb, Elia Kazan and John Garfield. It was, according to Brook Atkinson, 'not very well acted by the Group Theatre, which seemed unable to master the form. The show was admired without being liked'.[4] It ran for sixty-eight performances.

Meanwhile, *Der Weg der Verheissung* was being subjected to yet further delays. The piece had been designed to arouse interest in the Jewish tradition and was to have been given as a charity performance with the proceeds going towards helping the persecuted Jews in Germany. However, it soon became clear that, given the scale of the production, the lengthy rehearsal period (the opening night was postponed ten times in all) and the escalating costs (which eventually rose to $540,000) – the show was unlikely to make any profit for anyone. In an attempt to save the piece, both the score and the play were subjected to savage cuts. Even then, when the mutilated version of *Der Weg der Verheissung*, now entitled *The Eternal Road*, finally opened at the Manhattan Opera House on 7 January 1937 the four-act play ran until three o'clock the following morning. During the weeks after the première yet more of Weill's score and Werfel's play was cut in order to reduce the, by now thoroughly mutilated, work to manageable proportions. The press, overwhelmed by Reinhardt's lavish production, gave the piece rave reviews and the show ran for 153 performances. Although it played to packed houses throughout and there was not a single empty seat for the whole run, it was a financial disaster and made a loss of $5,000.

By the summer of 1937 Weill had decided not only to remain in America but also to become an American citizen. This decision necessitated his leaving and re-entering the States, and, in order to fulfil these immigration requirements, he dutifully left New York for Canada in the late summer and crossed the border back into America

73

on 27 August 1937.

At the same time Weill was again approached by Paul Green, the author of *Johnny Johnson*, about the possibility of his writing a score for *The Common Glory*, a piece commissioned by the government-sponsored Federal Theatre – a short-lived project set up in 1935, as part of the New Deal work-creation scheme, for the purpose of creating a national American theatre. Weill began but never completed the score.

A new, more hopeful, project was begun in March of the following year when Weill started work on a political satire about New York in the 1880s based on Washington Irving's book *Dietrich Knickerbocker's History of New York*. The idea for this piece, which became *Knickerbocker Holiday*, seems to have come from Weill, who saw the subject as a means of commenting upon the rise of Fascism in Europe. Maxwell Anderson, one of the leading American dramatists of the time, was asked to write the libretto. Weill had met and become friends with Anderson at a performance of Anderson's *Winterset* which the composer attended soon after his arrival in the States. Anderson agreed to write the text and the Playwrights' Company, a company recently founded by Anderson and four other writers as a means of producing their own plays without the help of commercial managements, agreed to mount the work in its first season. Anderson was to become Weill's closest collaborator during the remaining years of the composer's life.

In Anderson's play for *Knickerbocker Holiday* Washington Irving, having decided to write a history of Old New York, is transported from the early nineteenth-century to seventeenth-century New Amsterdam. Irving's arrival coincides with that of the new governor of New Amsterdam, Peter Stuyvesant. Adopting dictatorial methods of government, Stuyvesant gradually abolishes the freedom and liberties of the people, sentencing to jail any who protest. When the town is invaded by Indians, Brom Broeck, a protester with whose girl friend Stuyvesant is in love, escapes from jail and leads the fight against the attackers. Accused by Broeck of conspiring with the Indians, Stuyvesant sentences Broeck to death. Irving then intervenes and, reminding Stuyvesant of the way in which future generations will judge the action, wins a reprieve for Broeck.

The New York première of *Knickerbocker Holiday* took place at the Ethel Barrymore Theatre on 19 October 1938; the director was Joshua Logan, the conductor Maurice Abravanel, Weill's former pupil and the conductor of the first production of *The Seven Deadly Sins*. The star of the show, playing Peter Stuyvesant, was Walter

74

Huston for whom Weill wrote 'September Song', perhaps the most famous of his American numbers. According to Lotte Lenya, Weill decided to write this piece after hearing Huston sing on the radio one night: 'He was singing a famous patter song "I haven't got the Do Re Mi" and Kurt suddenly said, "You know, I'm going to write for him the most romantic song I can possibly write". From Walter's crackling voice Kurt heard something in the night.'[5]

Knickerbocker Holiday, the first of Weill's Broadway scores, was a considerable success (it ran for a respectable 168 performances) and, as the second piece to be staged by the Playwright's Company in its first season, it helped establish the new company as a viable concern. It was not, however, a 'smash hit' – Weill had to wait another three years, until the première of *Lady in the Dark*, for his first Broadway hit.

David Drew has suggested that Weill passed through some kind of personal crisis during the years 1939-40.[6] If this is so (and the fact that, as Drew has pointed out, *Lady in the Dark*, Weill's next Broadway show, inhabits a radically different world from that of his previous American works[7] lends weight to the suggestion) it may well have been a crisis occasioned by the course of events in Europe.

On 1 September 1939, following the annexation of Austria in March 1938, the Munich Agreement of September 1938 and the consequent annexation of Czechoslovakia in March 1939, Hitler began his invasion of Poland. The British and French declared war on 3 September 1939. The spring of 1940 saw the first of a series of German victories which led, in a little over two months, to the German domination of almost the whole of Western Europe. By June 1942 Norway, Denmark, France, Holland, Belgium and Luxembourg had fallen to the German army. Weill must have realized that, whatever the outcome of the war, the Germany and the Europe that he had known had disappeared for ever.

For whatever reason, Weill wrote few substantial works in the two years that followed *Knickerbocker Holiday*. Two large-scale projects – a folk-opera on the subject of Davy Crockett with a libretto by Charles Allen and a musical play entitled *Ulysses Africanus* with Maxwell Anderson – were begun and abandoned. The only deeply personal work of this period is the short cantata *Magna Carta* (also on an Anderson text) which Weill wrote at the beginning of 1940 and which received its first performance on the CBS 'Pursuit of Happiness' programme on 4 February that year. Otherwise, the works of this two-year period consist of routine pieces written to fulfil the various commissions which Weill's growing reputation now attracted: two film scores (one for the *Goldwyn Follies*, an MGM spectacular directed by George Marshall, and one for *You and Me*, a film directed by Fritz Lang), the incidental music to *Madam Will you Walk*, a play by Sidney Howard, and a musical pageant *Railroads on Parade*, with a text by Edward Hungerford, written for the New York World Exhibition and given its première on 30 April 1939. As a result of these commissions Weill was able to buy the house, with large grounds and a private brook, at New City, Rockville County, in which he lived for the rest of his life.

In 1940 Weill began work with Moss Hart and Ira Gershwin on a new musical, *Lady in the Dark*. For Hart it was the first play he had written without the collaboration of his usual partner George S Kaufmann; for Gershwin it was the first piece to be written after the death of his brother George. The story of *Lady in the Dark* deals with the psychological problems and fantasies of the lady editor of a successful fashion magazine. Troubled by recurring dreams, which feature the four men in her life, and by the attempts to recapture a melody from her childhood, the heroine finally relates her dreams to a psychoanalyst and is able to recognize her love for one of the men.

Gershwin, who lived in California, moved up to New York and for four months during the hot summer of 1940 the three men worked – in New York during the week and at Hart's summer home in Bucks County at the week-ends – on the new piece. Gershwin then returned home and Weill retired to his house in New York State to orchestrate the music.

With such an experienced and skilful team of writers, with a cast that included Gertrude Lawrence (in what proved to be one of her most memorable rôles) and the young Danny Kaye, and with lavish production numbers elaborately mounted on the revolving stage, the show could hardly fail to be a success. *Lady in the Dark* had its preview in Boston and opened at the Alvin Theatre in New York on 23 January 1941. The show ran for two seasons, with a total of 467 performances in New York and then moved to Los Angeles in the autumn of 1943.

In 1944 Paramount, who had paid $300,000 for the rights – the highest sum Hollywood had ever paid for a Broadway musical – made *Lady in the Dark* into a film starring Ginger Rodgers and Ray Milland and directed by Mitchell Leisen.

In December 1941, following the Japanese attack on Pearl Harbor,

America entered the war, and from January 1942 to May 1943 – while *Lady in the Dark* was drawing enormous audiences to the Alvin Theatre – Weill devoted himself to helping organize lunch-time shows for factory workers.

Modelled on the British ENSA entertainments, these lunch-time shows, which came to be called the 'Lunchtime Follies', were simply mounted on a small platform equipped only with a piano and a couple of microphones. Originally lasting for about half-an-hour, the shows were reduced to twenty minutes as the war advanced and the lunch-time breaks were shortened. The show included a mixture of songs, dance numbers, sketches (the first show also presented a new sketch entitled 'The Man who came to Russia' by Kaufmann and Hart) and, usually, one serious item about the war. One such, frequently performed, serious item was Maxwell Anderson's dramatization of Commander Shea's letters to his son.

The 'Lunchtime Follies' were organized by Weill, Moss Hart, the composer Harald Rome and Kermit Bloomgarten (the leader of the Group Theatre) from a small office above the Lyceum Theatre. Delighted at being able to help the war effort, Weill took particular pleasure in the immediacy of the audience contact which these shows afforded; the opening of the first show he later described as 'one of the most exciting moments in my theatrical life'.[8] Characteristically, Weill saw these popular lunch-time entertainments as suggesting new directions in which theatre might move in peacetime.

During 1942 Weill also composed a number of other patriotic pieces: a ballad for baritone and chorus, on a text by Archibald MacLeish, entitled *Song of the Free*; *Recitations*, a melodrama for speaker and orchestra which employed patriotic themes and texts drawn from poems by Walt Whitman; and four *Walt Whitman Songs* for baritone and orchestra. He also set two German texts by Mehring and by Brecht which he and Lotte Lenya performed on a Voice of America broadcast in support of the war effort.

Many of Weill's Berlin friends were living in the United States during the war and, in 1942 and 1943, a number of them made attempts to revive the collaboration with Brecht who was then living in California. In autumn 1942 Brecht, who had been working in Hollywood on Fritz Lang's *Hangmen also Die*, paid a four-month visit to New York to see Erwin Piscator who was planning to produce a version of Brecht's *The Private Life of the Master Race* in the spring of 1943. Weill and Brecht met on 1 October 1942, their first meeting since 1935 when Weill had just arrived in America. Earlier in 1942 T. W. Adorno had attempted to interest Brecht and Weill in doing a production of *The Threepenny Opera* but the plan had been abandoned. In early 1943 Aufricht, the man who had commissioned *The Threepenny Opera*, tried to bring Brecht and Weill together again to write a musical based on Jaroslav Hašek's *The Good Soldier Schweyk*. Again the plan came to nothing. The reason for this was that apparently Piscator was also engaged on an adaptation of the Schweyk story and Weill seems to have decided to abandon the project rather than risk widening the already serious rift between Piscator and Brecht.[9] Brecht continued to work on the adaptation by himself and it eventually became the play *Schweyk in the Second World War*. A further plan, for Weill to write the incidental music for Brecht's *The Good Woman of Setzuan*, was also discussed and abandoned.

Weill's involvement with the 'Lunchtime Follies' ended in May 1943 and he spent the summer of that year working on a new musical comedy called *One Touch of Venus*, with a text by S J Perelman and lyrics by Ogden Nash. The rather absurd plot of the work concerned a newly discovered statue of Venus which, displayed in a museum, comes to life and falls in love with a naive barber who chances to visit the museum. Having won the young man, and having lured him away from his girl friend, the goddess realizes that she cannot change herself into a mortal and turns back into stone. The work ends with the arrival of a new girl who is identical to the statue of Venus.

Continuing the atmosphere of the war-time shows, *One Touch of Venus*, with its light, witty score and its musical and verbal parodies, became Weill's longest-running Broadway show. Opening at the Imperial Theatre on 7 October 1943, *One Touch of Venus* ran for 567 performances. The conductor was, again, Maurice Abravanel; the director Elia Kazan. The star of the show, appearing in her first starring Broadway part in a rôle which had originally been intended for Dietrich, was Mary Martin, the future star of *South Pacific* and *The Sound of Music*.

Reviewing the show for the November issue of *Modern Music*, Elliot Carter offered some perceptive observations on both the strengths and weaknesses of Weill's Broadway work in general:

> Kurt Weill's new score for *One Touch of Venus*, coming after last year's *Lady in the Dark*, reveals his mastery of Broadway technique. Apparently he can turn out one success after another with a sure hand. Weill, who orchestrates and

arranges his own work, whose flair for discovering and using the stylistic earmarks of popular music is remarkable, has finally made himself at home in America. Where in pre-Hitler days his music underlined the bold and disillusioned bitterness of economic injustice, now, reflecting his new environment and the New York audiences to which he appeals, his social scene has shrunk to the bedroom and he has become the composer of 'sophisticated' scores.

The present one represents quite a piece of research into the phases of American love-life expressed in popular music – the barber-shop ballad, the bar-room song dripping with bloody murder, the serious and comic parodies of Cole Porter, an uproarious mock-patriotic 'Way Out West in Jersey' in the best college spirit style. Even the orchestration, with its numerous piano solos in boogie-woogie and other jazz styles, constantly recalls night-club atmosphere. Traces of the mordant composer of *Die Dreigroschenoper* and *Mahagonny* occur rarely and only in places where Weill is not trying to make an impression. Compared to his other American shows, the music is neither as ingenious and as striking as *Johnny Johnson*, nor as forced as his made-to-order jobs for *The Eternal Road* and the railroad show at the World's Fair. But in the atmosphere of Broadway, where so much music is unconvincing and dead, Weill's workmanlike care and his refined sense of style make up for whatever spontaneity and freshness his music lacks.[10]

One Touch of Venus, Weill's greatest Broadway success, was followed by the greatest disaster of his American career, the two-act operetta *The Firebrand of Florence* which took as its unlikely subject an episode from the life of Benvenuto Cellini. Cellini is suspected of having played a part in a conspiracy but he manages to convince the Duke of his innocence, thus winning the hand of his beloved Angela. The story is based on a book by Edwin J Meyer which had already formed the basis of a moderately successful 1924 musical, and with lyrics by Ira Gershwin, *The Firebrand of Florence* opened at the Alvin Theatre on 22 March 1945 – a fortnight before the end of the war – and ran for only forty-three performances.

David Drew sees *The Firebrand of Florence* as marking a real crisis in Weill's creative life and has described what he calls the 'crushing reception' of the work as being the point at which Weill was 'finally defeated'.[11] Certainly the period following *The Firebrand of Florence* saw another radical shift in Weill's musical style and in the final years of his life he deliberately abandoned the slicker techniques and glossy style of the Broadway musical to cultivate a simpler, more consciously American folk style. The next work which Weill wrote was a score for the film *Where Do We Go from Here*, but the first fruits of the effects which *The Firebrand of Florence* had on him appear in the one-act folk opera *Down in the Valley* which he wrote in September 1945.

Deliberately simple in both its musical and dramatic style *Down in the Valley* employs the characteristics of the American square-dance, barn-dance, folksong and church music to tell the story of Brack Weaver who, condemned to death, escapes from prison to be reunited with his girl friend. *Down in the Valley* was intended to be the first of a series of folk operas commissioned by commercial radio. In the event, the scheme collapsed and, in 1948, Weill and Arnold Sundgaard, the author of the text, rewrote the piece as an opera for performance by 'non-professional groups'. The work had its première in this form on 14 July 1948 at the University of Indiana campus at Bloomington.

Another folk work, the Broadway opera *Street Scene*, was composed in 1946. Based on Elmer Rice's 1929 Pulitzer Prize-winning play, *Street Scene* is set in front of an East Side tenement in New York City. The main story line of the work concerns an affair between Mrs Maurrant, one of the tenants, and the milkman. When, towards the end of the opera, Mrs Maurrant's husband learns of the affair he shoots his wife and her lover and is captured by the police. More important than this story, however, is the general picture of tenement life which the work attempts to convey, of the routines, the pastimes and the hopes, fears and dreams of those who occupy the building. Weill had first approached Rice about the possibility of setting *Street Scene* during a rehearsal for *Johnny Johnson*. Now he suggested the idea again:

> On a hot summer day in 1945, as we were leaving a Dramatists' Guild meeting together, we started talking about *Street Scene* again and decided that now was the time to do it. The Broadway musical scene had changed quite a bit in the ten years since we had first discussed the plan. Broadway composers had become more 'book conscious'. Opera was now a popular entertainment; the public had become interested in singing.

Before the second drink arrived (we were planted in a
cool bar by this time) Elmer and I had made up our minds
to go ahead with *Street Scene*. We decided to do it as a
musical version of the play, to cast it entirely with singers,
so that the emotional climaxes could be expressed in music,
and to use spoken dialogue to further the realistic action.
In discussing the problem of lyrics for a show in which
music had to grow out of the characters, we decided that
the lyrics should attempt to lift the everyday language of
the people into a simple unsophisticated poetry. We choose
Langston Hughes for the job.[12]

The backers of the project were far from enthusiastic and were not
encouraged by the try-out in Philadelphia, which Lotte Lenya
has described as having been 'a disaster'. 'There were, maybe, 250
people in the audience and next door *Finian's Rainbow* was playing to
standing room only.'[13] Billy Rose, the producer, attempted to per-
suade Weill to shorten some of the numbers and to make the operatic
elements less important: 'Right after the show opens Mrs Maurrant
sings an aria that takes perhaps eight or ten minutes. When he heard
it, Billy Rose came to Kurt and said, 'Kurt, it's impossible. You have
to shorten it – nobody will listen.' Kurt was very quiet and said to
Billy: 'If that aria doesn't work then I haven't written the opera I
wanted to write. I won't change a note.'[14] The backers were particularly worried about its being called an 'opera' ('the word opera
frightened everybody on Broadway', remembers Lotte Lenya) and,
when the show opened at the Adelphi Theatre on 9 January 1947, it
bore the subtitle 'a dramatic musical'. Few critics were misled by this
attempted disguise; Olin Downes, the critic of the *New York Times*, for
example, unequivocally described it as an 'opera' and called the
work 'the most important step towards significantly American opera
yet encountered in musical theatre.'[15] Weill himself regarded the
piece as having a special place in his output and said, 'Not until *Street
Scene* did I achieve a real blending of drama and music in which the
singing continues naturally when the speaking stops.'[16] *Street Scene*
was not the hit of the season. *Finian's Rainbow*, which opened in New
York on the night after *Street Scene*, ran for 725 performances and
Brigadoon, opening two months later, for 581. Nevertheless *Street
Scene* ran for 148 performances – a respectable number for an
opera. Writing about Weill some two years after the première, Hans
Heinsheimer chose to refer to *Street Scene* as one of the two American

81

works his readers were likely to remember. By that time Weill was, said Heinsheimer,

> probably the most successful of the many European composers who came to the United States in the last decade. Weill is the composer of *Lady in the Dark* and *Street Scene*; he is a distinguished member of the Playwrights' Company . . . when you want to see him he has first to consult a calendar and will then ask you to be his guest for lunch at the Oak Room of the Plaza Hotel on the second Friday of next month 'unless I call you – I might have to go to Hollywood'.[17]

In June and July 1947 Weill went to Palestine to see his parents, visiting England, France, Switzerland and, for a few days only, Germany *en route*. It was his only visit to Europe in the fifteen years between his arrival in America and his death in 1950.

Returning to America at the end of July, he began work immediately on a new piece, originally called *A Dish for the Gods* and eventually entitled *Love Life*. The six episodes of *Love Life* were to depict the gradual erosion of the institution of marriage by presenting the different stages in the breakdown of a single marriage spread over some 150 years. Beginning in 1791 with a young, happily married couple, the various episodes gradually move forward in time towards, in the second act, the date at which the work was first performed, and show the increasing stress, cynicism and bitterness to which the relationship between the couple is subjected and which, eventually, leads to the final breakdown of the marriage. The book and the songs were by Alan Jay Lerner, the author of *Brigadoon* who was later to write *Paint Your Wagon* and *My Fair Lady*. *Love Life*, Weill's most ambitious Broadway show, opened at the 46th Street Theatre on 17 October 1948. The director was Elia Kazan. Unfortunately, the run of the piece was seriously affected, as were all the other shows being played at the time, by a prolonged ASCAP strike and it had only 258 performances.

For his last completed Broadway work Weill returned to Maxwell Anderson, the writer of his earliest Broadway musicals, and to the kind of social themes that had dominated Weill's earlier works but had disappeared in his slicker commercial pieces. Described as 'a musical tragedy', *Lost in the Stars* was based on Alan Paton's novel *Cry the Beloved Country* and tells the story of a rural black preacher,

Stephen Kumodo, and his wife who go to Johannesburg in search of their son Absalom. When discovered, the son is under arrest for his involvement in a robbery, in the course of which a young white man was killed. Of those implicated, Absalom alone confesses his guilt in court and is sentenced to death. Moved by the honesty of Absalom's confession, the father of the dead youth approaches Kumodo and some kind of reconciliation is affected between the two fathers and the two races.

Directed by Rouben Mamoulian and presented by the Playwrights' Company, the work opened on 30 October 1949 at the Music Box Theatre in New York. For a work with a tragic story and a serious social message it had a considerable success and ran for 273 performances. Nonetheless it received a mixed critical reception, the *New York Times* finding it 'not altogether successful';[18] the *Herald Tribune* describing it as 'magnificent . . . moving to its climax inexorably with a tremendous crescendo';[19] while the *New Yorker* critic, who thought that the 'tragedy never rises above the level of a melodramatic device', admitted to being 'one of a small, wayward minority'.[20]

The effect which it had upon the public can perhaps be best judged from a review by Henry Hewes (who saw the original production) of the 1972 revival at the J F Kennedy Centre for the Performing Arts. He described how he and other 'old timers' were both moved by the performance of 'the season's best and most thrilling musical' and also 'moved by the memory of how they had felt in 1949'.[21]

At the end of 1949 Weill was full of plans for future projects including a musical play of Twain's *Huckleberry Finn* on which he and Maxwell Anderson began work in December. Although Weill completed five songs the score was never finished, for at the end of March 1950 he had a heart attack and was taken to the Flowers Hospital in New York where he died on 3 April. He was buried in Haverstraw Cemetery overlooking the Hudson River on 5 April 1950.

The Sidney B. Coulter Library
Onondaga Community College
Rte. 173, Onondaga Hill
Syracuse, New York 13215

Part Two
Assessing the Music

Chapter 6
The Early Instrumental and Vocal Music

The Italian composer Luigi Dallapiccola has described an occasion, in March 1942, when the name of Kurt Weill cropped up during the course of a conversation between himself and Anton Webern. The usually mild-mannered Webern reacted violently:

> Webern suddenly explodes. He points his finger at me (although I had not been the one who introduced the name of the composer he disliked) and asks me: 'What do you find of our great Middle-European tradition in such a composer – that tradition which includes the names of Schubert, Brahms, Wolff, Mahler, Schoenberg, Berg and myself?'[1]

In the diary in which he recorded the event, Dallapiccola admits to having been surprised by the fact that Webern saw his own music as part of the Middle-European tradition; to Webern, observed Dallapiccola, it was not 'a question of aesthetics and of taste that separated him from Kurt Weill, but rather the fact that Weill had refused the Middle-European tradition.'[2] It is indicative of the misunderstanding which Weill's music suffered in his lifetime, and has continued to suffer since, that Dallapiccola did not, for one moment, question Webern's assumption that Weill had broken with 'Middle-European tradition'.

In fact, both Webern and Weill grew up and developed their musical styles within the same Middle-European tradition and were deeply influenced by the same late romantic, hyper-expressive branch of that tradition. Weill's writings (such as the articles in which he describes how many of his ideas on music theatre sprang from his study of the works of Mozart, Beethoven, Weber and Bach) reveal the extent to which he himself regarded even the apparently icono-clastic, jazz-influenced work of the late 1920s and 1930s (presumably the works against which Webern's outburst was directed) as belonging to that same Austro-German tradition.

Much of Weill's earliest music remains unavailable. However, from what is available it is clear that the most important influences on these early works were Mahler, Schoenberg, Strauss, Schreker (with whom Weill had once thought of studying) and the other late romantic composers; influences of the kind which, at a time when expressionism dominated German music as well as the visual and literary arts, one might expect to find in the music of any talented young composer eager to become acquainted with and to assimilate the newest and most advanced ideas of the day.

Indebted to Mahler in its emotional atmosphere, to Schoenberg in its formal design and to both these composers – and others, such as Strauss and Liszt – in its typically German concern with thematic transformation and motivic integration, the First Symphony of 1921 clearly demonstrates Weill's musical origins in the post-Wagnerian German tradition.

Formally the First Symphony attempts to weld the usually distinct three or four movements of a traditional symphony into a single large-scale structure. Schoenberg had attempted such integrated single-movement structures in his First Quartet and First Chamber Symphony by spreading the different sections of the traditional sonata-form movement throughout the work in such a way that the sonata exposition and first reprise might be separated by the slow movement; the first reprise and development sections by a scherzo and the development and recapitulation by an allegro Finale. The twenty-one-year-old Weill certainly knew these works, just as the eighteen-year-old Weill had, apparently, known Schoenberg's *Pelleas und Melisande* when, as a pupil at the Hochschüle, he had composed the Rilke tone poem.[3] Much of the instrumentation of the First Symphony, the chords built of perfect fourths which open the piece and the chains of fourths which form the melody of the *Sehr wuchtig* section, are immediately reminiscent of Schoenberg's First Chamber Symphony. Influenced by the design of the Chamber Symphony and similar works of Schoenberg, Weill also attempts an ingenious, if not entirely successful, formal structure in which the three movements, linked by recurring motifs, themes and occasionally sections, are juxtaposed to form a single span.

The first movement proper is preceded by an introduction in which are stated the two most important themes of the work ('a' and 'b' in Ex 1 below, and a variant of 'b', the cell 'b¹') which give rise to other important thematic ideas. These themes occur constantly throughout the work and are subjected to numerous transformations. The first movement itself begins with a relatively traditional sonata exposition (the themes of the two subject groups being derived from, or including, those of Ex 1). The usual development section, however, is replaced by two episodes while the recapitulation is confined to a reprise of the first subject group and a reprise of the first of the two central episodes. The other sections of the movement are then recapitulated during the course of the other two movements, the second of the two episodes appearing in the middle of the *Andante Religioso* second movement and the second subject group, followed by a re-statement of the introduction to the first movement, reappearing at the end of the third and final movement; the whole work is bound together by the appearance of diminutions, augmentations, inversions and other transformations of the themes of Ex 1.

Ex 1

The influence of Schoenberg, which is so strong a feature of the First Symphony, appeared early in Weill's output and survived, in some form, throughout his student years; it is an influence that is still faintly discernible in the Violin Concerto of 1924 and in the pre-Brecht operas. Thereafter, it disappeared from Weill's music, although Weill himself remained an ardent admirer of Schoenberg, recognizing both his historical significance and his courage in facing the consequences of post-Wagnerian chromaticism. *Pierrot Lunaire* Weill regarded as a 'work that has brought about a new epoch in music history'[4] and, in two essays written in 1926, he described Schoenberg as 'the purest, most lofty-minded artistic personality and the greatest intellect of present-day life . . . he is the only one who has unflinchingly held fast to the pursuit of his goal. His full significance for the musical public will probably only become clear after another decade.'[5] He wrote an equally generous review of Berg's *Wozzeck*, describing its première in December 1925 as 'the greatest event in Berlin's musical life for many years'.[6]

While the influence of Schoenberg's music gradually waned, that of Mahler never disappeared from Weill's work. On a technical level the lasting influence of Mahler can be seen in Weill's orchestration, in which the simultaneous use of strongly differentiated timbres (the contrasting, rather than the blending, of colours within a small group of instruments) in the latter European pieces springs from the use of 'opposing timbres' and the 'soloistic, almost chamber music-like' handling of the orchestra in Mahler's works; Weill himself commented on these features in his review of a performance of Mahler's Ninth Symphony,[7] On an expressive level Mahler's influence remains not only in those gestures and passages that have a typically late romantic emotional intensity (and such passages appear even in Weill's works with Brecht) but, more importantly, in Weill's later use of 'popular' music as a means of expressing a moral attitude. Weill's gradual development of a simpler, more accessible musical language in the late 1920s will be discussed in the following chapter, but it is worth pointing out, while considering Weill's musical roots, the extent to which Mahler, as the first composer deliberately to exploit the emotional associations of 'cheap' popular music, anticipated a technique that was to become the basis of Weill's later style. It is perhaps more than a coincidence that while Weill's early music is firmly Teutonic in inspiration and reveals nothing of his Jewish musical ancestry (indeed *Der Weg der Verheissung*, and a few occasional pieces written when Weill had fled his native country, are the only works in which he seems to have consciously exploited his Jewish musical background) it is, like that of his fellow Jews Mahler and Schoenberg, deeply concerned with moral and religious themes. The religious element in the programme which lies behind the First Symphony is clearly indicated by its subtitle 'A People's Awakening to God'. David Drew has described the extent to which the *Divertimento* (with its 'feeling of religious fear' of the 'vengeful Jehovah of the old Testament')[8] and the *Sinfonia Sacra* continue this religious pre-occupation. The purely religious aspects of Weill's First Symphony were to disappear from his music within a few years of the work's completion; the moral and social concerns which are also implicit in the Symphony's full subtitle were to be a constant preoccupation of his work.

Unlike Webern, who, as a pupil of Schoenberg, was brought up only in the mainstream of the Austro-German tradition, Weill was also affected by influences outside this Middle-European tradition. Undoubtedly the most important of these influences was that of his teacher Ferruccio Busoni, whose ideas brought about a radical change in Weill's already-formed musical style. 'We young musicians', wrote Weill in a tribute to his teacher, 'were filled with new ideas and new hopes but we could not find the form for our content. We had burst the chains but we could do nothing with the freedom we had won . . . then Busoni came to Berlin.'[9]

Busoni's influence on Weill's view of music theatre will be discussed in the following chapter but many of Busoni's ideas, in particular his belief in the possibility of employing some kind of expanded tonality rather than turning to atonality and his opposition to the highly emotional atmosphere of the German post-Wagnerian composers, had a deep effect on Weill. Busoni is said to have loathed Wagner and all that he stood for to such an extent that he 'could hardly bring himself to write down the name'.[10] Busoni had a particular horror of the lush textures of Wagner's music and of the eroticism of Wagner and the post-Wagnerian composers; Wagner, he declared, had 'ruined music with his lasciviousness'[11] while the openly erotic operas of a composer such as Schreker, whose *Die Gezeichneten* he saw in 1921, 'aroused in him an almost moral indignation'.[12]

In challenging the hyper-emotionalism of the expressionist composers Busoni advocated a cool, objective music and a classicism based upon what he described as 'the masterly sifting and exploration of all the achievements of past experiments and their embodiment in fixed and beautiful forms.'[13]

Busoni's 'young classicism' was in accord with a general musical trend towards the exploitation of the styles, figurations and forms of earlier music. This trend, which has become known as neo-classicism (although the models to which its adherent turned were more frequently those of the baroque than those of the eighteenth century) had both purely musical and social causes.

91

During the course of the nineteenth century, the gradual extension of the time span over which a piece operated, coupled with the growing complexity of the harmonic and melodic language, had undermined the long-term organizational function of tonality which had been a feature of the music of the classical period. By the early years of the twentieth century, the further development of post-Wagnerian chromaticism and the gradual appearance of music in which tonal criteria no longer operated, had led to a point at which the tonal system – the system which had been the basis of Western musical thought and expression for over three hundred years – seemed about to collapse. Faced with this prospect, many composers turned back to the music of the past in an attempt both to find something stable to which they could cling and to find a way out of the predicament. Busoni's call for a 'sifting' of the achievements of the past and his advocacy of some kind of 'expanded' tonality, as opposed to atonality, are characteristic manifestations of the attitude of those composers who rejected Schoenberg's more radical solution to the problem. But neo-classicism was not simply a negative reaction to the musical crisis which seemed imminent; it was also one aspect of that positive rejection of the self-contemplation, the inturned, subjective emotionalism of the expressionists which characterized much art after the First World War and which has been discussed in general terms in Chapter Two.

Under Busoni, Weill turned away from the extreme expressionistic style of his earlier atonal works and towards the cooler, more objective idiom advocated by his teacher – a neo-classical idiom characterized by clearer melodic and rhythmic patterns, more lucid instrumental textures and a more rigorous and cleaner contrapuntal style. The sudden neo-classical interest in strict 'Bachian' contrapuntal thought and the use of Bach-like figurations, is particularly striking in the works which Weill wrote during his student years, many of which have movements based on specifically baroque forms. Thus, the String Quartet op 8 has a Chorale Fantasia as its last movement, the *Divertimento* a Chorale Prelude and the *Sinfonia Sacra* a Passacaglia.

Weill's change of style is immediately apparent if one compares the First Symphony of 1921 with the music of *Der Zaubernacht* and the orchestral *Quodlibet* which Weill drew from the ballet, or with the charming *Frauentanz* of 1923: the atonal emotional language of the Symphony has given way to an overtly neo-classical tonal idiom, the expressionistic gestures and complex rhythmic patterns to simple melodic and jaunty rhythmic figures, the complex, multi-layered orchestral thought to simple textures and unmixed timbres (favouring wind and brass) which look forward to the later Weill.

In opposing the Germanic, late-romantic tradition in which Weill had been brought up, and in which he had first established some kind of musical identity, Busoni created within Weill a creative conflict which took many years to resolve. The extent to which this stylistic conflict is apparent in the works which Weill wrote during the mid- and early 1920s varies from piece to piece – the *Quodlibet* and the *Frauentanz*, for example, are fairly assured works in the new neo-classical style; it is, nevertheless, a conflict that runs, in varying degrees, throughout much of Weill's music of this period. The effects of the conflict are, for example, clearly apparent even in the Violin Concerto of 1924, written after the *Quodlibet* and the *Frauentanz*, when Weill was already involved in planning *The Protagonist*, the work which was to mark his almost total abandonment of instrumental music.

Though separated into three distinct movements (the second of which is itself subdivided into three 'character pieces') the Violin Concerto seems more diffuse, less of a total entity than did the First Symphony, with its complex single-span structure. Thematically undistinguished and incessantly 'busy', the generation of activity seems in the Violin Concerto (as in much neo-classical music) to have become an end in itself and a substitute for real ideas. The confidence of the First Symphony has disappeared but the old style has not been replaced by anything which seems to elicit the same degree of assurance. Instead of the unified musical language of the earlier work, one finds a heterogeneous collection of stylistic influences, remnants of the influence of Schoenberg and Mahler rubbing shoulders with that of Busoni, Stravinsky and Hindemith. It is perhaps symbolic of this inner conflict that the rather dry and arid String Quartet op 8 should attempt to draw into its neo-classical world material from the First Symphony.

If such pieces as the Violin Concerto and the Quartet op 8 seem characterless when compared to the First Symphony one must re-member that these pieces, like all Weill's instrumental music with the sole exception of the Second Symphony, are the works of a young immature composer whose musical ideas have been overturned at a crucial stage of his development. Perhaps the stylistic conflict which Busoni precipitated in Weill's music mirrored a deeper conflict between the romantic and anti-romantic elements within the character of Weill himself. At any rate, Weill never fully renounced the subjective, late romantic expressionist influences which had formed the style of his earliest music or fully embraced the objective neo-classical style advocated by his teacher. Instead, the objective and subjective elements of the two styles – and of Weill's own nature – produced a conflict which was to become the creative impulse behind, and is still one of the chief fascinations of, his mature musical style.

The only purely instrumental work of Weill's mature years, the Second Symphony of 1933-4, is a graphic demonstration of the extent to which the new musical language, which he forged in the stage works which followed *The Protagonist*, grew out of the conflicting demands of neo-classicism and expressionism. Although it employs no single cyclic theme throughout, the Second, like the First Symphony, makes considerable use of Lisztian thematic transformations. Thus, the trumpet theme which closes the introduction to the first movement (Ex 2a) is transformed into the second movement theme shown in Ex 2b, while another second movement theme (Ex 2c) reappears, in turn, as a jaunty third movement figuration (Ex 2d). Similarly, the coda of the third movement has its origins in the melodic idea which opens the second movement (Ex 2e and f).

Ex 2

Such devices for ensuring the thematic unity of the piece, the Mahlerian march with which the work opens, and the closely integrated motivic relationships which spring from this opening figuration, are immediately reminiscent of the techniques of the late romantic composers. In the Second Symphony, however, such thematic and motivic relationships operate within a formal design that is much more traditional and much clearer than that of the First Symphony. The complications that appear – such as the disassociation of the return to the home key and the traditionally simultaneous return to the original material in the first movement, or the Haydnesque introduction of the first movement coda long before its allotted place[14] – operate within the outlines of the traditional symphonic structure.

Above all the Second Symphony, with its Mendelssohnian finale and its Mahlerian rhythms and instrumental effects (such as the trombone solo in the second movement) reveals, far more clearly than do the stage and the vocal works of the same period, the extent to which Weill's mature 'popular' language has its roots in that German tradition the influence of which is so clearly seen in his early instrumental music.

Chapter 7
The European Dramatic and Vocal Works

The première of *The Protagonist* in March 1926 established Weill, almost overnight, as one of the leading theatre composers of the day. After *The Protagonist* the twenty-six-year-old Weill only once, with the Second Symphony, returned to purely instrumental composition; the rest of his life was to be entirely devoted to the composition of either stage works or of vocal works, many of which had strong dramatic associations.

Weill's characteristic, and highly individual, approach to the relationship between music and text and the beginnings of that deliberately simpler musical style that is a feature of his best known music can already be seen in *The Protagonist* and the works which immediately followed it. It is not suprising, perhaps, that the first signs of this simpler style should coincide with the beginnings of Weill's career as a theatre composer: music that is effective in the theatre tends to employ broader, less intricate, gestures and to operate over a larger time span than music conceived for the concert hall. In Weill's case, however, the search for a simpler style was to lead, not to a modification of the style employed in his earlier music, but to a radically different kind of music.

Since this new, simpler and more popular style first came to fruition in the *Mahagonny Songspiel* and *The Threepenny Opera* – that is, in the first of the works which Weill wrote in collaboration with Brecht – it is frequently assumed that the change in style was entirely due to Brecht's influence. This assumption is encouraged by a number of coincidental factors: by the fact that the scores of many of Weill's works have for long been unobtainable (some of them, including some of the key works in Weill's development, having been either lost

Kurt Weill and Lotte Lenya at their home in New City, Rockville County, 1942

ABOVE *Franz Werfel, the author, Max Reinhardt, the director, and Weill, during the preparations of* The Eternal Road, *New York 1935-36* BELOW *The Group Theatre's production of* Johnny Johnson, *directed by Lee Strasberg, November 1936. Morris Carnovsky (centre) as the Psychiatrist and Russell Collins (right) as Johnny Johnson* ABOVE LEFT *The Princesse Edmonde de Polignac, who was one of the great patrons of new music during the first half of the twentieth century and who commissioned Weill's Second Symphony* BELOW LEFT *Scene from the première of* Marie Galante *at the Théâtre de Paris, December 1933*

ABOVE *A production still from the* The Eternal Road. *The photograph gives some idea of the size of the spectacular multi-level set created for Reinhardt's lavish production* OPPOSITE ABOVE LEFT *The opening of* The Eternal Road. *A cartoon by B. F. Doblin for the New York Post of January 8th 1937 showing Werfel and Weill (top), Norman Bel Geddes (the designer), Max Reinhardt and Meyer Weisgall (producer)* OPPOSITE ABOVE RIGHT *Weill with Maxwell Anderson, the writer of* Knickerbocker Holiday *and* Lost in the Stars, *New York 1949* OPPOSITE BELOW *Walter Huston as Peter Stuyvesant in the original production of* Knickerbocker Holiday *at the Ethel Barrymore Theatre, New York 1938*

LAUNCHING "THE ETERNAL ROAD"

ABOVE *Gertrude Lawrence and Victor Mature in the 'Circus Dream' sequence of* Lady in the Dark. *The show ran for two years on Broadway before transferring to Los Angeles* ABOVE RIGHT *Weill and Agnes de Mille, the choreographer, at a rehearsal of* One Touch of Venus, *1943* BELOW RIGHT *Weill and his parents Albert and Emma Weill at Nahariya, Palestine, in the summer of 1947, looking at the newly published score of Weill's* Street Scene

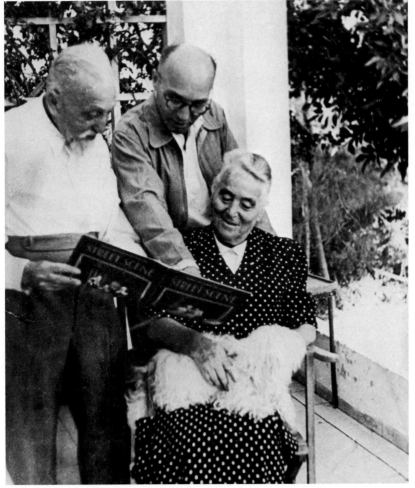

TOP LEFT *A scene from Weill's 'musical tragedy'* Lost in the Stars, *his last completed work. From left to right: William Greaves, Gloria Smith, Sheila Guyse, Lavern French and Van Prince* TOP RIGHT *Playbill from the original production of* Street Scene *at the Adelphi Theatre, New York* ABOVE *Polyna Stoska as Anna and Anne Jeffreys as Rose at the end of* Street Scene *in its original production*

or destroyed), and an overall view of Weill's European career has been impossible to obtain; by the fact that, despite the brilliance of the earlier pieces, the first Brecht scores are also Weill's first fully mature works, and that, as David Drew has pointed out,[1] a certain fashionable nostalgia for the Berlin of the 1920s and 1930s has drawn people towards those Weill-Brecht pieces that seem to reflect what is now regarded as the spirit of that period with the result that the works which do not employ jazz or popular elements (including a number of works with libretti by Brecht) have been ignored. At the same time musical developments in Europe since the Second World War have taken a course to which Weill seems to have little relevance and there have, therefore, been few purely musical studies of Weill's work. The additional consideration that much (though by no means all) of Weill's American music is, without doubt, of a lower standard than his European works has reinforced the popular view that Weill could produce works of any value only when inspired and guided by Brecht.

But perhaps Brecht's own writings, and the writings of the large number of Brecht scholars, have been the most important influences on the formation of the view that sees Weill merely as Brecht's musical factotum. Given the lack of any biographies of Weill until very recently or of any edition of Weill's writings (as compared to the innumerable translations, discussions and commentaries on Brecht); given the fact that we live, at least in Britain and America, in a culture that is literary rather than musical in its orientation, and given, also, Brecht's own flair for self-publicity, it is hardly surprising that Weill's contribution has been regarded as minimal.

Brecht was always cavalier in his treatment of both his sources and his collaborators and it is difficult not to view his biased accounts of the relationship between himself and Weill as being deliberate attempts at enhancing his own stature and achievements. Thus, in an interview published in Copenhagen in March 1934, Brecht suggested that it was because of his understanding of the requirements of a work and his ability to impose his ideas upon others that his musical collaborators gained any success; he once said: 'I had my own composers who knew how to write exactly in my style'.[2] Similarly, in his essay *On the Use of Music in an Epic Theatre*, Brecht implied that it was thanks to him that Weill saw the error of his earlier ways and was thus able to create a new popular style in keeping with the requirements of the drama:

97

This type of song was created on the occasion of the
Baden-Baden Music Festival of 1927 . . . when I asked
Weill to write new settings for half-a-dozen already existing
songs. Up to that time Weill had written relatively complicated music of a mainly psychological sort and when he
agreed to set to music a series of more or less banal song
texts he was making a courageous break with the prejudice
which the solid bulk of serious composers held.[3]

Such claims by Brecht have been almost universally accepted as
factual descriptions of the relationship between Brecht and Weill.
Thus, Otto Friedrich quotes Nicolas Nabakov as saying, 'Brecht was
much the stronger of the two. He had to force Weill to write differently'[4]
and John Gutmann, the critic of the *Bösen Courier*, as remarking,
'Weill started out as an academic revolutionary. His early works, the
Violin Concerto and *The Tzar Has His Picture Taken*, were all atonal.
Nobody will ever want to hear them unless he's writing a dissertation
on Weill. Brecht wasn't interested in that kind of thing.'[5]

It would, of course, be wrong to suggest that Brecht had little or no
impact on Weill. Nonetheless, the view of the relationship between
the two men which assumes that Weill not only changed his style to
suit Brecht's requirements, but also that he had no view on the
theatre and the rôle of music in the theatre other than those which
originated in Brecht, shows little understanding of Weill's artistic
and intellectual development. In fact, in the years immediately
preceding his first collaboration with Brecht, Weill had not only
begun to simplify his musical style but had already employed a
number of those techniques which were later to be associated with
Brecht's epic theatre.

Although the concept of an epic theatre – the essential point of
which 'is that it appeals less to the feelings than to the spectator's
reason'[6] – appears in Brecht's writings in 1927, the first full exposition
of the idea appears in his 1930 article 'Note to the Opera *Aufstieg und
Fall der Stadt Mahagonny*'. In this article he criticizes traditional opera
and theatre which, he argues, are designed to entertain the spectator
by providing him with sensations and encouraging him to become
involved in and experience at second hand the events on the stage.
Previous attempts at renovating opera have been misguided because
they have accepted the apparatus of the form and have thus accepted
that the primary function of opera is to provide an evening's entertainment. In place of such 'entertainment' Brecht advocates a new

'epic' theatre and opera in which the listener is forced to view the action as a detached observer, criticizing, judging and making decisions about what is happening on the stage. Emotional involvement, which would interfere with the listener's capacity to make objective judgments, is to be discouraged by means of various alienating devices: the Wagnerian concept of a *Gesamstkunstwerk* – in which music, text, stage direction, costume and all the other elements of a theatrical production work together to produce a total artistic experience – is to be replaced by an opera in which the different elements are clearly separated; the composer is to demonstrate a political and moral attitude rather than express an emotion and the music is to set forth, rather than heighten, the text. Some idea of the ways in which Brecht's theories were to be put into practice can be gained from the descriptions, quoted in earlier chapters, of the first productions of *The Threepenny Opera* and *Der Flug der Lindberghs*.

The '*Mahagonny* Notes' were written after Brecht and Weill had finished the opera, at a time when Brecht's ideas were changing and when the collaboration between the two men was virtually over. Weill was not consulted on the text of the 'Notes' and, in fact, probably disagreed with much that Brecht says in this essay. Nonetheless, many of the alienation techniques which Brecht describes in this article had already been employed – and employed for reasons similar to those put forward by Brecht – in Weill's pre-Brecht works.

For some years before his meeting with Brecht, Weill had been arguing the need for a thoroughgoing re-assessment of the nature and function of opera and for the renewal of operatic form. By 1925-6 Weill had already arrived at many of the ideas which were to characterize his later works. The decisive influence on Weill's conception of opera was his teacher Busoni whose two mature operas, *Arlecchino* (1917) and *Doktor Faust* (1925) stand in direct opposition to the Wagnerian musical and dramatic techniques that dominated German opera in the first decades of the twentieth century. An opera, like a symphony, argued Busoni, should have a musical form that was independent of words or action. It should deal only with those subjects that were incomplete without music and should not attempt to portray what could already be seen on the stage itself. To attempt to describe something in music was to assign to the art a task which lay outside its nature.[8] In rejecting the conventions of the Wagnerian music-drama Busoni advocated a return to the moral and ritualistic attitude of works such as Mozart's *The Magic Flute* and demanded:

99

a casting off of what is 'sensuous' and the renunciation of subjectivity (in favour of an objectivity which comes from the author standing back from his work – a purifying road, a hard road, a trial by fire and water) and the reconquest of serenity. Neither Beethoven's wry smile nor Zarathustra's 'liberating laugh' but the smile of wisdom, of divinity and of absolute music. Not profundity, and personal feelings and metaphysics but music which is absolute, distilled and never under a mask of figures and ideas which are borrowed from other spheres.[9]

Edward Dent described the effect of Busoni's 'reforms' in *Doktor Faust* in terms that are immediately reminiscent of those which Brecht employs in his description of the aims of epic theatre. *Doktor Faust*, says Dent, has 'something of the puppet play in its remoteness from everyday sentiments and sentimentality: the figures in the drama do only what is necessary and no more . . . there is no chance for the actors to endear themselves to the audience . . . to appeal to the affection rather than the intellect of the spectator.'[10]

Busoni's views, and his demonstration in the music of *Arlecchino* and of *Doktor Faust* of how these theories could be made to operate in practice, had a deep influence on Weill.

By 1925-6 Weill had already written a number of articles in which he had publicly rejected the dramatic and emotional ethos of late nineteenth-century opera with its would-be psychological profundity:

for here the experience of the inner soul was so complicated or so superficial that the simplest, the most basic, the oldest and yet the newest emotions were forgotten. It is just these emotions, however, which move us. In this context we can understand why Wagner had to create the form of the music drama, for how could the string quartet, the symphony or the opera suffice when the only function of his art was to mirror the sentiments of larger than life figures, gods, kings and heroes? But we can understand the reasons for his success: for the brutality, the eroticism, the criminality of these works did not express the noblest, but rather the most common human emotions of the pre-war generation.[11]

He stated his belief that the 'music dramas of the past decades' had led opera away from its true goal because they had encouraged 'the abandonment of a purely music framework':

100

Musical form is more than just an assemblage of isolated pieces: it is a means of expression every bit as important as the other active components of a composition, and to renounce it, or even to subordinate it, has the effect of significantly curtailing the possible means of musical expression.[12]

The new opera, declared Weill:

will not be confined to the mere underlining of a dramatic event through expression, tempo, musical pitch and dynamic: it goes far beyond that. It is a unique and purely musical art form, developed in close proximity with the theatre, and cannot be merely the adding of a theatrical expression or Gest to a musical event, nor of illustrating a dramatic plot with music. The interaction of a plot which enhances the music, or of music which only provides a commentary to the events on stage, does not make an opera.[13]

As an example of the way in which music and drama could combine to produce a new form of heightened theatre, a 'reinterpretation of naturalistic effects', Weill cites the 'alienating' effect achieved at the moment in Busoni's *Doktor Faust* 'when Mephistopheles murders the believers at the gate; the music leaves the interpretation of the outrageous event to the imagination of the listener and contents itself with a gesture of gentleness and freedom.'[14]

It is in his 1926 article on Busoni's *Doktor Faust* that Weill uses, for the first time, the word 'Gest', a term that occupies an important position in the development of Brecht's ideas on epic theatre but does not appear in Brecht's own writings until the '*Mahagonny* Notes' which were written in 1930. The term denotes 'an attitude, or a single aspect of an attitude, expressible in words or actions'. In 1929 Weill published an essay '*On the Gestic Character of Music*' and, in the same year, published another article in which he developed the ideas he had first stated in his Busoni article of 1926:

The new theatrical form, in which the chorus again plays an important role, creates a wholly new set of conditions for the use of music in the theatre, for this type of theatre is mainly concerned with the outward going 'gestures' of the production and, therefore, it leaves a great deal of scope for the musical score – not to illustrate or advance the plot,

101

but to grasp and underline the basic ideogrammatic attitudes expressed in a series of separate scenes . . . it is no
longer enough merely to add a few images and the pre-
requisites of modern living to the existing form of music
drama; nor is it enough to adopt a frivolous attitude to the
problems of form in the use of music theatre. The subject
matter of the time must find its equivalent in the form of
contemporary music theatre.[15]

By the time the above essay had been written, Weill and Brecht had
been collaborating for over three years (indeed, the collaboration
was almost over) and each had, undoubtedly, influenced the other's
views. Nonetheless, the ideas expressed in this article are not only
those expressed in the articles written in 1925-6 but those which
Weill demonstrated in a number of compositions written before he
began working with Brecht.

The Protagonist, Weill's first theatrical success, was the first practical
demonstration of the kind of 'new operatic form' which he had
advocated in his writings. The story of the opera concerns the leader
of a troupe of actors in Shakespearean England – the Protagonist
himself – whose sense of identification with his fictitious theatrical
rôles becomes so great that it invades, and eventually destroys, his
sense of reality. The work is thus directly concerned with one of the
basic ideas underlying Brecht's theories of epic theatre – the extent to
which emotional involvement in an art can obscure both a sense of
reality and an ability to make moral judgments. In order to emphasize
the subject of the opera, and to prevent the kind of emotional
involvement which the work itself condemns, Weill deliberately
distances the listener from the drama by writing music which is quite
distinct from the stage action which it accompanies. Perhaps the
clearest and most startling example of Weill's techniques comes at
the very end of the opera when art and reality have finally become
one to the Protagonist and, having murdered his own sister, he
pleads to be allowed to give one last, great performance in which
there will no longer be 'any distinction between real and feigned
madness'. Avoiding the traditional 'distracted' mad scene, in which
the music would merely illustrate the mental state of the Protagonist,
Weill chooses to accompany the stage action at this point with music
of the most simple, triadic kind – the little fanfares for the on-stage
wind band shown in Ex 3. Coming after the complex chromaticism of
the earlier music, this triadic music has a clarity and a triviality

102

which forms a fitting comment on the banality and emptiness of the Protagonist's own artistic beliefs; by going against, rather than simply illustrating, the stage action the music demonstrates a moral attitude towards the dramatic events.[16]

Ex 3 The Protagonist

The similarity between the techniques which Weill employs in this, his first performed opera and those which Brecht was to advocate in his 1930 '*Mahagonny* Notes' hardly needs pointing out. *The Protagonist* already demonstrates many of the elements of Brecht's epic theatre and all the leading critics of the time were quick to observe the effectiveness and the novelty of Weill's approach. Writing about the première of the work for the Berlin *Bösen Courier*, Oskar Bie remarked on the anti-romantic aspects of the piece: 'The romantic aching is over, scenic and spiritual shadows are brightly lit and the expression of feeling in the music is somehow hardened'[17] while Maurice Abravanel observed that Weill:

> full of enthusiasm and inspired by the objectivity of the Russians, has composed an opera that is without concession and without triviality . . . Weill does not weep at the death of the sister and nowhere does he invite us to take part in the despair of the hero – he satisfies himself with showing it, but does so with an accuracy that thrills the listener. This gives the work its peculiar value. *The Protagonist* is, as far as I know, the first successful attempt in opera to move the audience without engaging its sympathy.[18]

Adorno spoke of the fact that the music 'in no way mirrored the drama' but worked through disassociation, and was the key to the 'deep-lying dramatic intentions'[19] of the piece. All the critics recognized the work as being what Heinrich Strobel described as 'the beginning of a new development which clearly and resolutely leads to a new type of opera'.[20]

While developing his ideas on the relations between music and text in the 'new opera' Weill was also beginning to re-examine the nature of his musical language. Writing about *The Protagonist* in 1926 he said that his work on the opera had shown him not only that the 'stage had its own musical form which grows out of the course of the stage action' but also that 'on the stage, meaningful things can only be said with the simplest, most inconspicuous of means.'[21]

The triadic music at the end of *The Protagonist* had been a theatrical 'effect', a musical comment depending for its force on the complex, chromatic nature of the music which preceded it. In the works which followed *The Protagonist* – *Royal Palace*, *The New Orpheus* and *The Tsar Has His Photograph Taken* – Weill began deliberately to simplify his musical style and to create a new language in which triadic formations became the norm, in which the rhythmic figurations and the phrase structures became more immediately comprehensible, in which the frequent changes of bar length disappear and in which the accompanimental figures acquire a distinctly 'popular' feel. Already in these works the music is within striking distance, if not of the more overtly jazz-based *Threepenny Opera* and *Happy End*, then at least of that mixture of wiry neo-classicism and popular music which characterizes *Mahagonny*. As the following two examples demonstrate, the ostinato patterns and the melodic figurations of these works are often strikingly similar to those of the later *Mahagonny*:

Ex 4 a Der Zar

b Mahagonny

Ex 5, also from *Der Zar*, shows an early example of the kind of peculiarly Weillian side-step that is so typical of his later music:

Ex 5

Particularly interesting are such passages as that, from *Der Zar*, shown in Ex 6 below:

Ex 6

In this passage the highly chromatic melodic line, with its angular and unpredictable contour, seems to look back to the Schoenbergian expressionism of the early instrumental works while the other elements of the music – the rhythmic patterns, the neatly balancing, four-square phrase structures and the vamp-like accompaniment figuration – are clearly derived from the kind of popular model that Weill was to employ in his later pieces. Such passages are audible demonstrations of the link between his early and mature styles: once one has heard such a passage it is not difficult to understand how the sudden harmonic shifts and the unexpected melodic turns which characterize Weill's later work came about as a result of the bringing together of such apparently opposed influences as popular music, Viennese expressionism and Busonian neo-classicism. *Der Zar* and the two Goll works also mark the first appearance of jazz and popular elements in Weill's music. However, in all three works popular music is employed as a 'special effect', for specific dramatic purposes. In *Royal Palace* the jazz-influenced numbers accompany a film scene which depicts the heroine's pursuit of various fashionable pleasures – a train journey to Constantinople, a visit to Nice, to a ball, to the Russian Ballet, by aeroplane to the North Pole. In *Der Zar* the jazz number is a tango which, played on a gramophone, accompanies the Tsar's attempts to seduce the young lady photographer who, unknown to him, has come to assassinate him. Although satirical in effect, the function of these jazz numbers is, therefore, comparable to that of the triadic music which ends *The Protagonist*. The popular elements are employed as 'quotations', references to a musical style outside that of the main body of the piece, which thus make their effect through their incongruity. Like the triadic music of *The Protagonist* the jazz numbers of these pre-Brecht works express a moral attitude to the events happening on the stage. They condemn the frivolous and empty life of the heroine of *Royal Palace* and comment on the Tsar's sensuality and gullibility in *Der Zar*.

It is unfortunate that the music of the opera *Na und . . .* has almost completely disappeared since this piece might well have proved to be the key work in an attempt to understand Weill's development during this period. According to David Drew, the few remaining sketches for *Na und . . .* show that Weill later used many of the musical ideas from the piece in *Mahagonny*.[22] As it is, *The Mahagonny Songspiel*, *The Threepenny Opera* and, above all, the *Mahagonny* opera stand as the first works in which popular elements are fully assimilated into Weill's music and become the basis of a new and more easily comprehensible style. In these works the popular elements are no longer employed, as they are in the earlier operas, as deliberately incongruous, and thus satirical, features. The moral attitude expressed by the jazz music of *Royal Palace* and *Der Zar* is, however, implicit in Weill's use of popular music in the later works.

The nature and purpose of the simpler and more popular style towards which Weill was moving during the mid-1920s, and which he first fully adopted in the Brecht works, has been frequently misunderstood. Jazz and popular elements form only a small part of this new style. However, since general interest in Weill's music has been, almost exclusively, confined to those works which exploit popular music elements, it is a part that has attracted considerable attention.

Weill was not alone among serious composers in expressing an interest in jazz. For a while many composers – including men of the stature of Ravel, Debussy and Stravinsky, as well as lesser composers such as Krenek, Milhaud and the other members of Les Six – experimented with the possibility of employing some aspect of jazz in their music. Even the members of the Second Viennese School were affected by this trend. Both Schoenberg and Webern employed jazz instruments in at least one work each, although Berg was the only one of the three Viennese composers to use anything resembling the actual rhythms and figurations of jazz in his music. In some cases, such as that of Stravinsky, an interest in jazz seems to have been occasioned by a purely intellectual interest in its rhythmic techniques. In other cases the interest may have come about because, since the decline of tonality inevitably raised questions about the rhythmic, as well as the pitch, organization of music, dance rhythms of all kinds seemed to offer a way of generating some sense of momentum; in such cases an interest in jazz was comparable to the neo-classical composers' interest in baroque dance forms.

Weill's interest in jazz and popular music falls into neither of these categories. Nor can his jazz-influenced works be regarded simply as one manifestation of the idea, popular in the Germany of his period, of 'Zeitoper' or 'opera of the time' – of opera which, using jazz and the other fashionable music of the day, dealt with modern people in realistic, modern settings doing modern, up-to-date things. Krenek's 1927 'jazz opera' *Jonny spielt auf* is perhaps the best known example of Zeitoper. Although Weill is often regarded as one of the leading representatives of the Zeitoper composers, he himself resented the term, believing it suggested that topicality and 'relevance' in the arts meant nothing more than fashionable sensationalism. He regarded the idea of Zeitoper as an excuse for avoiding a thorough re-examination of operatic form.

Attacking the naive idea that there was a simple correlation between theatrical 'relevance' and mere fashion, Weill argued, in an essay on *Aktuelles Theater* (written in 1929), that the influence of the events of the time was clearly recognizable in the dramas of all periods and that the great spiritual and political movements of the day had always been handled by the theatre. Though based on historic truths, works such as Mozart's *The Marriage of Figaro* and Beethoven's *Fidelio* expressed a moral and spiritual truth, and thus had an enduring topicality, that placed them far above the genre of 'Zeitstücke' or period pieces. In an article on *Mahagonny*, Weill specifically rejects the idea that the catchwords 'Zeitoper', 'Jazz opera' and so on, as they have become understood are applicable to the work. 'Zeitoper', 'Zeittheater', 'Aktualität' and all such terms, argued Weill, had become catchwords, presented as though they represented the main problems of the theatre of the day:

> In this the situation in the theatre generally accords with the political situation in Germany, in that a concept that could have had a positive value and produced some kind of movement forward has, through the levelling effects of coalition politics, become a reactionary danger . . . These cheap forms of 'actuality' have been seized on by the conservative theatre; they alter nothing of the traditional forms; they don't change the way in which one really perceives anything and their effect on the box office is minimal . . . everything that we have experienced in the last year of 'the rhythm of the machine', the 'tempo of the city', the 'melody of the skyscrapers' and such like belong to these cheap forms.[23]

Weill published two articles on jazz. The first, entitled *Dancemusic: Jazz* was written in March 1926, two months after he had completed *Royal Palace*, the work in which the influence of jazz is first clearly observable. This article thus predates Weill's meeting with Brecht by precisely one year and the composition of the *Mahagonny Songspiel* by some fourteen months. In the article Weill draws attention to both the social significance of popular music and to the distinction between jazz and dance music:

> Today, because it is one of the few activities which can make city dwellers forget their humdrum everyday lives, dance has a significance that it did not possess in earlier times. It has, on the one hand, led to the growth of a light music industry which has little to do with art; on the other hand, however, some parts of dance music so completely define the spirit of the age that they could exert a lasting influence over a specific part of serious 'art music'.
> The rhythm of our time is jazz. In it the slow but sure

Americanisation of all our physical life finds its most notable manifestation.

Unlike art music, dance music reproduces nothing of the perceptions of the exceptional individual who stands above his times; instead it mirrors the instinct of the masses. And a glance into any of the dance halls of any continent shows that jazz is as precise the external expression of our time as was the waltz of the nineteenth century.

Even the inveterate opponent of this 'spirit of the time' will admit that, in those places which give forth dance music all evening, the shimmy outweighs everything else.

But if one plays a syncopated 2/2 bar underneath, it still doesn't make it jazz. The negro music, from which the jazz band originally sprang, is full of a rhythm complexity, of deft harmonic traits, of timbral and modulatory niceties of a kind that most of our dance band leaders are simply incapable . . . We have, for some weeks now, had a chance to hear real jazz bands on the radio for whole evenings . . . everything else that the radio offers us as dance music is surrogate.[24]

In his *Article on Jazz*, written in 1929 when he had already composed many of those jazz-based pieces on which his popular fame rests, Weill observed:

Jazz appears, within a time when artistry is increasing, as a piece of nature, as the most healthy and powerful expression of an art which, because of its popular origins, has immediately become an international folk music of the broadest possible consequences. Why should art-music isolate itself from such an influence? It depended on the strength of those individual talents who were approached by jazz, whether or not they could maintain their position under this influence; and for the serious European musician it was out of the question to imitate American dance music, let alone ennoble it.[25]

The distinction which Weill draws, in the first of these articles, between popular dance music and pure jazz is an important one. Weill's music has little relation to true jazz. The jazz influences that appear in his music are those which appeared in the popular dance music of the time; the tempo directions and the markings that stand at the head of each number in *The Threepenny Opera*, and which are not in the usual Italian, all relate to popular dance forms of the period, such as the foxtrot, the shimmy, the Boston and the tango.

To Weill, the main attraction of such popular music was that it produced an 'international folk music of the broadest consequences'; it provided him with a musical style which reflected 'the instinct of the masses', upon which he could build an individual and easily comprehensible style capable of dealing with the 'great ideas of the age'.

As a member of the Novembergrüppe, Weill subscribed to the group's belief in the social function of art. His social, political and artistic beliefs thus demanded that he write music that was comprehensible to a large body of people, and not simply to a small élite. An awareness of the social obligations of the artist informs all Weill's music from 1925 onwards and also runs through his writings. From the outset his articles as Berlin correspondent of *Der Deutsche Rundfunk* concentrate on the social responsibilities of the radio as an instrument which is directly in touch with a large section of the population.

Writing, in 1929, about *The Berlin Requiem*, Weill described the emergence of his new style as being determined by both social and technical considerations:

> The cantata *The Berlin Requiem* is one of a number of works that were, to a certain extent, thought of as studies for the opera *The Rise and Fall of the City of Mahagonny*.
>
> These works employ a certain type of vocal style with a small orchestra which is handled in such a way that the piece can be presented in the concert hall, in the form of a cantata, but can equally well – because of the attempt to make the musical speech clear and because of the way in which the gestic aspects of the content are determined – be presented in the theatre. It cannot be difficult to develop such a form, which meets equally the demands of the theatre and the concert hall, to meet the requirements of the radio. The bases of a radio art are: a strong musical structuring which suits the spiritual content of the work and which has the potential for a scenic production, but is compelling enough musically to enable the listener, without the help of the stage, to see in his mind a picture of the people who speak to him. It is thus handled here not as a lyric and not as the description of a condition but as the representation of a model. Having to write these pieces of

110

music for radio obviously meant that I had to know about the acoustic restrictions of the broadcasting studio; about which instrumental and orchestral possibilities the microphone favoured; about the spread of vocal registers and the harmonic limitations which radio imposes. Several years' observation of listeners to radio music and some experiments of my own, have shown me that it is the clarity and the transparency, rather than the refinement of the instrumental sound that is important. The radio presents serious musicians today, for the first time, with the problem of writing works which can be assimilated by a large group of listeners. The contents and the form of these radio compositions must, therefore, capture the interest of a large number of people of all sorts while the means of musical expression must present no difficulties to the inexperienced listener. Without doubt, the contents of *The Berlin Requiem* mirror the feelings and fears of a large majority of people. It is an attempt to express what the city-dweller of our time has to say about the idea of death.[26]

The simplification of Weill's musical style in the mid 1920s (a simplification which, as we have seen, began some time before his meeting with Brecht) was not therefore simply the result of the different musical demands of the theatre as opposed to the concert hall. It was also a response to what Weill, in common with his fellow members of the Novembergrüppe and many other artists in the Weimar Republic, regarded as the social demands of the time. Art had a social function which could not be met by writing for an élite, but only by developing a language which would be generally comprehensible. Weill is reported to have said 'I am not struggling for new forms or new theories, I am struggling for a new public.'[27]

Weill's purpose in employing jazz and popular elements was not, therefore – as is often suggested – parodistic. It was not his intention to mock either those popular forms which he used as his models or the conventions of traditional opera. Weill clarified his attitude to parody in an interview he gave in April 1930 on *Der Jasager*. When Dr Hans Fischer, the interviewer, remarked that it was those 'parodistic elements' of Weill's music, which were lacking in *Der Jasager*, that had made his earlier works so successful with young people, Weill replied:

Perhaps we should talk of a serious-ironical style, for the irony in *The Threepenny Opera* is meant seriously. People are mistaken if they have understood *The Threepenny Opera* only as a parody, as 'a lark'. Modern composers are not, in general, parodistically inclined – as the public and critics seem to believe. We are serious in subject and in music.[28]

Direct parodies of popular music appear in Weill's music only when dramatically justified. Thus, the banality of the refrain which accompanies the various self-indulgences in Act II of *Mahagonny* is itself a deliberate comment on the futility of the lives led by the characters involved. Similarly the cheap emotionalism of the dreadful 'Maiden's Prayer' in Act I of the same work (a number which elicits an enraptured 'That is eternal art' from one listener) is a reflection of the emotional shallowness of those characters. Parodies of the conventions of traditional opera are almost completely absent, as one might expect given not only Weill's love of Mozart and other eighteenth- and nineteenth-century operas but also his views on the seriousness of the form. Perhaps the only overt parody of operatic convention in Weill's work is the 'Jealousy Duet' between Lucy and Polly in Act II of *The Threepenny Opera*, a number which is as much an affectionate reference to operatic conventions as is Mozart's parody of the excesses of *opera seria* in Fiordiligi's distraught aria in Act I of *Così Fan Tutte*.

In describing Weill's work as 'music with a smouldering vividness and, at the same time, a mortally sad and faded background, music with a circumspect sharpness which, by means of its leaps and side-steps, makes articulate something that the song public would prefer not to know about,'[29] Adorno has pointed to the real relationship between Weill's music and that of the popular music of the time. Frederic Ewen has remarked that 'Post-war Germany had constructed out of America a fabulous, visionary domain, partly concocted out of reality, mostly built out of fantasy.'[30] The American dollar was 'seen as a sort of radiant vision against the background of the nightmare collapse of the mark', and there was:

> the American dream of Walt Whitman, the American West of the Indians, the grand adventure of the open prairies, buffaloes, cowboys and, not least, the lure of the great American cities with their skyscrapers. Everything that was American – American dances, Negro jazz, American drinks, American gangsters, American boxers, American speech – enjoyed a fashionable vogue.[31]

112

In taking these popular American forms as his models Weill relates not to the dance hall and the Amusierenkabaret, where such forms were most popular, but to the true literary tradition of the German cabaret. Cabaret style and techniques were, of course, an important influence on both Weill and Brecht. Brecht had himself set up a cabaret, *Die Rote Zibebe*, in Munich in 1922 and had made his first appearance in Berlin singing in cabaret to the accompaniment of his own guitar. One of Brecht's earliest writings is a description of a cabaret performance by Frank Wedekind: 'A few weeks ago he sang with his guitar, with a brittle voice, monotonous and untrained. Never has a singer so moved and inspired me.'[32]

The extent to which Brecht modelled his own cabaret style on that of Wedekind can be judged by comparing the above description with Lion Feuchtwanger's description of Brecht's own cabaret performances:

> He planted himself in the middle of the room and with open effrontery, in a horrible, loud shrill voice began to deliver his ballads to the twanging of a banjo, pronouncing his words with an unmistakably broad accent.[33]

Brecht's use of the word 'song' in the title of the *Mahagonny Songspiel* is a deliberate attempt to indicate that the pieces are cabaret rather than art songs. Both *The Threepenny Opera* and *Happy End* were written for, and originally performed by, cabaret singers and actors rather than trained singers. But the cabaret influence in these works is much deeper than its effects on performance techniques. Weill's use of his popular music models is directly comparable to the way in which Wedekind, Tucholsky, Mehring and the other great cabaret writers employed popular and immediately recognizable literary forms as the vehicle for the most searching examination of the political and social ills of the period.

Weill regarded his use of the popular forms and idioms of the time as being an essentially traditional technique that was in no way different from Bach's use of baroque dance forms, Beethoven's use of the minuet or Brahms' of the waltz. In many ways Weill's appropriation of popular idioms can be seen, not as part of a general interest in jazz, but as an extension of the neo-classicism which he inherited from Busoni. The way in which Weill employs his popular models is remarkably similar to the way in which the neo-classical composers of the period employed their chosen baroque or classical models.

In his essay on *The Threepenny Opera*, Adorno analyzed Weill's techniques by comparing the 'foreground' – the music Weill actually wrote – to the implied popular background in which 'the fatuous diminished seventh chords, the chromatic alteration of diatonic melodic steps, the espressivo that expresses nothing, all sound false to us.' So, Adorno says:

> Weill makes the chords themselves false by adding to the triad another note which sounds as false as did a true triad in the dance music of the 1890s, he distorts the melodic steps, he shows the stupidity of the modulation which doesn't go anywhere or shifts the modulatory emphasis in such a way as to upset the harmonic proportions so that a compositional style which includes a modulation from nothing to nothing itself collapses into an abyss of nothingness. There is a very clear path from such techniques to the best radical Stravinsky, such as *The Soldier's Tale* or the piano duets.[34]

Adorno's remarks suggest that he regarded Weill's intentions as being essentially parodistic (it is significant that he chooses as a comparison the little piano duets which are amongst the most overtly parodistic of Stravinsky's works). Nevertheless, his perception of the similarity between Weill and Stravinsky, and of the relation between foreground event and background model in the music of each composer, is quite accurate. Although working against very different background models, both Weill and Stravinsky employ these models in a similar way and both are careful to select only those aspects of the original models that will further their own creative ends. With both composers the result is a series of pieces in which the chosen 'model' acts as an ever-present and recognizable background against which the music operates; the works make their effect through the listener's perception of the difference between the 'heard' foreground and the 'understood' background. Moreover, in both Weill and Stravinsky the effect of this technique is to produce an emotional objectivity, a 'distancing' or – to use a term that has become particularly associated with Brecht – a sense of alienation which encourages the listener to consider and think about, rather than become emotionally involved in the music. The sense of objectivity which these techniques produce is, in itself, an indication of the extent to which Weill's music accords with the spirit of neo-classicism and of much of the art of the period.

Neo-classicism in music was a positive rejection of the hyper-

114

emotional romanticism of much post-Wagnerian composition; a rejection of expressionism in music, akin to that rejection of expressionism in the literary and visual arts which took place after the First War. In France, in *Le Coq et L'Arlequin*, Cocteau called for 'an end to music in which one lies and soaks', to music 'which has to be listened to with one's face in one's hands', and demanded 'Musical bread', 'music I can live in like a house',[35] suggesting the music hall, the circus and American negro bands as things which might fertilize an artist's imagination. Cocteau's pamphlet inspired much of the music of Les Six and set the tone of French music in the 1920s. In France the anti-romanticism of Les Six and their colleagues often resulted in facile and self-indulgent triviality; Weill's aims were more serious and purposeful.

Ian Kemp, in what, as yet, remains the only serious study of Weill's techniques, has defined a number of the elements which contribute to the ambiguous and peculiarly Weillian emotional climate of the works of the 1920s and 1930s. On the harmonic level Professor Kemp observes that 'whereas such figures as Stravinsky, Hindemith, Prokofiev and Milhaud tended (in returning to tonality) to reject traditional harmonic usage, Weill proceeded to develop a largely triadic harmony, paring down his vocabulary to the most basic chords and progressions.'[36] Professor Kemp has elsewhere observed that:

> the harmonic novelty in Weill's works lies in the way in which simple harmonies are juxtaposed; such juxtapositions creating a 'directional ambiguity', a sense of inner dissonance more disturbing than the overt dissonances of many works which may sound much harsher . . . from the consequent tension between the sophistication of the harmony and the simplicity of the phrasing arises a part of that strange ambiguity which pervades the entire structure and feeling of Weill's music . . . its compelling strength owes much to a tension between the familiar . . . and the striking novelty of the harmonic palette.[37]

Two examples from *Mahagonny* will serve to illustrate the extent to which the kind of tensions described by Professor Kemp operate at all levels of Weill's music.

The 'Alabama Song' consists of two contrasted halves. The opening of the first is shown in Ex 7a; and of the second in Ex 7b.

115

Ex 7 a

Ex 7 b

Melodically the first half employs only the very simplest and most confined of patterns – three notes, descending in step, which together cover the interval of a minor third; the minor third C – A in the phrases for solo voice, mirrored by the minor third A – F sharp in the alternating chorus phrases. Only at the very end of the first half of the song, as the music moves towards the cadence which introduces the 'refrain' of the second half, does the melodic line momentarily break out of these narrow limits. The simplicity of this melodic pattern, and its initial presentation as two regularly balancing, symmetrical phrases (the four-bar phrase, marked 'x' in Ex 7a, on the solo voice, answered by the complementary four-bar phrase 'y' for the chorus of six girls) acts as a fixed and easily recognizable norm against which the less predictable elements operate.

Through its very obsessiveness the constant repetition of this simple, rather matter-of-fact, opening pattern creates a certain tension. A further tension is introduced into the repetition of the opening melodic line, at bar ten, when the regularity of the previously symmetrical phrase structures is broken by the unexpected extension of the second solo phrase to create an asymmetrical seven-bar phrase ('z' in Ex 7a). At the same time the descending three-note pattern C, B, A shifts its position in the bar, thus disturbing the established relationship between the melodic figuration and the downbeat or rhythmically strong first beat of the bar.

This opening melodic line is supported by an orchestral accompaniment which, in terms of key, is highly ambiguous and constantly refuses to confirm or deny a stable tonality. Considered in isolation the vocal melody of this first half seems to imply a clear A minor tonality, the solo phrases being centred around the tonic A and the chorus phrases around the dominant E. However, such an interpretation is undermined at the outset by the fact that the opening figure in the accompaniment suggests C minor – a suggestion that is never confirmed since the harmonies throughout the first section are ambiguous, while the chief harmonic and tonal event of the opening twenty-four bars is the side-step in the bass from the opening C – G pedal to a pedal on C sharp and F sharp (a side-step between two extremely remote tonal areas which are separated by the interval of a tritone).

Ambiguous in its direction and unstable in its tonality, the opening half of the song acts as a long upbeat into the 'refrain' of the second half when the tonal uncertainties are finally resolved and the piece settles into a clear G major. In contrast to the confined melodic line of the first half, the vocal line (now completely symmetrical in its construction) becomes much more lyrical and wide-ranging in the second half, frequently covering an octave (and sometimes more) within the space of a few bars. The vocal lyricism of this second half takes place, however, against a flat, emotionally neutral accompaniment consisting of simple chords (enlivened only by some internal chromaticism and, when repeated, a few fragmentary melodic figurations) stated as a mechanically-repeated rhythmic figuration. The vocal line moves in long four-bar phrases in which one feels the move towards the strong downbeats at the beginning of the first and third bars; the accompanying figure is much more terse, covering only half a bar and appearing on the downbeat. The simultaneous use of a romantically lyrical vocal line and an accompanying figure which studiously avoids the upbeat – with its feeling of leaning towards the next bar and its traditionally expressive connotations – is a typically Weillian ambiguity. Together the melody and the accompaniment undermine, and consequently neutralize, one another. The emotional ambiguity and the sense of ironic objectivity produced by this fusion of romantic and anti-romantic gesture lies at the heart of the peculiar fascination exerted by Weill's music of the 1920s and 1930s.

It is interesting to compare the 'Alabama Song', one of the first numbers in the opera, with the 'Benares Song', the 'companion piece' which occupies a similar position at the end of the work. Here again a sixteen-bar introduction (more tonally stable than that of the 'Alabama Song' but similarly marked by surprising side-steps to remote areas) leads – via a peculiarly disorientating *a capella* chord sequence – to a lyrical refrain. Both sections of the song are accompanied by the same repeated rhythmic pattern.

The relationship between the lyrical melodic line and the terse, mechanically repeated accompaniment figure is similar to that found in the refrain of the 'Alabama Song' and produces a similarly 'distancing' effect. In the slow tempo of the 'Benares Song', however, the brashness of the 'Alabama Song' gives way to a sense of tragedy and disillusionment.

The refrain of the 'Benares Song' is shown in Ex 8. Here, in contrast to the 'Alabama Song', the movement towards the downbeat is emphasized both by the placing of the accompaniment's rhythmic figuration and by the yearning suspensions in the upper two vocal lines. The lyricism of these two vocal lines is further emphasized by their moving together in sensuous parallel thirds, by the ecstatic upward leap of a seventh (at 'a' in Ex 8) and by the subsequent descent to the double suspension on to the tonic F major which follows this leap.

Ex 8

Having temporarily achieved this clear F major the harmony then clouds over as it moves back towards the minor key at the final cadence. Here, in the sweetness of the parallel thirds and the luxuriance of the suspensions, Weill subtly employs and exploits the traditional conventions and the emotional associations which these conventions carry. The contrast between the yearning vocal line and the flat, objective rhythmic figuration which accompanies it reveals that the Benares 'where the sun is shining' is nothing more than a romantic and unobtainable dream. By this point in the opera Jimmy, the leading male character, has been sentenced to death and it is clear that the city of Mahagonny can no longer survive. If *Mahagonny* is a criticism of the emptiness of everything that the mythical America represented to the German imagination of the period, then the 'Benares Song' is the number in which the final disillusionment with this myth is most clearly stated. The music itself reveals the emptiness of the illusion. After the move back from the momentary warmth of the F major at the centre of the refrain to the darkness of the F minor cadence, we hardly need to hear that 'Benares is said to have perished in an earthquake' to know that the dream of an escape from the harshness of reality to some imagined paradise has been destroyed forever.

The two songs discussed above demonstrate two of Weill's most characteristic technical procedures: the underpinning of a romantically expressive melodic line by an unemotional, anti-romantic, accompaniment figure and the use of straightforward, regularly balanced phrase structures and simple diatonic melodies in conjunction with ambiguous harmonic formations. These formations tend to side-slip unexpectedly into remote tonal areas, especially those that are a semitone or a tritone away from the previous key centre. In his review of *The Protagonist* Abravanel perceptively points to the influence of the Russian composers on Weill's view of the relationship between text and music in the opera. There is little mention of the Russian composers in Weill's writings, and no mention of Mussorgsky, but the influence of Mussorgsky's modal harmonic procedures is evident in much of Weill's music and, like Mussorgsky, Weill tends to prefer relationships that lie outside the traditional diatonic system of Western music. In places the influence of Mussorgsky invades Weill's melodic, as well as harmonic, patterns; the recurring motif of *The Seven Deadly Sins*, which is discussed below, is instantly reminiscent of sections of Mussorgsky's *Boris Godunov*, while the melody which opens the first movement of *The Berlin Requiem* (shown in Ex 9 below) seems to be a direct quotation of part of Varlaam's song in Act II, Scene 1 of *Boris* (Ex 10).

Ex 9 Berlin Requiem No 1 Grosser Dank Chorale

Lo-bet die Nacht! Lo-bet die Nacht Lo-bet die Nacht und die Fin-ster-nis.

Ex 10 Mussorgsky: Boris Godunov Act II

Mussorgsky, the most original and individual of the Russian Nationalist composers, had, of course, been dead for almost forty-five years when Weill wrote *The Protagonist* but his music was, nonetheless, almost unknown in Germany. The French composers of the late-nineteenth and early-twentieth century, and especially Debussy, felt a particular affinity for Russian music. At a time when Debussy was, quite consciously, trying to free himself from the influence of Wagner and the Central European tradition which dominated Western European music, the work of the Russians in general, and of Mussorgsky in particular, seemed to offer a possible alternative. Debussy's harmonic innovations – his use of remote tonal relationships, of parallel triads, of unresolved discords and of the chord as a sonorous object in its own right – were deeply indebted to Mussorgsky's example.

However, although German film and theatre of the Weimar Republic were affected by the examples of the Russians, German composers (deeply conscious of belonging to the great Austro-German musical tradition) remained almost entirely unaffected by Russian influences. Of the German composers of his time, only Weill seems to have understood and absorbed the significance of the music of Mussorgsky and the Russian Nationalists; as in Debussy, it is in Weill's individual handling of harmonic and tonal relationships that this influence reveals itself.

Weill's instrumentation plays a particularly important rôle in achieving the kind of emotional ambiguity discussed above. Adorno referred to *Mahagonny* as 'music with a sonority that is filtered by a handful of instruments and that possesses a power of expansion that

routs and leaves behind the diffuseness of a much larger orchestra.'[38]
I have already referred to Weill's interest in Mahler and to the
possible influence that the chamber-music-like orchestration and the
bringing together of clearly contrasted 'unblended' timbres, which
one finds in late Mahler, might have had on Weill's orchestral
techniques.

To some extent, Weill's use of a small instrumental ensemble in
the works of the late 1920s and the 1930s is, of course, an imitation of
the sonority of the dance and cabaret bands of the time. However, it
is also a reflection of that trend away from the large orchestras of the
late-nineteenth century and the early-twentieth century that was
general among the composers of the period. To some extent this
trend was forced upon composers by purely economic considerations;
given the difficult financial situation in Europe after the First World
War, a new work for a small instrumental group had more chance of
being performed than had a new work which required large orchestral
forces. At a deeper level, the reaction against the sumptuous and
luxuriant sonorities of the late-romantic orchestra was yet another
aspect of the general anti-romantic movement in the arts of the
period. Weill's liking for wind and brass timbres is a characteristic
manifestation of this anti-romantic trend. Like Stravinsky – and for
the same reasons – Weill tends to avoid the string instruments, with
their 'expressive', 'romantic' connotations, preferring the more
objective, more clearly articulated, non-vibrato sound of the wind
instruments. Of the works written in collaboration with Brecht, the
scores of *Happy End*, *The Berlin Requiem* and *Der Jasager* include none of
the usual orchestral strings; *The Threepenny Opera* and *The Lindbergh
Flight* employ only a single cello. Even in those works, such as the
Mahagonny opera and *The Seven Deadly Sins*, that use a full complement,
strings are employed as rhythmic and percussive, rather than cant-
abile instruments. They are used 'in quotation marks' for consciously
romantic effects or are used in such a way that their expressive timbre
is neutralized by the simultaneous use of more acerbic timbres. Such
a use of the string instruments itself gives rise to that emotional
ambiguity, that tension between the romantic and anti-romantic
gesture, that is so characteristic of Weill's music.

In the following short passage from *The Seven Deadly Sins*, for
example, the almost Mahlerian yearning of the string line is negated
by the terse, jazz-like figurations of the wind and muted brass which
accompany it:

Ex 11

The clear, sparse textures of the Weill-Brecht works, the lack of any 'filling-in' parts and the sharp, unmixed timbres act as part of the distancing process. There is no indulgence in rich sonorities 'for their own sake': no 'wash of sound' which the listener can allow to flood over him. Any large-scale, rhetorical gesture is immediately reduced in size, and called into question, any romantically expressive figuration immediately endistanced and objectified by being played on such a small group of cleanly articulated, non-expressive instruments.

The popular view of Weill as a composer whose talents lay in his ability to capture the cynical and rather sleazy atmosphere of the Berlin of the Twenties and Thirties in tart little cabaret songs, is based almost entirely on the music of *The Threepenny Opera*, *Happy End* and, to a lesser extent, on the *Mahagonny Songspiel* – the three works in which the music most closely resembles that of cabaret songs and in which, for a variety of reasons, the moral stance of the authors is most easily ignored or misunderstood. Not only is the musical structure of all three works such as to encourage the performance of numbers as separate items removed from their dramatic context (so that the music of these works is best known as a series of unrelated songs) but, even within context, the social and moral implications of these works remain somewhat ambiguous. *Happy End*, for example, is most easily understood as a simple farce (Frederic Ewen, in his book on Brecht, dismisses the work as 'an unhappy farago' which 'were it not for the brilliant songs of Kurt Weill . . . might well be forgotten'[39]) while the libretto of *The Threepenny Opera* is, as all Brecht commentators have observed, so equivocal that the work can be easily accepted as little more than a brilliant *jeu d'esprit*.

The full-scale *Mahagonny* opera, on the other hand, presents a more difficult problem for those who wish to see Weill in this limited, and relatively comfortable, light, for in this piece the listener cannot avoid facing the issues which the work presents. The popular song style remains, but the individual numbers are far less easily divorced from their dramatic context than are the songs of *The Threepenny Opera* and this context, unlike that of the earlier work, is quite unambiguous in its moral and social position. The opera tells the story of the city of Mahagonny, a city of pleasure and of 'gin, whiskey, girls and boys', built to attract the gold flowing in from Alaska and the American west.

In Mahagonny everything is obtainable and everything is permissible if one has money. Act II of the opera illustrates some of the activities which make up the pleasurable existence of the inhabitants of Mahagonny: drinking, frequenting brothels, watching prize fights (the one shown on stage ends in the death of one of the combatants), eating until they kill themselves. Rape, murder and other crimes are regarded as trivial misdemeanours but lack of money is punishable by death. When, in the final Act of the work, one of the inhabitants can no longer pay his bills, he stands trial, is condemned and executed. God appears to the people of Mahagonny, but is unable to punish those who have already built a hell for themselves and the city is destroyed by flames.

Unlike *The Threepenny Opera*, *Mahagonny* is uncompromising in condemning the society which it presents. Ferocious both dramatically and musically, *Mahagonny* has none of the apparent bonhomie of the earlier work. It remains one of the most uncomfortable and disturbing of operas, as much because of Weill's oblique approach to his task as because of Brecht's text. In setting the scenes of self-indulgence in Act II and the horrifying final scenes of the opera to music of a deliberate banality, Weill was continuing that technique of distancing the listener by composing 'against', rather than 'with' the stage action that he had first employed in *The Protagonist*.

It is a technique that runs a high risk of defeating its own ends since the coming together of such horrifying stage action and such banal music can have an effect that is so shocking, and produce an alienation that is so brutal, that it may force the spectator to reject the work in equally aggressive terms. Perhaps no opera has aroused such hatred in its audience as has *Mahagonny*. The violent reaction of its earliest audience indicates not a misunderstanding of the piece but a clear understanding, and a rejection, of its message. Today, most people know *Mahagonny* and the 'popular' works of Weill through recorded, rather than staged, performances and it is, therefore, possible to ignore the oblique relationship between music and stage action. Divorced from its context, the music can be taken at its face value and its power reduced to manageable proportions. The present method of dealing with the almost unbearably painful images of *Mahagonny*, by regarding the music as a slightly cynical but amusing 'period piece', shows less understanding than was demonstrated by the work's first audiences.

I have earlier compared Weill's attitude to popular music with Stravinsky's attitude to the classical and baroque music which act as the models in his neo-classical works. Such a comparison seems fair when applied to the brilliant, often garish, music of *The Threepenny Opera*, *Happy End* and, to a lesser extent, *Mahagonny*, but it cannot be equally applied to the other works which Weill wrote between 1927 and 1935.

In *The Threepenny Opera* and *Happy End* Weill had used a simple sequence of cabaret songs as the vehicle for his newly established musical language. During the years that followed, the simple formal structures of these works disappeared, together with many of the more obvious external trappings of this new language, as Weill moved from an overtly 'jazzy', cabaret style to a less restrictive musical style.

The harmonic and many of the melodic features remain. These are the characteristic Weillian thumb-prints of the earlier works and it is not difficult to find passages in the later works that are directly reminiscent of the first Brecht-Weill pieces, as the following example demonstrates:

Ex 12 a Mahagonny   Act II

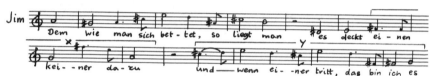

b Seven Deadly Sins   No 6 Unzucht

However, the more energetic jazz rhythms, the bright colours and what Drew has called 'the twentieth-century demotic expressions'[40] of popular music which are found in *The Threepenny Opera, Happy End* and parts of *Mahagonny* disappear. The move away from the overt cabaret, song style was a move towards a style that was more controlled, more flexible and at the same time less restricted. It was a move towards a style that retained the simple language and popular feeling of *The Threepenny Opera,* but was also capable of the austerity of *The Berlin Requiem,* the classical detachment of *Der Jasager* and the direct tragic statements of *Die Bürgschaft.* Above all, perhaps, it was a style that allowed for the development of larger musical structures.

In these post-*Threepenny Opera* and post-*Mahagonny* works the popular, jazz elements no longer form an implied 'background' against which the composed foreground operates. In works such as *The Seven Deadly Sins* the popular elements have become as much, and as natural, a part of Weill's style as was the folk element in the music of Haydn. To a large extent the movement towards this more flexible, more controlled style corresponds to a re-emergence of those neo-classical elements which had been present in Weill's earlier instrumental music. In fact, neo-classical influences had never completely disappeared from Weill's music (they can be seen, in particular, in *Mahagonny* in such things as the canon which accompanies the hurricane in Act II, in the chorale prelude which follows it and in the subtle polyphony of the 'Crane Duet') but had merely been obscured by the cabaret style of *Happy End* and *The Threepenny Opera.*

If Weill's instrumental works (other than the isolated Second Symphony) and the pre-Brecht operas can be considered as an attempt to fuse the two distinct influences of his early musical life – the expressionism of Mahler, Schoenberg and the late romantics and the neo-classicism of Busoni – into a unified musical language, then the works written after *Mahagonny* can be similarly viewed as an attempt to reconcile the new simpler and more popular language of the late 1920s with the neo-classicism of his earlier music.

The most obvious sign of Weill's move towards a more classical style is his gradual return to a more orthodox instrumental ensemble. The *Berlin Requiem* includes parts for banjo, guitar and two saxophones, but the saxophone is prominent in only one movement, and is elsewhere used as a member of a brass ensemble, while the banjo makes only a single appearance. The guitar, used as a popular rather than as a 'jazz' instrument, provides a simple chordal accompaniment to the ballade of the second movement, while the percussion consists only of timpani and, very sparingly employed, side drum and cymbals. By the time of *Der Jasager*, the saxophone and the banjo have disappeared and the piece has a purely Stravinskian ensemble.

Along with the polyphonic writing of these less specifically jazz-orientated ensembles there returns the polyphonic writing which was a feature of Weill's early instrumental music. Now it is a strong, muscular contrapuntal writing adapted to the demands of the new, popular language; Bachian figurations appear which, as in baroque music, are consistently and systematically exploited throughout a movement; baroque sequences and textures; baroque techniques (particularly canon which now forms the basis of almost all Weill's choruses) and a sense of rhythmic momentum and of thematic construction and extension that is clearly baroque in character.

On occasions the references to earlier music are quite specific. Both the text and the music of the finale number of *The Berlin Requiem* (the *Zweiter Bericht über den unbekannten Soldaten*), the opening of which is shown below, deliberately allude to the recitative style of the Bach Passions, an allusion that is intended to suggest a parallel between the subject matter of the *Requiem* and that of the Bach Passions.

Ex 13 Berlin Requiem No 1: Zweiter bericht über den unbekannten soldaten

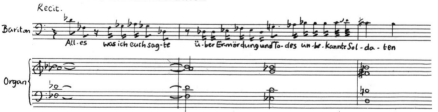

Such specific references are unusual, although they also occur in *Der Jasager* and the *Lindbergh Flight*; more important is the extent to which the neo-classical influence is completely absorbed into Weill's new popular, but now no longer specifically cabaret-style, language.

These other post-1927 European scores are marked by a classical sense of balance and by a technical and emotional restraint that is absent from the three better known Weill-Brecht works. In *Mahagonny* the savagery of the libretto is reflected in the ferocious bitterness of much of Weill's score. In *Die Bürgschaft*, on the other hand, the savagery is, as David Drew has pointed out, confined to the stage.[41]

Die Bürgschaft is about the way in which trust and friendship are corrupted by money and power. Act I of the opera is concerned with the subject on a personal level. Act II, in which the mythical country of the opera's setting is occupied by the forces of a totalitarian power, examines the relationship between the individual and the state. Act III portrays the effect which the new regime has on both the population as a whole and on the relationship between the two men whose story opened the opera. The final scene of the work, in which one man hands over his friend to be killed by the mob, is as horrifying and remorseless as anything to be found in opera. Yet, as Drew remarked, this act of 'consummate perfidiousness' is accompanied by music of an 'almost unbearable serenity.'[42] In *Der Jasager* a young boy joins an expedition through the mountains to the city so as to obtain medicine for his sick mother. In the course of the journey the boy himself falls ill, and, unable to continue, threatens the success of the expedition. He elects to die according to ancient custom by being thrown over the cliffs so that by his death the expedition can continue.

In both *Die Bürgschaft* and *Der Jasager* Weill's habitual practice of writing 'against' rather than 'with' the dramatic action – a technique which appeared in his first performed opera – is put to new ends. The sentencing and the execution of Jimmy Mahoney in *Mahagonny* is given an additional horror by being accompanied by music of a deliberate banality; the death of Johannes Mathes, at the end of *Die Bürgschaft*, and the sacrifice of the young boy in *Der Jasager* are accompanied by music which, by opposing the dramatic action, endistances and causes us to question, rather than experience, the morality of the violence shown on the stage; 'the music', as Weill himself observed in his comments on Busoni's *Doktor Faust*, 'leaves the interpretation of the outrageous events to the imagination of the listener and contents itself with a gesture of gentleness and freedom'.[43]

In both *Die Bürgschaft* and *Der Jasager* the characters are treated as stylized models, many of them are nameless (as in the expressionist drama of the period) and are simply identified by their function or status, with which (as in the Nō plays upon which Brecht based *Der Jasager*) they introduce themselves on their first appearance. The stylized, anti-naturalistic, nature of the two works is further emphasized by the music itself which, in both material and structure, recalls the conventions of baroque opera and oratorio. The final scene of *Die Bürgschaft*, for example, alternates *ritornelli* and episodes in the manner of a baroque concerto, while, in both works, the action is framed and punctuated by formal and dramatically static choruses. The chorus of *Der Jasager* is employed, in the manner of a Greek chorus, as a group which both participates in and, on other occasions, comments on or points out the moral of the stage action. In *Die Bürgschaft* the rôle of the chorus as disinterested commentator is emphasized physically by one chorus being on stage and a smaller, more important, 'commenting' chorus being seated, raised, in the orchestra pit or on the side of the stage.

Like Busoni, Weill believed that opera required a musical structure which existed independently of the dramatic action, a belief based – again like his teacher – on his experience of the operas of Mozart and Verdi. The formality of the musical design of *Die Bürgschaft* is not, therefore, an attempt to achieve the kind of fusion of 'abstract' musical forms and the dramatic demands of through-composed opera that Berg had achieved in *Wozzeck*. Like all Weill's work, from the *Threepenny Opera* onwards, *Die Bürgschaft* and *Der Jasager* are 'number' operas that totally reject the aesthetics and the techniques of the Wagnerian opera. Whole numbers and large, clearly defined, blocks of music (such as the choruses which frame Act I of *Die Bürgschaft*) reappear but such recurrences simply underline the formality of the musical and dramatic design. The Wagnerian *leitmotiv* has no place in Weill's dramatic works. Recurrent musical cells and shapes may appear, but these have a purely musical, rather than a 'literary', significance. The melodic pattern which opens *Der Jasager*, for example, is transformed to produce the theme of the chorus which greets the boy's decision to die; but the connection between the two musical ideas (which is stressed by the repetition of the opening section immediately after the related chorus) has no 'psychological' significance. When themes, rather than whole numbers, return they are isolated in such a way that the listener's attention is drawn to them; one such example is the passage, singled out by both its placing and orchestration, which ends numbers two and six and then becomes the basis of the seventh number of *The Seven Deadly Sins*.

As in Stravinsky's *Oedipus Rex*, with its equally objective commenting chorus, the symmetry and the formal design of these post-*Mahagonny* works is part of their stylized, monumental and deliberately ritualistic nature. Although Brecht dismissed *Die Bürgschaft* as 'bourgeois', the opera is as true to Brecht's conception of epic theatre, and as true to Weill's own belief in the necessity of evolving a new form of opera, as is the aggressive and more overtly iconoclastic *Mahagonny*.

Chapter 8
The American Works

To most admirers of Weill's European works, his output during the last fifteen years of his life comes as a profound shock. In these late works Weill the European intellectual, Weill the ironic observer of the political and social ills of his time, Weill the moralist – even Weill the composer with a limited but nonetheless individual and disturbing voice – seems to have disappeared. Instead, there emerges a picture of a composer willing to adopt the musical clichés of the Broadway musical and only too eager to embrace its commercial values. The picture also shows a composer happy to provide glossy, undistinguished music to libretti that are not simply apolitical but, in some cases, seem to condone all the attitudes that his earlier work critized. Inevitably, many people who value Weill's European works regard his American works with bewilderment, if not with horror.

The popular explanations of this apparent *volte-face*, of the 'problem' of Weill's American works, fall into two categories. Those who are interested in the European works primarily for literary, social or political reasons tend, as David Drew has pointed out,[1] to favour explanations that suggest that Weill could only compose when inspired by Brecht (or, on very rare occasions, some other forceful writer) and by the kind of social and political conditions found in the Germany of the inter-war years. Those who value Weill's earlier works for musical reasons find it impossible to believe that the sophisticated composer of *Mahagonny* could have employed the naive, and frequently sentimental, musical language of the American works with any degree of sincerity and, therefore, regard the American Weill as someone who betrayed his ideals by 'selling out'. The more charitable of these admirers may excuse this 'sell out' on the grounds

132

that Weill had, after all, to make a living. The less charitable will regard him as a cynical opportunist or as someone corrupted by the financial rewards available to anyone willing, and able, to produce a slick commercial product. Amongst the latter group may be numbered Otto Klemperer who, when asked 'why Weill went to pieces as a composer in America' replied: 'He was very interested in money, that's the reason. He got too involved in American show business and all the terrible people in it.'[2]

None of these explanations does justice to Weill or shows any understanding of the complicated process by means of which the European Weill was transformed into the rich and famous Broadway composer of the late 1940s – a process in which Weill's social and musical beliefs, his complex psychological make-up and the historic events of the period all play a part.

I have already discussed the extent to which Brecht's aims have been mistakenly assumed to be those of Weill also. Weill's main concerns were always social, humanistic and musical, rather than directly political. Unlike Eisler, Weill was never willing to subjugate his musical ideals to the expression of a clear and unambiguous political message and, indeed, the break between Weill and Brecht came at the point at which Brecht's political ideas began to interfere with what Weill regarded as the musical necessities of the work.

Once the true nature of Weill's aims is recognized it becomes possible to see that, far from betraying his ideals, Weill pursued both his musical and social aims in these American works with what, given the new cultural environment within which he was working, was remarkable single-mindedness.

Weill's output in America can be conveniently divided into three groups, each group covering a period of five years. The first group of works, written between 1935 and 1940, includes *Der Weg der Verheissung*, *Johnny Johnstone*, and his first Broadway musical, *Knickerbocker Holiday*. The second, covering the period 1941-45, consists of *Lady in the Dark*, *One Touch of Venus* and *The Firebrand of Florence*. The final group covers the last five years of his life and includes the folk opera, *Down in the Valley*, *Street Scene*, *Love Life* and *Lost in the Stars*.

To those familiar with Weill's European works, the second of these groups is, at least in terms of subject matter, the most problematic. Pure, commercial Broadway shows, it is difficult to detect any social or humanistic concerns behind the stories of *Lady in the Dark* (which deals with the psychological problems and fantasies of the editoress of a fashion magazine), *One Touch of Venus* (in which a statue of Venus comes to life and falls in love with a barber) or in *The Firebrand of Florence* (about Benvenuto Cellini's attempts to win the hand of the girl he loves). These three works are exceptional, however, and all Weill's other American works deal with social and moral subjects that reflect concerns as topical and relevant to the American audiences of the period as were those of the earlier works to his European audience. The theme of war, for example, is dealt with in the anti-militaristic *Johnny Johnstone*; racial tensions in *Lost in the Stars*; tenement life in *Street Scene* and politics in *Knickerbocker Holiday*. Certainly Weill never again found a librettist as poetic, as dramatically skilled or as hard-hitting as Brecht. Nonetheless, if the handling of these social themes seems timid, rather naive and often peripheral to the more obviously commercial aspects of the story, we must recognize that, given the state of the commercial Broadway theatre of the time, even to tackle such subjects was a brave innovation.

The simple, popular style which Weill had adopted in the European works of the mid-1920s had been an attempt to achieve a musical language which would be immediately comprehensible to a large number of people, which would, in Weill's own words, 'enable meaningful things to be said with the simplest, most inconspicuous of means'[3] and which would enable the 'new opera' to reach a 'new public'. In the radical and experimental atmosphere of the Germany of the inter-war years, it had been possible for the development of the new language and new forms to take place within the confines of the established opera houses and the serious theatre. In the United States Weill found himself faced with a culture which did not allow for such possibilities. The serious 'play with music' – the form which, well-established in Europe, gave rise to *The Threepenny Opera* and *Der Silbersee* – was almost unknown in America, while American opera houses (of which, compared with Germany, there existed a mere handful) catered exclusively for one particular, élite section of the population.

In *Down in the Valley*, a work intended for performances by non-professional groups, the preface in the score says:

> [it] can be performed wherever a chorus, a few singers and
> a few actors are available. The physical production can be
> as simple as a 'dramatic' concert performance where the
> principal act their scenes in front of the chorus without any
> help of scenery. If scenery is used it should consist of some

> simply painted frames indicating the place . . . the leading
> parts should provide good training for the specific type of
> singing actor who has become such an important asset of
> the musical theatre.

This work represented one attempt to reach a wider popular audience. If *Down in the Valley* has behind it none of the didactic political intentions of a Lehrstück such as *Der Jasager*, its intentions of providing some kind of musical training are similar, and are directly in line with the aims of the Gebrauchsmusik of the Germany of the 1920s. The extent to which *Down in the Valley* succeeded in achieving its aims can be judged by the fact that the piece received over 1,600 productions (and some 6,000 performances) in the first nine years of its life.

Such things as *Down in the Valley* and the 'Lunchtime' shows, in which Weill took such pleasure, were, however, a response to a specialized and specific social demand. To reach a truly popular audience Weill had to work within the mainstream of the American music theatre and this, inevitably, meant the Broadway musical.

'A composer must know for whom he is composing',[4] Weill observed, and in order to reach an American public Weill had to find a new, and specifically American, musical language which would be as generally comprehensible as had been the language of his later European works. During the period from 1941-45 this language was that of the Broadway musical; after 1945, and after the disastrous reception of *The Firebrand of Florence*, the language was more consciously based on the melodic and rhythmic inflections of American folk music and on the popular music of the streets, rather than on commercial popular music. Langston Hughes, the black American poet who wrote the lyrics of *Street Scene*, has described how Weill went with him to hear authentic blues numbers in different parts of Harlem and studied American children's games and songs in order to achieve a 'national idiom' that would be understood by the American people.[5] In the obituary of Weill which appeared in the *New York Herald Tribune* on 9 April 1950, Virgil Thomson acknowledged Weill's success in creating such a national idiom, saying of *Down in the Valley* that, 'it speaks an American musical dialect that Americans can accept'.

If Broadway seemed to offer Weill the chance of reaching a popular audience it also, more than anywhere else, seemed to offer the possibility of creating both new forms of music-theatre and large-scale musical structures approaching those of opera.

A few weeks after his arrival in the United States, Weill attended the dress rehearsal of Gershwin's *Porgy and Bess*. According to Weill himself, the experience made him realize that, 'the American theatre was well on the way to the more integrated form of musical theatre that we had begun to attempt in Europe. That gave me the courage to start work on a serious musical play for the American stage – *Johnny Johnson*.'[6] However, Lotte Lenya's memories of the occasion suggest that Gershwin's achievement in *Porgy* had a more far-reaching effect on Weill: 'He listened very closely and he said, "you know, it is possible to write an opera for Broadway".' From that point onwards, said Lenya, Weill was, 'always consciously working towards an opera'.[7] There can be little doubt that Weill, who had urged the necessity for a 'new type of opera' in the Germany of the 1920s, felt the need for a similarly new type of American opera. Moreover, it was clear to him that such a new type of opera could not develop in the United States within the confines of the opera house. As early as 1937, shortly after the production of *Johnny Johnson* and before his first Broadway musical, Weill had declared his belief that:

> If there will ever be anything like an American opera, it is bound to come out of Broadway. To start a new movement of American musical theater, you cannot go to the Metropolitan. They haven't got the audience. Broadway represents the living theater in this country and American opera, as I imagine it, should be part of the living theater. Opera has lost contact with the theater and leads the existence of a museum piece, toilsomely preserved by its devotees.[8]

Few of Weill's American works were pat 'formula', 'sure-fire', musicals. Within the context of the commercial Broadway musical theatre both the subjects and their musical treatment were unusually adventurous. There were, for example, few precedents within the tradition of the musical for such things as the 'Greek' chorus of *Lost in the Stars*, the confining of the music of *Lady in the Dark* to the dream sequences (in themselves miniature, self-contained operas) or the ensembles of *Street Scene*.

It is difficult today to realize the extent to which a work such as *Street Scene* differed from the other, more commercial musicals of its time. Contemporary critics, however, were in no doubt that the work, with its complex ensembles and large musical structures, its single set and simple costumes, its lack of dancers, chorus, comedians and lavish production numbers represented a step towards 'a significantly American opera'. During the last five years of his life Weill seems to have been more and more consciously attempting to create an indigenous operatic tradition based on the classics of American literature. At the time of his death he was working on a version of Mark Twain's *Huckleberry Finn* and Lotte Lenya remembers finding on his desk a list of equally 'classic' subjects including *Gone with the Wind* and Melville's *Moby Dick* that Weill was considering using as the bases of future works.

In his *New York Herald Tribune* obituary Virgil Thomson referred to Weill's attempts to found an American operatic tradition and described him as, 'a workman who might have bridged for us the gap between grand opera and the singspiel'.[9] Five years later, the critic Gilbert Chase acknowledged the stature of Weill's achievements in the late works, saying that Weill had given the American theatre 'works that transcend the level of popular entertainment'.[10] That we, today, find it difficult to accept the folksiness, the sentimentality and the rather self-conscious 'messages' of these late works may simply indicate that the spirit which these pieces embody no longer forms a part of our mental attitude: the cynicism of the European works is more in tune with our way of looking at the world than is the innocence and naivety of the American works.

It is easy to overlook, or ignore, how consistent and how brave, given the cultural context, were Weill's attempts to retain his integrity. The tenacity with which he continued, in these American works, to pursue his life-long musical, social and humanistic beliefs gives the lie to the idea that the American Weill betrayed the ideals which he had promoted in his earlier European works. Weill's belief in the necessity for a new form of opera never changed; nor his belief that this new opera should reach a new public. Only his ideas about the way in which these ends were to be achieved had undergone a transformation.

There remains, however, what, to anyone whose interest in Weill is primarily musical, are the most perplexing and problematic aspects of his American music. That most of the American works are of a lower musical standard – often of a much lower standard – than Weill's European works is, I think, undeniable. Comparing Weill's

137

European and American works, David Drew, the most perceptive and sympathetic of commentators on Weill, has said; 'I know of no composer, indeed no creative artist of any kind, in whose work there is so great a gulf between the best and the worst',[11] and has observed of *Down in the Valley* that 'even the technique is deficient; shoddy modulations abound, simple tunes are decked out with meaningless counterpoints, empty *ostinati* do service of real invention.'[12]

Equally, and perhaps more, disconcerting than the standard of the music, is the nature of the change in Weill's musical language in the works written in the last fifteen years of his life. The change of style which took place in Weill's music during the 1920s is startling but not only is it possible to see the links between the atonal Weill of the Violin Concerto and the popular, jazz-based Weill of *The Threepenny Opera*, it is also possible to understand the changes in his style in terms of the more general artistic and musical trends in Europe of that period. As I have tried to show, the popular style of Weill's later European music has its roots in the European tradition within which he grew up, and in the developments within that tradition which were taking place during his formative years.

If Weill's works from the years 1927 to 1935 represent an extension – albeit an extension in a surprising and unpredictable direction – of the European tradition, the American works seem to represent a complete rejection of this tradition; a denial, rather than a development, of Weill's earlier style. The nature of the American commercial theatre and the desire to write for an American audience in a musical language which it would understand, could explain a change in the more superficial aspects of Weill's musical style; they cannot explain a change as profound as that which actually took place.

Despite Drew's remarks on the technical weakness of *Down in the Valley*, the American pieces are rarely less than the works of a skilled and totally professional craftsman. Even at their best, however, they are works of a kind that could have been written by a number of competent Broadway composers. In these works the individual voice of the European Weill seems to have disappeared into an anonymous stylistic greyness.

Since Weill, as reticent as ever about his inner thoughts and feelings, left no indication as to why this profound change in his language took place, one can only surmise the deep psychological and personal factors which led him to cultivate this apparently deliberate anonymity. Some attempt at this is necessary if one is to approach an understanding of Weill's American career.

It is difficult to overestimate the profound effect which emigration had on those forced by circumstances to leave Germany in the 1930s. Despite his total silence on the subject, the extremity of Weill's response is a measure of the depth of the psychological and emotional effect which the experience had on him.

We know from Lotte Lenya that, once in America, Weill never spoke German again – even his dying words were in English.[13] Similarly, we know that he refused to have anything to do with his fellow refugees, even with those, such as Hindemith, who had previously been amongst his closest personal friends. Lotte Lenya has said:

> The old timers were always talking about the past, they would always talk about how marvellous it had been in Berlin . . . Weill didn't want to have anything to do with refugees. He never saw any of them again. Never . . . Kurt never wanted to look back.[14]

Lenya has suggested that Weill's refusal to speak his native language or talk about his earlier life came about because he 'was always looking ahead', but there can be little doubt that it was also a part of Weill's reaction to the experience of emigration. Driven from his homeland, Weill rejected everything that that homeland represented.

It was not by chance that the various attempts by Adorno, Aufricht and others to revive Weill's European works or to suggest new projects on which Weill and Brecht might once again collaborate, came to nothing. Virgil Thomson remembers that, soon after Weill and Lotte Lenya had arrived in the United States, he and a number of other people:

> thought that it would be good to produce in Hartford Weill's German opera made with Brecht, *Mahagonny*. We took Weill there to see the theatre, and I even played through the score with him for setting tempos. But quietly the project was dropped and one came to understand that Weill's working association with Bertolt Brecht . . . was to be buried. And buried it remained until his death.[15]

Thomson suggests that Weill wanted to hide 'a possibly Communist-tainted past'. It seems more likely, however, that Weill simply wanted, as Lenya has remarked, 'to forget everything German'.

In any event, the Germany that Weill had known had disappeared.

In May 1938, while Weill was working on *Knickerbocker Holiday*, his first Broadway musical, the scores of his European pieces were being displayed in Dusseldorf as part of the Nazi Ministry of Propaganda's exhibition of 'Debased Music'. *Magna Carta*, Weill's declaration of human rights, was written in the early months of 1940, by which time the French and British governments had declared war and the German military high command was preparing for its spectacular spring offensive. By May 1940 the Germans had overrun all the countries to the west of them and Weill's Europe – his background and his roots, the culture which had formed him, everything that he had stood for and believed in – had been destroyed.

Rejected by the society within which he had been brought up, betrayed by the culture of which he had regarded himself a part, the American Weill had to re-establish not only his career but his very identity. The use of ancient Jewish modes in *Der Weg der Verheissung*, the occasional pieces written to celebrate the founding of the state of Israel, and the liturgical setting of *Kiddush* for cantor, mixed chorus and organ, demonstrate the extent to which exile and the experiences which led to it, forced Weill, as it did many other Jews, to recognize and reassess their identity as members of the Jewish race.

Alongside the psychological rejection of everything to do with Germany, and the recognition of his racial identity, Weill also had to assert his new national identity as an American. Following the publication of a review of *Street Scene* in February 1947, Weill wrote to *Life* magazine to complain of their description of him as a German composer:

> Although I was born in Germany I do not consider myself a 'German composer'. The Nazis obviously do not consider me as such either and I left their country (an arrangement which suited both me and my rulers admirably) in 1933. I am an American citizen and during my dozen years in this country have composed exclusively for the American stage . . . I would appreciate your straightening out your readers on this matter.[16]

Weill wanted, Lenya has said, 'to absorb America; he really wanted to get into America'[17] and to become a true American, not an American 'simply on paper'. Weill could only establish his new identity as an American citizen, as opposed to an expatriate German, by adopting the standards and the values of his new home.

It is not, perhaps, surprising that Weill threw himself with such eagerness into helping the American war effort (it is significant that the only settings of the German language which he composed while in the United States were specifically written for propaganda broadcasts) nor that, following the end of the war and the disastrous reception of *The Firebrand of Florence*, he should have become even more determined to submerge himself in the culture of his new country and create a truly 'American' music for the American people.

If this adoption of American values necessitated the renunciation of his earlier musical language and of the European culture which that language represented, if his rejection of 'everything German' necessitated the denial of his previous musical identity and what seems to have been the deliberate cultivation of an anonymous 'American' style, then these were the prices that Weill was prepared to pay.

Perhaps some insight into Weill's attitudes during the last fifteen years of his life can be gained by seeing the way in which his compatriot George Grosz responded to the cultural and social trauma of emigration. In her book on Grosz, Beth Irwin Lewis observes:

> He did not find paradise in America, though he tried desperately hard to become a complete American. He was determined not to live like an exile, living in the past and waiting to return to Germany. He intended to shed his German identity and sink his roots into the new land. He threw himself with enthusiasm into becoming a practical, money-making American but the ties with Germany were too strong. He wrote some time later, 'I really haven't brought it off. I can never become a genuine American. Thus, I am, after all, nothing more than – yes, a demoralized and forgotten German.'[18]

In both his art and his outer life Weill shed his German identity more successfully than did Grosz; indeed, in his American works Weill actually demonstrated the gradual shedding of his old identity and the acquisition of a new one in the clearest way available to a composer. Whether Weill, like Grosz, felt demoralized, whether he too felt that he had not 'brought it off' is something that he never revealed but he, at least, was not a 'forgotten German'. As Lotte Lenya has remarked, 'He had success all his life. One cannot say, in his case, that when he died, he died misunderstood.'[19]

There is, nonetheless, a bitter irony in the fact that Weill's greatest

American success came a few years after his death, not with a work written in his later 'American' style but with a piece from that period of his life that he had tried to forget. When *The Threepenny Opera* was revived at an off-Broadway theatre in 1954 it ran for a record breaking 2,707 performances – a run that surpassed not only the runs of Weill's own Broadway shows but also the runs of such legendary musicals as *Oklahoma, The Sound of Music, South Pacific* and, as a final irony, the Weill-Brecht inspired *Cabaret*.

CHRONOLOGICAL LIST OF WORKS

The following list of works includes all Weill's major compositions, whether published or unpublished. Excluded are the many works which Weill began and never completed, the numerous individual songs and the various arrangements which Weill made of his own and other composers' pieces.

Pre 1919
: *Schilflieder* song cycle (unpublished)
Piano pieces (unpublished)

1919
: *Die Weise von Liebe und Tod des Cornets Christopher Rilke*, symphonic poem for orchestra (unpublished)

1919-20
: String Quartet in B minor (unpublished)
Sonata for 'Cello and Piano (unpublished)
Nina der Lenclos, opera in one act (unpublished, lost)
Das Hohe Lied, opera in one act (unpublished, lost)
Shulamith, oratorio (unpublished)

1921
: Symphony No. 1 (Universal Edition, Vienna)

1922
: *Divertimento* for orchestra and male chorus (unpublished)
Sinfonia Sacra op 6 (unpublished)
Die Zaubernacht, ballet for children (unpublished)

1923
: *Recordare* (unpublished)
String Quartet op 8 (Universal Edition, Vienna)
Quodlibet op 9 (Universal Edition, Vienna)
Frauentanz op 10 for voice and instruments (Universal Edition, Vienna)
Stundenbuch for voice and orchestra (unpublished, lost)

1924
: Concerto for violin and wind instruments (Universal Edition, Vienna)
Der Protagonist, opera in one act on a libretto by Georg Kaiser (vocal score: Universal Edition, Vienna)
Der neue Orpheus, cantata on a text by Ivan Goll (vocal score: Universal Edition, Vienna)

1926
: *Royal Palace*, opera in one act on a libretto by Ivan Goll (vocal score: Universal Edition, Vienna)
Herzog von Gothland, incidental music for a radio play (unpublished)
Na und . . ., comic opera (unpublished, lost)

1927
: *Gustav III*, incidental music for a stage play (unpublished)
Der Zar lässt sich photographieren, one-act opera on a libretto by Georg Kaiser (vocal score: Universal Edition, Vienna)
Mahagonny Songspiel, text by Bertolt Brecht (Universal Edition, Vienna)
Vom Tod im Wald, for bass and wind instruments. Text by Bertolt Brecht (unpublished)

1928
: *Konjunktur*, incidental music for a stage play (unpublished)
Katalaunische Schlacht, incidental music for a stage play (unpublished)
Der Dreigroschenoper (The Threepenny Opera), a play with music. Text by Bertolt Brecht (Universal Edition, Vienna)

144

	Kleine Dreigroschenmusik for wind (Universal Edition, Vienna) *Das Berliner Requiem*, cantata on poems by Bertolt Brecht (vocal score: Universal Edition, Vienna)
1929	*Der Lindberghflug* (Der Ozeanflug), radio cantata on a text by Bertolt Brecht (vocal score: Universal Edition, Vienna) *Aufstieg und Fall der Stadt Mahagonny* (The Rise and Fall of the City of Mahagonny), opera in three acts on a libretto by Bertolt Brecht (vocal score: Universal Edition, Vienna) *Happy End*, comedy with music on a text by Elisabeth Hauptmann and Dorothy Lane. Songs by Bertolt Brecht (Universal Edition, Vienna) *Petroleuminseln*, incidental music for a stage play (unpublished)
1930	*Der Jasager*, school opera in two acts on a libretto by Bertolt Brecht (Universal Edition, Vienna) *Mann ist Mann*, incidental music for a play (lost)
1931	*Die Bürgschaft*, opera in three acts on a libretto by Caspar Neher (vocal score: Universal Edition, Vienna)
1932	*Der Silbersee*, a play with music by Georg Kaiser (vocal score: Universal Edition, Vienna)
1933	*Der Sieben Todsünden der Kleinbürger* (The Seven Deadly Sins of the Bourgeoisie), ballet by Bertolt Brecht (Universal Edition, Vienna)
1934	Symphony No. 2 (Schotts Söhne, Mainz) *Marie Galante*, a play with music by Jacques Deval (songs published by Heugel et Cie, Paris)
1935	*Der Kuhhandel*, comic operetta on a play by Robert Vaubery (two songs published by Chappell and Co., New York) *The Eternal Road*, dramatic oratorio on a text by Franz Werfel (vocal score: Heugel et Cie, Paris)
1936	*Johnny Johnson*, a musical play by Paul Green (vocal score: Samuel French, New York)
1938	*Knickerbocker Holiday*, musical comedy by Maxwell Anderson (vocal score: De Sylva, Brown and Henderson)
1939	*Railroads on Parade*, dramatic pageant (unpublished) *Ballad of Magna Carta*, cantata (vocal score: Chappell and Co., New York)
1941	*Lady in the Dark*, a musical play by Moss Hart, lyrics by Ira Gershwin (Chappell and Co., New York)
1942	*Three Walt Whitman Songs* (Chappell and Co., New York)
1943	*One Touch of Venus*, a musical comedy by S J Perelman and Ogden Nash (songs published by Chappell and Co., New York)
1945	*The Firebrand of Florence*, musical play by Edwin Justus Meyer, lyrics by Ira Gershwin (songs published by Chappell and Co., New York)

1946	*Kiddush* for cantor, chorus and organ (published in 'Synagogue music by contemporary composers', Schirmer, New York)
1947	*Street Scene*, an American opera by Elmer Rice, lyrics by Langston Hughes (Chappell and Co., New York)
1948	*Down in the Valley*, a folk opera by Arnold Sundgard (vocal score: Schirmer, New York) *Love Life*, a vaudeville by Alan J Lerner (songs published by Chappell and Co., New York)
1949	*Lost in the Stars*, a musical tragedy based on Alan Paton's 'Cry, the Beloved Country' by Maxwell Anderson (vocal score: Chappell and Co., New York)
1950	*Huckleberry Finn*, unfinished musical play by Maxwell Anderson (five completed songs published by Chappell and Co., New York)

DISCOGRAPHY

At present most of the recordings of Weill's music are of the most popular of the works which he wrote in collaboration with Bertolt Brecht; there are, therefore, no available recordings of *Die Bürgschaft*, *The Protagonist*, *Der neue Orpheus*, *Royal Palace*, *Der Zar lässt sich photographieren*, *Der Jasager* or *Der Ozeanflug*.

Of the popular Brecht-Weill works there exist complete, but rather old, recordings of *The Rise and Fall of the City of Mahagonny* (R77341) *The Threepenny Opera* (R78279) and *Happy End* (R73453) conducted by W. Bruckner-Ruggenberg and with a cast that includes Lotte Lenya. There are also fascinating historic recordings (made in 1930) of excerpts from these three works sung by the original cast, played by the Lewis-Ruth Band and conducted by the original conductor Theo Mackeben on AJ 641911.

The most representative selection of Weill's European music is to be found on the Deutsche Grammophon recording of the London Sinfonietta conducted by David Atherton. This boxed set includes the Violin Concerto, the *Berlin Requiem*, *Vom Tod im Wald*, the *Kleine Dreigroschenmusik*, the first Pantomime from *The Protagonist* and the *Mahagonny Songspiel* (DGG 2740-153). A further performance of the *Mahagonny Songspiel* with the Jerusalem Symphony Orchestra conducted by Lukas Foss can be found on Turnabout TV 34675. A recording of *The Seven Deadly Sins* sung by Lotte Lenya and conducted by W. Bruckner-Ruggenberg can be found on R73657.

A recent recording of the New York City Opera's version of *Der Silbersee* appears on Nonesuch DB 79003.

Of Weill's early, that is to say pre-Brecht works, there are recordings of the *Quodlibet* op 9 (played by the Westphalian Symphony Orchestra conducted by Siegfried Landau on TV 37124) and the First Symphony (in two performances: one by the BBC Symphony Orchestra conducted by Bertini on ZRG 755, one by the Leipzig Gewandhaus under Edo de Wart on 6500-642) in addition to the Sinfonietta performance of the Violin Concerto mentioned above. Both recordings of the First Symphony couple it with performances of the Second Symphony by the same artists.

Of Weill's American works there are in existence old, in most cases the original, recordings of *One Touch of Venus* (with Mary Martin, conducted by Maurice Abravanel on Decca DL 79122) and *Lost in the Stars* (DL71920). Selections from *Lady in the Dark*, sung by Gertrude Lawrence, are coupled with a version of *Down in the Valley* conducted by Peter Adler on RCA LPV-503. A complete performance of *Down in the Valley*, conducted by Maurice Levine, can be found on Decca DL 74239.

BIBLIOGRAPHY

BOOKS

Appignanesi, L *The Cabaret* (Studio Vista, London 1975)
Atkinson, B *Broadway* (Cassell, London 1971)
Bullock, A *Hitler: A Study in Tyranny* (Penguin Books, London 1969)
Carter, E *The Writings of Elliot Carter* (ed. by E and K Stone) (Indiana University Press, Bloomington/London 1977)
Dent, E J *Ferruccio Busoni* (E Eulenberg, London-reprinted 1974)
Drew, D (ed.) *Über Kurt Weill* (Suhrkamp taschenbuch, Frankfurt 1975)
Drummond, A *American Opera Libretti* (Scarecrow Press, New Jersey 1973)
Eisler, Hanns *A Rebel in Music* (ed. M Gruber) (Seven Seals Publications, Berlin 1978)
Ewen, F *Bertolt Brecht* (Calder & Boyars, London 1967)
Eyck, E *A History of the Weimar Republic* (Oxford University Press, Harvard University Press 1964)
Friedrich, O *Before the Deluge* (Michael Joseph, London 1974)
Gay, P *Weimar Culture* (Penguin Books, London 1974)
Gershwin, I *Lyrics On Several Occasions* (Hamish Hamilton, London 1977)
Green, S *The Encyclopedia of Musicals* (Cassell, London 1977)
Hamilton, George Heard *Painting and Sculpture in Europe 1880-1940* (Penguin Books, London 1972)
Heinsheimer, H W *Fanfare for Two Pigeons* (Doubleday & Co., New York 1951)
Heinsheimer, H W *Menagerie in F Sharp* (T V Boardman & Co., New York 1949)
Hitchcock, Henry Russell *Architecture: Nineteenth and Twentieth Centuries* (Penguin Books, London 1971)
Innes, C D *Erwin Piscator's Political Theatre* (Cambridge University Press, 1972)
Jackson, A *The Book of Musicals* (Mitchell Beazley, London 1979)
Kemp, Ian *Paul Hindemith* (Oxford University Press, 1970)
Marx, H (ed.) *Weill-Lenya* (Goethe House, New York 1976)
Milhaud, D *Notes without Music* (Alfred A Knopf, New York 1952)
Slonimsky, N *Music Since 1900* (Cassell, London 1971 – 4th edition)
Thomson, V *Virgil Thomson* (Weidenfeld & Nicholson, London 1967)
Walter, B *Theme and Variations* (trans. J A Galston) (Hamish Hamilton, London 1947)
Weill, K *Ausgewählte Schriften* (ed. D Drew) (Suhrkamp Verlag, Franfurt 1975)
Willett, J *The Theatre of Erwin Piscator* (Eyre Methuen, London 1978)
Willett, J (ed.) *Brecht on Theatre* (Eyre Methuen, London 1978)
Zweig, S *The World of Yesterday* (Cassell, London 1943)

BIBLIOGRAPHY

ARTICLES

Adam, P 'Lotte Lenya: September Song' *The Listener* 24 May 1979, pp 707-9

Aufricht, E J 'Die Morität vom Mackie Messer' *Melos* November 1966, pp 359-63

Branscombe, P 'Brecht, Weill and *Mahagonny*' *Musical Times* No 102, August 1961, p 483

Downes, O 'Musical Sociology' *New York Times* 4 April 1954, sect. 2, p 7

Drew, D 'Brecht versus opera' *Score* No 23, July 1958, pp 7-10

Drew, D 'Happy End' notes to CBS record 73463

Drew, D 'The History of *Mahagonny*' *Musical Times* January 1963, pp 18-24

Drew, D 'Kurt Weill', notes to DGG record 2740 153

Drew, D 'Kurt Weill and his critics' *The Times Literary Supplement* 3 and 10 October 1975, pp 1142-1198

Drew, D 'Music Theatre in the Weimar Republic' *Proceedings of the Royal Musical Association, vol 88 1962*

Drew, D 'Topicality and the Universal' *Music and Letters* No 39, July 1958, pp 242-55

Drew, D 'Two Weill Scores' *Musical Times* No 107, September 1966, pp 797-8

Drew, D 'Symphony 1' preface to published score, Universal Edition, Vienna

Drew, D 'Symphony 2' preface to published score, Universal Edition, Vienna

Drew, D 'Weill's School Opera' *Musical Times* No 106, December 1964, pp 897-9

East, L 'A Festival of Weill' *Music & Musicians* March 1977, pp 36-40

Engelmann, H U 'Kurt Weill-heute' *Darmstadter Beträge* No 3, 1960, pp 87-95

Helm, E 'Weill's *Bürgschaft*' *Saturday Review* No 40, 16 November 1957, pp 35-9

Hewes, H 'The Theatre' *Saturday Review* No 55, 6 May 1972, pp 64-5

Horowitz, J 'Lotte Lenya recalls Weill's "Street Scene"' *New York Times* 26 October, 1979

Kemp, I 'Harmony in Weill: Some Observations' *Tempo* 10 April, 1973, pp 11-15

Kemp, I 'Symphony 1' notes to record ZRG 755

Koegler, H 'Kurt Weills amerikanische Bühnenwerke' *Melos* March 1956, pp 67-70

Lenya, L 'In conversation with Steven Paul', notes to DGG 2740 153

Padmore, E 'Kurt Weill' *Music & Musicians* October 1972, pp 34-40

Redlich, H 'Kurt Weill' *Music Review* 11 August 1950, p 208

Reinhardt, M 'Brecht und das musikalisches Theatre' *Musik und Bild* No 3 November 1971, pp 522-5

Weill, K 'Aktuelles Theater' *Melos* 37, July/August 1970, pp 276-7

Weinraub, B 'Lenya on Weill: The Memory Lingers On' *New York Times* 25 October, 1964

Other Sources:

For information on Weill's American career the following are useful sources:

Chronologies in the New York Goethe House's 'Weill-Lenya' produced as a booklet to accompany their 1976 exhibition in New York.

Kowalke's notes for the booklet of the 1979 New York City Opera production of *Street Scene*.

NOTES

CHAPTER 1

1 see Drew, David 'Introduction and Notes' in booklet accompanying the Weill Symphony No 1 (Argo ZRG 755)
2 *ibid.*
3 see Kastner, Rudolf *Weill und Busoni* reprinted in Drew, David (ed.) *Über Kurt Weill* (Suhrkamp Taschenbuch, Frankfurt 1975, p. 11)
4 see Drew, David 'First Symphony' in notes accompanying the Weill Symphony No 1 (Argo ZRG 755)
5 *ibid.*
6 Stuckenschmidt, H H *Ferruccio Busoni* (Calder & Boyars, London 1967, p. 178)
7 Dent, E J *Busoni* (E. Eulenberg, London 1974, p. 127)
8 Weill quoted in Stuckenschmidt, *op.cit.*, p. 196
9 *ibid.*
10 Wasserman, Jacob quoted in Stuckenschmidt, *op.cit.*, p. 63
11 Selden-Goth, Gisella quoted in Stuckenschmidt, *ibid.*, p. 64
12 Dent, E J *op.cit.*, p. 287
13 Kastner, Rudolf *op.cit.*, p. 10
14 see Drew, David 'First Symphony', *op.cit*
15 Heinsheimer, Hans *Menagerie in F Sharp* (T V Boardman & Co., New York 1949, p. 131)
16 *ibid.*
17 see Drew, David (ed.) *Vorwort* in *Kurt Weill: Ausgewählte Schriften* (Suhrkamp Verlag, Frankfurt 1975, p. 13)
18 Weill, Kurt *Der Protagonist* in *Kurt Weill; Ausgewählte Schriften*, *op.cit.*, p. 53
19 Lenya, Lotte 'In Conversation with Steven Paul' in booklet accompanying Kurt Weill, London Sinfonietta, DGG 2740-153
20 compiled from Lenya, Lotte *ibid.*, and Lenya, Lotte 'September Song' (*The Listener*, 24 May 1979, p. 707)
21 Lenya, Lotte, *ibid.*
22 Weill, Kurt *Meine Frau* in *Kurt Weill: Ausgewählte Schriften*, *op.cit.*, p. 9

CHAPTER 2

1 Zweig, Stefan *The World of Yesterday* (Cassell, London 1943, p. 298)
2 Walter, Bruno *Theme and Variations* (Hamish Hamilton, London 1947, p. 276)
3 Zweig, Stefan *op.cit.*, p. 312
4 Walter, Bruno *op.cit.*, p. 277
5 Zweig, Stefan *op.cit.*, p. 311
6 Bullock, Alan *Hitler: A Study in Tyranny* (Penguin Books, London 1969, pp. 90-1)
7 Zweig, Stefan *op.cit.*, p. 301
8 *ibid.*, p. 292
9 *ibid.*, p. 313
10 Kessler, Count Harry *Tagebücher 1918-1937* quoted in Friedrich, Otto *Before The Deluge* (Michael Joseph, London 1974, pp. 37, 51)
11 Zweig, Stefan *op.cit.*, p. 361
12 *ibid.*, p. 361
13 Lenya, Lotte 'In Conversation with Steven Paul' in programme booklet accompanying Kurt Weill, London Sinfonietta (DGG 2740-153, p. 8)

14 Walter, Bruno *op.cit.*, p. 296
15 Hulsenbeck, Richard *Die Dadaistische Bewegung. Eine Selbstbiographie*, quoted in Raabe, P *The Era of German Expressionism* (Calder & Boyars, London 1974, p. 352)
16 Piscator, Erwin 'The Proletarian Theatre: Its Fundamental Principles and Tasks'. First published in *Die Gegner*, October 1920; reprinted in translation in *Culture and Agitation: Theatre Documents*, Howard, Roger (ed.) (Action Books, London 1972, p. 42)
17 Hulsenbeck, Richard *op.cit.*, p. 352
18 Hindemith, Paul quoted in Kemp, Ian *Paul Hindemith* (Oxford University Press, 1970)
19 Eisler, Hanns 'Our Revolutionary Music' first published in *Illustrierte Rote Post*, March 1932, Berlin; reprinted in translation in *Hanns Eisler: A Rebel in Music* (Seven Seas Books, Berlin 1978, p. 59)
20 *ibid.*
21 Eisler, Hanns 'On Stupidity in Music' *ibid.*, p. 189
22 Willett, John *The Theatre of Bertolt Brecht* (Eyre Methuen, London 1967, 3rd edition, pp. 107-8)
23 Innes, C D *Erwin Piscator's Political Theatre* (Cambridge University Press, 1972, p. 30)
24 Piscator, Erwin 'New Red Stage' February 1932 quoted in Innes, *ibid.*, p. 31
25 Piscator, Erwin programme to *Hoppla, Wir Leben!* quoted in Innes, *ibid.*, p. 62
26 Innes, *ibid.*, p. 5
27 *ibid.*, p. 187
28 *ibid.*, p. 185
29 Vakhtangov quoted in Willett, *op.cit.*, pp. 111-2
30 Brecht, Bertolt letter to Piscator, March 1947 quoted in Innes, *op.cit.*, p. 198
31 *ibid.*, p. 198
32 *ibid.*, p. 25

CHAPTER 3

1 Heinsheimer, Hans *Menagerie in F Sharp* (T V Boardman & Co., New York 1949, p. 132)
2 Abravanel, Maurice *Le Protagoniste* reprinted in Drew, David (ed.) *Über Kurt Weill* (Suhrkamp Verlag, Frankfurt 1975, p. 18)
3 Heinsheimer, Hans *op.cit.*, p. 133
4 Heinsheimer, Hans *op.cit.*, p. 134, 136-7
5 Heinsheimer, Hans *op.cit.*, p. 137
6 Lenya, Lotte 'In Conversation with Steven Paul' in programme booklet for Kurt Weill (DGG 2740-153 p. 8)
7 quoted in Willett, John *Brecht on Theatre* (Eyre Methuen, London 1978, p. 86)
8 Weill, Kurt *Anmerkungen zu meiner Oper 'Mahagonny'* in Drew, David (ed.) *Kurt Weill: Ausgewählte Schriften* (Suhrkamp Verlag, Frankfurt 1975, p. 56)
9 Lenya, Lotte quoted in Friedrich, Otto *Before the Deluge* (Michael Joseph, London 1974, p. 262)
10 Drew, David 'The History of *Mahagonny*' (*Musical Times*, January 1963, p. 18)
11 Lenya, Lotte quoted in Friedrich, *op.cit.*, p. 262
12 Lenya, Lotte quoted in Padmore, Elaine 'Kurt Weill' (*Music & Musicians*, October 1972, pp. 35-6)
13 Friedrich, Otto *Before the Deluge*, *op.cit.*, p. 268
14 Aufricht, E J *Die Morität vom Mackie Messer* (*Melos* 33, p. 359)

15 Lenya, Lotte quoted in Friedrich *op.cit.*, p. 265
16 see Aufricht, E J *op.cit.*, pp. 359-63
17 Heinsheimer, Hans *op.cit.*, p. 138
18 *ibid.*, p. 140
19 Lenya, Lotte quoted in Freidrich *op.cit.*, p. 270
20 Heinsheimer, Hans *op.cit.*, p. 140
21 Lenya, Lotte quoted in Friedrich *op.cit.*, p. 140
22 Heinsheimer, Hans *op.cit.*, p. 139
23 *ibid.*, p. 134
24 Lenya, Lotte quoted in Friedrich *op.cit.*, p. 271
25 quoted in Willett, John *op.cit.*, p. 85
26 Lenya, Lotte 'In Conversation with Steven Paul', *op.cit.*, p. 8
27 Heinsheimer, Hans *op.cit.*, pp. 146-7
28 Weill, Kurt *Notiz zum Berliner Requiem* in Drew, David (ed.)
   Kurt Weill: Ausgewählte Schriften (Suhrkamp Verlag, Frankfurt 1975, p. 139)
29 Brecht, Bertolt 'An Example of Pedagogics' in Willett, John *op.cit.*, p. 31
30 *ibid.*, p. 32
31 see Drew, David 'The History of *Mahagonny*', *op.cit.*, pp. 18-20
32 see Drew, David 'Notes to *Happy End*' accompanying *Happy End* recording
   (CBS 73463)
33 Lenya, Lotte quoted in Adam, Peter 'September Song' (*The Listener*, 24 May
   1979, p. 707)
34 Lenya, Lotte 'In Conversation with Steven Paul', *op.cit.*, p. 19
35 see Drew, David 'Notes to *Happy End*', *op.cit*

CHAPTER 4

1 Weill, Kurt *Über meine Schuloper 'Der Jasager'* reprinted in Drew, David (ed.) *Kurt Weill: Ausgewählte Schriften* (Suhrkamp Verlag, Frankfurt 1975, pp. 61-3)
2 see Drew, David 'Weill's School Opera' (*Musical Times*, No 106, December 1964, p. 934)
3 Heinsheimer, Hans *Fanfare for Two Pigeons* (Doubleday & Co., New York 1954, p. 177)
4 see Drew, David *op.cit.*, p. 935
5 Warschauer, Frank 'Die Weltbühne' 8 July 1930, quoted in Ewen, Frederic *Bertolt Brecht* (Calder & Boyars, London 1967, p. 247)
6 Heinsheimer, Hans *Menagerie in F Sharp* (T V Boardman & Co., New York 1949, p. 174)
7 *ibid.*
8 *ibid.*, p. 173
9 *ibid.*, p. 175
10 Lenya, Lotte quoted in Friedrich, Otto *Before The Deluge* (Michael Joseph, London 1974, p. 328)
11 Lenya, Lotte 'September Song' (*The Listener*, 24 May 1979, p. 707)
12 Brecht, Bertolt reprinted in Willett, John *Brecht on Theatre* (Eyre Methuen, London 1978, p. 87)
13 Lenya, Lotte 'September Song' (*The Listener*, 24 May 1979, p. 708)
14 Völker, Klaus *Brecht: A Biography* (Calder & Boyars, London 1979, p. 59)
15 Willett, John *The Theatre of Bertolt Brecht* (Eyre Methuen, London 1967, 3rd edition, p. 156)

16 Brecht, Bertolt *Diaries 1920-1922* (Eyre Methuen, London 1979, p. 65)
17 *ibid.*
18 anonymous review, 9 March 1932, reprinted in Drew, David (ed.) *Über Kurt Weill*
     (Suhrkamp Taschenbuch, Frankfurt 1975, p. 77)
19 Zweig, Stefan *The World of Yesterday* (Cassell, London 1943, p. 361)
20 Bullock, Alan *Hitler: A Study in Tyranny* (Penguin Books, London 1962, p. 213)
21 *ibid.*
22 'L. St.' 20 February 1933 reprinted in Drew, David (ed.) *Über Kurt Weill, op.cit.*,
     p. 108
23 *Volkischer Beobachter* 24 February 1933, reprinted in *ibid.*, pp. 110-11
24 Milhaud, Darius *Notes without Music* (Alfred A Knopf, New York 1952, p. 236)
25 Vuillermoz, Émile *Candide* 15 December 1932, reprinted in Drew, David (ed.)
     Über Kurt Weill, op.cit., p. 101
26 More, Marcel *La Politique* 1932 reprinted in *ibid.*, p. 98
27 Mehring, Walter 1933 reprinted in *ibid.*, p. 118)
28 Kessler, Count Harry *Tagebücher* reprinted in *ibid.*, p. 18
29 Huth, Anno *Der Weg der Verheissung* reprinted in *ibid.*, p. 122

CHAPTER 5

1 Lenya, Lotte 'September Song' (*The Listener* 24 May 1979, p. 708)
2 Atkinson, Brook *Broadway* (Cassell, London 1971, p. 342)
3 *ibid.*
4 *ibid.*
5 Weinraub, Bernard 'Lenya on Weill: The Memory Lingers On' (*New York Times*,
    25 October 1964, 114:17 section 2)
6 see Drew, David 'Two Weill Scores' (*Musical Times*, September 1966, p. 798)
7 see Drew, David 'Kurt Weill and His Critics – 2' (*Times Literary Supplement*
    10 October 1975, p. 1198)
8 Weill, Kurt 'Lunch Time Follies' reprinted in Drew, David (ed.) *Kurt Weill,
    Ausgewählte Schriften* (Surhkamp Verlag, Frankfurt 1975, p. 87)
9 see Willett, John *The Theatre of Erwin Piscator* (Eyre Methuen, London 1978,
    p. 153)
10 Carter, Elliot *The Writings of Elliot Carter* (Indiana University Press, Bloomington
     1977, p. 95)
11 Drew, David 'Two Weill Scores', *op.cit.*, p. 789
12 Weill, Kurt 'A Musical Play About New York' reprinted in *Weill-Lenya* (Goethe
     House, New York 1976)
13 Lenya, Lotte quoted in Horowitz 'Lotte Lenya Recalls Weill's *Street Scene*' (*New
     York Times*, 26 October 1979)
14 *ibid.*
15 Downes Olin, quoted in Kowalke, Kim '*Street Scene*: A Broadway Opera'
     New York City Opera Playbill, 1979, p. 51
16 Weill, Kurt quoted in Drummond, Andrew H *American Opera Librettos*
     (Scarecrow Press Inc., Metuchen, New Jersey 1973, p. 107)
17 Heinsheimer, Hans *Menagerie in F Sharp* (T V Boardman & Co., New York 1949,
     p. 130)
18 Atkinson, Brook *New York Times* 6 November 1949, quoted in Drummond,
     Andrew H, *op.cit.*, p. 103
19 Barnes, Howard *New York Herald Tribune* 31 October 1949, quoted in
     Drummond, Andrew H, *ibid.*

20 Gibbs, Woolcott *New Yorker* 12 November 1949, quoted in Drummond, Andrew H, *ibid.*

21 Hewes, Henry *Saturday Review* 6 May 1972, p. 64

CHAPTER 6

1 Dallapiccola, Luigi, *Incontro con Anton Webern* Florence 1945, quoted in Moldenhauer, Hans *Anton Von Webern: A Chronicle of His Life and Work* (Gollancz, London 1978, p. 537)

2 *ibid.*

3 see Drew, David *First Symphony* notes accompanying Argo ZRG 755

4 Weill, Kurt 'Schoenberg: *Pierrot Lunaire*' reprinted in Drew, David (ed.) *Kurt Weill: Ausgewählte Schriften* (Suhrkamp Verlag, Frankfurt 1975, p. 124)

5 Weill, Kurt 'Arnold Schoenberg' reprinted in *ibid.*, pp. 119-20

6 Weill, Kurt 'Alban Berg: *Wozzeck*' reprinted in *ibid.*, p. 154

7 see Weill, Kurt 'Gustav Mahler: Symphony IX' reprinted in *ibid.*, pp. 121-2

8 see Drew, David 'After the First Symphony' notes accompanying Argo ZRG 755

9 Weill, Kurt, *Busoni und die neuen Musik* reprinted in Drew, David (ed.) *Kurt Weill: Ausgewählte Schriften, op.cit.*, pp. 20-1)

10 Dent, Edward *Ferruccio Busoni* (E Eulenberg, London 1974, p. 280 – reprint)

11 *ibid.*, p. 281

12 *ibid.*

13 Busoni, Ferruccio 'Young Classicism' *Frankfurter Zeitung*, 1920

14 see Kemp, Ian *Second Symphony* notes accompanying Argo ZRG 755

CHAPTER 7

1 see Drew, David 'Music Theatre in the Weimar Republic' *Proceedings of the Royal Musical Association* vol. 88 1962

2 'Interview with an Exile' reprinted in Willett, John *Brecht on Theatre* (Eyre Methuen, London 1978, p. 65)

3 *ibid.*, p. 86

4 Friedrich, Otto *Before the Deluge* (Michael Joseph, London 1974, p. 261)

5 *ibid.*

6 Brecht, Bertolt 'The Epic Theatre and Its Difficulties' in Willett, John *op.cit.*, p. 23

7 see Brecht, Bertolt 'The Modern Theatre is the Epic Theatre' in Willett, John, *ibid.*, pp. 33-42

8 see Dent, E. J. *Ferruccio Busoni* (E Eulenberg, London 1974, p. 305)

9 Busoni, Ferrucio 'Young Classicism' letter to *Melos* quoted in Slonimsky, N *Music Since 1900* (Cassell, London, 1971, fourth edition, p. 351)

10 Dent, E J *op.cit.*, p. 297

11 Weill, Kurt *Bekenntnis zur Oper* reprinted in Drew, David (ed.) *Kurt Weill: Ausgewählte Schriften* (Suhrkamp Verlag, Frankfurt 1975, p. 30)

12 Weill, Kurt *Busonis Faust und die Erneuerung der Operform*, reprinted in Drew, David, *ibid.*, pp. 31-2

13 *ibid.*, p. 31

14 *ibid.*, p. 32

15 Weill, Kurt *Aktuelles Theater*, reprinted in Drew, David, *ibid.*, pp. 48-9

16 this passage in *Der Protagonist* is discussed in detail in David Drew's 'Music Theatre in the Weimar Republic', *op.cit.*, pp. 98-9

17 Bie, Oskar *Der Protagonist* reprinted in Drew, David (ed.) *Über Kurt Weill* (Suhrkamp Taschenbuch, Frankfurt 1975, p. 15)

18 Abravanel, Maurice *Der Protagonist*, reprinted in Drew, David, *ibid.*, p. 18

19 Adorno, T W *Protagonist und Zar* reprinted in Drew, David, *ibid.*, p. 26

20 Stobel, Heinrich 'Kurt Weill 1920-27, reprinted in Drew, David, *ibid.*, p. 28

21 Weill, Kurt *Der Protagonist* reprinted in Drew,. David (ed.) *Kurt Weill: Ausgewählte Schriften, op,cit.*, p. 52

22 Drew, David 'The History of *Mahagonny' Musical Times*, January 1963, p. 18

23 Weill, Kurt *Aktuelles Theater* reprinted in Drew, David (ed.) *Kurt Weill: Ausgewählte Schriften, op.cit.*, p. 46

24 Weill, Kurt *Tanzmusik, Jazz* reprinted in Drew, David *ibid.*, pp. 132-3

25 Weill, Kurt *Notiz zum Jazz* reprinted in Drew, David, *ibid.*, pp. 132-3

26 Weill, Kurt *Notiz zum Berliner Requiem* reprinted in Drew, David, *ibid.*, pp. 139-40

27 Heinsheimer, Hans *Fanfare for Two Pigeons* (Doubleday & Co., New York 1954, p. 177)

28 Weill, Kurt *Aktuelles Zweigespräch über die Schuloper* reprinted in Drew, David (ed.) *Kurt Weill: Ausgewählte Schriften, op.cit.*, p. 67)

29 Adorno T W quoted in Drew, David 'The History of *Mahagonny', op.cit.*, pp. 21-2

30 Ewen, Frederic *Bertolt Brecht: His Life, His Art and His Times* (Calder & Boyars, London 1970, p. 113)

31 *ibid.*

32 Brecht, Bertolt quoted in Ewen, Frederick, *ibid.*, p. 66

33 from Feuchtwanger, 'Success' quoted in Ewen, Frederic, *ibid.*, p. 90

34 Adorno, T W *Zur Musik der Dreigroschenoper* reprinted in Drew, David (ed.) *Über Kurt Weill, op.cit.*, p. 42

35 Cocteau, Jean *Le Coq et L'Arlequin* translated by Myers, R (Egoist Press, Paris 1921)

36 Kemp, Ian 'Harmony in Weill: Some Observations' *Tempo* no. 104, 1973, p. 11

37 Kemp, Ian 'Second Symphony' notes accompanying recording of Weill's symphonies on Argo ZRG 755

38 Adorno, T W *Zur Musik der Dreigroschenoper* in Drew, David (ed.) *Über Kurt Weill, op.cit.*, pp. 39-44

39 Ewen, Frederic *op.cit.*, pp. 185-6

40 Drew, David 'Weill's School Opera' *Musical Times* no. 106, December 1964, p. 934

41 see Drew, David 'Topicality and the Universal: The Strange Case of Weill's *Die Bürgschaft, Music and Letters*, vol. 39, July 1958, pp. 242-55

42 see Drew, David, 'Weill's School Opera', *op.cit.*, p. 899

43 Weill, Kurt *Busonis Faust und die Erneuerung der Operform* reprinted in Drew, David (ed.) *Kurt Weill: Ausgewählte Schriften, op.cit.*, p. 35

CHAPTER 8

1 see Drew, David 'Two Weill Scores' *Musical Times*, September 1966, p. 798

2 Heyworth, Peter (ed.) *Conversations with Otto Klemperer* (Gollancz, London 1973, p. 64)

3 Weill, Kurt *Der Protagonist* reprinted in Drew, David (ed.) *Kurt Weill: Ausgewählte Schriften* (Suhrkamp Verlag, Frankfurt 1975, p. 53)

4 Weill, Kurt quoted in Kowalke's '*Street Scene*: A Broadway Opera' New York City Opera programme booklet, October 1979, p. 50

5 Hughes, Langston *My Collaboration with Kurt Weill* reprinted in German translation in Drew, David (ed.) *Über Kurt Weill* (Suhrkamp Taschenbuch, Frankfurt 1975, pp. 141-5)

6 Weill, Kurt 'A Musical Play About New York' reprinted in Marx, Henry (ed.) *Weill-Lenya* (Goethe House, New York, 1976)

7 Lenya, Lotte quoted in Horowitz, Joseph 'Lotte Lenya Recalls Weill's '*Street Scene*' *New York Times* 26 October 1979

8 Weill, Kurt 'The Future of Opera in America' quoted in Kowalke, *op.cit.*, p. 48

9 Thomson, Virgil *New York Tribune*, 9 April 1950

10 Chase, Gilbert 'America's music from the Pilgrims to the Present' quoted in Drummond *American Opera Librettos* (Scarecrow Press Inc., Metuchen, New Jersey 1973, p. 29)

11 Drew, David 'Two Weill Scores', *op.cit.*, p. 789

12 *ibid.*

13 see Lenya, Lotte 'September Song' *The Listener*, 24 May 1979, p. 708

14 see Horowitz, *op.cit.*

15 see Thomson, Virgil, *op.cit.*

16 Weill, Kurt letter to *Life Magazine* reprinted in Marx, Henry (ed.), *op.cit.*

17 Lenya, Lotte in Horowitz, *op.cit.*

18 Irwin Lew, Beth *George Grosz: Art and Politics in the Weimar Republic* (University of Wisconsin Press, Madison/London 1971, p. 233)

19 Lenya, Lotte 'September Song', *op.cit.*, p. 708

ACKNOWLEDGEMENTS

The publishers would like to thank the following for the loan of photographs and other illustrative material used in this book.

Akademie du Künste, Bertolt Brecht Archiv, Berlin-DDR.

BBC Hulton Picture Library.

Norman Bel Geddes Collection, Hoblitzelle Theatre Arts Library: Humanities Research Centre, University of Texas at Austin, by permission of the Executrix of the Norman Bel Geddes estate, Mrs Edith Lutyens Bel Geddes.

Bettman Archive Inc., New York.

Bildarchiv Preussischer Kulterbesitz, Berlin.

Casparius Collection, London.

Culver Pictures Inc., New York.

George Grosz Estate, Princeton, New Jersey.

Hoblitzelle Theatre Arts Library: Humanities Research Centre, University of Texas at Austin.

Robert Hunt Library, London.

Keystone, London.

Lichtbildwerkstatte Alpenland, Vienna.

Kugal Meyer – New York Public Library.

Photo Library Collection, Museum of City of New York.

Popperphoto, London.

The Post.

The Billy Rose Theatre Collection, New York Public Library.

Alison and Peter Smithson.

Springer/Bettman Film Archive, New York.

Maria Steinfeldt, Berlin-DDR.

Theatermuseum des Institute für Theaterwissenschaft der Universität Köln.

Theatre Collection, Museum of City of New York.

Ullstein, Berlin.

Universal Edition A. G., Vienna.

Roger Viollet, Paris.

Wilde World Photos, New York.

INDEX

Abravanel, Maurice 18, 39, 68, 69, 74, 78, 103, 121
Academy of Art, Berlin 14-15
Adorno, T W 78, 103, 112, 114, 122-3
Aktuelles Theater 107-8
'Alabama Song' 7, 42, 115-19
Allen, Charles 75
Anderson, Maxwell 74, 75, 77, 82, 83
Arrau, Claudio 18
Article on Jazz 109
Atkinson, Brook 73
Aufricht, Ernst Robert 43-5, 51, 64, 78
Aufstieg und Fall der Stadt Mahagonny, der 42-3, 50-1, 57-60, 63-4, 104, 106, 112, 115-21, 122-3, 125-6, 129; *see also* Mahagonny

Baden-Baden Music Festival 41-3
'Ballets 1933, Les' 68
Beggars Opera, see Dreigroschenoper
Bel Geddes, Norman 71
'Benares Song' 119-21
Berg, Alban 90
Berlin Neue Musik 1930 Festival 56
Berlin Requiem 49, 110-11, 121-2, 123, 128
Bie, Oskar 103
Bing, Albert 14
Bloomgarten, Kermit 77
Book of Poverty and Death 17
Brecht, Bertolt 9, 35, 37, 41-6, 49, 50, 51-2, 55, 56, 59-62, 68, 77-8, 96-9, 113
Bullock, Alan 27, 66
Bürgschaft, die 62, 64, 129, 130
Busch, Ernst 37
Busch, Fritz 18, 39
Busoni, Ferruccio 14-18, 91-3, 99-100, 101

Cabaret 37, 113
Carter, Elliot 78-9
Cellow Sonata, *see* Sonata
Chase, Gilbert 137
Cocteau, Jean 115
Common Glory, The 74
Concerto, Violin 8, 89, 93
    Violin and wind band 19
'Crane Duet' 51, 59

Dada 30, 33
Dallapiccola, Luigi 87

Dancemusic: Jazz 108-9
Darrieux, Marcel 19
Debussy, Claude 122
Dent, Edward 15, 100
Dessau Opera House 14
Deutsche Rundfunk, der 18, 110
Divertimento 17, 90, 92
Doktor Faust 100, 101, 129-30
Down in the Valley 80, 133, 134-5, 138
Downes, Olin 81
Dreigroschenoper, die 7, 18, 44-8, 65, 72, 96, 106, 111-12, 113, 114, 123, 124, 125, 142
Dresden State Opera 39
Drew, David 9, 42, 56-7, 67, 75, 79, 90-1, 97, 106, 127, 129, 132, 138

Ebert, Carl 64, 65
Ebert, Friedrich 23-4
Eisler, Professor Hanns 34-5, 56, 60
Engel, Erich 45
Eternal Road, see Weg der Verheissung
Ewen, Frederic 112, 125
Expressionism 32, 35, 91

Felix Mendelssohn Foundation 14
Firebrand of Florence, The 79, 80, 133-4
First Symphony, *see* Symphony
Flug der Lindberghs, der 49, 123, 129
Frauentanz 17, 92, 93
Friedrich, Otto 98

Gebrauchsmusik 34, 135
Gershwin, George 72
Gershwin, Ira 76
Gielen, Josef 39
Goldwyn Follies 76
Goll, Ivan 20-1, 36, 105
Good Soldier Schweyk, The 78
Good Woman of Setzuan, The 78
Green, Paul 72, 74
Grosz, George 27, 141
Group Theatre of New York 72-3
Gustav II 43

Happy End 51-2, 113, 123, 124-5
Hardt, Ernest 14
Hart, Moss 76, 77
Hartlaub, Gustav 34
Hauptmann, Elisabeth 44, 51, 52

Hauptmann, F A 66
Hauspostille 42, 43, 49
Heinsheimer, Hans 17, 39, 40, 45, 48, 57-8, 81-2
Hertzka, Emil 17, 39, 48
Herzog von Gothland 40
Hewes, Henry 83
Hindemith, Professor Paul 34, 49
Howard, Sidney 76
Huckleberry Finn 83, 137
Hughes, Langston 136
Hulsenbeck, Richard 33
Humperdinck, Engelbert 14
Hungerford, Edward 76
Huth, Arno 69

Innes, C D 36
International Society for Contemporary Music (ISCM) 19
Irving, Washington 74

Jasager, der 49, 55-7, 67, 111, 123, 128, 129, 130
Jazz 106-9, 126-7
'Jealousy Duet' 112
Jessner, Leopold 36, 43
Johnny Johnson 72, 73, 133, 134, 136

Kaiser, Georg 18-20, 41, 66
Kastner, Rudolf 16
Katalaunische Schlacht 43
Kazan, Elia 78, 82
Kemp, Ian 115
Kessler, Count Harry 29, 69
Kestenberg, Leo 14, 57, 65
Kiddush 140
Kingdom for a Cow, see Kuhhandel
Kleine Dreigroschenmusik 49
Klemperer, Otto 133
Knickerbocker Holiday 74, 75, 133, 134
Koch, Friedrich 14
Konjunktur 43
Krasselt, Rudolf 14
Kuhhandel, der 70

Lady in the Dark 75, 76, 133-4, 136
Lane, Dorothy 52
Lenya, Lotte 19, 21, 31, 41, 42-3, 48, 52, 58, 59, 60, 69, 70, 75, 136, 139, 141
Lerner, Alan Jay 82
Lewis, Beth Irwin 141
Lindbergh Flight, see Flug der Lindberghs

Loch, Tilly 69
Logan, Joshua 74
Lost in the Stars 82-3, 133, 134, 136
Love Life 82, 133
Lüdenscheid 14
'Lunchtime Follies' 77, 135

'Mack the Knife' 7, 44
Mackeben, Theo 45
MacLeish, Archibald 77
Madam Will You Walk 76
Magna Carta 75, 140
'*Mahagonny* Notes' 42, 98, 99, 101
Mahagonny opera, *see Aufstieg und Fall der Stadt Mahagonny*
Mahagonny Songspiel 33, 41-3, 67, 70, 96, 106, 113, 124
Mahler, Gustav 90
'Maiden's Prayer' 112
Mamoulian, Rouben 83
Manhattan Opera House, New York 71-2
Marie Galante 70
Massnahme, die 56, 60
Mehring, Walter 69
Meyer, Edwin J 79
Milhaud, Darius 67
More, Marcel 68
'*Moritat*' *see* '*Mack the Knife*'
Mussorgsky, Modest 121-2

Na und . . . 40, 106
Nash, Ogden 78
Nazism 30, 63, 65, 67
Neher, Caspar 42, 61, 64, 69
Neinsager, der 57
Neo-classicism 92-3, 114-15
Neue Orpheus, der 20-1, 40, 104
Neue Sachlichkeit 34
New Objectivity, *see* Neue Sachlichkeit
New Opheus, see Neue Orpheus
Nino de Lenclos 14
No-Sayer, see Neinsager
Novembergrüppe 17, 32, 110

Ocean Flight, see Flug der Lindberghs
On the Gestic Character of Music 101
One the Use of Music in an Epic Theatre 41, 47-8, 59, 97-8
One Touch of Venus 78-9, 133-4
Ozeanflug, see Flug der Lindberghs

Perelman, S J 78
Petroleuminseln, die 49
Pierrot Lunaire 89-90
Piscator, Erwin 35-7, 43, 77-8
Playwrights' Company 74, 75, 83
Pledge, The, see Bürgschaft, die
Polignac, Princesse Edmonde de 68
Protagonist, The 19, 20, 39, 93, 96, 102-4, 121

Quodlibet 17, 92, 93

Railroads on Parade 76
Recordare 17
Reinhardt, Max 36, 70, 71
Rice, Elmer 73, 80
Rilke, Rainer Maria 14, 17, 20, 88
Rise and Fall of the City of Mahagonny, see Aufstieg und Fall der Stadt Mahagonny
Rome, Harald 77
Rose, Billy 81
Royal Palace 40, 41, 104, 106

Salzburg Festival 17
Schilflieder 13
Schoenberg, Arnold 88-90
Schreker, Franz 91
'September Song' 7, 74-5
Seven Deadly Sins of the Bourgeoisie, The 68-9, 70, 121, 123-4, 127, 131
Silbersee, Der 66-7
Sinfonia Sacra 17, 91, 92
Six, Les 115
Sonata, Cello 14
Song of the Free; Recitations 77
Stiedry, Fritz 64
Stines, Hugo 28
Straram, Walter 19, 67
Strasberg, Lee 73
Stravinsky, Igor 114
Street Scene 73, 80-1, 133, 134, 136-7
String Quartet in B minor 14
Op 8 17, 92, 93
Strobel, Heinrich 103
Studenbuch 17

Sudermann, Hermann 15
Sundgaard, Arnold 80
'Surabaya Johnny' 7
Symphony, First 8, 16, 88-9, 90-1, 92
Second 68, 69, 70, 94-5
Szigeti, Joseph 19

Thomson, Virgil 136, 137, 139
Threepenny Opera, see Dreigroschenoper
Tonality 92

Ulysses Africanus 75
Universal Edition 17-18, 48, 51, 67

Violin Concerto, *see* Concerto
Vom Tod im Wald 43, 49
Vuillermoz, Émile 68

Wagner, Richard 91
Walt Whitman Songs 77
Walter, Bruno 26, 27, 31, 70
Way of the Promise, see Weg der Verheissung
Webern, Anton 87
Weg der Verheissung, der 70, 71, 73, 90, 133, 140
Weill, Albert 13
Weill, Emma 13
Weise von Liebe und Tod des Cornets Christopher Rilke, die 14
Werfel, Franz 70
Where Do We Go from Here 80
Willett, John 35, 61
Wozzeck 90

Yes-Sayer, see Jasager
You and Me 76

Zar Lässt sich Photographieren, der 41, 42, 104-5, 106
Zaubernacht, die 17, 20, 92
'Zeitoper' 107-8
Zemlinsky, Alexander von 64
Zweig, Stefan 23-4, 26-7, 28, 30, 65
'Zweiter Bericht über den unbekannten Soldaten' 128